"Lee writes candidly about her adventurous—a   ̶   ̶   ̶ ̶ ̶ ̶y
through life. Her vivid prose draws you into that journey. Her passion makes you
want to stay for the ride."—**Valorie Burton**, AUTHOR OF *What's Really Holding You Back?*

"With an open heart, Cara Lopez Lee relates her round-the-world journey to self-
discovery with the unabashed, dazzling honesty of a good friend telling you her
innermost secrets over a cup of coffee. The backdrop of intriguing cultures and
landscapes further enriches Lee's bold memoir, *They Only Eat Their Husbands*."

> —**Rose Muenker**, WINNER OF THE SOCIETY OF AMERICAN TRAVEL WRITERS GOLD
> AWARD TRAVEL COLUMN

"Lee gets it right about life and love in the Last Frontier in *They Only Eat Their Husbands*.
Her adventures on the road had me laughing out loud with a heart-tugging message
we can all relate to."

> —**Lauren Maxwell**, ANCHOR OF *CBS 11 News This Morning*, ANCHORAGE, ALASKA

"Lee takes you on a fun, fabulous adventure—perfect for any woman who wishes she
could escape 'life' to travel the world."

> —**Susan Kim**, ANCHOR, *Live at Daybreak*, TODAY'S TMJ4, MILWAUKEE, WISCONSIN

"Lee's ill-advised romances with a cast of Alaskan rogues had me alternately laughing
and wanting to shout, 'No, don't do it!' Meanwhile, her descriptions of the unusual
people and exotic locations she encountered on her travels made me eager to experience
them myself . . . until I remembered Asian rats and European robbers are not my thing."

> —**Mark Graham**, AUTHOR OF *The Fire Theft*

"Lee's compelling personal journey is told with a modesty that downplays the many
achievements she has accomplished and the sometimes painful lessons she has learned
throughout her life. The pages turn easily with vivid descriptions not only of the places
she travels through but of the lovers, friends, and people she travels with."

> —**Jeffrey Moore**, PRODUCER, *Destination Wild*, FOX SPORTS

"A witty and moving story that truly captures the sense of wonder, self-discovery, and
adventure that unfolds when one throws caution to the wind and ventures out into
the world alone. This is what travel is really all about...experiencing real life through
unfiltered eyes, embracing the unknown, challenging yourself, and never losing your
sense of humor in the process."

> —**Anne Fox**, CITIZEN PICTURES, PRODUCER *Giada's Weekend Getaways*, FOOD NETWORK

CONUNDRUM PRESS A Division of Samizdat Publishing Group.
PO Box 1353, Golden, Colorado 80402

They Only Eat Their Husbands: Love, Travel, and the Power of Running Away

Conundrum Press edition.

For information, email info@conundrum-press.com.

ISBN: 978-1-942280-00-2

Library of Congress Control Number: 2014951807

Conundrum Press books may be purchased with bulk discounts for educational, business, or sales promotional use. For information please email: info@conundrum-press.com

Conundrum Press online: conundrum-press.com

THEY ONLY EAT THEIR HUSBANDS

LOVE, TRAVEL, AND THE POWER OF RUNNING AWAY

A MEMOIR BY CARA LOPEZ LEE

A Division of Samizdat Publishing Group

Author's Note

Although this book is a true account, I've taken minor precautions to protect the people who appear in it, and I've taken minor poetic license to serve the audience who reads it. To respect people's privacy, I've changed the names of most characters. To further protect a few of those people, I've altered minor details of appearance or profession. To streamline the book, I've combined a few minor characters, blended a few conversations, and condensed the timing of a few events. All that said, the events and dialogue in this book provide a much more accurate representation of my experiences than you might expect, thanks, in part, to my extensive journals. However, some of the quotes should not be taken as verbatim; rather, they provide my best recollection of what was said or the types of things that were said. Others might recall the events in this book differently, and I respect that. Memory is always colored by individual perception and by time. I don't profess my memory to be perfect, only that I've striven to be honest and fair in sharing it.

For Mom, who opened three doors:
to books, to her home, to the world.

ALASKA ESCAPE PLAN

Running away is vastly underrated.

I learned that long before I came to Alaska, before I discovered the isolation that comes with the darkness of winter, before I began to contemplate the severe curvature of the globe where I've spent nine years living out of sight from the rest of the world. I always believed that people who said running away never solved anything were simply people who stayed put.

When I was a child living in the suburbs of L.A., on the days when I felt that no one cared about me, I packed my little blue suitcase with a toothbrush, a single change of clothes, and a small stuffed lion named Leo and ran away from home, sometimes for hours. I returned only to realize no one knew I'd left.

When I was twenty-six, one night shortly before I left Denver, I had another in a string of arguments with Aaron, the boyfriend I lived with. After the initial shouting died down, I tried to explain all the things he did, and failed to do, that made me feel he didn't care about me. He crawled into bed, closed his eyes, and listened for a very long time, then said in a calm, cold voice, "Cara, when you keep going on and on and on like that, it makes me think about guns . . . and knives." He didn't say another word. Terrified, I fell silent, and waited.

I heard the unmistakable change in his breathing that signaled sleep and tentatively whispered his name. No answer. I grabbed a sleeping bag and a change of clothes and ran away to a friend's house. I was back before Aaron woke the next morning. Like my family, he never noticed I'd left either.

It was not, I think, unreasonable for me to let my imagination take his threat to its insane but logical conclusion. Once during an argument, Aaron pulled his gun out of the closet, grabbed me, forced the gun into my hand, and urged me, "I can't take this any more. Just put me out of my misery

1

now. Go ahead, just shoot me!"

I dropped the gun on the couch and pulled away, shaking with fear. "Please stop it! Please! You're scaring me!"

He rolled his eyes. "Oh, quit making a big deal out of nothing. I was just kidding. It's not loaded. See?" He picked up the gun and opened the chamber. It was empty.

Usually our arguments were your basic screaming matches. But, once, he shoved me against the wall with his hands around my throat and said, "Don't push me"; once, he shook me until I could feel my brains rattling inside my skull; and, just once, he threw me across the room, although he was thoughtful enough to aim my body at the bed for a soft landing.

It wasn't the latent violence that upset me most. It was the insults, always delivered as jokes. One night, when I visited him at the nightclub where he tended bar, he pointed out a sexy young cocktail waitress with measurements of about 36-24-34—compared to my less notable 34-27-36—and said, "If you had a body like that, I'd marry you in a heartbeat."

Aaron was the funny, friendly, popular guy everybody loved, who would never turn his back on a friend, or stranger, in need. No one knew what happened between us in private. He told me I was the one with "problems." Having fewer friends than he did, no outside frame of reference, and no actual bruises, for a long time I believed him.

By the time I realized that, no matter whose problem it was, I had to leave, I'd already begun to rely on him financially. Working part-time as a nightclub DJ and restaurant cashier while finishing college, I was low on ready cash. I felt too humiliated to ask my family for help. In my last semester of school and getting straight A's, I just wanted to hold out until graduation.

Then, just before I graduated, Aaron was diagnosed with testicular cancer. In my feeble understanding of relationships, this earned him my unqualified forgiveness. How could I stay angry? Bald and puffed up from chemotherapy, with one lonely testicle as lost in its sack as a new divorcé in a king size bed, he was even more difficult to resist than when he'd first turned on his blond, fit, oversexed charm. That he should lose one of his balls was ironic, given his indiscriminate lechery toward other women, marked by such pithy lines as "I'd like to turn you upside down and lick you like an ice cream cone."

Yet he turned his loss to advantage, tossing a twinkling blue-eyed wink at this or that pretty young thing and saying, "I used to be nuts. Now I'm just nut." Maybe the joke was lame, but his self-effacing acceptance of the cheap joke life had pulled on him was sincere, and even looking like hell he continued to charm everyone, including me.

But when I began to insist he make a commitment, or at least stop throwing his cigarette butts in the kitchen sink, and he began to insist I move out, or at least stop letting the water puddle outside the shower, the tension grew. It seemed to me I was someone else, the day he dragged me through the living room by the arm, my body knocking over his fuzzy blond furniture along the way, as he screamed his outrage at my inability to drop a subject. God knows what the subject was. I absently worried that my arm might pull out of the socket, but my more persistent thought was, "This can't really be happening to me—I have a college degree."

We finally fell to the floor, physically and emotionally exhausted, and he apologized, more or less: "I'm sorry. No one since my ex-wife has ever driven me that far before."

Later, when I tried to suggest that he had an anger management problem, he yelled, "Don't give me that! I never hit you." Technically that was true; he never hit me. I only wished he had; it would have made the choice to leave so much clearer.

In December of 1989, I began making plans to run away for good. It had been more than a year and nearly seventy-five rejection letters since I'd graduated from college with a degree in broadcast news. I resolved that if I didn't get a job by January 1, I was going to join the Peace Corps; I'd saved several brochures and had begun to form vivid mental pictures of a thatched hut and a difficult but satisfying life in some torpid South American jungle.

But on Christmas Eve, I received a call in the cashier's booth at work from a TV news director in Alaska. The station in Juneau needed a news anchor/reporter immediately, and the job was mine if I could fly there in two days. I asked for a week. I hung up the phone and stared into space, stunned at this unexpected resolution to my problems. My picture of a thatched hut in the jungle morphed into a metal Quonset hut in the frozen arctic.

A coworker asked, "Cara, are you okay?"

"Yes . . . Do you know if they have some kind of atlas around here?"

"What're you looking for?"

"Juneau, Alaska."

When I flew to Alaska, on New Year's Day 1990, I didn't think of it as running away. But running is a secret I've discovered hidden inside. It's a secret I share with thousands of Alaskans who've moved here from elsewhere, who, whenever someone asks, "What brought you to the Last Frontier?" answer, "Adventure."

In a land of runaways, adventure is both escape and salvation. The questions follow you here: buried in the hot heart of a glacier, riding the stubborn bore tide up Turnagain Arm, or perched atop the elusive peak of Denali. The answers are here, too: in the inquisitive eyes of a stalking black bear, the circling arms of a dip-netter calling a salmon to his death dance, or the soft pad-pad-pad of a sled dog's feet on the snow of the Iditarod Trail. Running away solves everything. It has to, because when you stand at Point Barrow, at the top of the world, and see the arctic ice stretching before you for thousands of miles, you realize there's nowhere else to run.

Yet ever since I got here, I've been trying to get back out—for nearly nine years. I once met a woman of forty who'd lived here for fifteen years. "I have an Alaska escape plan," she said, "but I never seem to get around to it." Like her, I both love and hate Alaska with equal passion.

In the years I've spent plotting my next escape, I've discovered the power of darkness, the purity of cold, and the secret of love. I've never lived in an igloo, but I've slept in a snow cave. The man who showed me how to build it taught me that a blizzard with wind-chills to ninety below zero is not very brutal at all, that nothing is as brutal as what we put ourselves through to hold onto love.

Imagine for a moment what it would be like to run as far as possible from all you know, to a land north of reality, a fantasy of emerald green and icy white, a place where pioneers still live. Imagine that when the arctic air has sapped your soul of all possible warmth, you will find a love that appears to give light and heat in a frozen world, only to discover that the love you've found is an illusion. Imagine that after you've lost everything, you can finally hear the heartbeat of the land. And, if you're lucky, you will rediscover your own heartbeat.

But first, you must imagine that you are brave enough to run away.

THIRTY-FIVE YEARS OLD—ANCHORAGE TO PALMER, ALASKA

After nine years in the Last Frontier, I'm running away again.

My name is Cara Lee, and this journal is the record of two journeys: today, I began the first leg of a trip around the world, alone; today, I also began the first leg of a trip into the world within me, the tiny world inside my skull, which is still filled with the boundlessness of Alaska. It has taken me until this moment, as I leave the Last Frontier, to summon the guts, the hindsight, and perhaps most importantly, the time alone, to reflect on my life here. As I hit the road out of the state, I can finally, clearly see the path I rode in. For me, these two journeys have become one: I couldn't dare to travel the earth alone if I hadn't come to Alaska, and I couldn't see Alaska plainly if I didn't get some distance.

First, let me tell you about leaving Anchorage today, and give me a moment to steel myself before I tell you about arriving in Juneau nine years ago. I promise I'll reveal everything, in time. I've never been one to hold back, even when it might have served me better.

You probably think I have good reasons for leaving. Don't be too sure. I'm not. I can only tell you that somewhere along the way, amid all my running, I seem to have misplaced my life. Thirty-five arrived much faster than I expected. I once thought that by this time I'd have a husband, one or two kids, and a house, or at the very least, a dog—maybe a golden retriever. Instead, I have an apartment with a no-pets policy and my last boyfriend just left town. I once planned that by this time I'd land a six-figure contract as a TV news anchor in a major market. Instead, I'm a small market reporter with a six-inch stack of rejection letters. I once hoped to save the world, or at least a friend. So far, I haven't so much as saved myself. Hell, I haven't even lost those last five pounds. It's not the life I once imagined. But with no attachments and no mortgage, I have nothing to lose. I'm free.

The idea of escape has often comforted me through trying times, but deciding to actually skip town feels like admitting defeat. Although I spent my childhood in L.A., I grew up in Alaska, the first place that ever felt like home. But even in this homelike place, I have yet to find the love and peace I yearn for. So now that I'm grown up, I've decided to head out for one more search.

My itinerary is pretty sketchy. To start, I'm taking my car on a slow crawl south from Anchorage to L.A.—the place where I first packed my little blue suitcase—to see the family I left behind. After that, I'll fly overseas for six months. Where? I've yet to decide. I plan to travel light, at least to the eyes of a casual observer; my stuffed lion is long gone, and my angst is too bulky to fit into a backpack.

The heroes of ancient Greek mythology underwent tests of strength, courage, and character to prove their worth. Each was typically on a noble quest to rescue others. I'm only trying to save myself. This may sound ignoble, but it's the torch of modern psychology, isn't it? The idea that one cannot help anyone else until he or she has first brought home the Golden Fleece of self-actualization. So, either I'm embarking on the next phase of a noble quest, or the most self-involved ego-trip ever.

★ ★ ★

I'd planned to leave Anchorage this morning. But, reluctant to spend hours trapped in a car with only my thoughts for company, I lingered with the evening sun and my friend Kaitlin.

Kaitlin and I are near opposites. We look different. I'm a short woman with short dark hair, large dark eyes, and a vaguely multi-ethnic look that usually raises questions—the short answer is Mexican, Chinese, Irish, English, Swiss, French, and Cherokee. "Cute" is the adjective I hear most often. Kaitlin is seven years older, but a head-turner with long blond hair, wide-set green eyes, and an unselfconscious giggle that could set a man's pants on fire. We like different things. I like skiing, hiking, and camping; Kaitlin doesn't like the feeling of cold wind on her ears, being sweaty, or sleeping outdoors. I've romanticized my career as a journalist into a crusade for truth and justice; Kaitlin enjoys selling real estate, because, she gushes, "It's like taking someone on a shopping trip to Nordy's, only better."

We live in different worlds. I've never married and have no children; Kaitlin has had three marriages and four children. She has no problem dating a man just for sex and companionship, yet keeps winding up with men who want to marry her. I want to fall in love and get married, yet keep winding up in relationships based on sex.

In spite of having so little in common, our mutual acceptance has never wavered. Yet I didn't realize how close we were, until her eighteen-year-old daughter's body was found in McHugh Creek four years ago.

Someone had raped April, then chased or pushed her off the cliff above. Murder drew a stark chalk outline around my friendship with Kaitlin. Then again, maybe she didn't become my closest friend until that time, when she needed me and I felt the Elysian gift of being needed. I can still see Kaitlin doubled over and howling, as if she recalled the agony of labor pains eighteen years distant and felt her daughter being ripped from her again. At that moment, my friend was more exposed than if she were naked; sharing that moment would bond us for life. Whatever connected us, for the past few years we've managed to talk for an hour almost every day, crying and giggling and divulging every last secret.

This evening, as our voices bounced off the white, nail-scarred walls of my empty apartment, the rooms echoed with the distance that would soon separate us. Trying to escape the hollowness, we locked up the apartment and walked to Westchester Lagoon to watch the sunset. Somebody had drained the water from the lagoon. It was an ugly, swampy hole, instead of the sparkling lake where, until yesterday, I used to go on my daily run—past purple fireweed and Canadian geese, down to the Coastal Trail that runs alongside the cold, metal-colored water of Cook Inlet.

"Westchester Lagoon is empty and Cara's leaving. What a terrible day," Kaitlin said.

"I called Chance the other day to say goodbye," I said.

Chance is not only my ex, he's the ex before my last ex. So I imagine most people would have replied, "What made you do a stupid thing like that?" But Kaitlin isn't that kind of friend. Besides, I think she's always felt guilty that she introduced me to Chance, even though I've always reassured her that I didn't blame her. Whatever she was thinking, she merely asked, "So, how'd that go?"

"He told me he and Sheila are buying a house together. But in my mind what I heard him say was, 'You see, I can make a commitment to the right woman, just not you.'"

"Yeah, well if she's his idea of the right woman, you're well rid of him." Even if his new girlfriend were a missionary, Kaitlin would have found something wrong with her, and for that I was grateful.

"At least my relationship with him helped me grow in a lot of ways."

"Really? It seems more like you shrank. I think he destroyed your self-esteem."

We slowly walked back to my car, which was piled high with clothes and luggage. Kaitlin handed me a box. "I got you a going away gift. Don't worry, it's not another self-help book. I know you've sworn off them. But I had to get you some kind of self-help." It was a road safety kit for my car. We laughed too hard and held each other too tight.

"It doesn't seem real, that I'm leaving," I said. "I can't believe I won't get to talk to you every day anymore."

"Give me another hug," she said, threw her arms around me, then pushed me away. "Now leave, before we start crying."

As I pulled away, I rolled down my window and called out, "Thanks for being my friend!"

On my way out of the city, I stopped downtown to take photos of familiar sights, the things I'd always considered too ugly or depressing to photograph before: the homeless Alaska Natives on 4th Avenue, less painful to think of as parodies instead of people; the misshapen Performing Arts Center with its garish trim of flashing red and green rings, which the people of Anchorage boast is one of the ugliest buildings in town; the condemned, pink McKay Building, which the city keeps threatening to blow up but never does, much to the disappointment of the TV news community— we love it when people blow shit up, without the guilt of death of course.

As with all my relationships, the city's uglier aspects seemed to disappear as I left. The fading sunset cast a glow of longing over Cook Inlet, illuminating the gold Arco building, as the city hung suspended in semi-darkness. Across the inlet, a veil of twilit shadows softly blanketed Sleeping Lady; many people argue that Mount Susitna doesn't look like a lady at all, but tonight I could see her.

The increasing dusk suited my mood as I turned my back on Anchorage and headed up the Glenn Highway toward the Matanuska-Susitna Valley. Yellow and gold fall colors fled past my windows. Like me, they too had lingered in town well past their season.

I took the Old Glenn Highway turnoff, where river and mudflats glistened in the faint glow of the Alaskan night. The Mat-Su River had eaten away more of its banks this summer, and continued to threaten people's homes. During my time in Alaska, several houses have fallen into that changeling waterway, as mighty hunks of bank have given way to the river's hidden power. Several people have tried to sue the borough for failing to inform them that a giant river on a floodplain might have the temerity to change course over time. But tonight the river looked almost tame, as a gentle rain began to fall in the valley.

I only drove for an hour before stopping in Palmer for the night; the sky was turning a blacker shade of dark and I didn't want to miss a last glimpse of anything on my way out of Alaska. I checked into this flea-bag motel, then drove to Carr's and bought a pint of coffee-and-fudge ice cream. I devoured the entire pint while sitting up in my squeaky motel bed, watching a repeat of *The X-Files*. With each spoonful I began relegating Alaska to the past.

I've changed since I first came north, in ways that I needed to change. Nonetheless, I'm leaving the same way I came: alone. I used to think that if I strove to become a better person, life would become easier, the answers more apparent. Not true. I've only succeeded in emptying the 5-foot 2-inch vessel I once thought of as me. Westchester Lagoon is empty, and so am I.

But surely the lagoon won't stay empty forever. Surely it only waits to be cleansed by the next tide. Maybe as I continue down the highway, the world outside my car windows will fill me with a new vision, as refreshing as clean, cool, clear water.

THE LAST FRONTIER
TWENTY-SIX YEARS OLD

As the tires on my red Honda Civic propel me into the future, the world outside my window is a mirror of the self I hope to become: moving forward, ever-changing. But as my thoughts wander, the world of memory is the only mirror in which I see myself as I am. So I keep looking in the rearview mirror, peering into my past, trying to see how I ended up on this road.

When I first arrived in Alaska on January 1, 1990, I had to redraw my grandiose self-portrait of the courageous adventurer. Southeast Alaska was not the frozen wasteland I'd expected. The region's most pervasive feature was the Tongass National Forest, a mountainous, temperate rainforest threaded by fjords. In winter, the dark green mountains and islands of the Inside Passage were laced with heavy snow; in summer, they were an effusive tangle of verdant life wrapped in heavy mist.

In the capital city of Juneau, the cracker-box houses and shops were a whimsical chalk painting, perpetually melting in mushy snow or drizzly rain. In winter, state lawmakers buzzed with a pioneer passion for democracy. In summer, towering white cruise ships dwarfed Gastineau Channel and flooded the city with tourists. There was a movie theatre, a McDonald's, and a mini-mall, although furniture had to be ordered from "Down South."

I didn't live in the kind of place I'd pictured: a metal Quonset hut hung with icicles and beset by cruel winds. Instead, I rented a room on Douglas Island, in a three-bedroom zero-lot-line, which I shared with a man, a woman, a German shepherd, a black lab, and a green parrot. The perfidious parrot's rousing pre-dawn chorus of, "Good-morning-accckkkk! Good-morning-accckkkk!" eliminated the need for me to set an alarm.

When I first arrived, I was so immersed in the mist-cloaked, emerald mystery of Juneau that at first I didn't sense its edges. It's not possible to get in or out of Juneau by any means other than boat or plane. After a few months, it hit me: I couldn't simply hop in my car and drive somewhere else when the mood struck, as if I'd checked into the Hotel California. When I felt that way, I'd take my car north on the main drag as far as I could go— about forty miles. This was called going "out the road," a road that never could take anyone out of town, but only mimic the feeling. Juneau is one of the most beautiful places I've ever known, but even paradise should have an escape route that doesn't require a plane ticket.

Yet what I felt wasn't claustrophobia, because in another sense, Alaska was bigger than imagination could contain. Beyond the mountains that hemmed Juneau in sat one of the largest ice fields on the planet. Sometimes, after work, I drove up Douglas Island and parked my car across the channel from Mendenhall Glacier. As I stared at the glacier, which glowed like a medieval ice spirit in the dusk, I felt dawning in me a belief in my own secret possibilities. One clear night as I drove home from work, the sky came alive, undulating and eddying in ethereal shades of red and green that appeared and disappeared like capricious spirits. Leaning over the steering wheel to stare up through the windshield, I nearly drove off the road. I swerved just in time, but continued to gaze up at the hypnotists that had nearly killed me. They were merely the northern lights, but I couldn't shake the idea that I was watching angels dance.

For the first few weeks I was fascinated with maps and globes. I'd moved to a place so far away that makers of U.S. maps usually relegated it to a box in the South Pacific, so that millions of schoolchildren spent years under the erroneous impression that Alaska was an island next door to Hawaii. On globes, Alaska curved along a different horizon from the world I'd known, reinforcing my feeling of dissimilation from the people who lived in that other world.

Many locals seemed suspicious of outsiders like me, which was understandable because we rarely stayed in Alaska long enough to be worthy of their attachment. Newcomers received the disdainful Native nickname, Cheechakos; old-timers received the prized nickname, Sourdoughs. My Cheechako shortage of friends and Juneau's damp, windy cold often kept me indoors, where I immediately gained ten pounds gorging on the four basic comfort foods: mac-and-cheese, spaghetti, pizza, and chocolate. I wallowed in suffering as if I had discovered it.

Like many Alaskans, from Cheechakos to Sourdoughs, I indulged in the belief that I was unique and extraordinary. There are Alaskans who deserve such adjectives: the Alaska Natives, who've carved an exquisitely hard existence from ice and tundra; and the pioneers, who came to the Last Frontier to rediscover harmony with nature, forge an independent lifestyle, or build a new enterprise. In my case, the belief that living in Alaska made me special was pure conceit: I only came here because I couldn't land a job anywhere else. But I needed that minor conceit to survive; being special was the only thing I could balance against the cabin fever and overwork that soon threatened to release the oddball who lived inside me, endlessly pacing and yammering to herself.

The weird engineer who wore his bedroom slippers to work at the TV station, even in the snow, was a reminder never to indulge in too much time alone with my thoughts. So I made the only friends I easily could: other journalists. Some were firmly planted in Juneau and suspected that I planned to ditch them as soon as a better opportunity came along, which, of course, I did. Others, like me, came to Alaska for their first job and first big adventure, and didn't plan to put down roots. Our camaraderie had the intensity of friendships made during military boot camp—a shared, but fleeting, trial by fire. We got together to sing karaoke at The Waterfront, eat Tex-Mex at The Armadillo, engage in conversation and debate at the

Heritage Coffee Company, and bond over our banishment from normal life.

I retained but one connection to my previous life: deep fear and stress. Only the source had changed: the seemingly simple task of making it to air every night. When I first arrived, the news director had just given his notice. It was such a tiny news department that he also happened to be the only other reporter on staff. For one week he showed me the ropes. Then he left. The following week, another reporter showed up.

Cheryl was a tall, perfect-breasted beauty with auburn hair, studious but sin-tempting hazel eyes, and the barest hint of sultry Louisiana bayou on her otherwise citified tongue. She had no idea, until she walked in the door and I threw myself at her in panicked greeting, that she and I and one photographer would be the only people putting on an entire newscast.

Cheryl and I did all the reporting, writing, and producing, most of the video editing, and some of the shooting for the nightly news. She also anchored sports, while I covered weather. On our first day together, a pair of powerful hands seized my heart as I thought, "We're not going to make it!" On the heels of that panic came a cool, determined calm, as another self replied, "Of course you'll make it. Because six o'clock will come, whether you're ready or not, and you will be on the set."

It was a realization that would help me in the months to come, as Cheryl and I literally ran through town covering the legislature, Alaska Native rights, gay rights, halibut fishing, timber clear-cutting, salmon spawning, and garbage bears. I stood among piles of processed human shit at the town's sewage dump, while Cheryl waded through the bullshit of state government and told me the local gossip: which lawmakers were sleeping together, which reporters smoked dope, the dozens of men who asked her out.

She was attracted to brilliance, and fell for a newspaper reporter with a knack for metaphor. Tender hearted, but sharp-tongued regarding fools, she vociferously disapproved of everyone I dated.

We became friends quickly as we lived several years of experience in nine short months. Together we plowed through the stress that threatened to plow through us. We regularly laughed, cried, shouted, swore, and threw things—we had no idea that those last three gave everyone around us the mistaken impression that we hated each other.

One day, as we argued over the best way to cover a story, a young administrative assistant turned to us with doe eyes and said in a tremu-lous voice, "I wish you two would stop fighting and try to get along." She sat down in a huff. Cheryl and I stared at each other and burst out laughing. Neither of us thought of it as fighting, but as lively debate. This wouldn't have been a problem in a regular newsroom, but the station was so small that sales, accounting, and news were all carried on in one large room. Often, we were still putting on make-up when the control room hollered, "Sixty seconds!" and we rushed to the desk to shove microphones up our blouse fronts and welcome the audience to *The Southeast Report*, without a second to spare.

In the middle of one newscast I turned to do a live interview with an assembly member and, after introducing him, drew a complete blank: "Thank you for joining us. The first thing I'd like to ask you is . . . uh . . . is . . . ahem . . . excuse me . . ." I shuffled my scripts, trying to find the cheat notes I kept for just such an emergency. But that evening, in my crazed rush to get to the news desk on time, I'd buried my notes beneath my scripts, and a quick search wouldn't yield them. My face started to burn. I stared at the assemblyman in horror. He didn't look any too thrilled either. The faint sounds of laughter drifted down the hall from the control room, where the director had fallen out of his chair and was on the floor giggling and kicking his feet.

It lasted a gut-twisting twenty to thirty seconds, an eternity in TV news. Then the assemblyman saved me. "I'll bet you want to ask me . . ." I don't remember the subject. I only remember smiling at him like an idiot and saying, "Yes," in a tone suggesting that was exactly what I'd planned to ask all along and my career wasn't flashing before my eyes.

Cheryl, though more poised and together than I, was not immune to the foibles of small town news. One night, she was getting ready to tape on the set, frustrated as usual with one technical problem or another, and didn't realize her microphone was prematurely live. In the middle of a family sitcom the word "Fuck!" blasted through living rooms all over town.

Cheryl was a savvy journalist, who liked the work. Yet she confessed she never could completely shake her inner Louisiana girl, who'd rather be shucking peas on her grandmother's porch than racing to make a live feed. That girl occasionally popped up in the newsroom. Perhaps the most memorable time was the day she came flying into the studio on roller blades to tape an interview with the governor, who was already on the set. Both she and the governor laughed heartily, as she barreled into the news desk, unable to brake.

"I'm a Type-B personality in a Type-A career," she once confessed to me. "Sometimes I don't know why I'm doing this to myself."

I *was* a Type-A personality, and I didn't know why I did *any* of the things I did to myself. The worst thing I did to myself had little to do with work. One reason I came to Alaska was to escape a terrifying man. It didn't occur to me I might have run in the wrong direction.

★   ★   ★

I didn't come to Alaska to find a man. But there were just so many of them, it was hard to avoid tripping over a few.

In the Lower Forty-eight, the belief that Alaska has an excess of men has given hope to many a lonely single woman that, if all else fails, she can always pack up and head north. In some small villages the "more men myth" is true, with ratios as high as four or five guys to one gal. But there are few careers for a single woman to pursue in the Alaska Bush. In bigger towns, the manhunt fantasy falters, as the numbers hew closer to one-to-one, although yes, there are a few extra men.

Both in the city and in the bush, there's a well-known saying about Alaska's male-to-female ratio: "The odds are good, but the goods are odd." Many of the extra males are the same kind of men who, once upon a time, would have been toothless gold prospectors, grizzle-haired hermits, or drunken roustabouts. Among the rest, there do exist passionate, exciting men with a sense of adventure, and only a few are actually dangerous, but good luck sorting them out.

A married couple living in Juneau once told me their small town was such a tough place for a single man to meet someone, that they knew guys who went to the airport to pick up women, "because they'd already dated every woman in town." For me, it's never been hard to meet men; if I stand still in one place long enough, an alcoholic is sure to find me.

Joe and I first met when a small group of journalists got together for lunch at a popular hippy-food restaurant called The Fiddlehead, named for the ferns that proliferate throughout the Tongass. Joe was a freelance journalist, but his rumpled clothing rode a fine wrinkle between aspiring poet and flat-out bum. He was obviously older than I, but how much older was hard to say. His long, dark, floppy bangs, bushy beard, and mustache obscured most of his face as effectively as a ski mask—as if he didn't want to be noticed. In fact, what first caught my attention was how little he spoke. His mud-and-grass colored eyes clearly took in much, but gave away little. It would be weeks before I realized he was very opinionated, dismissing most people as either witless liberals, ignorant conservatives, or just plain idiots.

The few times he opened his mouth, he spoke in a gentle basso that almost fell below the range of hearing. As I leaned forward to catch his words the sound struck me as distractingly sexual, in odd contrast to his short, stocky frame. In the end, I blamed it all on the voice.

Joe lived on a sailboat in Juneau harbor, and on my first Fourth of July in Alaska, he invited a handful of reporters and photographers for a nighttime sail to watch the fireworks over Gastineau Channel. Until the Fourth of July cruise, it was always the stunning colors of fireworks that thrilled me most. But that night it was the sounds. The explosions bounced back and forth between the mountains of Douglas Island and Juneau with thunderous repeating echoes, as if the small pleasure boats bobbing around us were the ghosts of long-ago battleships. The strains of Jimi Hendrix playing his out-of-bounds rendition of "The Star Spangled Banner" floated to us from the shipboard radio. A pack of journalists ran around the deck like rowdy teens, waving sparklers that sizzled like bacon.

Joe, our captain, was the only one who remained silent throughout most of our brief cruise. Every shadow seemed to intersect in the place where he stood at the helm, so it was difficult to read his face. Later he confessed, "I had that party for *you*. Didn't you know? I watched you all night," so that now, in my memory, I see his curious eyes hidden in the shadows, following my every move.

At the time, I was unaware of his unspoken lust. How could I have known he even liked me? He barely spoke to me. As for my feelings toward him, he struck me as gnome-like in appearance and offbeat in manner, so that at first I had no more idea of lusting after him than a monk. However, I fell in love with the memory of that night.

After the fireworks, we all sang several ribald rounds of "Barnacle Bill the Sailor," cracked tasteless jokes about Joe Hazelwood (captain of the ill-fated Exxon Valdez oil tanker), and poked fun at Alaska's state lawmakers.

"Senator Fox told me his idea of the perfect way to spend the Fourth was sitting on his back porch with a six-pack and shooting off his gun," Cheryl said.

We all laughed. But Joe, never one to let down his political guard, couldn't leave it at that. "You should've mentioned that in your story last night."

Cheryl gave him a puzzled frown. "It didn't have anything to do with habitat protection."

"You don't think people would be interested to know that one of the lawmakers making decisions on their environmental policies is a gun-toting redneck who doesn't even care about local ordinances against discharging firearms in a residential area?"

"Not unless there's a salmon stream nearby," Cheryl said. "Okay, it might have made a great bit of character nuance, but I only get two minutes to tell a story. Which part would you suggest I leave out?"

"That's the problem with TV news, I guess: no time for the whole story." He looked around him at several pairs of staring eyes and fell silent, although I noticed him studying me under his lashes, as if gauging my reaction.

When the party broke up, he stood on the dock and gave me a hand out of his boat. It was the only private moment we shared all night. As I jumped from deck to dock, my hand in his, this time he made no attempt to disguise his intense stare, which threw me off balance.

A few days later, when he asked me to go with him on a hike to Ebner Falls, I was lured by the remembered image of him leaping back onto his boat like an affable pirate. If I considered that he might be hiding a hook, it only intrigued me more.

★ ★ ★

The pirate set his hook with his element of choice: water. Joe couldn't have found a better way to catch me than with a hike to a cascade. Water has always called out to that ancestral part of me that was born ages ago in its deep, wet womb. But Ebner Falls was the first glacier-fed Alaskan water to ever astonish me. Its color was the natural effect of glacial silt, but it called to my mind the unreal blue-green of an over-chlorinated swimming pool, roaring with a pure white froth.

The falls were just part of the scenery Joe and I passed as we hiked the

Perseverance Trail. The trail was layered in twenty impossible shades of green: stilt-walking old growth spruce, hemlock, cedar, giant skunk cabbages, and curling fiddlehead ferns. Clouds draped themselves low and languid on the mountainsides, as if laden with secrets.

"Well," Joe sighed, "this is pretty much what it looks like at any given point in the Tongass."

"Yeah, all these miles and miles of natural beauty must seem really redundant after a while," I retorted.

As we moved up the trail, past rusted equipment from the old Perseverance Gold Mine, Joe talked to me in the way of most news hounds, drilling me with questions as if he were interviewing me for a story. He seemed quietly impressed by all I said, while I was captivated by his attention. He apologized for his previous impertinent remarks about TV news, saying he thought the amount of work I produced in one day was phenomenal. "I'm amazed you can cover so many stories and still manage to eke out any information that makes sense."

The more we walked, the more Joe found his voice, wedging bits and pieces of himself into the few openings I gave him in the mostly me-sided conversation. He told me he was the youngest of three children and the black sheep of his family. "My sister thinks I should get married. My brother thinks journalism is just a hobby and I should find a more respectable profession. I think they're just worried someday I'll show up penniless on their doorstep and embarrass them in front of the neighbors."

"I'm the black sheep of my family, too," I said, "which is a neat trick, since I'm an only child. My dad thinks I'll never amount to anything with just a bachelor's degree, my grandmother thinks I'll never get married because I hate to cook, and my stepmother just thinks I'm a lousy daughter."

"Why?"

"I borrowed two thousand bucks from my dad to ship my car and some of my other stuff to Alaska—the TV station wouldn't pay moving expenses. Anyway, I didn't realize how high the cost of living was up here, so I've only been able to pay back a few hundred bucks so far. So my stepmom thinks I'm a flake."

"I disagree. I think it takes a lot of character to come this far away from everything you know and start a new life."

"Or it takes a real flake."

He paused, then said, "They say everyone who comes to Alaska has a dream. So, what kind of dreams do flakes have?"

"I want to work as a reporter in Alaska for a year or two, then work my way up to a top-twenty market in the Lower 48."

"So, you're another one of those people who just came here to grab the oil money and run?"

To a non-Alaskan his accusation might not make sense, but Alaska's economy is driven by oil, and everyone who lives here benefits from it, directly or indirectly. Plus, Alaskans don't pay state taxes. Instead the state pays *them*; every resident is entitled to dividends from the state Permanent Fund, an investment account created with oil royalties. After a year, I was eligible for my first check. During my time in Alaska, the size of my annual dividend check has surpassed the thousand-dollar mark.

But I refused to be labeled a mercenary. "That's not it at all. I came here because it was the only place I could get a job. And I'll have to leave if I want to advance my career."

"A dedicated journalist doesn't do it for money."

"You mean we're the fourth arm of government, defenders of truth, freedom, and democracy? I believe in all that, too. That's why someday I'd like to have the resources to do more in-depth stories, and that'll never happen at a small-town TV station."

"I understand. I guess I'm just being selfish. I was hoping you'd stay."

"So, what about you?" I asked. "What kind of dreams do black sheep have?"

"I want to take my boat sailing around the world. And I'd like to visit Ukraine. That's where my ancestors are from." He went on, "I did a story once in the Russian Far East, and one night I sat around a campfire with a bunch of locals. It was freezing, but they passed around a bottle of vodka and told stories and laughed all night, while I sat there shivering. Anyway it got me thinking, someday I'd like to visit my grandfather's village and pass a bottle around a fire." He smiled disarmingly. His smile wasn't remarkable of itself, except for its bright contrast to his otherwise intensely serious demeanor. By that measure, it was a knockout.

After our hike we went to the Red Dog Saloon, where I drank a beer and stapled my business card to a wall plastered with them, while Joe practiced his vodka-drinking and storytelling skills on me and anyone else within earshot. They weren't "stories" so much as loud, rambling pontifications on nothing in particular—although at one point I think he said something about fighting to hang onto "the Alaskan way of life." Customers gave him irritated looks. I shushed him, and he loudly insisted I not shush him.

When we left, he walked me to his office near the docks. It was a transparent move to impress me with his dashing profession. The office looked like that of an absent-minded professor, mismatched second-hand furniture barely visible beneath stacks of magazines, newspapers, and photographs stained with coffee rings.

I sat in a swivel chair and turned slowly to take in the black-and-white photos that peppered-and-salted the walls. There was an Alaska Native girl, Tlingit I think, cutting fish with an *ulu*: a curving, fan-shaped blade set into a bone handle. There was a weathered-looking commercial fisherman standing below a haul of halibut hanging from a winch: each huge and hideous fish had a pair of bulging eyes on one side of its head, which seemed to stare accusingly at its killer. But the photo that struck me most was of a pair of trumpeter swans flying over a sparkling wetland: lovers in flight captured by the lens of a loner.

As I stilled the office chair to gaze at the swans, Joe stepped behind me and massaged my shoulders, his hands so fast and clumsy that, instead of relaxing me, it agitated me. I stood abruptly and turned around, hoping he'd stop. Mistaking this signal, he kissed me, gobbling at my mouth like a cannibal. His mouth tasted of stale booze, and the room closed in as I tried not to gag. Insidiously, it was at that moment more than any other that I was hooked, lured by the potential to explore this man's inner depths. He must have them; why else would a creative and intelligent man drink?

Two weeks later, we spent the night on his boat in the harbor, talking and making love until dawn to the hiss and glow of an oil lantern, the murmur of Joe's baritone whisper, and the sensual sway of the sea.

Before I drifted off to sleep, I finally got the courage to ask his age. He was thirty-eight, eleven years older than I. "Is that a problem?" he asked. "Of course not," I said. I still felt like a child and I hoped hanging around with a grownup might rub off, though I didn't say so.

Cheryl later told me, "Be careful, Cara. He's got quite a reputation."

"You mean with the ladies?" I asked with genuine surprise.

"No, as a drunk."

"He doesn't drink *that* much. And he's a lot different than I thought he'd be. Once you get him talking he's really interesting, smarter than anyone I've ever dated before. He can be sweet, too, and very romantic."

"That makes sense. He is a journalist. Creative people can be very romantic. I'm sure he's very exciting. Just . . . be careful."

But the warning itself, "Be careful," only added to the attraction. That's what someone always tells you just before the fun begins.

★ ★ ★

The allure of a glacier is that it's not merely beautiful, but also overwhelming and potentially dangerous. A glacier is best understood if you stand silently and listen to its creaking, groaning heart. Its beauty is the result of intense pressure. A glacier forms when the weight of tons of snow forces the snow beneath it to compress into ice. The pressure is so extreme it heats up the molecules and melts them into liquid in the instant before they form ice. That is why a glacier flows: however cold and forbidding it may appear, there is a place inside that burns.

It was Joe who took me to see my first Alaskan glacier up-close. Juneau's Mendenhall Glacier undulated toward the lake like an icy tidal wave, thrusting its way through the surrounding mountains, carving valleys in its powerful wake. I stared in neophyte awe at the wall of deep blue-upon-white, tortured and lovely, monstrous in size, frightening to consider, with man-eating crevasses lurking across its expanse.

Joe told me he'd once hiked across a glacier and fallen into a crevasse. "That may have been the scariest moment of my entire life. I had no idea how far I was going to fall. Some of those crevasses can go down more than a hundred feet." He didn't fall that far. A fellow hiker pulled him out.

He handed me his camera and taught me how to take better photos. He stood at my shoulder, and his soft-spoken words tickled my ear, "If you want less camera shake, take a deep breath . . . then, as you press the shutter, exhale slowly." Ironic, that this advice came from a man who I remember most vividly from the moments when he was unsteady and swaying.

He was not gentle and quiet then.

Those were the times when he attacked my professional worth: "Why don't you become a real journalist instead of a TV reporter? Are you afraid of coming up with sentences that have more than three words? Afraid to expose how little you really understand?"

Sometimes his comments didn't make sense, things like, "If I wazh a sailor I'd drink the ocean. But *you* wouldn't unerstan' 'cause you don't know what it's like to sail."

"What are you talking about?"

"You know exackly what I'm talking aboud. Don't pull that lunatic crap on me! You're just like my fugging family."

"Joe, have you been drinking?"

"What does that have to do with your ignorance?"

The next day a tormented Joe would whisper a tender apology, still sounding confused. I think he often didn't remember what he was apologizing for.

Of course I thought about telling him to take a hike. But Joe was my guide to falling in love with the Last Frontier. He seduced me with his passion for Alaska.

One night as we lay awake on his boat, rocked by gentle waves, Joe said, "I love you, Cara."

I was silent.

He turned my face to the moonlight to confirm the tears swimming in my eyes. "That's supposed to make you happy. It's not supposed to make you cry."

I knew the usual response was supposed to be, "I love you, too," but I wasn't there yet. Still, I felt a mournful tenderness for this man who walked out of step with the rest of the world, so I came up with the oblique response, "Except for time, I'm already in love with you." In the manner of a man in love, he did not question this inane line of crap.

I knew that falling in love with Joe was likely to get me into trouble, and only partly because I was leaving to start a new job in the big city, which locals jokingly referred to as Los Anchorage.

★ ★ ★

At Thanksgiving, Joe flew to Anchorage for a visit. He arrived stumbling drunk. The moment he stepped off the plane he began bowing deeply to total strangers, waving his Russian-style fur hat with a flourish and loudly pretending to speak Russian. We went out to dinner, where I begged him to take off the hat and stop drinking.

"You need to pull your head out of your ass and have some fun," he said.

In the morning he apologized again, kneeling beside my bed like a penitent child. His apology was vague, referring only to "last night" and his "behavior." It was clear that, once again, he had no real recollection of what he'd done.

On Thanksgiving Day he drank a fifth of alcohol, whiskey I think. He was so drunk I refused to let him help me shop for the meal. I wouldn't let him help me in the kitchen either.

"You're treating me like a little kid," he said.

"It's just that I can't concentrate if anyone else is in the kitchen," I lied.

He wasn't fooled, but he gave up and retreated to the living room to drink and sulk.

I'd invited my roommate Max and one of his friends to join us, and they soon came out of Max's smoke-filled room to socialize. They seemed oblivious to the tension in the air, probably thanks to the generous appetizer of marijuana they'd inhaled.

At the time, possession of an ounce of marijuana for "personal use" was still legal under Alaska law, thanks to the state constitution's strong stand on the right to privacy. There were still laws against buying and selling it, so how anyone was supposed to obtain this supposedly "legal" dope was a mystery.

During my first few months in Anchorage, Alaskans debated the ballot issue that would make marijuana possession illegal in the state. When the measure passed, I said goodbye to my roommate. He was a sweet guy, docile as a kitten, but I was a reporter with high ambitions, and I didn't want to risk being linked to someone engaged in illegal activity, no matter how legal it had been a week before. Besides, his room was kind of scary, and the smell of dope was slowly permeating the entire apartment.

But on that Thanksgiving, I was grateful that Max, his friend, and their dope were all present to mellow out the rough edges of the drunk I'd invited to stay. By mealtime, I'd had a couple of glasses of wine myself in the spirit of assimilation and in the hope of picking up the strange rhythm of the sporadic conversation. Joe talked politics, which regularly reminded Max and his buddy of some sophomoric movie that had made them "fall on their asses laughing."

The dinner turned out perfectly. The two men with the raging munchies showered me with compliments, until even Joe had to admit the turkey was delicious. Triptophan perpetuated everyone's dull stupor late into the evening, and gave me the one thing I was most thankful for that Thanksgiving: the moment when Joe passed out.

The next day, Joe and I went cross-country skiing in Russian Jack Springs Park and stopped to watch several moose munch on birch bark just off the trail.

As we continued down the trail, he said, "If you have to live in Anchorage, I can see how this greenbelt would be a compensation. Too bad you can still hear the traffic, though."

"You really do hate Anchorage, don't you?"

"It's just that it's not really like living in Alaska. I mean, if you want to live in a city, why not go to Los Angeles?"

He was scheduled to stay for four days. He left after three. I barely stopped the car long enough to let him out at the airport and drove away without looking back.

If I'd known that moment at the airport was the end of our relationship, I might have come up with a scathing tongue-lashing, or at least burned rubber as I drove off. However, a few months later I was grateful I'd refrained from saying anything I might have regretted.

It was while ripping *Associated Press* wire copy in our newsroom that I first learned what happened to Joe. According to the *AP*, he was found unconscious and bleeding in an out-of-the-way corner outside a building in Juneau. Muggers had stabbed him in the neck and left him to die. He was drunk, which might be why they'd targeted him.

I called Cheryl. She told me what the *AP* didn't say: that Joe was so drunk the surgeons were sure he would die because it was too risky to give him anesthesia for the surgery he needed. They feared the combination of alcohol and anesthetics might put him under forever. "They finally operated, and he came through it. But he's still not out of the woods," Cheryl said.

I wanted to cry, but instead launched into irate invective: "I'm sorry, but this whole thing really pisses me off at Joe. It was his own stupid fault. If he hadn't been drinking they probably wouldn't have attacked him. He might as well have slit his own throat."

Cheryl warned me against that kind of talk. "That's just a way of re-victimizing the victim. However drunk Joe was, the animals who stabbed him and left him to die were to blame, not him."

When he regained consciousness, she called me back. "I went to visit him. He looked so terrible it was hard not to cry. You know, hardly anyone has gone to see him. A lot of people are talking like he deserved it. Even his family didn't come. You should call him."

So I did. His voice was as hoarse as a tonsillectomy patient's, and he didn't say much except to repeat how glad he was I called. I told him I was grateful he was okay. I refrained from telling him I was furious with him for almost getting himself killed. He's the one who said it: "I know if I hadn't been drinking this might not have happened. I know I have to change or I'm going to die. I know I'm killing myself."

His words filled me with pity, but I resisted the urge to hop a plane to see him. It wasn't that hard to resist. I knew Joe found pity annoying. I knew we'd ultimately find each other annoying. I knew our different visions of Alaska were taking us down different paths, and I was already gone.

*   *   *

To Alaskans like Joe, the only good thing about Anchorage was its location, "just twenty minutes from Alaska." To me, the Anchorage Bowl looked like a 1970s strip mall in the midst of a resplendent castle: the city's hasty architecture seemed out of place against the rugged turrets of the Chugach Mountains and the shining moat of Cook Inlet. Like other cities, Anchorage had tall office buildings and trailer parks, corporate lawsuits and gang warfare, indoor plumbing and cable TV. There was not a single MacDonald's. There were ten.

But the rush-hour-gridlocked, car-exhaust-hazed exterior didn't fool me for long. Somewhere within Alaska's biggest city, thrumming beneath the heaving, pot-holed asphalt, there lay a deeply primitive place. Moose and bears still roamed among us, and sometimes they killed. Every winter, ice and snow tore the lines right off the road, frost cracked open the pavement, and people plugged in their cars to keep them from freezing.

Anchorage had no more snowfall than many cities in the Lower 48. The thing was, it never seemed to melt. For six months, plows pushed snow into towering berms that never shrank, but grew and multiplied in winter the way dandelions do in summer. I loved the mounting snow; in the darkness of winter, it reflected and amplified the meager light of the brief daytime sun and the electric lights of the long winter nights.

Of course, Anchorage wasn't nearly as cold and forbidding as the Arctic, several hundred miles to the north, where the freezing air was usually too dry to snow. Anchorage wasn't even as cold as some places in the Lower 48, thanks to the Japanese Current—I never fully understood how this Pacific Ocean phenomenon worked, just obediently repeated the phrase "Japanese Current" to anyone from "Outside" who asked me, "Isn't it cold up there?"

It wasn't the cold that I struggled to survive. It was the dark.

Someone once told me that living through an Alaskan winter was like turning the lights off for six months. For six months, we lost a few seconds to a few minutes of light each day until we reached the winter solstice and fewer than four hours of daylight. Then, for the next six months, we gained a few seconds to a few minutes of light each day until we reached the summer solstice and more than twenty hours of daylight.

"The summers make up for the winters," Cheryl said. "You get all that sunlight back." Certainly the long days of summer were energizing. In fact, by summer solstice, I felt manic. I remember going out with friends to Chilkoot Charlie's, where the city's middle class dressed down and its sleazy dregs dressed up to play bad pool, dance to cover bands, and drink away the few hours of darkness. The sun was barely beginning to set when we walked in after eleven p.m., and dawn was just teasing the sky when we left at three a.m. I often couldn't sleep at night, for all the light sneaking into my room beneath the curtains. Some people put aluminum foil on their windows to block the light, but those homes always made me feel as if I were sitting inside a casserole dish.

So, no: for me the lost sleep of summer did little to make up for the long sleep of winter. Over the years, the effects of the darkness seemed cumulative, so that each winter felt more depressing than the one before. Like fungus, all my festering disappointments grew in the dark. I wasn't alone. At the TV station, I reported one story after another in which Alaskans outpaced the national average in alcoholism, drug abuse, domestic violence, and suicide. Most suicides happened in spring, but only because killing oneself required more energy than anyone could muster in winter. I blamed it all on the clinging night. But, like other Outsiders who yearned to belong, I embraced my suffering as the hazing ritual required to make me a member of the club. Surviving the darkness was Alaska's secret handshake.

At first I felt disappointed that the dramatic six months of total darkness promised to me by friends who'd never set foot in Alaska was not as
they'd advertised. Then, as a reporter covering the rural Alaska beat, I flew
north to Barrow, to do a story on the year's last sunset, prelude to the longest night in the world.

Point Barrow is truly the northern edge of the earth. As the photographer and I stood on the shore staring at the junction of the Chukchi and
Beaufort Seas, my brain refused to register that there was any kind of sea
before my eyes. All I saw was a white expanse of ice so vast it made me
want to cackle like a madwoman. Strangely, I was reminded of an endless
wheat field in Kansas, the only image I could think of that was remotely
akin to this. The only things that prevented the frozen sea from appear-
ing flat and monotonous were the random humps and ridges of shifting
ice. I might take off across that ice, enter another dimension, meet God,
continue walking for eternity, and never reach any destination; or I might
walk for five minutes and end up back where I started—all without the
least surprise.

At 12:35 in the afternoon on Sunday, November 18, we turned our eyes
east to watch the last sunrise of the year. A tiny, distant ball of glowing
embers shyly lifted itself to peek over the horizon, then swiftly crawled a
few inches across that imaginary line. Tiny crystals of ice fog gave the air
a sparkling, reflective quality. In the hour and twelve minutes from sunrise to sunset, the sun's feeble rays turned the ice fog into rainbow dust
shivering atop the arctic plain.

At 1:47, the sun disappeared off the edge of the earth. It would not rise
again until January 23, more than two months later—not six months, as
my friends "down in America" believed. Still, that was a helluva long night.

"It's so eerie," I muttered. "It's like we're standing at the end of everything."

It was a powerful ending, the death of the sun at the end of the world.
Although the sight moved me, the immensity of the pitch-black night that
followed was almost disturbing. I never again romanticized the notion of
living in darkness for six months. As it was, the semi-darkness of an Anchorage winter was enough to suffocate joy, and each succeeding plunge into
the long winter night fed my ultimate desire to escape.

ALASKA ESCAPE PLAN
THIRTY-FIVE YEARS OLD—HAINES, ALASKA TO BELLINGHAM, WASHINGTON

Last night, lying in a motel room in Haines, waiting to catch the ferry south to Bellingham, Washington, grief over my unleashed past and fears over my unplanned future pressed inexorably on my brain. My mind felt like a wad of over-chewed gum, and I had no energy left to keep chewing. I've discovered that only one thing can make me feel better when I get that wound up: talking to Sean, the last Alaskan man I tripped over. Until he left the state last month, Sean was alternately my lover and best friend.

He barely answered the phone before I began weeping uncontrollably. I said that I felt close to a nervous breakdown, that I wasn't sure I could even make it to Seattle, that there was a chance someone would have to come scrape me off the floor. The perfect listener, he didn't tell me everything would be all right. He simply allowed me to fall apart.

After I moved uninterrupted from hysteria to repetition to exhaustion, he said, "I wish I could be there with you. I wish I could help. I don't know what to say."

"That's all I needed to hear. Just talking to you always makes me feel better."

"Well, I didn't do anything, but I'm glad you feel better. You know, sometimes I worry about you. Then I think about it and I realize you'll always be okay, because you're an amazing person, Cara. But if you ever need to talk, you can call anytime. I really miss you."

When I hung up I felt stronger, just knowing that someone in the world missed me tonight and that he thought I was so amazing I could survive anything, even my darkest thoughts. My eyes swollen and my emotions drained, an uneasy post-storm calm settled over me and I fell into a restless sleep.

THE LAST FRONTIER
TWENTY-NINE YEARS OLD

I wonder how different my relationship with Sean might have been if I'd seen celibacy versus sex as two ways to express a relationship, rather than two ways to avoid one.

Six years ago, Kaitlin and I decided to take a martial arts class. I chose aikido, which roughly translates as "the art of peace." This appealed to my aspiration to achieve enlightenment, which tended to surface between boyfriends. Still, I was impatient to kick ass and a little disappointed that, before we could learn to fight, we had to learn to fall.

My impatience soon vanished, when Sensei Sean was assigned to teach us how to roll. When Sean approached us on the mat, I didn't know he was a third-degree black belt and a sensei. I only sensed his high rank because he was one of the few people wearing a hakima (a pair of intricately tied, loose black pants that looks like a skirt). I elbowed Kaitlin and rolled my eyes in our silent shorthand for the teenybopper shriek, "Oh my God, he's sooo cute and he's coming this way!" He had a stocky body, a strong chin, and tattered curls of brown hair. I had to make a conscious effort not to stare into his perpetually amused eyes, which were an impossible shade of blue—were those colored contacts?

"We teach you to roll first because we spend a lot of time being thrown on the mat. Safety is most important," he said. He then demonstrated, flowing low across the mat like a sudden rush of water. I followed, slamming across the mat like a bag of rocks: elbow, shoulder, head, spine, ass . . . bang, bam, whap, ouch, oof. We rolled throughout the entire class, until I felt like a mass of bruises and my shoulder throbbed.

"I keep hurting my shoulder," I told him.

"I see that. It looks painful."

"Is there a better way to protect my shoulder?"

"Don't leave it out there."

"Thanks."

Afterward, I told Kaitlin I thought he was handsome and funny.

"Yes, I noticed you asked for an unusual amount of instruction," she said.

I went on as if I hadn't heard her, "But I think he knows he's cute. He seemed kind of arrogant."

THIRTY YEARS OLD

Over time, I discovered that Sean was far from arrogant. Off the mat, he was a shy, diffident man who preferred to listen and observe. I discovered something else: off the mat, he had a girlfriend. So, on the mat, I became just another admiring student.

Sean was an excellent teacher who conveyed a sense of wonder, as if he'd discovered each move just a moment ago. He spoke about "staying in the moment" and "letting go of the mind" in ways that made those ideas sound tangible. When he trained with the other high-ranking udansha he spun like a dervish and flung his small body through the air like an acrobat, his face full of a Puckish mischief that tickled the watching students into spontaneous laughter.

The time came for my first test. I was too naive to realize that a properly humble beginner would never have the audacity to ask a Ni Dan (third-degree black belt) to be her uke (the training partner who is continually thrown during a test). Too polite to point out my faux pas, Sean agreed to be my uke, telling me he felt "honored" that I'd asked.

He trained with me patiently, full of silliness and wisdom. "Do you see what's happening here?" he asked as I tried to escape his grasp. "You're pushing right back into my strength. We'll be here all day. Now, if you work around it . . . See? You're no longer fighting my strength, but working with it . . . Then, you can redirect it, and . . . stick your finger in my ear."

The day of my exam, he brooked no nonsense. Shortly before the test, I was standing amid a crowd of practicing students, hands folded in front of me in a self-conscious Eve pose, when Sean appeared and his fist flew into my clasped hands. I flinched and grabbed my stinging knuckles, staring at him saucer-eyed. "Don't ever stand like that," he said. "You'll get hurt. You should always stand in a ready stance. Relaxed, but ready. Work on your awareness." I never stood like that again.

During the test, it felt like we were dancing in a graceful pas de deux, except for the sweating and grunting and the bodies slamming into the mat. I passed.

A few days after my aikido test, he came to my thirtieth birthday party, which I'd dubbed "A Funeral for my Youth." Sean was one of the few who dressed in black, as per the party invitation, and I thanked him for remembering. "Don't give me too much credit," he said. "Black is my favorite color. I probably would've worn it anyway."

I'd also asked the guests to submit advice for people over thirty. Sean's contribution was a list of "new pick-up lines for over-thirties" such as, "Hi, I'm a martial artist and I'm here to help." I'd asked everyone to skip gifts, but he brought one anyway: a traditional sake set. As he presented it, he said, "It's not really a birthday gift. It's a tradition for the uke to give the nage a gift after the test." The way he smiled sideways made me realize that the tradition was quite the opposite; I should have been the one to give him a gift.

I allowed him to let me save face, with a dip of my head and a penitent smile. "Thank you, sensei. By the way, I realize now that I was overstepping my place by asking you to train with me. You must've thought I was a brazen little thing."

"No, I thought you were pretty brave. Most people would've been afraid to ask. But you don't seem to have any fear."

"Oh, I'm afraid of everything. But I just ask myself, 'What would I do if I wasn't afraid?' Then I do that."

"Now *that*," he said, "is living in the moment."

He hadn't brought his girlfriend to the party. They had a reputation for being on-again, off-again. But there was no point in wondering about their current status, because by then I'd started dating someone else. Tommy was at the party, too, but he spent most of the night hiding somewhere by the pony keg and said very little to me all night. Tommy wasn't so much a boyfriend as a placeholder. But, at age thirty, I thought it important to entertain all options.

Sean used to say, "The life you live, you make all these choices, all these decisions. But in the end, it's all about timing."

THIRTY-ONE YEARS OLD

After the stifling cabin fever of my fifth Alaskan winter, the spring sun came hollering at my window, begging me to come out and play. For the first time, Sean's girlfriend was off-again at the same time I was sans placeholder. Emboldened by spring fever, I asked him to join me for a bike ride.

We rode Anchorage's Chester Creek Trail out to Cook Inlet. The inlet and the still-snowy mountains looked gorgeous in the newborn sunshine, but I was distracted by Sean's muscular thighs, outlined in skin-tight bicycle shorts. I didn't have much chance to stare, however, as he spent most of the time riding behind me. That was a matter of politeness on his part; he was the stronger cyclist and wanted to keep me in sight.

Sean was amused that I could keep up a steady stream of chatter while pedaling at, what was for me, a furious pace. "How can you breathe?" he asked.

"I'm fine!" I turned to shout over my shoulder, almost zigging off the path.

"Shouldn't you keep your eyes on the trail?"

"I'm fine!" I turned to shout again, zagging the other way.

We talked about everything from the weather to the meaning of death, and one thing became clear: while his ex was off-again, Sean was still *on*. Every subject reminded him of something funny Ann said this one time, or something interesting he and Ann did together this other time, or something or other about Ann at one time or another. Although we went out together a few more times, removing his ex from our conversation was like trying to pull flies off a no-pest strip.

It didn't bother me all that much. I'd had three relationships in three years and I'd begun to wonder if I was destined to forever be the ultimate antidote to love. I decided that, until I felt more optimistic, I'd keep my relationships with men platonic. I told Sean all I wanted was friendship. Still, part of me hoped he might inspire me to give up this latest attempt at celibacy—my third, or was it my fourth?

Soon after that, my celibacy experiment failed. But not with Sean. I met someone else, or rather, two someone elses. Sean didn't seem to mind when my new love life became part of our conversations. He didn't have a hidden agenda; friendship I asked for, friendship I got. It was kind of refreshing, getting what I asked for. I told myself that it was better this way, that if Sean and I had consummated my fantasy it would have killed our friendship.

ALASKA ESCAPE PLAN
THIRTY-FIVE YEARS OLD—THE INSIDE PASSAGE, ALASKA

Today, at my ferry's last stop on the Inside Passage, I discovered a woman with no sentimental illusions about sex. The ferry anchored for three hours in Ketchikan, and I spent most of that time walking around Creek Street—the old red light district. Boardwalks amble over the creek, where old clapboard brothels and new replicas rise above the water on wood pilings. Creek Street has transmogrified, from a pack of flesh and booze merchants, to a gaggle of souvenir merchants. Just one little house refuses to give up its ill repute: Dolly's House.

Ketchikan's most fondly remembered madam, Dolly Arthur, nee Thelma Copeland, was born in Idaho in 1888. Thelma left home at thirteen, moving first to Montana, then Vancouver. At first she waited tables, but soon discovered she could make more money from the attentions of her many male admirers. She moved to Ketchikan, changed her name to Dolly, and at thirty-one, set up her Creek Street establishment. Back in 1919, the surplus of Alaskan men was no myth at all, making the Last Frontier the perfect place to ply her new profession.

During prohibition in the Roaring Twenties, Dolly did a booming business. She considered herself higher class than common whores, whom she claimed to detest. She called herself a "sporting woman" who sold booze and conversation. If she also happened to like a good roll in the sack, that was another matter. She was known to say, "I just liked men and they liked me, too!" She had the kind of beauty that was in vogue in Mae West's era: big and busty with blond doll curls, which she wore well into old age.

Today, Dolly's pastel green home is a cloying anachronism. With its peeling pink-flowered wallpaper, pink lampshades, pink-shrouded brass bed, and the secret liquor cache in the closet, it recalls a time of innocent dissipation and good clean lechery—a time that never was.

Creek Street was a rough place during its red-light days, which lasted into the 1950s. The little wooden bordellos were filled at various times with fishermen, loggers, and miners. Every night, music, ribald laughter, and rough voices floated over the water, while piss, bottles, and the occasional body floated *in* it.

Ultimately, what set Dolly apart from the other girls on the boardwalk may simply have been that she stayed long after the party was over. After World War Two, Dolly shared her home with a man named Lefty for twenty-six years, off and on between loud and lusty fights. Lefty was a raffish longshoreman who called on more than one of Creek Street's other gals, but Dolly took the philosophical view that at least "he always came back."

When the red-light district was put out of business in the fifties, Dolly became a respected member of the community. She had a foul mouth and foul temper, but she was generous, always paid her bills, and gave the town something to talk about long past her prime. She continued to receive gentlemen callers for many years after she retired.

Dolly lived in the house at 24 Creek Street into the early seventies. She died in 1975 at the age of eighty-seven, leaving her home and furnishings to the town to use as a museum. It may be the only museum in the world that features bathtub curtains decorated with multicolored flowers made from French silk condoms.

I don't know if she came to the Last Frontier to find a man, but she certainly came to take advantage of their overabundant presence. In those days the odds were, indeed, good. And if the goods were odd, what could a sporting woman expect? I'm sure the idea of living a celibate life while surrounded by a passel of men would have made Dolly laugh.

THE LAST FRONTIER
THIRTY-ONE YEARS OLD

If I'm going to face the truth—and sitting on a ferry for three days is giving me more time for that than I ever wanted—I have to admit I probably wouldn't be leaving Alaska if it weren't for Chance.

The first time I saw Chance, his body was flying upward into a pale blue spring sky. Kaitlin had invited us both to dinner, and when I arrived I spied him in the backyard, jumping on a trampoline with her two youngest kids. He was doing flips and giggling harder than Josh and Alexandra, who were eleven and twelve.

So when Chance came into the house, breathless, bright-eyed, and tousle-haired, it's no wonder I assumed he was younger than I was. I was thirty-one; I figured him at about twenty-five. He had frat-boy hair, flirty blue eyes, and a prankster grin. He was very gentlemanly as Kaitlin introduced us. Then he ran back outside to play.

"So what do you think?" Kaitlin asked.

"Jesus, Kaitlin, let's see, based on our thirty seconds of introduction . . . he's cute, and he's charming, but he's too young and too good-looking for me. He looks like a Ken doll. He reminds me of the popular boys who used to make fun of me at school."

He wasn't twenty-five. He was thirty-three. And, as the evening drew on, he kept climbing out of the box I'd drawn to contain him. He'd traveled to exotic places and thrown himself into dangerous adventures and he knew how to tell a story. At dinner, we couldn't stop laughing when he told us about his days as a trouble-making army brat: in the Philippines he had a pet monkey that sat on his shoulder and went with him everywhere; also in the Philippines, he once tried to make chocolate-covered lizards by dipping live geckos in chocolate sauce; in Florida, on a dare, he tried to swim through an underground drain and almost drowned.

Growing up didn't change him. On a snorkeling trip somewhere in the tropics, a small octopus wrapped itself around his hand and a battle ensued: "So I'm trying to shake the octopus off, but he won't let go. Then I try to pull him off, but he just latches onto my other hand. So I try to bite his head off. Suddenly he turns and pushes his tentacles against my face. So I yank him off—STHLUPP! But the tentacles wrap around my hand again. Now I'm mad, so I try biting his head off again—STHLUPP! He grabs my face again." He finally pried the octopus off, though we wouldn't have tired of the story if the octopus had fought him for another fifteen minutes.

Although I was amused by this oversized man-child, that wasn't enough to convince me to try hooking up with him. For the next couple of weeks, Kaitlin pestered me to call him. I said if he were interested he'd have to call me.

"It's not like you gave him a lot of encouragement," she said.

"I don't know if I'm ready to date again. I need to get my confidence back up. I'll tell you what, if someone else asks me out first, then later, down the road, I might have the courage to call him."

* * *

Two months passed. Chance didn't call me; I didn't call him. I forgot about him and resumed the celibacy dance with Sean. Then, as the summer days stretched out, I grew restless.

I read somewhere that there were people who, unencumbered by romantic entanglements, actually enjoyed spending time alone. So on the Fourth of July, instead of trying to wrangle an invitation to someone's, anyone's, barbecue, I set out to prove to myself that solitude was not just a test of character to endure, but an opportunity to celebrate. To prove it, I spent the day with the largest horde of strangers I could find.

Every July Fourth, tens of thousands of Alaskans swarm to the tiny fishing town of Seward to party in the streets, and to watch three hundred men and three hundred women run up and down Mount Marathon in separate races. Mount Marathon emerges from Resurrection Bay with the sudden thrust of all Alaska's seaside mountains—a steep, grueling, three-thousand-foot dare. For Southcentral Alaska, the race is an Independence Day icon.

I wedged myself into the crowds at the bottom of the mountain, to watch men wearing paper numbers leap down the mountainside. Even as all that sweat-soaked, dirt-stained testosterone rushed past me, it never occurred to me that coming to Mount Marathon to celebrate my celibacy might be a mistake.

After the race, I wound my way through the crowded festival booths and went to the beach for a walk. The shore was packed with hundreds of people fishing and camping, children playing ball, and a circle of teens kicking a Hacky Sack. Looking past all those people to the sun-washed bay, I smiled, thinking, "What a great companion I've found in myself, a woman full of interesting thoughts, compatible and undemanding. Spending time alone really is satisfying." Then a cute guy rode past me on a bicycle.

Our eyes met, and he did that corny Hollywood double take that I thought no one ever did in real life. Later, when I turned to walk back toward the docks, we crossed paths again. This time I did the double take and we both laughed.

"Did you just finish the men's race?" I asked.

"Yeah, I did." He turned his bike around and backpedaled to cruise alongside me.

"I'm impressed!"

"It's not like I was a top finisher or anything. I don't usually do stuff like that."

"Well, you look like you do . . . I mean you have a runner's body . . . I mean . . . " I was surprised at how flustered I was.

He was short and wiry, and I admired his athletic good looks. I also admired his love of challenge and the outdoors, which I assumed had brought him here. He smelled overly ripe, but I figured any guy would after running up and down a mountain on a hot day. As I listened to his slow laugh and stared into his arrestingly large, sea-colored eyes, I forgot how great it was to be alone.

Scott was a living checklist of Alaskan cool: a carpenter who'd just designed and built his own house, a backpacker who'd traveled to exotic countries, a dog lover who owned a powerful Akita. He was the kind of dreamer who did something about it, and it was easy to imagine myself going along for the ride. So what if that ride was in a smelly old truck full of dog hair?

He lived in Kenai, even farther from Anchorage than Seward. But in Alaska, so many towns are spread so far apart that Alaskans don't think of a three-hour drive the way most people do. So we exchanged numbers. There was no reason to call Chance now. Scott seemed perfect, without the terrifying excess of charisma.

A couple of weekends later, Scott drove to Anchorage—ostensibly to visit a friend, but he spent most of the weekend with me. We went on a bike ride along the Coastal Trail, my usual modus operandi as a serial first-dater. The sight of a moose on the trail, the sound of shifting gears, and the condensed versions of our life stories filled the day with companionable noise, and I was hooked. When we went to a movie the next day and he awkwardly held my hand in the darkened theater, I noticed he smelled like a men's locker room. But I put it down to nerves.

I drove to Kenai for a visit and he took me to see the house he was almost finished building. It stood on a wooded bluff overlooking the beach. The house was an airy, sunlit space of pale wood and clear glass, its cirque of oversized windows a paean to both the rising and setting sun.

"It's beautiful," I said. "I never knew anyone who designed their own house before."

"Well, my dad helped a lot. And hopefully it'll only be my house for a few years. What I hope to do, as soon as I move in, is to immediately start work on the next one. Then I'll sell this one, move into the next one, then start another one, and turn the whole thing into a moneymaker. Then I won't have to work for other people ever again."

"Your own person," I said thoughtfully. I looked around me, imagining a tall plant in this corner, a large print on that wall, and myself curled up with a book next to the bay window.

We went for a walk on the beach with his dog, Avy. The broad-shouldered Akita was theoretically under voice command. But when we passed a female golden retriever, Avy ignored his master's voice and tried to mount her. The retriever's owner, a young woman sunbathing in her panties and bra, jumped up and began screaming and uselessly flapping her arms. "Oh my God! Do something!" she shrieked.

Scott jumped in and pulled off his dog. Then he turned to me and said, "Excuse me. This may look kinda strange." My mouth dropped as Scott grabbed Avy by the front paws and flipped the huge dog on his back. He then straddled the animal until they were nose-to-nose, gripped Avy's snout in his hands, stared the dog down, and shouted, "No! Bad behavior! No!" The dog tried to rise, but Scott forced him backward again, holding that position until the dog stopped struggling, whimpered, and licked his face. Only then did he allow his pet to rise. Scott then turned to me and smiled sheepishly. "I learned that from a dog trainer. Avy sees me as his alpha male, and if I want to teach him right from wrong I have to treat him the way an alpha male would by establishing a dominant position."

During the rest of our walk, Scott talked not about dogs, but about relationships. He told me his mother was an alcoholic and his father was a co-dependent, his ex-girlfriend was a co-dependent who recently went back to her abusive ex-boyfriend, and he (Scott) was a co-dependent with a habit of falling for women who treated him badly. He and his father had recently joined a twelve-step program together and Scott was an overflowing vomitory of the language of recovery: enabling, self-awareness, letting go, one day at a time, higher power . . . I'd never known a man who talked so much about relationships. I assumed it was a good sign: maybe someone so interested in the subject would be good at it.

Back at his house—the dark and dingy one he was living in until the wood-and-glass dream house was completed—the walls were filled with photos of foreign countries he'd visited. On one wall, a group of Vietnamese children laughed down at me as my latest experiment with celibacy came to an end. I'd planned to wait, at least until I could convince Scott to put on deodorant, but I changed my mind for two reasons: long repression in the company of Sean, and the long drive home from Kenai.

Some women would have called my next two months with Scott a whirlwind romance. It was more like a tornado of sex. I believed I was falling in love. But, after two months of whirl, we ran out of wind. First our conversations turned dull. Then he stopped calling. I didn't bother trying to find out why.

"I'm okay about it," I told Kaitlin. "It's not like he was perfect. He kept talking about his old girlfriend, and the new self-help program that was helping him get over his old girlfriend, and how he was never again going to make the same mistakes he made with his old girlfriend. Besides, he had really bad B.O. Get this: he said he didn't believe in antiperspirants or deodorants, because he read an article that said they interfere with the natural sex pheromones that attract women."

"Ewww! I could never date someone who had bad body odor. How could you stand it?"

"I figured after we were together a little longer I could break it to him gently, tell him his pheromones weren't as sexy as he thought. I just never got the chance."

Kaitlin was sympathetic, for about five minutes. Then she couldn't restrain herself: "Okay, you said if someone asked you out first, to build your confidence, you'd call Chance."

"It's been too long."

"I've got an idea. Chance does this sport called paragliding. Why don't you call and tell him you want to do a feature story about paragliding?"

"I'm not going to do that!" I said.

"Why not?"

"It sounds unethical."

"Paragliding?"

"No, calling him on the pretext of doing a story."

"No it's not. It's a legitimate feature. It's a very cool sport, and it hasn't been around that long. It's perfect for TV, very visual. So, you'll *really* do the story. Then later, if he seems interested, you can ask him out."

"Okay, okay. But what's paragliding?"

* * *

After Kaitlin sold me on the paragliding story, I called Chance and stammered my way through a pitch. I'd been a reporter for five years, and I was known for being aggressive, yet I couldn't seem to remember what I usually asked on these calls.

He said he'd put me in touch with someone from his paragliding club. Then he changed the subject. "I've been meaning to call you, but I never got your number. I thought about calling the TV station, but I didn't want you to think I was a stalker."

"You could've just asked Kaitlin."

"I thought about that, too, but I was kind of embarrassed. Anyway, I was wondering, would you like to go with me to see *Phantom of the Opera*? I've been wanting to see it and you're the only person I could think of that I'd want to take."

When I told Kaitlin, she said, "You see? He has class," as if she were already taking credit for her matchmaking success.

"And he has this sexy voice," I said. "Not deep, but warm and soothing. He gives you this feeling like he's hanging onto your every word."

Phantom didn't open for a few weeks, and now that it came down to it, I didn't want to wait that long. So, that weekend I invited him to—what else?— go for a bike ride along the Coastal Trail. I later found out that he borrowed a bike for the occasion, because he didn't want to admit he didn't own one. He picked me up, showing up at my doorstep with a platter of fresh fruit, which we dug into before we started. *Kaitlin's right, he has class*, I thought.

During the bike ride, I was nervous as a schoolgirl. I chattered incessantly, pulling out every exciting reporter anecdote I could think of: flying with a bush pilot to cover the Iditarod Trail Sled Dog Race, driving through forest fires, getting stuck in a blizzard in Bethel. I went on and on, until I thought he was convinced I was either a superhero or the most pretentious woman he'd ever met. Instead, my stories seemed to excite him, and gave him openings to talk about his adventures as a paramedic. We were both addicted to the adrenaline-rush of our jobs.

"Your job sounds amazing," he said.

"But I don't save lives."

"I don't do that as often as you think."

It never occurred to me that Chance might have a hero complex, or that a strong woman might not offer enough opportunities for a hero to strut his stuff. I was lonely, and, for the moment, that was something from which he could rescue me.

We spotted a Ptarmigan, and he stopped his bike. "*Shhh!* Watch this. These birds are so dumb. It's the only bird you can hunt with a broom."

Without looking at the bird, he began sidling up to it, mimicking the walk of a Ptarmigan, bobbing his head and craning his neck. The downy brown bird sat very still, trying to blend in with the dirt. "He thinks if he sits still we can't see him," Chance whispered. Then he very slowly reached out and touched the bird. In a sudden flutter, it flew away. In that moment I knew: I was in the same danger as that dopey Ptarmigan. This goofy guy had me mesmerized. I'd never met anyone who could be so unabashedly weird and still retain such deadly sex appeal.

After the Ptarmigan flew away, Chance smiled at me and said, "I haven't felt this good in a long time. I'm having so much fun my smile muscles hurt." He stopped smiling when his pager started beeping. He looked at the phone number and sighed with irritation. He explained, "It's this guy from work who I asked to trade shifts. The thing is, I don't know if I want to switch with him after all, because he called it a 'favor.' I just don't want him to think I owe him. I don't like to be in someone's debt."

My smile faltered, too, as a tiny doubt tugged at a corner of my mind. I projected to some moment in the future when I'd give too much to this man and he'd resent me for making him feel indebted. But I shook it off. *You're always borrowing trouble from the future*, I told myself. *He's the most exciting guy you've met in a long time. Relax.*

On our second date we went to a movie, and afterward he said, "I've been reading the new dating manual, and it says that on the second date you're supposed to kiss me."

So I did.

On our third date we went for a walk, and I said, "I bought a copy of that dating manual, too, and it says on the third date you're supposed to hold my hand."

So he did.

The first time I saw Chance truly fly was on our fourth date. We were at Hatcher Pass with maybe a dozen other paraglider pilots, their girlfriends, boyfriends, families, and dogs. The sky was a rainbow of paraglider canopies drifting back and forth along the cliffs.

Chance giggled like a school kid on the first day of summer as he rolled out his blue nylon canopy. "I hope you don't mind if I rush off. The conditions are incredible!" He strapped on his harness and started running. His bright blue wing rose behind him, and he jumped off the cliff. Air filled the canopy and lifted him into the sky, where he continued to rise, higher and higher, and farther and farther away, until he disappeared around the hill. He sailed back and forth above the ridge again and again, along with the other pilots. Everyone was laughing and hollering. I could almost smell the adrenaline in their wake.

"Three hundred feet above launch! Can you believe it!" he shouted at his friends as he returned to earth. Then he turned to me, "I'm sorry, I know you don't understand, but going three hundred feet above launch, that's amazing! It's like being a bird, just soaring on the updrafts."

Once my image of him took to the sky, there was no bringing it down. Soon after that, Chance invited me into his apartment. I didn't want to make the mistake of moving too fast, like I did with Scott, but I thought it would be okay if we stayed in the living room. I didn't know that his living room doubled as his bedroom. We rented old episodes of *The Outer Limits* and flopped on his futon to watch. Afterward, we barely stayed within the limits of the dating handbook.

When I felt my self-control slipping I pulled away and said, "I just want you to know, there's this guy I was seeing up until a few weeks ago, and we never really split up. He just stopped calling . . . "

"You mean, you have a boyfriend and you're here in my bed?" Chance slipped me a sly grin and kissed my neck.

"I wouldn't exactly call him my boyfriend anymore. But it was sort of serious, and then it suddenly stopped. And this is all happening a little quickly for me."

"Look, I'm not planning to have sex with you, if that's what you're worried about—not that I don't want to . . . I mean, you're very attractive. It's just that I've kind of got a new dating rule: no intercourse. At least, not for a long time. Really. I can draw a line if you can."

True to his word, he didn't try to insert tab-A into slot-B, although we certainly went farther than I planned. His kiss was as simultaneously calming and exciting as his voice, driving smelly Scott from my mind. I hadn't felt this way since I was eighteen. I'd only settled cynically for its recurring counterfeit, because I was someone who always wanted to be in love.

When I stood in his doorway to say goodnight, he said, "I like you a lot, so I just want to warn you: I'm not very good at commitment. I wouldn't call off that old boyfriend just yet."

My face burned with humiliation. *That was stupid,* I thought. *Did I ever ask him about his feelings?* I gave him a cursory hug and left, feeling like an accessory to my own violation.

⋆ ⋆ ⋆

After we got only half-naked and stopped short of spending the night together, Chance stopped calling. Two weeks went by. I decided it was a no-fault breakup, like being let go during the probationary period at a new job. That's when Scott called.

Out of a warped sense of loyalty, and a perverse desire to blot Chance's rejection from my mind, I decided to give Bachelor Number One another chance. When Scott invited himself to my place for the weekend, I accepted. Hadn't Chance said, "I wouldn't call off that old boyfriend just yet"? Hadn't I once come to the covert conclusion that I could marry Scott? Surely he'd stop talking about his old girlfriend sooner or later. Surely as soon as I explained to him that his pheromones made me a little nauseous he'd rush out and buy deodorant.

When Scott arrived at my doorstep on Friday night, I dragged him into my apartment and we made up with a vengeance. I noticed that making love with this ultra-athletic guy was kind of like competing in an Olympic sport for which I'd never trained; I just couldn't keep up with his high-speed performance. And I couldn't push Chance out of my mind.

Afterward, we went to a country-western bar with a couple of my friends, where I stared at Scott's innocent eyes and tried to figure out why the feeling that had seemed so real a few weeks ago had vanished. Mistaking my stare, Scott sealed our fate by saying, "Don't go getting all mushy and start falling for me, now."

Indignant, I decided he needed to be taken down a peg. Maybe he was an outdoorsy Alaskan man who'd built a house in the woods and seen some interesting places, but once the exciting image wore off he was just another presumptuous, smelly guy with issues. In spite of the compulsion I felt to hang onto yet another placeholder until Mr. Right arrived, I chose to forego another qualifying run in the sack. Whatever flimsy thing had been between us was now gone. That night I told him our relationship wasn't going anywhere. In the morning he left and didn't return.

Later, I realized that Scott wasn't a bad guy. His biggest problem was that I wanted someone else.

* * *

The day after Scott left, Chance called. My heart started beating with the same silly eagerness as a puppy's tail thumping the floor. He invited me for a hike up Flattop, a popular mountain just half an hour outside town. Without asking why he hadn't called in two weeks, without stopping to think about his last words to me, I leapt at the chance to see him again.

Flattop was always the handiest place to remind myself that, although I lived in a city, I still lived in Alaska. It only took forty-five minutes to hike to the top of the 3500-foot mountain, and it was a relatively easy trail for anyone in decent shape. Yet it was also an easy place to achieve a sense of accomplishment, with steep rises and a hand-over-foot scrabble up craggy rock, leading to an incredible view. The top looked as if someone had chopped the peak off with a cleaver, giving Flattop its name. The flat surface seemed to confuse the ever-shifting, swirling air, leaving the top invariably cold and windy.

Just in case the winds might be in his favor, Chance packed his paraglider on his back. But as we rose above the twisted hemlock of the lower slopes, the wind was already whipping us. So he hid his paraglider in some bushes on Blueberry Hill, to retrieve on our way down. Now that he was empty-handed, he offered to carry my daypack. "I'm okay for now," I said. "But I may take you up on that later."

A short way up the trail, he said his throat was sore. "I put some cough drops in the top of your pack, can I grab them?" I waited as he stepped behind me and unzipped my pack to rummage around for a lozenge. Later, when we reached the steepest section of the hike, I said, "Okay, I'll take you up on that offer—you can take my pack now." His face twitched in a mischievous grin as he took my pack, put it on the ground, and unzipped it. "Okay. But first . . . I won't be needing this anymore." He reached into the pack, pulled out a huge rock, and tossed it to the ground, where it landed with a thud. It weighed at least five pounds. Then he innocently tossed the pack onto his shoulders. Chance had never needed that cough drop. I stared at the rock, slack-jawed, then pummeled him. As we stood there giggling, I realized I was in love with him. That damned rock seemed to seal it.

A short time later, we pulled ourselves over the final crag and onto the abbreviated peak. The wind nearly knocked us over.

"Isn't this great!" Chance shouted over the shrieking air. "I love extreme weather."

"Yeah, it's great, but my ears are freezing!"

We ran for cover behind a cairn, where Chance huddled behind me, cupped his hands over my ears and blew on them. His breath felt hot, in exciting contrast to the cold. When we felt warm enough to stand, we took in the 360-degree view: graceful saddles led in several directions to the severe alpine beauty of the Chugach Mountains, while below us Alaska's largest city looked like a toy model and Cook Inlet gleamed in the sun. No one else was on the mountain and we ran around like children, giddy with the freedom of having this windswept view to ourselves.

When we were too cold to stand it anymore, we scurried down the mountain and back to his place. We curled up together on his futon while Chance talked, his soothing voice buzzing in my ear. I relaxed into a feeling of warm contentment and, in characteristic fashion, spoke my thoughts aloud without stopping to consider them: "Chance, from now on I don't want to be with anyone but you."

The comment came from my desire to completely attach myself to Chance. Yet that comment severed me from him in a way I didn't expect, because this guy who'd told me he was lousy at commitment had assumed I'd already made one. His body stiffened with anger.

"What do you mean? Have you been with someone else? Did you see your old boyfriend again?"

"Well, yes. You stopped calling and I thought I wasn't going to hear from you again. So I thought I'd give him another chance. But that's my point: when I saw him, I realized I didn't want to be with him, I wanted to be with you. So I told him it was over."

He sat up and pushed me away. "When exactly did you tell him this?"

There was no getting out of this situation. I have a profound aversion to lying, based less on merit than on ingrained defensiveness over being wrongly and regularly accused of lying as a child. I could refrain from speaking, but he would know the answer by my silence.

As my mind raced for a reply, he repeated, "When was the last time you saw him?"

"Friday night."

"Did you sleep with him?"

I sat in embarrassed silence.

"Damn it!" He jumped off the couch as if I'd burned him. "You have no idea what a turn-off that is for me. So you broke up with him, but you sent him away with a big smile on his face, didn't you? And I was starting to think I'd met someone who was so different. I thought this was special."

I'd thought so, too, and I could feel it irretrievably slipping away. I babbled, "Don't you see? I tried to give my old boyfriend a second chance, but it didn't work because I realized I was falling for you."

"Then how could you do that with him?"

"I'm sorry. I just want you to know . . . I really did have a wonderful time today. And . . . I'm so sorry. Goodbye." I started to leave.

"So now I don't even get a hug?"

Puzzled, I turned back and gave him a hug. He held me tightly. I felt confused by his mixed signals. I remembered him telling me he wasn't good at commitment. What had he expected? Then again, what had *I* expected? I pulled away and left.

★ ★ ★

The next day, I called to apologize. It took me several tries before he answered the phone.

"Can I come over and talk with you?" I asked.

"This just isn't a good time."

"I really am sorry."

"No, it's not that. It really isn't a good time."

"Why? What else is wrong?"

"I've been drinking."

"What do you mean? A lot?"

"I had nine beers."

"Oh, I see," I said softly.

In spite of what popular wisdom had to say on the subject, I blamed myself for upsetting him. Surely he didn't drink nine beers on a regular basis? He looked and acted so respectable; he was so well-spoken and polite.

He called back later, after he sobered up, and invited me over after all. When I arrived he was throwing out his trash. I heard the clanking of bottles, a loud after-the-frat-party noise. God, how I hate that sound. My head began to ache and my heart began to pound. I wanted to run.

But when he returned from the garbage bin, he didn't seem drunk, just tired. He sat down, pulled me onto his lap, and pressed his forehead to mine.

"Cara, I won't pretend you didn't hurt my feelings, but I think we can get past this. I think I can understand. All I know is I thought about you all day, and I couldn't stand the thought of not seeing you again."

I spent the next two years trying to get back to that feeling on the mountain. Sometimes I think I'm still looking for it, even as I leave Alaska behind.

ALASKA ESCAPE PLAN
THIRTY-FIVE YEARS OLD—THE INSIDE PASSAGE, ALASKA

The ferry made no stops today. On the third day of our journey through the Inside Passage we drifted through an elegy of rain. Low clouds caressed the sea with longing.

I'm staying in the solarium on the back deck, where it looks as if a hippie subculture has set up a little village. Tents stand lined up like a row of squat soldiers at the rear, while deck chairs draped with sleeping bags sit gathered in small groups under the roof. Backpacks lie scattered everywhere. The solarium is a hive of college kids returning from summer jobs, families finishing vacations, fishing guides, the young, the old, the searching, the lost. I've been sitting in my deck chair, opening and closing a Russian nesting doll painted in shades of pink abandon. I bought the wood doll a couple of days ago in Sitka as a gift for Iliana, my two-year-old half-sister in L.A. I know she'll probably lose the tiniest dolls, but I don't care. I just want to see her reaction when she opens each doll to see what's inside, one after another.

Even on vacation, I'm usually driven by a compulsion to do something, hounded by my grandmother's voice in my head: "I never saw anyone so lazy!" But today the voice stopped, knowing that, even if I wanted to, there wasn't much to do. I spent the morning playing Scrabble with an older woman camped next to me in the solarium. Then I spent the afternoon talking with two fellow travelers, Pete and Sam, until lazy began to feel good.

Pete's a sightseeing pilot. He's thirty-five, but has the optimistic smile of a man ten years younger. Sam is a fishing guide. He's the same age as Pete, but has the saturnine demeanor of a man twenty years older, someone who's seen it all and found much of it disappointing. When I told them that I'm traveling around the world, the two of them helped me cobble together an incoherent travel philosophy, each offering very different advice.

Pete suggested, "Take plenty of pictures. And write down what they are. I can't tell you how many photos I have that are like, 'well, this is a mountain somewhere.'"

Sam advised, "Don't let your view of the world narrow down to the tiny square of your camera's viewfinder. Stop taking photos sometimes and just look around."

Pete said, "Be open to getting to know local people. Some of my best travel experiences have been with people who offered to show me around, or invited me to their homes."

Sam said, "There are a lot of con artists out there, and people who'd love to take advantage of a woman traveling alone. Trust no one."

Later, there was a stir of excitement among the passengers when twenty to thirty porpoises began leaping next to the boat. I called Sam over to take a look; Pete was nowhere in sight. Sam sauntered over and leaned against the rail in a James Dean slouch. As we watched the sleek gray bodies torpedo through the water, I thought I heard one give a squeaky call. Then I turned and stared suspiciously at Sam as he gazed seriously off into the distance. "Is that you?" I asked. He started laughing, and I elbowed him in the ribs.

Tonight, as we sailed south into clearing skies, the northern lights appeared. Almost everyone on the back deck was asleep, except Pete, who sat in a chair out in the open, staring up at the sky. "You know," he said, "studies have shown that, when the northern lights appear on this side of the pole, there's a mirror image on the other side." We both fell silent as we watched the silky green and red cape cast itself trembling and crackling across the cold, dark sky.

Alaska is not just a place. It is an idea. For those who are cast adrift, it is a place to drop anchor. For those who wander, it is a place to call home. For those whose lives are defined by longing, it is a dream of desire fulfilled. If my soul had a name I would call it Alaska, the Last Frontier. I'll be gone before winter puts Alaska to sleep again. But this place, this idea, will forever imbue my black-and-white dreams with shifting colors, as the angels that dance in the Aurora Borealis whisper, "You can leave us. You can leave it all. But we will never leave you."

A good thing they won't. It's lonely traveling on my own, and a little company couldn't hurt—real or imagined, friend or stranger.

COMING HOME

My contacts burned and phlegmy grit coated my throat as I was swallowed by the omnipresent brown cloud of Los Angeles. Home—as if this impersonal place that has chewed up and spit out so many dreamers could have nurtured anyone. I wasn't eager to reach my father's house, where I always forget who I am, instead becoming the person he and his wife think I am. But this time his wife would no longer be there. So who would I be?

While the idea of my own death has always left me alternately curious and petrified, the death of others only embarrasses me. I've heard that I need not weep for the dead because of the hope of heaven. Yet whenever someone dies, I fear that my inability to exhibit feelings of sorrow or pity will only raise suspicions I might be a sociopath. The death of others only puzzles me. A person was here; now he or she is not. How odd. The only emotional reaction I've ever been certain of in the face of death has been to realize my connection to those left behind.

Los Angeles began to lure me back several months ago. My father made the phone call telling me my stepmother had cancer, but I knew it was really the voice of the great smoggy beast gurgling, "Bring me more flesh on which to feed."

Dad said I couldn't tell her I knew because she'd made him promise not to tell anyone. It was a secret they'd kept for nine years. "But I don't think that's right," he said. "I think family should know these things. Anyway, now the doctors say it's touch-and-go, and I didn't want you to be surprised if I called with bad news."

He avoided the word "dying." It seemed I wasn't the only one who found death embarrassing. Maturity might make us comfortable being caught in any number of unintentional crudities: flatulence, stray boogers, bad dancing. But my stepmother didn't want to be seen dying, and my father didn't want to be seen losing it.

Dr. Alex Lopez is a stoic, coolly analytical genius whom I've never known well. By the time he was twenty-seven—when I was six years old—he was already a university professor of psychology and Mexican-American studies. Even then, he had salt-and-pepper hair, thick glasses, and an erect bearing so that from my earliest memories he had the appearance of unquestionable intellectual authority. My father's booming baritone and biting sarcasm have always driven the saliva right out of my mouth. I feel destined to forever make silly remarks that result in eye rolling as my brilliant father explains the error of my thinking.

When I was a child, the only way he felt comfortable showing affection was by tickling me until I giggled so hard I couldn't breathe, or by calling me pet names like *fatso*, *ugly*, and *dingbat*, followed by more tickling, apparently to assure me these weren't insults but endearments. Even though I hated it, I learned to laugh, because it was the only time my daddy laughed *with* me.

My parents divorced when I was two. My mother feared she couldn't raise me alone, and then she married a man who didn't want stepchildren. So I spent most of my childhood with my father's parents. Actually, I spent most of my childhood being tossed around like a hot potato.

The first two times Daddy remarried—when I was four, and again when I was seven—I temporarily moved out of my grandparents' house to move in with him and each new "Mommy" as he attempted to draw a new family circle. Only on weekends and in the summers was I allowed to stay with the family I knew: Grampa, who built a loft bed in my bedroom and taught me to roller skate by pulling me around the driveway with a broomstick, and "Mom," who listened to me read Dr. Seuss books while I sat on her lap and watched old Judy Garland movies with me on TV. Every Sunday night, when my grandparents brought me back to Daddy's, I cried myself to sleep.

On weeknights, when Daddy and Step-Mommy Number Two worked late and couldn't find a babysitter, I stayed home alone. One night when I was seven, I watched Steven Spielberg's *Duel* on TV. I was terrified to go to sleep for fear a stranger would come in and try to kill me like the crazy trucker who chased that poor man in the movie. When Daddy came home at midnight to find me sitting up in his bed still watching TV, he blew up.

"I was too scared to sleep," I said, crying. "The noise makes me feel better."

"Don't lie to me! I know you just want any excuse to watch TV."

He and Step-Mommy Number Two said that a lot: "Don't lie to me!" Every day after school, "Mommy" would ask if I'd gotten in trouble again for talking in class. If the answer was yes, she'd pull down my panties and spank my bare butt red; if the answer was no, she'd say, "Don't lie to me!" pull down my panties and spank my bare butt red. That divorce was a relief.

Age nine: I lived with Dad's girlfriend while he worked a second job and lived alone in his apartment. Age ten: I moved in with his girlfriend's parents. I spent a lot of time with her mother, who spoke only Spanish. I only understood a few phrases, which made me feel frustrated and isolated. But she smiled a lot, made me homemade tortillas, and shook her head at my dad when he yelled at me, so I understood she was my friend. That didn't last either. One Sunday night when I was eleven, I lay in bed listening to Daddy and Grampa shout in the living room. A week later I was happily living with my grandparents again.

I suppose another child would have figured out by then that happiness never lasts. When I was twelve, Grampa left. That same year, my mother disappeared—my real mother.

You know the old joke: my parents moved and didn't tell me? From age five until age ten, I used to fly to Phoenix to stay with my mother and her husband for two weeks every summer. When I was eleven, they divorced and she returned to Southern California, where I saw her more often—for a while. When I was twelve, on Mother's Day, I phoned to tell her I had a gift for her. A recorded voice informed me that her number was "disconnected or no longer in service."

Hoping it was a mistake, I called the number for weeks. All that summer, the gift I'd bought her sat atop a bookshelf, waiting: a tiny cactus planted in a clear plastic pot, featuring a fluorescent colored sand painting of a palm tree. One day, a friend of mine accidentally knocked it over, and the orange, green, and pink sand spilled out. I carefully poured the grains back into the pot, but the sand painting had erased and I couldn't recreate it. I stared at the blurred lines in the sand and started to cry, because I knew at that moment that my mother wasn't coming back.

I grew determined to hang onto my grandmother, the woman I'd always called "Mom," before, during, and between the rest.

By then my dad had become, not a Sunday father, but a birthdays and holidays father. In school, I earned mostly A's, but Dad only noticed when I got a B. He didn't get angry, just asked, "What happened?" When he visited Mom and me the Christmas of my sophomore year, I proudly showed him a report card with three A-pluses and two A's. He absently said, "That's nice," and changed the subject. Hardly the opening of the heavens I'd busted my ass for. With the absurd logic of an angst-addicted teen, I chose a new approach: I'll show you, I'll screw me.

By the time I graduated I'd earned several C's, a D, and an F, gotten stupid drunk and crazy stoned on multiple occasions, had sex (with a man I loved, of course) in my grandmother's bathroom while she napped in the next room, and had an abortion at fifteen. It was easy to hide these things, because my grandmother was always working or sleeping and my father rarely visited.

To his credit, for graduation Dad gave me a much-undeserved car, a vintage VW bug. I accepted it and confessed nothing, believing it was a pittance compared to the blood he owed me.

On my sixteenth birthday, I began applying for work. Two weeks later, it was Father's Day. I still hadn't landed a job, so I bought dad's gift with my allowance. When he opened the box and saw the tie clip, his jaw twitched with rage. I was shocked when he thrust the box back at me, saying it was time I got a job and he didn't want any gift from me that I hadn't paid for with money I'd earned.

"But Cara *did* earn that money, by doing chores," my grandmother said.

"Mom, she shouldn't be paid for housework. That's an expected part of being a member of a family. Look, I don't want to hear from Cara again until she's found a job." With that, he stalked out of the house, before I could remind him that it had only been two weeks since I'd reached the legal age to work, before I could explain that I'd applied for two dozen jobs and simply hadn't been hired yet, before I could ask if he thought homemakers deserved a share of the family income, since housework was "an expected part of being a member of a family."

By the time my dad married Christina, I was seventeen and beyond the desire to name another stranger "Mommy," especially one as close to *my* age as she was to my dad's. Christina was a twenty-six-year-old Mexican

beauty just shy of a bachelor's degree (which my father encouraged her
to finish). She had dark, Siamese cat eyes and a girlish giggle that sounded
like music to those she loved and an automatic weapon to those she suspected were fools. I never heard the music.

Christina hated me. I'll admit by that point there wasn't much to like. I
was an embittered, self-centered, self-righteous teenager who spent most
nights hanging out with my friends at a coffee shop until three a.m. We
were actors and musicians, and we spent hours discussing how to save the
world through art. When I told Christina that I planned to be an actress,
she aimed her giggle weapon at me and fired sharp machine gun bursts
of titters.

When I started attending my father's university, she accused me of being
ashamed of my Hispanic heritage since I refused to use Dad's last name,
Lopez. This wasn't true; it wasn't my heritage I was rejecting, but the
father who had rejected me. My grandfather, my dad's step-dad, had the
last name Lee, and I used that name because I considered him my father. I
didn't explain this to Christina, sure it would only make her hate me more.

When I was nineteen, at Thanksgiving, Christina made her first overture
of friendship in two years. She suggested we make tamales together on
Christmas Eve. Equal parts excited and terrified at the prospect of spending
time alone with her—in the kitchen, no less, where she was an undisputed
master of the art of Mexican cooking and I felt like a klutz—I accepted.

Then, during the month before Christmas, I had what used to be called
a nervous breakdown. Today you'd call it depression, although nervous
breakdown sounds more like it felt: as if every nerve in my body had broken down. Nobody noticed.

It started shortly before Thanksgiving, when I got suspended from my
waitress job because too many of my customers walked out without paying. Then my roommate moved out and I couldn't find a new one. All I
had in the fridge was a package of bologna and a carton of milk. Then
my car broke down and I couldn't afford the repairs. I was a commuting
student and didn't know anyone who could give me a ride. All this during
my first semester attending the university where my father not only had
a lofty reputation, but the power to crush my will: "Do you know what
the odds are of making it in the film industry? Who's going to hire a philosophy major? What do you mean 'communications'?" Broke and jobless,

without a ride or roommate, powerless and invisible, I withdrew for the semester and moved back in with my grandmother.

That's when my birth mother called. Her only comment about the missing seven years: "I heard you've been looking for me."

My two grandmothers had recently exchanged letters on the subject of my mother's disappearance, and my mother's mother had only this to say about the reason: "Jennifer said she called Cara one day, and Cara was in a hurry to rush off with some friends. Jennifer said she realized her daughter had her own life now and didn't need a mother anymore." Her twelve-year-old-daughter. That's why, when my mother finally called and we made plans to get together, I was afraid to ask for explanations or voice recriminations, lest I scare her off again.

She took me shopping and bought me decadent amounts of clothing. We looked at each other in dressing room mirrors, each trying to find a glimpse of herself in the person standing next to her. At forty-one, my mother's pale, freckled European-American beauty was still youthful, although the shiny dark hair she still piled on her head in a 1960s hairdo was streaked with gray, and her hazel eyes darted around nervously—as if she didn't trust the world around her to remain constant. Our conversation rose and fell, from non-stop laughing chatter to nervous silence. As I moved in and out of fitting rooms, we tried to fill each other in on the last seven years of our lives. I was in love with a twenty-two-year-old business major I'd been dating for a year. She'd married her third husband, an engineer, four years before.

Shortly after our visit, the engineer called, crying, to tell me that my mother had become an alcoholic and that he thought I was a key to solving her problem. I tried to sympathize, but I began to wish my mother had stayed "disconnected or no longer in service." This woman had never taken responsibility for me, and now I was supposed to help her? She and I briefly talked about it, and she explained that her husband's emotional abuse had driven her to drink. By silent agreement, we treated her drinking the way we treated her disappearance: we acted as if it never happened.

Shortly after that, my boyfriend dumped me. He said I was too needy. Years later he confessed he was so high on cocaine during our relationship that he didn't remember most of it.

At that point, although I continued to work sporadic temp jobs, I spent the bulk of my time in a sleepwalking triangle: from bed, to fridge, to TV, and back again. One day a couple of friends came over, and my grandmother sent them to my room to coax me out. They found me lying in bed shredding the pair of nylons I was wearing; I'd started pulling on a runner and gotten carried away. I looked up sheepishly from the frayed nest of tan thread spread around me and we all laughed. Maybe if I hadn't laughed someone would have noticed I was unraveling.

So you see, I kind of forgot about Christina's tamales. In my defense, I will say she didn't mention them for weeks.

I was surprised, the night before Christmas Eve, when I came home from a party after midnight to find a note in my grandmother's angry handwriting. My friends used to joke that I had the only mom who knew how to yell in a note, with furiously dark scribbling, underlines, and exclamation points. The note said, "Christina and your dad called and they said to show up at their house at 9:00 a.m. *sharp tomorrow morning, <u>or don't bother coming at all!</u>*"

I was incensed at this rude demand that presumed I had no other life beyond the one my occasional family ordered. I had plans. In an effort to rejoin the world, I was baking Christmas cookies in the morning to take to friends, including my estranged boyfriend, and I'd already called to tell everyone I was making rounds. So I decided to take Christina and my dad up on the "don't bother coming at all" part of the message. If it was a joke, it obviously meant that it was okay to show up anytime. If it was serious, screw them!

On Christmas Eve day, after burning the cookies and getting burned by the ex—he loved the cookies, but not me anymore—when I showed up at Dad's house he ran outside and met me at the car to tell me Christina was furious. I tried to explain my take on their note, but it sounded kind of stupid once I said it out loud. He "strongly suggested" I apologize.

If I was terrified of Christina before, now I could barely breathe. It was a long walk up the stairway to their Spanish style house with the antique terra cotta roof—my dad once told me those tiles weighed several tons. Inside, my heels echoed on the wood floor as I made my way to the kitchen, where Christina was stirring something on the stove.

"Excuse me, Christina," I said, and hesitated.

"Yes?" She turned to me. Ice chips flecked her eyes.

"I just wanted to say I'm sorry . . ." I'd planned to say more, but my own sobs caught me by complete surprise, a wet and gasping implosion that hit with the ferocity of an asthma attack. I thought about the boyfriend who'd dumped me, the mother who'd dumped me, the restaurant customers who'd walked out on those checks, and the parade of stepmothers who'd walked in and out of my life. I wanted to tell her all that had happened in a few weeks. I wanted to say that her message had given me the feeling she didn't want me there. I wanted to say I was terrified of women. But I couldn't explain anything, because likely she would tell me I'd brought it all on myself, and because, worst of all, maybe I had. So instead of spewing the effluvia of nineteen years of emotional exile and self-pity, I only cried . . . and cried, and cried, until, in a voice cracked and dry as a desert, I came up with the empty explanation: "I'm sorry, I had a bad day."

She put her arms around me and awkwardly patted my shoulder, carefully holding her body away from mine, so that at first glance someone might have thought we were demonstrating proper frame for a ballroom dance. Then she said, in a voice thick with irritation, "All right, Cara, all right. Don't torture yourself. It's okay."

For the next few hours, the house filled with the tension of a battlefield during a ceasefire. After dinner, I offered to help Christina wash dishes, but she refused. So I sat in the breakfast nook with my dad and grandmother, while my stepmother attacked the dinnerware.

As she furiously scrubbed a pot, my father asked, "Christina, is something wrong?"

She thrust the pot into the suds as if she wished to drown it, and said, "I'm just tired of this game Cara's playing with me."

Sensing I was about to be as thoroughly scoured as that little pot, I wanted to run. But I was trapped. "Come on, Mom," my dad said to my grandmother, as he rose from the table. "We should leave these two alone." Silently, with a look over her shoulder at me, a look I couldn't read, my grandmother followed her son out of the room. As Christina sat across from me, I felt a deep lethargy. There was no room inside me for any more pain.

She explained that her invitation had been a gesture of friendship, and that my not showing up felt like a slap in the face. I explained that I *had* shown up, after I'd kept my other commitments, and that her ultimatum "or don't bother coming at all" felt like a slap in *my* face.

"Cara, I meant that as a joke."

"If it was a joke, why did you expect me to respond to it like a command?"

The bottom line was we didn't trust each other. I'd spoiled her fantasy about two women sharing a Mexican Christmas tradition. The significance was lost on me, because I had no memories of bonding with a woman in a kitchen. And, having only one foot in the world of Mexican culture, I didn't understand how difficult tamales were to make, so I didn't know why she needed more than a couple of hours of my help.

"I don't buy that," she said. "I think you left me high and dry to prove a point. You haven't wanted me around from the beginning."

Her comment took me by surprise. "I've always seen it the other way around. But okay, maybe I have seemed a little unapproachable. You have to understand, it's not easy for me to get close to women. My dad's been married a few times, and each time I believed that person was going to be my mother, and then she was gone. So, maybe I'm just a little cautious, you know?"

"Cara!" her thin voice sliced through the air, "I have no plans to be just another of your father's *wives*. I'm here to stay, so get used to it."

"I didn't mean it that way . . . " I felt the tears rising again, but they only enraged her more, because she saw them as part of my "game."

The only thing that ended the argument was the stroke of midnight, when Christina declared a truce because it was time to open presents. At midnight every Christmas Eve, my family traditionally opens one gift each. So we gathered around the tree in the living room, where my grandmother and father ripped into their gifts and self-consciously extolled the contents, while Christina and I carefully peeled away paper and muttered wooden thank-yous. I don't remember what my gift was. Shortly after one a.m., we all went to bed.

I lay awake on the fold-out couch in the den, listening to the familiar hum of L.A. traffic in the city below, staring up at the ceiling of this house in which I'd never lived, and imagining what it would be like if the tons of antique tile on the roof crashed through the ceiling and crushed us all. I realized that, if Christina had been wrong before, she was right now: I hoped she would leave him, like the others had. My body shook with cold, although the house was warm. This aching cold felt like hatred, and it frightened me. I tried to tell myself it was just a misunderstanding, but I couldn't stop the waves of resentment. I knew I'd have to do everything I could to hide my feelings, or risk being skewered again by her thin, girlish anger.

Over the years, I tried to make peace with her. My grandmother suggested that asking people for advice was a good way to win them over. So I often called Christina for advice about school and career, friendships and men. She gradually responded and we developed a grudging friendship. I found most of her advice lacking in perception, but not for lack of effort. She was an intelligent, emotional woman, who cared deeply for her other family members, but, like many people, she lacked the imagination to empathize with someone to whom she felt no connection.

My grandmother thought it was simpler than that. She believed Christina was jealous because I was a reminder that my dad had once fathered a child with another woman. Christina had tried to have a baby for years, but couldn't. Whatever the reasons, the tension remained.

Then, when she was forty-four, after she'd given up hope, Christina had a baby. Almost instantly, her attitude toward me softened. For the first time in years, she gave me a direct invitation to visit. I immediately took her up on it. I flew to L.A. as often as possible, not wanting to miss out on having a sister after thirty-three years as an only child. During those visits, Christina was so overflowing with love for her baby that she couldn't help splashing me with some of the excess affection. It was like jogging past a cold sprinkler on a hot day, a refreshing shock.

The second time I visited, when Iliana was a few months old, her mother told me, "Your sister just loves music. Watch this." She played a classical CD, and Iliana went quiet with elfin-eyed wonder. I picked up my sister and danced with her, and she smiled at me as we swayed around the floor. Love is a moment, like a pebble skipping across a pond. Iliana and I could not yet speak to each other, but it didn't matter. It didn't matter at all.

The third time I visited, my father said Christina had the flu and felt too sick to come out of her room. However, my grandfather stopped by. Although I didn't know it then, Christina had invited him over to see *me*.

I hadn't spoken to Grampa in years. This wasn't my choice. When he'd married his second wife, he'd never given me his phone number. Even after they'd divorced, he'd rarely responded to my letters or calls. During this unexpected visit, he admitted that Christina had scolded him for neglecting me. He later explained that he'd stepped aside to give me a chance to bond with my dad, never realizing that he was depriving me of the only father I truly knew. I never had a chance to tell Christina how grateful I was to her, for giving that father back to me.

I still didn't know she had cancer.

When Dad divulged her secret, first I pitied her, then I felt guilty, then I grew angry. Over the years she'd often accused me of being dishonest, of playing games, yet she'd spent nine years hiding the truth. And, because she wanted to maintain her lie, she left me stuck with the role of the biggest bitch in her life, and she in mine, even though those roles, too, were lies.

★ ★ ★

I can still smell the antiseptics and urine of the ICU, that halfway house of death. As Dad and I entered, my eyes scanned the beds, pausing at the sad sight of a tiny, shriveled, bald old man of about eighty, body twisted, arms twitching. That was the patient we approached. That little old man was Christina. As a reporter, I'd often seen the results of sudden, violent death. But nothing prepared me for the shock of sitting idle for two weeks, watching someone undergo a slow attack from within.

I told her I loved her, possibly the strangest truth of my life. If she weren't in a coma, perhaps she would have sat up to accuse me of falsehood one last time. I promised to look out for her daughter.

Christina never spoke, yet in my memory she whispers: "I was only forty-six. I had a two-year-old daughter. I didn't get to finish anything. I wasn't ready. I wasn't ready at all." For me, forty-six is eleven years away. I know there's no point in dwelling on death, which could come tomorrow, or sixty-five years from now. But whenever it comes, I don't want it to catch me waiting for my life to turn out. That was Christina's final gift to me, her unuttered advice, which for once I would follow. She convinced me not to wait any longer to do what I do best: run for it.

Some people say the definition of insanity is doing the same thing over and over and expecting different results. Other people call this persistence. Then again, there are some things that seem the same, but when you look closely, they aren't alike at all.

* * *

I arrived at my father's house tonight in the gloom of a warm and smoggy L.A. evening. My dad, baby sister, and I hovered in the doorway, smiling and embracing, our faces dressed up in the family joy people wear for photos. "But what are those grinning people thinking about, really?" you might ask, trying to spot the flaw in this American portrait.

The wood floors squeaked as we walked through the dining room, past the table littered with bills, where Christina's name stared belatedly from the little plastic windows of several envelopes. In the kitchen, the housekeeper had left two pots warming on the stove, organic beans and rice, macrobiotic fare the family had learned to eat in hopes of driving out the cancer in their midst. The patient was gone, but the diet remained, to beat back death for the survivors. Dad steamed organic vegetables and heated organic tortillas, and we all sat down to dinner in the breakfast nook where I'd once argued with Christina until midnight on a Christmas Eve.

While I helped my sister smear her mouth with bean drippings, I told my Dad about the high points of my road trip down the coast. When I spoke of the Hearst Castle, just outside San Luis Obispo, he smiled and said, "Christina and I went there once. She really enjoyed it. We took tour number one, but we talked about going back sometime and taking one of the other tours . . . " He trailed off. Usually I feel a compulsion to fill dead air, but this time I let it die.

My dad interrupted the chewing session to ask if I'd take Iliana to preschool in the morning. I readily agreed, relieved to have a task, to feel I'm earning my keep. I've touted this three-month visit to my father as mutually beneficial: I'll have a place to stay while planning the rest of my trip, and Dad and Iliana will have someone to fill in the blanks during a difficult transition. Yet, in spite of my good intentions, I feel like an interloper in this house of mourning.

After dinner, I watched Iliana play with the Russian nesting doll I bought her in Sitka. She made quite a show of unscrewing the top off each doll, eyes twinkling, as if she were about to show me a bit of magic. As she opened each one, she drew her mouth into a small round "o" and repeated, "There's more!"

I certainly hope so.

* * *

I offered to shop for Iliana's Halloween costume, but Dad said she had one. Last night I put it on her—a smiling, gap-toothed jack-o'-lantern. She looked even tinier in that puffy balloon of orange fabric, a monstrous mouth swallowing her middle, a fat green stem atop her little head.

Dad said, "Christina bought her that costume, before . . ."

"Oh . . . It's adorable," I said, pretending to be at ease with these creepy pauses.

Before we left the house, I took a photo of my sister with our dad. He stared into space, while she stared into the lens with a puzzled look. Perhaps she was wondering what it is he's always staring at, off in the middle distance.

Rather than take her trick-or-treating, which would have been about as fun as a funeral march, we took her to a party. In spite of the horde of sugar-rushing kids, it still felt like a wake. The presence of several small ghosts, angels, and skeletons did little to dispel the feeling.

The hosts served dinner as well as sweets, and Iliana asked to try my lemon garnish. I hesitated, but Dad said, "Let her try it. That'll cure her curiosity." Her comical pucker was followed by a look of delight and the sweet peal of giggles. "More!" she said. So I gave her another. "You've gotta love a kid who loves lemons," I said to Dad. But he was staring at his favorite ghost again, who was missing another of her daughter's firsts.

After dinner, the room became a headachy blur of orange cupcakes, miniature candies, and screaming children. I made Iliana a plate of goodies, and Dad and I stared as she turned her cupcake upside down, smeared frosting on her plate, and accidentally tipped over her punch. He angrily grabbed her arm, causing her to drop the cupcake on the ground as her eyes opened wide in terror. "Iliana! Why are you doing that?!" he shouted, inches from her face.

Tears rose in her eyes, while my heart leapt into my throat. I pulled her away from him and onto my lap. "She doesn't know why she's doing it, Dad!" I said. "She's doing it because she's two. Chill out!"

"All right."

"Think about how big your voice is, and how little she is! You scared the hell out of her."

"Okay. I get it."

"Jesus," I muttered. "You even scared me."

"I said okay, Iliana! Drop it. Why do you have to drag everything out?"

"Dad, I'm not Iliana. I'm Cara."

I looked around to see if anyone was watching. But the party roared on, unconcerned with our petty problems. I picked up my sniffling sister. "That's okay. It was an accident. Would you like another cupcake?" She gave me a hesitant nod, and I carried her to the table of goodies. A moment later she was laughing, but my heart was still slamming up into my windpipe.

As I contemplated my emotionally crippled father, I began to fear that history will repeat itself, that he'll abandon another daughter to be raised by relatives, that another girl will grow up feeling unwanted.

THE LAST FRONTIER
THIRTY-ONE YEARS OLD

Sitting in the passenger seat of Chance's Toyota Land Cruiser, I looked in the rearview mirror at Autumn and wondered why her friendly, gap-toothed smile made me nervous. The insubstantial but tempting warmth of Alaska's Indian summer had convinced Chance to plan an overnight camping trip at Kenai Lake. Autumn and two of her three sons, ages six and eight, went with us.

A few months before he'd met me, Chance had met Autumn through a multi-level marketing group. They'd become instant friends. Her upbringing with a single father and three brothers had given her an affinity for male company. She was a young, conservative Christian, whose opinions seemed mostly borrowed; the most biting commentary I ever heard her attempt was when she gave Jane Fonda the pithy nickname "Communist Woman." Although she wasn't a woman of broad information, she was witty, vivacious, and full of infectious laughter. Of Athabascan descent, she had high cheekbones, deep brown eyes, and cinnamon skin. Depending on the light and her mood, her face might look grey-shadowed and plain, or glowing and goddess-like.

Her husband had said he'd try to join us, but he never showed. Mike worked long hours in construction and preferred to end his days in front of the TV. He didn't approve of his wife's good-looking male friends, loud female friends, or the multi-level marketing cohorts who coaxed her into "gallivanting" at night. I suspected he was the blanket that had smothered Autumn's opinions before they'd had a chance to breathe. However, the few times we saw them together he was so quiet it was easy to forget he was there, except for his rare wisecracks. Once, when Autumn wasn't around, Mike joked about marrying her to make an honest woman of her. The look in his eyes, and the three children they'd had by their mid-twenties, lent truth to his jest. I thought the joke in poor taste and felt a little sorry for her.

I might have felt more sorry for her, except I could tell that Chance did, too.

At the lake, I grew increasingly jealous of Chance's attentions to Autumn. First he helped her set up her tent. Very thoughtful. Then they both insisted I relax while they made dinner. I clenched my jaw as they giggled over the near-conflagration they started while lighting the camp stove. After dinner, Chance invited her for an evening float on the lake in his new inflatable boat, just the two of them. I stayed onshore to watch the kids. I could hear Chance and Autumn's giggles echoing off the water, although I couldn't see them through the trees lining the shore.

Her boys had crawled into their tent to sleep, but after the first half-hour, the six-year-old started calling for his mother. I peeked in and told him she was still in the boat.

"Are you cold?" I asked. "Do you need another blanket?"

"I want my mom."

"I'm sorry. I'm sure she'll be back soon."

When they came back, I addressed Autumn in the flattest tone I could muster. "Your son was asking for you."

She ran to the tent.

"How long were we gone?" Chance asked.

"About an hour."

He wrapped his arms around me and kissed my forehead, "I left my baby doll alone all that time? I'm sorry."

I was only partially mollified.

That night, Chance and I slept in the back of his Land Cruiser. In the middle of the night, we heard tapping on the window. It was Autumn. She'd only brought a warm-weather sleeping bag and she was cold. She asked if she could crawl into the SUV with us. "Sure," Chance said. For the rest of the night, I only slept in angry little fits and starts, while Chance lay sandwiched between Autumn and me.

The next day, he invited her to hop into the inflatable boat with him again. The day was sunny and windy, and he'd hatched a plan to use his giant kite to pull them across the lake.

It was no small risk. This wasn't one of those little paper or plastic kites I'd flown as a kid, but a broad nylon wing designed much like his paraglider. I'd seen him fly the huge red kite on land and watched it pull him off his feet many times. The powerful canopy could easily drag him into the water, or capsize the raft. People have died of hypothermia falling into glacier-fed lakes within swimming distance of shore, their pointless lifejackets firmly fastened about them. But crazy chances were the dots that connected Chance's life, creating an alluring shape.

"We're gonna make history!" he said.

"No guts, no glory!" Autumn said. She was brave, if not original.

I wanted to go, despite the danger. But no one invited me, and the boat could only hold two. Chance handed me a camera to record the moment. I was hurt, but too embarrassed to protest. Once again, I was a reporter watching from the sidelines, recording events in which I could not take part. In spite of myself, I was captivated by the beauty of the red kite as it dodged and dipped and painted figure eights in the sky. Propelled by a stiff wind, the kite dragged the boat through the water so fast that a large white wave spilled across the front of the tiny vessel, threatening to swamp it. My heart raced with the raft as I realized Chance and Autumn were about to die before my eyes. When they reached the halfway mark, I gave up standing watch and drove to the other shore to pick them up. I brought the boys with me. What would I say to them if we arrived to find two bodies floating in the lake?

But Chance and Autumn were standing at the water's edge, wet and laughing. "Did you see that?" he said. "That was incredible!" Although they were giddy as kids, they were fish-eyed with a fear not yet shaken. As they dried off, Chance apologized to Autumn: "That was a pretty big risk. I should've let the kite go."

Maybe if I'd gone instead of her, my different weight or different reactions would have dumped us overboard and killed us. But that thought didn't help. I envied them this moment.

I never did get to try out that boat.

I did play with Chance and Autumn again, and again. I always felt as if they were the cool kids and I was the tagalong. The more this enraged me, the more I tried to fit in, and the more I tried to fit in, the more enraged I grew—until my emotions became a loaded gun, just waiting for someone to pull the trigger.

THIRTY-TWO YEARS OLD

I had to leave Los Angeles and Denver behind and move to the Last Frontier to first notice the sounds of violence in the streets. I didn't live in a bad neighborhood, yet the sound of gunshots at two a.m. became as unremarkable to me as the hum of a passing car. Anchorage cops told me that it was common at night for young people, often gang members, to drive around the city and shoot at each other, or just fire random shots for the hell of it, reveling in their power to dispense fear and death. I sat in Anchorage courtrooms and pondered the bewildered eyes of young men, boys really, who had shot and killed.

In spite of all that, life in Alaska taught me to appreciate guns. Maybe I picked it up by a sort of cultural osmosis; even if you subtract the gangs, Alaskan culture is, after all, a gun culture. That is to say, it's still a frontier, with an "I'll do what I damn well please and it's none of your business" attitude.

It was Chance who first took me to a firing range and taught me to shoot a handgun. I felt an almost sexual rush of adrenaline. *Maybe this is what people are so afraid of,* I thought. *Maybe something with the power to kill shouldn't be so seductive.*

A few months later that message hit home, the day Chance, Autumn, and I went to an outdoor firing range just outside town to shoot targets with his .45.

I'd made a concerted effort to become friends with Autumn. This was partly in self-defense—I thought if she learned to like me she would be less likely to cross the line with my guy—but it was also because I found her lively and likeable. Still, as my friendship with her grew, so did her friendship with Chance, and so did my jealousy.

That day at the firing range, Chance gave Autumn plenty of tutoring on how to fire his gun. He stood behind her, touching her arm, her shoulder, her waist, all ostensibly to help her learn proper body position.

Afterward, he and I returned to his condo alone. When I joined him in the basement to watch him clean his gun, I complained about his training session with Autumn. "You never help *me* that way."

"You never seem to want advice. You always tell me to leave you alone."

"Only because you're so critical and treat me like I'm stupid when I don't get something right away."

"Okay, you're probably right. Autumn even told me to go easy on her. She says I can talk kind of harshly when I'm giving advice. I'm sorry."

Just then, I heard a noise in the house. "What's that?" I whispered.

"What?"

"I heard something."

We both fell silent, listening to our own breathing.

"Crap! I think we left the garage door open," I said.

Then we both heard it, some kind of movement upstairs.

"Someone's in the house," I said.

Chance picked up the gun, loaded it, and pointed it toward the floor as he started creeping toward the stairway. Now all I heard was blood surging through my ears. I stood close behind him as he tiptoed up the stairs.

"Boo!" Autumn shouted, as she jumped down to the landing and found herself staring at the barrel of a gun.

"Shit!" Chance yelled, lowering his weapon.

For a moment we all stood transfixed.

Autumn broke the silence, "Oh my God. I'm sorry. That was really stupid. I'm so sorry. That was so stupid." She walked back upstairs to leave, shaking her head and mumbling to herself.

Chance followed her outside. I sat down on the stairs and stared into space.

A few minutes later he returned. "She's okay, just embarrassed," he said. Then he started rambling, "We should never have left the garage door open. But she knew we were out firing guns today! She knew she never should have snuck in the house like that. She said she thought it would be funny. You realize we did absolutely the wrong thing? If there's an intruder in the house, you're never supposed to go looking for them. You're supposed to wait for them to come to you."

I just sat and stared.

"Jesus!" he went on. "We were just a split second away from a terrible tragedy. What would I have told her husband? Can you imagine? We almost turned her kids into orphans."

"I need to go home," I said, and stood up to leave. Chance gave me a hug, and I burst into tears.

"Yeah, that shook me up, too," he said. "Are you okay? Oh God, I'm sorry."

The following year, Chance signed up for an Alaska license to carry a concealed firearm. He often wore a suit or blazer, and—tucked into the back of his pants under his jacket—his .45, waiting for the day some madman might attack us on the streets of Anchorage. He admitted it was unlikely, but if it ever happened, wouldn't I be grateful he wasn't like the other "mindless sheep that go around unprotected, never thinking ahead?"

I didn't fear madmen, gang members, or mindless sheep. I didn't even fear Chance, not yet. The only person I feared was Autumn, although I thanked God that Chance didn't actually shoot her. I can't imagine how we would have gone on from there.

★ ★ ★

It was months before I had the courage to confront Chance about my fears. He kept distracting me with his schizophrenic charm. He gave me a candy necklace made out of Sweet Tarts. He read me bedtime stories. One night we camped inside his condo: we put up a tent in the living room, built a fire in the fireplace, and slept in sleeping bags while listening to CDs of nature sounds like frogs, crickets, ocean waves, and rain.

But no distraction could make me overlook the disappearance of sex. And I couldn't come up with enough baked goods, backrubs, or martyrdom to halt the primitive emotional ambush waiting inside me. One night, he sat soaking in the tub with lit candles around him and a beer in his hand. I knelt by the tub and asked if I could join him. He turned me down.

I picked at a loose cuticle with obsessive concentration and said, "We rarely make love anymore. Why is that?"

"I just haven't felt like it lately. Do you want me to make love to you even if I'm not in the mood?"

"No. But you used to be in the mood a lot and now you're not. I was wondering why."

"Why do you think?"

"Maybe because I've gained weight?" I asked, thinking this was something I at least had some power to control.

"It's not the size of a woman's body that makes her attractive. You're probably one of those annoying women who hurts other women's feelings by always talking about how fat you are when you're really not, aren't you? Have you ever noticed that some fat women are very sexy, while some slim women with nice features are still unattractive because of their attitude?"

"So I'm not attractive to you anymore because of my personality? Is that the problem?"

"The problem is all these annoying discussions. You know how I hate this."

I explained that the annoying discussions hadn't started until after I'd noticed the distance between us. I told him I wanted to know what caused the distance in the first place. Looking back, it's so clear now that all my double-talk was just a way of fooling myself.

Chance wasn't fooled. "What's this really about, Cara?"

"Okay. I'm worried because you spend so much time with Autumn."

"Autumn's a good friend."

"Yes, but you're both human, and I don't think it's healthy for you to spend so much time together when her husband and I aren't around. It's too much temptation."

"You think Autumn and I are going to have an affair?"

"Yes. You might not plan on it, but . . ."

"Autumn would never do something like that. She's a nice person."

"I know she's a nice person. Chance, nice people have affairs. Of course nice people would be attracted to each other. Who wants to have an affair with a jerk?"

"You shouldn't worry about it. Look, I came in here to relax. Would you mind leaving me alone?"

He didn't get out of the tub until the water grew chill gray, and he didn't stop drinking beers until his face grew warm red. He passed out early in a deep, snoring stupor. If I was jealous of Autumn, I was even more jealous of alcohol because he spent more nights in its arms than in mine. I began to realize *that* was my real competition.

Lying next to him that night, I felt more alone than I ever did when I was alone. All my sexual frustration turned to boiling rage. I crawled over him, stood up, and yanked the covers off his body. When that only raised a mild grunt of annoyance, I tugged the pillow out from under his head.

"What the hell are you doing?" he grumbled.

I repeatedly kicked the futon, screaming, "Why are you doing this?! You fucking drunk! You're ruining everything! I hate you! I hate you! I hate you!" Each time I screamed the word "hate" I punctuated it with a swift kick to the futon.

"Great. You hate me. I got it," he said, his eyes narrow and flashing, like shards of broken glass. "Now can I sleep?"

Then I left.

I didn't know which was worse, that those words came out of my mouth, or that I was never sure if he even remembered them the next day, when he asked me to come back.

* * *

The four of us stood at the back of the water taxi—Autumn and Mike, Chance and I—watching Chance's yellow kayak bob through the water at the end of a towrope. It reminded me of a child's toy boat floating in a bathtub.

We were all there to play a role in Chance's newest heroic fantasy. "Autumn's always telling me how she and Mike are having problems," he said. "I think it'd be good for them to get out and do something fun together in the outdoors. And it'd be good for us to get to know another couple. Who knows? Maybe we can help save their marriage."

I knew he meant it. Chance's savior fantasy was fueled by a true desire to help, coupled with powerful self-delusion. He saved lives as a paramedic; perhaps he could resuscitate a drowning relationship. I wondered, too, if he was trying to rescue our relationship from the temptation Autumn presented. He was always trying to get the four of us together to do things. However, it was rare that both Autumn and her husband were available at the same time.

This time Chance's plan was a four-day, three-night kayak excursion in Kachemak Bay. I'd kayaked only once before. So, to prepare for our trip, I took a kayaking seminar with Chance. Autumn and Mike had never kayaked before, but they couldn't afford the seminar. In the unpredictable waters of Alaska, they'd be relying on Chance's relative experience.

The water taxi took us to Hesketh Island, where we picked up three more kayaks. We were supposed to meet the taxi at this spot again in three days.

After we pitched our tents, we went for an afternoon paddle. In the glittering sunshine, Kachemak Bay flung a generous swath of multifaceted beauty. Snow-robed mountains rose above sparkling fjords that raveled away into unseen distances. Evergreens walked down nearly to the water's edge, where translucent blue-green tidal pools hinted of glaciers tucked away among the folds of the fjords. We saw no whales or sea lions as I'd hoped, just a few otters, their wise and whiskered old gentlemen faces gazing at us with mild curiosity.

I relaxed into the uncomplicated labor of paddling as tiny waves nudged my kayak in a tranquil lullaby. The air was warm, but I never forgot that the frigid water could kill as fast as a weapon. If I fell in, I'd have only a few minutes to use my new skills to climb back into the kayak, or die of hypothermia. This knowledge added an undercurrent of tension to my reverie. With no real agenda, we set out for Elephant Rock, so-named for the obvious reason: the rock looked like the head, floppy ears, and dangling trunk of an elephant. Small waves surged through the narrow arch formed by the trunk, and we took turns surfing them in our kayaks. An electric thrill charged through me as each powerful little wave thrust me through the arch. Our laughter echoed through the rocky passage, then drifted away on the increasing wind.

Afterward, we paddled to a beach to take a break. "Where are the canned oysters?" I asked.

"Why?" Chance replied.

"Because I'm hungry."

"Those are for later. We're going to eat those as an appetizer with the crackers."

"Okay, but I need to eat something. I'm really hungry."

"Can't you wait until dinner?"

"Damn it! I told you I wanted to buy some food of my own, but you insisted you and Autumn would buy everything. Remember I asked, 'Do you promise I'll be able to eat whenever I need to?' And you said, 'Yes.' Now it's only the first day and you're already rationing me."

"No, I'm not. I'm just telling you to wait."

Autumn gave me a sympathetic look. "Chance, she's hungry. Let her eat something."

"I'm not giving her a whole damned can of oysters."

"I didn't say it had to be oysters," I said. "That's just something I remember seeing."

"Here, you can have my orange," Autumn said softly, with a scolding glance at Chance.

"No, that's okay. I'll wait. It's not like I'm going to starve to death. It just pisses me off. I hate begging. It's humiliating."

"I'm really not going to eat it," she said, and thrust the orange into my hand.

"Thanks." I accepted the fruit and, feeling deflated, sat on the beach to peel it. It was hard to swallow, each slice passing over a lump in my throat. So much for the ocean's lullaby.

★ ★ ★

In the morning, we broke camp and prepared to make our way to another shore. I packed my kayak carefully, balancing the weight for stability in the water. I'd just finished when Mike walked up, peeked into the hull of my kayak, and said, "Great, you have room." He then unceremoniously shoved something heavy into my kayak. It didn't fit at first, so he pulled something else out, then wrestled everything back in.

"Wait! I've got it all balanced," I said.

"I'm sorry, but I don't have room in my kayak."

"Okay, but let *me* put it in, so I can balance it with everything else."

"Cara, don't be so anal. You worry too much," he said, and walked away.

After he said that, I felt too embarrassed to reach in and rearrange the gear. A few minutes later we shoved off.

We made our crossing into the teeth of a stiff wind, pushing into waves stronger and taller than any of us anticipated: maybe two feet high. Later, I'd stare at a ruler, calculating, and think, *Okay, how is that a big deal?* But a ruler is a single, stationary object, and it's not rudely punching at my little kayak in angry bursts as I sway atop the dangerously chilly waters of Alaska. It might not have been so bad if the waves had been broad rollers we could ride up and down, rather than narrow chop that slammed into us over and again. I wondered if I was in over my head. I said nothing, but felt my eyes grow into the bulging state my friends call my "deer in the headlights" look.

Having been taught that it's safer to drive directly into a wave, I angled into the wind as much as possible while still making a course for shore. Having been taught nothing, Autumn was too frightened to push into the waves and, with a look of determination, she began paddling in the direction of least resistance . . . toward the vast open waters of Cook Inlet. The open water terrified me even more than the waves, so I continued toward shore. This soon created a gap between the group and me, as everyone else followed Autumn.

Chance paddled over to me. "Cara, we need to stay with the group."

"Chance, she's taking us out to sea. Besides, if I go that way, the waves are going to knock the side of my boat. We're supposed to go *into* the waves. It's not safe going that way."

"I know, I know. You're right, and I tried to tell her. But she's scared and she's not doing it, and it's even more unsafe if we get separated."

He was right. So, though it increased my terror, I turned to follow Autumn and Mike. As I'd predicted, the waves pummeled my boat, sending it lurching sideways. Also as I'd predicted, my boat rolled at a more alarming angle than anyone else's, because my load was heavier on the side most vulnerable to the persistent waves. Pissed at Mike for shoving his gear so haphazardly into my kayak, and more pissed at myself for not rearranging my load just because he'd called me "anal," I found it easier to deal with the situation. Anger was easier to deal with than fear.

In his gentlest, most persuasive voice, Chance coaxed Autumn to turn into the waves. I began to breathe again, as the open water that yawned before us shifted to my periphery.

When we reached the opposite shore, we paddled along the shoreline until we arrived at the mouth of Tutka Bay, where the air was calmer and the waves gentler. We passed small islands and rolling hills backed by powerful mountains, until we entered the passage to Tutka Bay Lagoon. The slender channel grew narrower and shallower until the water was just inches deep and my kayak scraped rocks on the bottom.

Just as I began wondering if we'd have to get out and drag the kayaks, we spilled out into the lagoon, where a small purse seiner was circling its net around a huge catch of pink salmon. We paddled into the midst of so many leaping salmon that there was never a moment when there wasn't one in the air. The sight made me laugh with childlike delight.

We set up camp on the shore. Then Autumn and Chance went fishing, while I explored the tidal pools for sea stars and Mike took a nap.

In the evening, Chance and I paddled into the darkened lagoon and floated there while salmon cavorted and splashed around us. The distant murmur of Autumn and Mike's voices was the only other sound. A fish leapt over the bow of my boat. "Whoa!" Chance said. "I hope one of them lands right in my kayak!"

After a brief silence he said, "I was proud of you today. You were so brave during that crossing. You were the calmest, quietest one in the group."

"That's because I was terrified."

"Really? It didn't show." He dropped his voice, "You know, I was scared, too."

"I'm glad I didn't know that, or I would have been more afraid."

"I was kind of pissed off at Autumn, too," he said. "That was dangerous."

"Really? I thought you were pissed at *me*."

"No. You were the only one doing the right thing. It's just that I knew we had to stay together."

We stopped talking for a long time and just listened to the fish leaping around us. Then he reached through the moonlight, took my hand to pull our kayaks together, and kissed me—the weightless, lingering kiss of falling in love. "This is way special, babe," he said. His blue eyes shone dark and liquid as the lagoon. The moon glistened on the water and in the scales of the salmon as they rose into the night.

★ ★ ★

The enchantment of that perfect night spilled over into the morning as we finished our tour down the long finger of Tutka Bay. Then we turned back to paddle for Hesketh Island, where we'd started two days before.

Along the way, we stopped at a wooden float and climbed out of our kayaks for lunch.

I pointed at the float and said, "Look at all those barnacles."

"I think those are mussels," Mike said.

"I've always wondered how you get mussels," Autumn said.

"You go to the gym," Mike said.

We all burst into laughter.

It was the last moment we truly shared. As we paddled on, we each drifted in our own little worlds. Mike and I pushed ahead. I looked back and saw that Chance and Autumn had pulled up side by side and stopped for a moment. He had his arm on her shoulder and they were leaning their heads together to share a private conversation. I turned away and paddled harder.

It took longer than we expected to reach the mouth of Tutka Bay. By the time we started the crossing to Hesketh Island, the sun was setting and a breeze was rising. At first it didn't seem so bad, but soon we found ourselves in windier, wilder conditions than we'd encountered on our first crossing—and this time dusk was closing in. By the time we recognized our danger we were already at the halfway mark. There was nothing for it but to press on.

The evening grew darker. The waves attacked more viciously, tossing freezing cold water at me until my face was so wet I decided it was safe to let the tears fall without fear of anyone noticing. We barely spoke. Reaching the far shore seemed in doubt. The danger was real. It was too dark, and the waves were not only taller—maybe up to three feet—but also steeper and choppier than before. My kayak was taking a bitch-slapping, and so was my nerve.

To regain a sense of control, I began cussing at the waves, calling them names as I beat them with my paddle: "You cocksuckers! Fuck you! You're not going to beat me, son-of-a-bitch! Fuckers! Fuck you, shitty little fucking waves! Take that! And that!"

Then, to distract my thoughts, I began the deep breathing I'd learned in aikido, breathing in rhythm to my paddle strokes: "In . . . out . . . in . . . out." Sensei Sean had always gotten after me to *"breeeeath"* and "stand up straight." I noticed I was hunching my back, so I sat up straighter.

The twilight deepened. The shore seemed as far as ever. I muttered the Lord's Prayer.

When we reached shore, wet, shivering, and triumphant, I thought, *Now I know I can handle anything.* As we unloaded our kayaks, I told Autumn I'd prayed during the crossing, fearful of what might happen. "That's funny. I never worry about stuff like that," she said. "I always know God will take care of me." The remark stung, as if she said my faith were inferior.

I brushed the subject aside and we started a fire and set up camp. I shivered through dinner, then went straight to my tent and fell asleep.

If only I could have slept through everything that followed.

★　★　★

In the middle of the night, I woke to the sound of two male voices pitched with so much tension it made my heart race. Mike and Chance were talking with a pretense toward calm that was more unbearable than straightforward yelling. It took me a moment to register what the conversation was about.

"It wasn't supposed to be like this. I never meant it to be like this," I heard Chance say in a choked voice. He spoke as if he'd caused an accident but had no idea how it had happened.

Then I heard Mike: "I told her I didn't like you guys spending so much time together. 'We're just friends,' she kept saying, and I trusted her. I should've known. You guys always sat too close together and leaned too close together when you talked."

"I wouldn't blame you if you wanted to hit me."

"I'm not going to hit you. That won't solve anything. I just want you to understand what you've done, how wrong it was."

It's funny how denial only seems obvious when other people are living in it. As I listened, the reality I'd been denying sank in: although Mike and I had thought there were only two couples on this kayak excursion, there were three. The pounding waves of our crossing seemed inconsequential now, compared to the pounding in my chest.

Later, Chance came into the tent to find me wide-awake. "Did you hear?" he asked.

"I heard enough."

He said nothing, just crawled into his sleeping bag. I remained silent for about an hour, until my chest burst open with a great heaving sob, then another, and another.

"Cara, be quiet! Cara, stop it! They'll hear you!"

"You're actually pissed at me?!"

"You're making a scene."

"Whose fault is that?"

"Try to think about somebody besides yourself," he said. "They'll hear you." It was as if he still believed he could save their marriage, by sparing them my tears.

The next morning we all crawled silently out of our tents and retreated in pairs to different parts of the small beach—Chance and I in one spot, Autumn and Mike in another—but always in sight of each other because there was nowhere to get away. The water taxi was scheduled to pick us up at two in the afternoon. That was several hours away.

After a couple of hours, Mike suggested we all needed to talk. For the first time in my life, talking was the last thing I wanted to do. But I was too numb to object. We sat on a couple of logs and twiddled our eyes for a moment.

Mike's voice was so quiet. "I've had a long talk with Autumn, and I told her I'd take her back. But she says she's in love with you, Chance. She says she wants to be with you."

"That's not what I said, Mike! You didn't listen to me."

"Well then, what did you say? Didn't you say you wanted to be with Chance?"

"Don't do this to me," she said, her eyes filled with tears, her jaw clenched.

"That's not going to happen," Chance said. "Whether or not you stay together, we never planned on being a couple. We just made a mistake. Anyway, it's over now. You guys can still work on your marriage. I don't want your marriage to break up because of me."

"You still don't get it!" Mike said. "Over the years there are bonds created in a marriage, bonds of trust. You've broken those bonds. They can't be repaired that easily—"

I cut him off. "I don't think we should talk about this now, because I don't even know everything you're talking about and a lot of this is none of my business. Some of it's just between you and Autumn, or you and Chance, or Chance and me. Anyway, I don't think this is the time or place." I was amazed at how calm I sounded.

As we retreated to our separate corners, Chance complimented me for handling everything with such calm maturity. I'd only made the calm, mature decision to bury my head in the sand. I was a dignified fool.

I pretended to myself that as soon as we got off this damned island I'd leave Chance, that I'd be my own hero, the woman who was no one's victim. But in the twisted, habit-formed places of my mind I was already formulating my plan to hang onto him. I would forgive him, he would owe me for that, and his guilt would make him mine. How could he leave me now?

Since my initial outburst, I'd remained dry-eyed, believing that more tears would only increase my humiliation. Meanwhile, Autumn wouldn't stop crying. I'd taken up a restless, directionless pacing, and as I walked past her she tentatively said, "Cara . . ."

"Yes?"

"I'd like to talk to you sometime."

"I'm sorry, but I don't really want to. If you feel the need, you can write me a letter."

I'd tried desperately to make her my friend, but standing in front of this swollen-eyed wife and mother, I realized I didn't know her. What good would it do trying to understand each other now?

During the long wait, Chance and I decided to occupy ourselves by making a banana cream pie. We rummaged in our dry bags for pudding mix, bananas, and other ingredients. After we mixed the filling and poured it into the pre-made crust, we dug a trench in the sand and filled it with ocean water. We floated the pie in the cold water to firm up the filling, and sat together silently watching it drift back and forth. When the pie was ready, Chance asked Mike and Autumn if they wanted any. They weren't hungry.

As I absently pushed bits of pie into my mouth, I started to smile. I realized I'd suffered the pain I most feared and it hadn't ended me. "I can't believe you're still smiling," Chance said, and put his arms around me. He rocked me, and with each gentle sway I hated him, then loved him, then hated him, then loved him, as we looked out at the bay.

Time burrowed into the sand and disappeared like a crab, the air thick with the smell of salt water and lies, the silence broken only by the muffled sounds of the surf reluctantly lapping the shore.

Hours later, riding back to Homer in the water taxi, Autumn tried to cover the awkwardness with a joke, "Hey, Mike, how do you get mussels?" We all just looked at her. She cast her eyes down at the boat deck. No one spoke again.

COMING HOME
THIRTY-FIVE YEARS OLD—LOS ANGELES, CALIFORNIA

Today a small package from Sean arrived in the mail. He sent me two books: Steve Martin's *Pure Drivel* and a book of poetry by Billy Collins. Inside the flyleaf of the Collins book, Sean had written a poem of his own:

> *I miss you.*
> *When the wind gently caresses the leaves into a song,*
> *I dream of you.*

He always gives the perfect gift: some little something that tells me he knows who I am, but something that also reminds me of him. I called to thank him.

"I've been thinking," he said. "I'm so sorry for all I've put you through. I do love you, Cara. The only reason I've never committed to you is because I've been afraid of fucking it up." He asked for another chance. He asked if he could come to L.A. to spend Christmas with me.

"I don't know. I think we should move on. After Christmas, I'm going to be traveling a long time. We're not a couple anymore."

"You're right. This is my own fault." He started to cry. I've heard him cry before, though not often. It always makes my heart hurt, as if whatever's happening to him is happening to me.

"It's not all your fault. I'm not sure I could have made the commitment either. I've always blamed men for never making a commitment, but maybe it's been me all along. By clinging to men who couldn't commit, I've always escaped that decision." I paused. "Look, this doesn't mean I don't love you, Sean. I'll always love you, and I'll always be your friend. My soul is connected with yours and it always will be."

"I know. But it'll never be the same, and you know it."

"No, it won't. But even if we ended up together, it would never be the same. Something always happens that no one expects. Nothing is ever the same. No matter what we do."

His offer is tempting. But I'm not ready to trust him. It's easier to think about trusting someone new, a man who hasn't yet let me down. I haven't given up hope on the man I have yet to meet, only on the ones I already know.

*   *   *

My jaw hurts. I've been clenching it at night again. This time the problem isn't Chance. It's not Sean either. It's another man.

The last time I lived in a house with my father, I was nine. It was no fun the first time, tiptoeing around the icy draft Dr. Lopez left in his disciplined wake. Yet here I am, by choice, nine all over again. This time he is making an effort, which is almost more annoying. It was less complicated when he took no interest in me and I felt free to simply hate him.

Today he took me to the USC-UCLA game at Pasadena's Rose Bowl Stadium. My dad now teaches public administration at USC and he's a big SC fan. I'm not big on football, but I couldn't turn down a chance at the father-daughter moment I used to dream about.

About a mile from the stadium we were bogged down in game-day traffic, amid a flotilla of flatbeds and convertibles full of fans dressed in cardinal-and-gold or blue-and-gold, waving signs and ululating good-natured battle cries. My father is not a patient man. After his car crawled only one block in five minutes, he decided to park in a nearby neighborhood, saying, "We can walk the rest of the way faster than we can drive it."

He certainly could. When I was a child I used to have to run to keep up with his brisk walk. "Hurry up, Cara!" he would say, rarely glancing back to see if I kept up, so that I always feared he'd lose me and never notice. Today, I did a sort of skip-jog. If I walked I'd lose him, if I ran I'd pull too far ahead. As usual he looked straight ahead, as if I weren't there, as we zigzagged between other pedestrians.

Then my father zigged when I zagged. I stepped on his heel and went down, slamming into the sidewalk as if I'd been tackled. My loud grunt of pain was accompanied by a chorus of "OHHH!" from some two-dozen college kids crammed into the vehicles idling on the street. If it hadn't been for their empathetic groans, I'm not sure my dad would have noticed.

He turned and said, "Oh my goodness!" (He's the only man I know who can say "Oh my goodness!" without sounding effeminate.) Then, echoing several nearby voices, he asked, "Are you okay?"

The fall had ripped open my leggings and torn a bloody hunk of flesh from my knee, but I said, "Yeah, I'm okay."

He apologized, and when we resumed walking he slowed his pace, although I still had to limp-hop to keep up with him. Several times in the ensuing half-mile, we caught each other's eyes and chuckled. He mimicked my lurching limp and gurgled, "Walk this way!" like Igor from *Young Frankenstein,* and our chuckles turned to giggles. When we reached the stadium, he went to the concession stand and got some ice for my knee.

During the game, he explained every nuance of the action, the strengths of each team, and the stats of the players without a trace of his usual condescension. Together, we rolled our eyes when SC fumbled for the umpteenth time, and laughed when mascot Tommy Trojan rode his white charger onto the field and the fan sitting next to us shouted, "Shoot the horse!" USC lost, but I didn't care. My father and I had laughed together, and this time the joke wasn't on me.

By the time we returned home, my knee was swollen. Dad said, "You'd better get some ice on that and put your leg up." A few hours later I was still in the TV room, happily lying on the couch with my leg up, when my father-daughter fantasy came to an end.

He sat down and asked how my travel plans were coming. Still relishing the attention, I did what I always do when I'm excited: I continued talking after I stopped thinking.

"There's so much to see in Italy," I said. "I can't possibly see everything I want to see in just four weeks."

"That's too much time. You'll see. You'll probably get bored."

"But I don't mind just hanging out and doing nothing. And I like doing weird stuff. Remember, I'm the weird one in the family."

"That's presumptuous, Cara."

He was right, as usual; I was showing off. That ended the conversation, so we did the only thing we always enjoy doing together: we watched a movie. This one was some B picture about a teacher working in a tough ghetto high school. There was rampant violence in the halls, and one girl offered to have sex with the teacher in return for good grades. My father— who always talks throughout movies but angrily shushes anyone else who dares do the same—told me the movie was stretching reality too far. He said such things rarely happen in schools.

"Sure they do," I said.

"Cara, I've spent a lot of time working with people in the school system. Such things may happen, but they're rare events."

"Not necessarily."

"'Not necessarily' isn't an argument," he said. "In any assertion, the exception of 'not necessarily' may already be assumed."

I grew defensive. "I only used the shorthand, 'not necessarily,' because I didn't want to get into a debate while we're watching a movie. But okay, you might have spent a lot of time in schools, but I've spent a lot of time with gang members in Anchorage—as a volunteer *and* a reporter—and I find it hard to believe L.A. gangs would be more tame. I've interviewed a fifteen-year-old kid who sold guns. I've covered cases of teachers who had sex with students. The movie might be using hyperbole, but filmmakers often use hyperbole to underline the truth."

"*All right*, Cara. Why do you have to be right about everything?"

I stared at him, taken aback, my mouth opening and closing like a beached fish.

"What's the matter now?" he asked.

"It's just that, when I describe you to people, that's the way I always describe *you*, that you always have to be right."

"Really?" he said. He looked genuinely perplexed.

"God. You have no idea. I've been so bitter." Choking on tears of rage, I stood up. "I've been struggling so hard to avoid this. I didn't want to be like those dysfunctional families who tear each other apart in movies. I didn't want to be another cliché. But here we are!"

The next moment, I felt guilty about my outburst, knowing he was still grieving for his dead wife. "I'm sorry," I said. "You were watching the movie and now I've made you miss it. We were having a good time and now it's ruined. My anger was way out of proportion to your comment. I should have chosen another time to tell you how I felt. I'm really sorry."

"Don't worry about it, Cara."

Neither of us said another word. I left the room.

I went to the kitchen and called Kaitlin to unload. "All these years I've been hoping someday my dad and I would have this great relationship. When I came here I thought this was my chance to fix everything. But maybe we aren't meant to get over our pasts. Maybe some things just can't be repaired."

"That's true," she said, "but it's only human that you'd hope for more. Every daughter wants her father to love her and be proud of her. The way I see it, any father would be proud to have a daughter like you. He just doesn't know how to show it. And you're right, you can't fix that. Only he can."

But my dad doesn't even know there's anything to fix.

One thing I'll say for Sean, whether or not he's able to repair anything between us, at least he's aware something is broken.

* ★ *

I'm beginning to wonder if death is the only thing powerful enough to illuminate my connection to the people I love. Sean has flown back to Alaska because his father is dying. Tonight I called him in Anchorage. We switched our usual roles: he talked, I listened.

Sean's dad, Stu, had fallen so deep into depression that he stopped eating and drinking. He became so dehydrated he wound up in the hospital, where he came down with pneumonia. Then complications set in. Sean told me that the doctors had to pump bile out of his father's stomach, that when they stuck the tube inside him they accidentally ruptured his spleen, that by the time they cut him open to repair his spleen it had stopped bleeding, that opening him up then led to an infection. Now he's on a breathing machine.

Sean said, "I have to get okay with . . . to get okay with the fact that I can't stay. I have to leave in a few days. I have to be okay that I was here for my dad." He repeated this several times.

"I know sometimes you worry that you're not a good son, but you *are* a good son. You know how you can know that, don't you?"

"They send you some kind of card in the mail?"

"You're there. You showed up. He knows you're there for him. You can't help it if you can't stay indefinitely. You moved away for a lot of good reasons, at a time when you had no idea your dad would get sick."

"That's true." He sighed. "I was going to call you today. I wanted to hear your voice . . . It's good to hear your voice."

"I feel bad for you that you don't have a girlfriend, or somebody to be there with you."

"Yeah, I was thinking about that. I miss you. I wanted you to know . . . because . . . well, because it's important."

As we spoke, I pictured him engulfed in an Anchorage winter. I could picture the hoarfrost covering that city in crystalline white purity. There are places in Anchorage that are just as dirty, dismal, and depressing as an L.A. ghetto. Yet L.A. never has enough frost to bathe it in innocence. For a moment I felt homesick for Alaska.

But although I miss Alaska, the truth is I've never truly felt at home anywhere. If Alaska seemed like home, it was only because so many other people there were lost and broken like me, like the castaway dolls and jack-in-the-boxes that *Rudolph the Red-Nosed Reindeer* found on the Island of Misfit Toys. I remember I once asked Sean's dad how he wound up in Alaska. He said, "They told me to turn left at Utah, and I turned right by mistake."

I thought about checking on flights to Anchorage, so I could be by Sean's side as he sits by his father's side. Then I realized it's not my place anymore. I don't know what is.

* * *

I've been considering canceling my trip overseas. I just spent a few days in San Diego, dipping down into Mexico for a day to complete my circuit down the coast. Then I returned to L.A. and discovered something that made me furious: my father went on a ski weekend with his new girlfriend. She isn't the problem. I'm glad he met someone. He no longer looks so lost.

When he met Jessie around the holidays, just four months after Christina died, he asked me, "Do you think it's too soon?"

I was surprised he wanted my opinion. Then I realized he was used to asking for Christina's opinion and that was no longer an option. I carefully considered my answer. "If you were someone else I'd probably say yes. But in your case, no, I don't think it's too soon. You're simply the kind of person who's happier when you're in a relationship. If you fall in love with someone new, that doesn't mean you didn't love your wife."

I have no problem with Dad having a girlfriend or going on a ski weekend. My problem is that he left *this* weekend. On Friday afternoon, even though his two-year-old daughter had an alarming cough, he left her in the care of an aunt. That night, her aunt took her to a doctor, who discovered that Iliana had an infection in both ears and had lost six pounds. She only weighed twenty-five pounds to start with. The next day, when I came home and saw my sister's listless face, the dark circles under her fever-bright eyes, and her thin little body, I wondered how he could leave.

When my dad called to check in, I shouted at him for the first time in my life, holding nothing back. "What are you doing in Mammoth when your daughter's sick?!"

"She wasn't that sick when I left. Why didn't anyone call me?"

"*That* sick?! You don't pay attention. For weeks she's been listless, she keeps crying, coughing, and whining, she barely smiles anymore. She's beginning to realize her mother's not coming back, and now you're gone most of the time. She doesn't understand what's going on, but she does get depressed whenever you're not here. I can see it on her face. And now she's sick and you're off skiing?!"

"She gets depressed when I'm not there? Oh, poor baby. Let me talk to her."

Iliana has a very modest vocabulary, so it was a pretty one-sided conversation. She looked perplexed listening to Dad's voice on the phone, maybe wondering how he shrank it to fit in there. My father then reassured me that he'd be home tomorrow, as planned, and that the housekeeper knew where to get in touch with him in case of emergency.

He wouldn't be back in time to see me off at the airport. This wasn't news. He'd never planned to.

After I got off the phone with my dad, I called Kaitlin to pour out my anger.

When my monologue devolved into tears, she said, "Cara, your father's doing it to you again."

"What do you mean?"

"He's abandoned you again."

"You mean the way he treats Iliana is making me relive the way he treated me?"

"No, I'm not talking about your sister. I'm talking about you. He's doing it to *you*."

It took me a moment to understand what she was saying. I hadn't thought of it that way. "You mean he's abandoned *me*? Left me here holding the bag?"

"Yes."

"But I'm not even holding the bag. Don't you see? I'm dropping it. I'm leaving to go to China, *to-mor-row*. Maybe I shouldn't go. Iliana already lost her mother, and now I'm going to leave. She'll think she was abandoned twice. I still don't think my father knows how to be there for a child. Maybe I should ask for custody, if he'll let me."

"Adopting her won't help. Whether she lives with you or her dad, she'll still be abandoned by her father and she'll still have lost her mother. And if you adopt her, she'll also lose her sister."

"I don't think my dad would abandon her. It's obvious he loves her, and he's very responsible. He's no Ward Cleaver, but he's not that bad."

"That's not what I mean. I'm talking about emotional abandonment. If you want to give him something to think about, you should ask him what he's going to do if his second daughter grows up to hate him as much as you do."

"I don't hate him."

"Cara . . . " she chided me.

"Okay, okay."

"Look Cara, you can't rescue anyone here. What you can do is be there for Iliana, as a *sister*. You're in a unique position. You can give her the kind of understanding no one else can because you were abandoned, too."

As her words sank in, I felt a power I'd never known before. It could be different this time. I never had a big sister when I was growing up, but Iliana would. The realization made me feel even guiltier about leaving.

But Kaitlin said that was a mother's guilt, not a sister's. "Grown-up sisters don't usually live at home. You've already done plenty. Giving up your life for someone isn't a gift—it's martyrdom. If you want to do something for your sister, be a role model. Go on your trip. How many girls have big sisters who have the courage to travel around the world alone?"

★ ★ ★

I've spent the past couple of weeks telling Iliana about my journey in the simplest words possible: "Your big sister is going on a long trip."

This afternoon, Grampa drove me to the airport. As I threw my duffel bag into his truck bed, I marveled that I've condensed my new life to fit into the thirty-five-pound backpack stuffed inside that duffel. All that's left of my old life are several boxes of books, photo albums, and clothes stored at Grampa's house. I've sold my car, and with that I no longer own a single key. For the next six months I'll be carrying everything I need on my back. I feel liberated. Almost.

Before I left, I picked up Iliana and carried her to the mailbox. She stared curiously at my face as I spoke to her. "I'm going now. I'm going on my long trip. But you see this mailbox? Wherever I go I'll be thinking of you, and just so you know I'm thinking of you I'll send you postcards, and they'll come in this mailbox. I'll write on them and Daddy will read them to you."

"Long trip," she chirped, smiling uncertainly. At least she didn't look as wan as she did yesterday.

"That's right. But—this is very important—*I will come back*. And when I come back I'll give you a big hug and a kiss, okay?"

My sister's nod was solemn, or maybe it was just a mirror. I kissed her goodbye.

Maybe I shouldn't worry so much about leaving her with our father. I remember once, when I was seven, I was in the car with Dad and one of my step-moms. It was raining and the windshield wipers were on. A tiny twig had gotten hung up in the wiper mechanism and was swishing back and forth, in sync with the wipers. My dad pointed at the twig and said, "Look, Cara, a baby windshield wiper!" We laughed so hard it felt like we'd never stop. But we had to get out of the car sometime.

THE BUTT OF THE LION

I'm sitting in the bar of a Beijing hostel, in the uncounted, insomniac hours of the morning, my only company the waitress sleeping on the couch behind me. I seem to be the sole person awake in the entire Jinghua Hotel. It's around noon yesterday in Los Angeles. I think. After crossing the international dateline, my internal clock is a mess.

Sitting among a maze of chair legs turned up on tables, I can easily imagine I'm in any bar in the world after hours. It hasn't quite sunk in that I'm in China—except that everyone here looks Chinese, everyone speaks Chinese, and every sign is written in Chinese.

I wish I could sleep; I need the rest. The rattling cough my family passed around over the holidays, which I thought was gone, has crept back into my lungs. That makes four weeks with this heavy hand squeezing my chest, and it's making me nervous. I don't want to end up in a hospital in a country where no one, but no one, speaks my language.

I've already learned a few polite Chinese words, such as "hello," "please," and the ever important "how much?" According to my phrasebook, "thank you" is *"xie xie,"* pronounced *"shyèh-shyeh"* with a soft "sh," a subtle sound like two chalkboard erasers rubbing together.

Last night in the hallway, I met a young American couple who live in China and they gave me some pointers for navigating both the streets and the communication gap:

"When you're getting on a bus, you have to rush forward as fast as you can and push your way into the crowd, or you can forget about making it on," the man said.

"And be careful crossing the big intersections," the woman said. "You probably already noticed, but it's every pedestrian for himself. They don't have right of way here. And if the street vendors get really aggressive, just remember: *Bú yào!*"

"*Boo Yow!*"

"Yeah, but you have to put the tones in the right place: *Bú yào!*"

"*Bú Yohw!*"

"Close enough."

"What's it mean?"

"The literal translation is 'don't want.' It more or less means 'leave me alone.'"

I thanked them and walked away muttering, "*Bú Yów, Bu Yòwww, Bù-yòw . . .*"

I could study my Chinese phrasebook to pass the time until sunrise, but I don't know how much good it will do. Even when I can make out the phonetics, I can't decipher the tones. Rising tones, falling tones, tones that fall then rise—or is that rise then fall? And if I rise when I'm supposed to fall, I'll say the wrong words. It's probably best to keep my mouth shut. That shouldn't be difficult today; my sleepless night in the bar may conspire with this surreal new world to turn my tongue to stone.

★ ★ ★

When the murmuring light of dawn stirred the stillness of the hostel, I left the bar to go outside and breathe the leaded fumes of Beijing's chill morning air. I bought a cheap breakfast from a nearby street vendor. It was Beijing's common fast food: an egg concoction spread into a thin pancake and fried on a griddle, then ladled with sauce and folded up in cheap paper for eating on the go. I have no idea what it was called, but the eggy-doughy consistency and salty-sweet flavor were so satisfying that I intend to become an addict.

As I ate, I gazed at the odd tableaux spread before me like some parenthetical scene from a David Lynch movie. Next door to the hostel stands a McDonald's fronted by a small square. In that square two small groups of people were taking two very different sorts of classes in the gauzy light of the early winter morning. At one end, a group was learning ballroom dance, slowly whirling to a waltz that emanated faintly from a boom box, tendrils of warm breath trailing behind them in the frozen air. At the other end, another group was slowly shifting through tai chi poses, making not a sound, pulsating like marionettes. In a wide lane beyond the square, hundreds of bicycles whirred by like the wings of countless insects. In the madcap lanes beyond that, automobiles sped past in a kill-or-be-killed frenzy while pedestrians wearing impassive expressions ran for their lives. The dancers and martial artists seemed out of place and time against the rush-hour pandemonium before them and the Western burger franchise behind.

An hour later, I boarded a tourist bus to the Great Wall of China. It was six hours round-trip to our particular destination, known as the Wild Wall. It was worth the long drive to leave behind Beijing's high-rise human car-tons, apartment balconies piled with boxes and bikes and laundry, and bare treetops flowering with the shredded pink and blue shopping bags carried aloft by the city's grimy winds. It was worth it to see the rugged section of the Great Wall that rolls up and down the dun, grassy, roller-coaster hills of Simatai.

Unlike Beijing, a few scattered huts were the only signs of civilization. Unlike the Great Wall in Beijing, the Wild Wall wasn't overrun with tour-ists and vendors. However, the moment our bus arrived, we were each selected by a local villager to be chaperoned for our walk along the wall, whether we wanted this service or not.

My chaperone was an elderly woman, with hair pulled back in a gray-streaked bun. She scurried silently behind me, until I remembered the advice of the American hostellers. I stopped, turned, and barked, *"Bú yào!"* (Don't want!) When my feet halted, her feet halted. But she only smiled and chattered to me in Chinese (or some other language). As soon as my feet resumed the uphill trudge, she began following again. I stopped again and shouted more aggressively, *"Bú yào! Bú yào!"* Again she politely halted, until I started walking. Then she resumed following. I gave up and simply ignored her as she trailed me up the wall like a shadow.

I didn't realize until we arrived that we'd be able to walk atop the wall. The steps were inconsistent: sometimes tiny and close together, forcing me to take mincing footsteps; other times giant-size, requiring me to scramble on hands and feet; yet other times so erratic it looked as if the builders had been working without sleep. The flowing ribbon of rough-hewn brick marched unevenly over hill after hill, indifferent to the terrain. Walking on those steps leading endlessly one into another, I wondered where my life was going.

I followed the wall over the crests of three hills, until my calves protested each uneven step: *"Bú yào, bú yào, bú yào."* Then the dry, dusty air and lack of sleep began to get to me. Feeling as if I were going to faint, I turned back.

I felt relieved when my shadow woman abandoned me and attached herself to someone with more staying power. But my luck didn't last. Another shadow adopted me for the return trip. This one was younger, maybe in her forties. Shadow Number Two kept grabbing my arm along the steep spots, saying, "Careful, careful." I would have felt safer if she'd left me the hell alone; the way she kept unexpectedly grabbing my arm threw me off balance. When I stopped to rest, she theatrically pointed to a village in the valley below and said, "Mon-golia," then she pointed the other way and said, "Bei-jing."

I bought a postcard from Shadow Number Two. It cost two yuan, a rip-off at local prices, but it was the only way to get rid of her before she mentioned her hungry children for the tenth time. This was a bad habit for a budget traveler to get into. I would see many more poor people on my journey and I didn't have enough money to save them. But I was too tired to resist.

Before I left Shadow Number Two behind, I turned for a last look at the wall. That's when I spotted a section on the wall's lower side where someone had written, in large letters, "I love you Nicky." What kind of person scribbles graffiti on the Great Wall of China? It must have been a man, I thought. Who else would try to express love with an act of destruction? *"Bú yào* to that!" I said to the wall. Shadow Number Two turned her mystified gaze to the unoffending wall. I turned and walked away. This time she didn't follow.

THE LAST FRONTIER
THIRTY-THREE YEARS OLD

Saying *"bú yào"* in any language has never worked well for me. Whenever I've said "don't want" to the men in my life, they've reacted like the Shadow Women of Simatai: halting for a moment, then following me again the moment they thought I wasn't looking.

After the kayak trip, I conjured up enough self-control to stay away from

Chance . . . for six whole days. Then Kaitlin came by my apartment for a visit and broke the spell.

I'd already told her the story, and she'd already told me several times that she wished she'd never introduced us. Still, I couldn't resist asking, "So, have you seen Chance lately?"

"Yes, and I hope I don't ever see that asshole again!"

"Why? What did he do now?"

"He had an appointment with me to look at some houses—and he brought Autumn with him! I was so pissed at him for putting me on the spot like that. It was incredibly awkward."

I barely spoke after that.

When Kaitlin left she took one look at my stony face and said, "Cara? You're going over there aren't you? Oh God, I knew I shouldn't have said anything. Don't go over there tonight, okay? Look, at least wait until tomorrow. Give yourself a chance to think."

But the moment she was gone, I drove straight to his place, my body a tight knot of pugnacious fury. It was late. He opened the door a crack to see who it was. I presented a front of perfect calm, my breathing even, my face void of expression.

"Cara . . . hi . . . " There was a note of confusion in his voice. "I was going to call you."

"Aren't you going to ask me in?"

"Sure." He opened the door wider, but studied my face with suspicion. I pushed past him to the living room, to the futon where he slept, half-expecting to see her there. She wasn't.

"What're you doing?!" he asked.

Not answering, I strode into the laundry room where he hung his keys, took his key to my apartment off the hook, and turned to face him, my consuming anger unmasked. "I don't want to see you! I don't want you to call me! I don't want you to even *think* of me again! And Kaitlin doesn't want anything to do with you!"

"What're you talking about?"

"Kaitlin told me. She told me about Autumn coming with you to look at houses. To look at *houses*?! With Kaitlin?! She's my best friend. How could you do that to her? How could you do that to *me*?"

"I didn't ask Autumn to come with me. She invited herself along."

"You couldn't say 'no'? I thought you said you weren't going to see her anymore."

As if someone had flipped a switch, his expression turned ugly. "Okay, that's enough! Get out!" He grabbed me by the collar and started hauling me down the hallway like a bouncer handling a belligerent drunk.

A moment earlier I would have been glad to leave, but I didn't want to be pushed. I started digging my feet in like a cartoon cat, skidding and sliding across the floor as he propelled me toward the door. My wrath dissolved, replaced by shameless pleading and clinging. "Wait a minute! Just tell me why! Make me understand! Wait! I deserve to know what happened."

He stopped, and we stood comically frozen in mid-struggle as he said, "Oh come on. You were there, that night on the island. I thought you said you heard."

"I said I heard *enough*. At that point I was still hoping Mike only caught you kissing. But you slept with her. It was an affair. Come on! I want to hear you say it. How many times?"

"I don't know. A few."

"Since when?"

"Maybe nine months or so."

"That's almost the entire time we've been together!"

He looked surprised.

"Are you in love with her?"

"Yes."

"That's not what you told Mike."

"I wanted to give them a chance to work things out. I kept meaning to end it."

"How did he find out?"

"He saw us together—we weren't making love, we weren't even kissing, but we were sitting way too close. It was obvious what was going on." Then it all came pouring out of him: "I never meant for it to happen. At first it made sense for us to spend time together, because I was giving her business advice. But it became clear there was an attraction. So we drew a line: we said we'd just be friends. But as a friend she was always telling me about her marriage problems. She told me it made her feel better to talk to me. She made me feel like a hero. I know we shouldn't have made love, but in some ways it made me feel like a good guy, because it seemed like she was neglected and abused, and she needed the love and attention I gave her."

"What about the love and attention *I* needed?"

"At the beginning, when you seemed so lonely, I felt like you needed me. But you don't really need me the way she does."

"So I have to be abused and neglected before my needs are worth your attention? So if I was more helpless, that would've done the trick? You don't think I needed you?"

"Yeah, but I'm not talking about being a black hole of emotional need. I'm talking about *really* needing me. All you ever do is complain."

"The only thing I complained about was the amount of time you spent with Autumn. Anyway, if I was so awful to be with, you could've left. When you started sleeping with her we hadn't been together that long. Why not dump me then?"

"For God's sake, can't you ever just listen? You wanted to know what happened—I told you. I'm not defending it. Anyway, whatever's wrong with you and me isn't her fault. If our relationship had been any good none of this would've happened. It's not Autumn's fault you can't nab a husband. And frankly, it's not my fault either. So stop trying to blame us!"

Devastated, I said nothing, just stared at him, my jaw working, my eyes hot and dry.

My silence only seemed to enrage him more. "Most people would see this as a cue to leave. What are you still doing here?"

With that, he dragged me toward the door again, and I dragged my feet again. When we reached the door, he flung it open and shoved me into the hall. I flew backwards, lost my footing, and fell. As my head slammed into the floor, I heard a loud crack, saw a flash of light, felt a jolt of pain. Then . . . nothing but cold, hard tile. I lay still for a moment, stunned. Then I curled into a ball and muttered to myself, "Oh my God."

"Oh get up! It's not that bad," Chance said and walked inside.

It was an accident. He had asked me to leave, and I had dragged my feet. He'd only meant to push me out the door, and I'd slipped. It wasn't fear or physical pain that kept me curled up on the floor. It was the realization of the depth to which I'd allowed my self-respect to fall. For perhaps two endless minutes I lay there, not knowing how to compose myself from my prone position into some dignified form of departure. The scariest thing was: I didn't *want* to leave.

"Cara," he whispered from inside the condo. "Cara, come here."

I slowly rose, floated inside like a sleepwalker, and sat on the falling edge of the futon.

His face was a miserable blur of pity and disgust. "How's your head?"

"I think I have a bump."

"Here, let's see . . ." He pulled me closer and gently rubbed the back of my head. "Oh! You really do have a bump . . . I'm sorry."

He put his arms around me and we didn't say much after that. Although his embrace was gentle, it wasn't comforting. Something in his touch made me itch to be alone. But my sudden need for solitude felt foreign to me, and I ignored it.

* * *

Autumn and Chance did stop seeing each other once Mike forbid it. Even after Autumn and Mike divorced, she and Chance still avoided meeting, because she didn't want to risk losing her kids in a custody battle and Chance didn't want to risk gaining her kids in the same battle. As for Chance and *me*, my guess is he couldn't bring himself to face the long winter nights alone. So, by default, I won custody of the boyfriend.

As I had predicted on the kayak trip, having wronged me, he felt he owed me. And as I had predicted on our first date, believing he owed me, he resented me. I only hoped that, with the competition out of the way, sooner or later he would get over his resentment and remember how great he used to think I was.

I grew determined to take Autumn's place as his sidekick, and I believed the best way to do that was to remind him of my adventurous spirit. Chance was more addicted to adventure than alcohol. So in late March, as winter grudgingly held onto spring, we drove to the World Extreme Skiing Championships in Thompson Pass. The skiing event was an annual excuse for Chance's paragliding buddies to get together for some winter flying. It would also give the two of us a chance to bond again while he taught me a fun survival skill: how to build a snow cave.

When we arrived at the pass, the afternoon light was stretched thin and we were road-weary and hungry. We hit the local lodge, hoping for a warm meal. The front door was off its hinges and a chill wind whistled through the joint. The kitchen had run out of about half the items on the chalk-board menu, including steaks, lettuce, and rice. The two scruffy gents who ran the place managed to scrape up a couple of burgers and half a cup of hot chocolate—with that, they were out of milk. When we tried to order dessert and heard, "Sorry, we're outta that, too," we couldn't stop giggling. Our laughter began to thaw the ice that lingered between us.

One thing the lodge never seemed to run out of was beer. So by the time Chance was ready to leave, it was dark and freezing outside, and he was less than evenly heeled. It was too late to build a snow cave, so he hatched a new plan. He began to create a makeshift tent on top of his Land Cruiser by attaching a pole to his roof rack and lashing a tarp to it. He wouldn't consider sleeping *inside* the SUV, because it was too full of food and gear.

"Is there anything I can do to help?" I asked.

"You leave everything to me!" he said with the borrowed good cheer of excess drink. "I'll have this up in no time."

A guy who was camping nearby shook his head at the sight of Chance's animated blue tarp gyrating and cursing atop the SUV. Bill—who was about our age with a tangled ponytail and a bird's nest beard—offered us his second tent. I was tempted, but Chance called out from inside the gesticulating tarp, "Thanks, but we've got everything under control here!"

Bill left.

About fifteen minutes later he returned, pointed behind me, and said, "It's there if you need it. You're more than welcome." He'd pitched his second tent anyway. Chance was still wrestling with the tarp.

"Thanks," I said. "But I know Chance. He'll never give up, even if it kills him."

"What if it kills you?"

Chance finally bullied his listing tent into place, flaccid tarp dangling from drunken pole. "There. Isn't it great?" he asked with the pride of a suburban dad who's just put up a sundeck.

I laughed with delight at the unusual sight.

"What?" he asked, looking downcast at my reaction.

"Nothing. I just can't believe you did it. I'm impressed." I really was.

Chance wrapped his arms around me, and we took a moment to stare up at the great wheel of stars that sparkled overhead.

Bill walked up to us and held out his binoculars. "Have you seen the comet yet?"

"Hayakatuke?" Chance asked.

"Hayaku*take*," I corrected him.

"Whatever," he said. I knew it annoyed him when I corrected him, but the compulsion was as hard to control as a sneeze.

"No, I haven't seen it," I said to Bill. "Thanks." I accepted the binoculars, and he directed my gaze toward the small streak of light inching across the sky. "That's amazing!"

"Just think: it'll take about 72,000 years for it to come around again," Bill said.

"Just enough time for you to put up another tent," I said to Chance.

"Very funny."

When the cold became unbearable, we bundled up in several layers of clothing, clambered atop the roof, and shimmied into our sleeping bags. The roof rack dug into our backs, and wind crept under the tent. When I began to shiver, Chance put his sleeping bag over me and mumbled, "Don't want my little treasure to get cold."

★ ★ ★

In the morning, we met several paraglider pilots at a nearby hill called Blue Ice Bump. Chance and his friends spent the next couple of hours attempting to turn disagreeable crosswinds and a slope of unremarkable height into an exciting day of flying. The struggle to get their canopies in the air was long and the flights down the abbreviated hill were short. Still, from a spectator's standpoint, the sight of ribbons of color falling through a crisp blue sky was satisfying.

Meanwhile, I strapped on my downhill skis and skied the humble little bump. The ride down lasted less than fifteen seconds, while the hike back up took at least five sweaty, tendon-stretching minutes. A lesser optimist would have given up after the first try. I skied it twice.

As the afternoon sun wore down to a pale wick, Chance and I realized we needed to get to work on the snow cave. We found a spot to build it on the backside of Blue Ice Bump. Chance produced a small shovel and started digging a hole in the snow, a satisfied look of concentration on his face. After digging down a bit, he started tunneling into the side of the hill. Then he carved out blocks of snow, and I climbed down into the hole to toss them out. After we established a tunnel, he widened the far end into a small cavern. We switched tasks a few times, and soon the only sounds were the muffled thuds of shovels and thrown blocks of snow, and our own heavy breathing.

Then the sky turned violet and the temperature began to drop. We'd been out in the cold for five hours and we'd been working on the cave for about an hour of that. We hadn't eaten since breakfast. My stomach growled, my muscles ached, and my clothes were damp and cold with sweat (despite my high-tech, moisture-wicking underwear). Chance asked if I wanted to stop. Before I could answer, he went on to say we should finish the cave before the evening grew much darker or colder. "Let's keep going," I said, knowing he hated it when I complained.

When another twenty minutes proved we weren't going to finish before pitch dark and extreme cold set in, I asked, "Do you want to stop?"

"Not yet. Let's keep going."

One of his friends set up a tent nearby and he stopped by to marvel at our masterpiece. Chance tossed off some proud puffery about our "humble little cave," along with a few pointers about how to build one. Then he went back to digging. Another twenty minutes passed.

After we'd been at it for two hours, I was shivering uncontrollably and my fingertips were numb. I said, in what I'm sure was a whining tone, "Chance, I can't do this anymore. I'm cold. I'm tired. I'm hungry. Please! Can we stop?" I was down inside the hole that served as the cave's entryway and he was standing above me. Without warning, he leapt down into the pit, grabbed me by the neck, and pushed my head downward. I shrieked in surprised fear. He leaned over me and growled into my ear between clenched teeth, "Stop . . . embarrassing me . . . in front . . . of my friends!" I assume he meant his friend in the nearby tent; there was no one else around. I said nothing, but cried icy tears as I doggedly resumed digging.

He said, "I don't know what you're complaining about, anyway. I wanted to stop an hour ago. You're the one who insisted on continuing." That statement flabbergasted me, and I've puzzled over it ever since. But, fearing he would jump me again, I said nothing.

A few minutes later he snatched my shovel from my hands and put his arms around me. "You look frozen. I'm sorry I worked you so hard. Let's go to the lodge and get you some food." I felt relieved the abominable snow ogre was gone, but never got over the uneasy feeling he might return at any time.

When we returned to the snow cave, the sky was black. We turned on a flashlight inside the tiny cave so Chance could finish digging. The final task was to build a sleeping shelf out of snow. While he did that, I stood outside, above the cave. A preternatural aqua glow rose from the snow where the light shone through the semi-translucent ceiling.

Inside the cave, the bluish-white ceiling was a series of geometric gashes and stumps, showing where blocks of snow had been removed. Chance lit a lantern, and its flame worked together with our warm breath and body-heat to coat the ceiling in a thin, glistening layer of slick ice. We lay our pads and sleeping bags atop the snow shelf, which kept us off the frozen ground and close to the ceiling, where we'd be more insulated. With four layers of clothing plus our sleeping bags, I convinced myself I was cozy and warm, although my nose was red and dripping. We were a lot warmer than we had been in the tent atop the car. It was probably thirty degrees inside the cave. That was warm enough for me. Any warmer and I wouldn't have been able to sleep for fear of drowning as our shelter melted around us.

The next day there were no paraglider-friendly winds to be found, so we drove to a rocky mountain with a sheer vertical drop to watch the Extreme Skiing Championships. A helicopter carried suicidal skiers to the top of the mountain where we followed their progress down the steep slopes with binoculars. One wrong move could easily spell death. It's happened before.

But that day, Chance and I exhaled in amazement as we watched skiers perform the impossible with brave style and athletic grace. There was a starting point and a finish line, but the route down was up to each contestant. They flew down narrow chutes between jagged boulders and jumped off rock ledges. The slope was more like a cliff, and I wondered just what was holding their skis to the mountainside—sheer force of will?

Crowds watched with us from the highway. Like me, many of them were avid skiers who would never dream of facing such a murderous precipice. I smiled to myself as I realized that most of them would never spend the night in a snow cave either. For a moment I saw myself not as a victim, but a survivor. Then I turned my gaze to Chance and the feeling left me. I knew I should have let him go after the kayak trip.

I was on a steep vertical cliff, holding on by sheer force of will. This was a scary ride, but I couldn't give up the rush. I was addicted to Chance.

* * *

After years of complaining about men who drink, on the Fourth of July, 1996, I took on an Alaskan challenge that started as a bar bet between two men. According to local tradition, back in 1915 one guy bet another guy that he could run up Seward's Mount Marathon and back in less than an hour. He lost, but only by a few minutes. That was the first Mount Marathon run. This time I would be one of the three hundred runners in the women's race.

The entire course, from downtown and back again, is only about three miles. But one third of that distance is straight up: the mountain rises from nearly sea level to 3022 feet in just one mile, one of the many hulks gathered around Resurrection Bay. A few years earlier, when I saw the event for the first time, I was shocked to see the front runners coming off the mountain caked not only in a cement-thick layer of mud, but also in their own blood and gore. I realized the story of the bar bet must be true; it would take a couple of drunk people to come up with a race like this.

I spent the night before the race aboard a friend's boat in the harbor, waiting for Chance to drive in from Anchorage to join me. He showed up just before midnight, threw down his duffle, gave me a quick kiss, and immediately took off for the bars. Sometime after two a.m. I heard him fumble his way down the galley stairs, flop down on the opposite bunk, and start snoring. I clenched my jaw and rolled over.

In the morning, while I checked in, Chance hiked up the mountain ahead of me to cheer me on and videotape my run. This time *he* would be the reporter watching from the sidelines, recording an event in which *I* would fully take part.

At the starting line I looked around and noticed that three hundred women make a very small group, as footraces go. In all the races I'd run before, there had been at least a thousand participants, usually more. I saw a woman I knew and, though we weren't close friends, I gave her a hug. She seemed embarrassed, but I didn't care. I felt connected to these women by a cheerful insanity of purpose. We weren't only about to hike up a mountain, we were about to rush up a mountain *as fast as we could*.

When the man giving us our countdown reached "3-2-1!" I tore off down the street as fast as I could, which wasn't very fast. When I hit the bottom of the mountain I was behind a bottleneck of fidgeting women, all waiting their turn to head up the narrow trail through the trees, single-file. At least the wait gave me a chance to catch my breath.

As we scurried up the path, it quickly became apparent that no one runs *up* Mount Marathon. They might run *down*, but on the way up, the best even the fastest runners can do is a slow jog. The best I could do was a fast walk as excruciating pain shot through my calves and fire filled my lungs. My mind kept repeating, "Just keep going. Just don't stop. If you stop, you'll never start again. Just keep going . . ."

It was a perfect day, warm and growing warmer as the morning clouds burned off. Early in the race, we passed a group of three men who'd climbed up a tree to watch. They sang a song about beautiful ladies climbing a mountain.

The sound of labored breathing drifted to me from ahead and behind, and to my amazement, the sound of talking! One woman was talking about her wedding plans. She was going to marry one of the men set to run the men's race in the afternoon. Smiling, I said, "This is so great! I bet the men don't talk like this during their race."

The young bride replied, "Don't you believe it! My fiancé talks with his friends all the way up the mountain. He says it helps pass the time."

As we rose higher, the conversations took on a note of light-hearted complaining:

"Remind me why we're doing this again?"

"Are we crazy?"

"Boy, I can't wait to have a beer."

I discovered that speed isn't everything. One woman had stayed well ahead of me for a long time, but I passed her when she pulled over to the side of the trail for a fit of dry heaves.

Soon the mountain was so steep I was forced to scramble on my hands. I was wearing bicycle gloves in anticipation of this and I didn't miss a beat . . . until I heard a familiar voice.

"Hi, Cara!"

I looked up to see Chance standing above me with his video camera rolling. "So, you didn't beat me to the top after all," I said, grinning at him as I passed.

Then I broke out of the trees into a field of rock and scree. We passed an official timer who told us we'd been going for close to forty-five minutes.

Someone said to me, "You're still smiling!"

"Yeah, it looks like a smile doesn't it?" It was a grimace, of both pain and determination.

Now that we were in the open, there was more room to pass. When I pulled almost even with the racer just ahead of me, she turned and said, "You're doing great!"

"Thanks. It doesn't feel like it."

The encouraging young woman, whose name was Hanna, was doing my pace just one step better, so I decided to make her my rabbit, sticking with her for the rest of the race. Each time she said, "Hey Cara, it's easier over here," I followed. As we neared the top, most of the women grew quiet, but Hanna continued to chatter.

When I pointed out that she seemed more upbeat and talkative than any of us, she said, "That's because I sing when I run."

"You what?"

"I sing when I run. It keeps me motivated, and it helps my breathing. If you want to make sure you're getting enough oxygen while you're running, you should run at a pace that allows you to speak. If you can't speak, your lungs aren't getting enough oxygen. Well, I don't always have someone to talk to . . . so I sing."

When a couple of other women started talking about the finishing time they were shooting for, Hanna said, "I just want to finish before the parade starts. Last year I took so long to finish I got stuck running behind the fire engine. I already felt like throwing up and then I was stuck behind that engine blowing exhaust in my face—blechhh!"

We were still a long way from the top when star Alaska runner Nina Kempel came flying down the mountain. And we were still a long way from the top when the sirens went off in town, announcing that Nina had crossed the finish line. Her winning time was 55:08. I arrived at the top about seventeen minutes later.

Then I started running down toward the "chute," deliberately bypassing firm terrain and heading straight for the slipperiest part of the scree slope. At this point the loose scree became my friend, as I tried to pick up time. I took Neil Armstrong leaps, my feet sinking into soft dirt and deep piles of tiny rocks. I was grateful for the duct tape I'd wound around my ankles, closing the gap between my shoes and socks; without it, my shoes would have filled with stones. When I felt as if I were going to pitch forward on the steep slope, I threw myself backward onto my butt and slid. When my legs got tired, I fell on my butt and slid. Just for fun, I fell on my butt and slid. Gravity was doing the work now and I was having an absolute blast.

On the way down, I spotted Chance again. He cheered me on and I threw my arms in the air in a corny victory sign.

I snatched a peripheral glimpse of Resurrection Bay below, blue interrupted by flashes of sunlight and tiny white fishing boats. Then several women in front of me started kicking up great clouds of dust, turning my contact lenses into sandpaper. So for the rest of the way down the rocky slope, I ran with my eyes shut, tears streaming down my dirty face.

Blinded, I was concerned I'd miss an important turn: one experienced Mount Marathoner had instructed me to keep to the left to avoid coming down above the Killer Cliff. Each year some runners leap off the cliff on purpose as a fast route to the bottom, but some people end up there by terrible mistake. I knew that at least one woman was once carted away from the bottom of the cliff in an ambulance. But how could I keep to the left if I couldn't see? I decided the best way to avoid the Killer Cliff was to keep following the blinding cloud of dust kicked up by the runners in front of me. The dust ended when I reached the stream. I splashed through it several times, squishing through mud and slipping across slick stones as I followed its course. One wrong move and I'd fall. But, high on adrenaline, I didn't slow my pace. I scrambled down a series of steep rocks and came careening off the mountain, along with Hanna and another woman.

The three of us emerged into a crowd of hundreds of spectators who greeted us with a rousing cheer. Inspired, I picked up speed, passing first Hanna, then the other woman. All along the streets, hordes of people applauded each of us as we passed, one by one. In the final block, a woman flew by out of nowhere and lapped me. My strength spent, I mentally cheered her on.

I surged through the finish line at 1:45:55. Hanna came in seconds later. We threw our grimy arms around each other in congratulations. I thanked her and said, "I don't think I would have done so well if it hadn't been for you."

I was caked in sweat and mud. I was not first, or tenth, or twentieth. I came in 155th. But during my final sprint through town, I'd overheard a couple of spectators say, "Look, she's still smiling!" And this time I was. I began to believe I might be an amazing person.

Afterward, as I walked the packed sidewalks of downtown, shaking off adrenaline and gulping down water, I spotted Scott, my smelly ex-boyfriend from Kenai. There was no avoiding him. He was walking toward me and he saw that I'd seen him. I was in an excellent mood, and I figured what could be more harmless than a brief chat on a crowded street with an old lover about whom I could no longer even summon a mild fantasy? So I stopped to say hello.

While Scott and I talked about the footrace we now had in common, Autumn floated into view. Even she couldn't ruin my high good humor that day. I smiled and said hello. She gave me a weak smile, said, "Hi," and sidled away. For a moment I wondered if she would run into Chance and report that she'd seen me talking to a good-looking guy.

So what if she did? For the first time, I didn't give a shit what Chance thought. I was no longer listening to Scott. Instead, I was imagining what it might be like to live my life without considering what *anyone* thought.

★ ★ ★

Chance's moods began to swing in a wider and wider arc. It was impossible to guess ahead of time which kind of night it might be. I began to learn that when he was drunk he was loving and generous and "Can we snuggle all night like two spoons?" When he sobered up, he was bitter and sarcastic and "You're not my girlfriend! I told you I never wanted a girlfriend!"

I often provoked him at the early, lighthearted stage, anticipating the rage to come and unable to bear the tension of waiting. These arguments made little sense, and he didn't understand why I started them. All he knew was that he'd been in a good mood until I'd brought him down.

The nights he asked me to stay with him, after he fell asleep, I kept my body as far away from his as possible. If one of my limbs touched him in the middle of the night he'd whine and kick. I lay there gritting my teeth and slept only intermittently. One night a loud voice startled me from sleep: "What are you, nuts?!" I was surprised to recognize my own voice actually berating me.

My jaw grew increasingly sore until it was so swollen and feverish I went to a doctor. The doctor told me I had TMJ, Temporo-Mandibular Joint disorder, from clenching my jaw.

I fantasized that alcohol was the root of our problems and that its removal from the equation would equal "happily ever after." I knew that the decision to quit had to come from him. But, never doubting he would make that decision, I decided to ride out the storm. I started going to Alanon meetings so I wouldn't have to ride it out alone. That only made him angrier.

"You think I'm a drunk! You think I'm a loser!"

"This isn't just about you. I'm going to those meetings because I keep ending up with the same problems."

"That's just another way of saying I'm not the first loser you've ever gone out with."

He had me there. But so what? For a long time I'd blamed myself for our problems, believing that if I'd been easier to get along with he would have been too happy to drink. But I was tired of blaming myself and tempted to blame someone else for a while.

I did leave him. Several times I walked away, with the heel-clicking, tire-screeching drama of a woman who would never return. Each time, I returned.

One night I called ahead to check the emotional weather. "So, should I come by?"

"Cara, it's over. Can't you take a hint?"

"What hint? *You* invited *me* over just last night. You said you loved me."

"You should know by now not to pay attention to what I say when I'm in a blackout."

"But, you made love with me."

"Don't give me that. You aren't some innocent victim. You wanted it as much as I did."

"Yes, I did. But it meant something to me." I felt like a duped high school girl instead of a thirty-three-year-old woman who should know better.

"Look," he said, "I'm only going to say this one more time. I don't want to see you any more, and I want you to stop calling me."

"I want you to say that to my face. I'm coming over." I hung up, and fifteen minutes later I was standing outside his house, repeating the same questions. "How could you use me like that?"

"You and I are close—I couldn't have sex with someone I didn't care about. But that doesn't mean we're a couple. And if you keep going on about it, well, I'm starting to regret that we did it at all."

"But you said you loved me!"

"Do you think if you keep repeating that, it's going to change anything? Cara, I like you, okay?—when you're not acting like a *Fatal Attraction* psycho bitch from hell. But . . . "

"What did you say?"

"You heard me." He repeated it slowly, over-enunciating each word: "*Fatal . . . Attraction . . . psycho . . . bitch . . . from hell.*"

You see, I thought, *isn't it so much better to have him say it to your face?* Without another word, I got in my car and drove away. As I made my sniveling way home, I realized I wasn't a victim so much as a tragic hero. Weren't they always the authors of their own undoing?

THE BUTT OF THE LION
THIRTY-FIVE YEARS OLD—KUNMING, CHINA

Yuantong Temple has been standing for more than a thousand years, and in such a venerable place I expected an afternoon of peaceful contemplation. But, without knowing the language, I feel destined to misinterpret this country, no matter what I do. I am an observer of people and sights I cannot hope to understand.

As I entered the temple, I saw signs saying that photos are forbidden inside the halls. But the guards in the main hall said nothing when flashes went off as several Chinese tourists took photos of an ancient Buddha. In the outdoor sections of the temple, photos are allowed, and I took several. In the midst of a large square pond stood a graceful octagonal pavilion linked to the surrounding complex by two stone bridges. The multiple arches of the bridges cast reflections in the water, creating a row of perfect circles that begged to be photographed.

Hundreds of Chinese on their New Year holiday swarmed the grounds. In the courtyard, they lit candles and incense and offered food and money before statues of Buddha. Although it was crowded by American standards, compared to the congested city outside its walls the temple was as serene as I'd hoped—until I took my final photo.

I was about to leave when I spotted a small hall I'd overlooked. Three golden Buddhas dominated the room where only a handful of people were meditating or praying. A shaft of sunlight pierced the dimness and turned the golden Buddhas into shining temptations. This room displayed no sign forbidding photos. Still, it seemed prudent to assume the rule applied here, too, and it seemed respectful not to snap photos inside a room where people were performing devotions. But after a few of the faithful left, an idea struck me. I decided to wait for the room to empty, step outside, and shoot a photo from there, catching just a glimpse of the golden altar in the background. Then there'd be no one to offend, and I'd technically be following the rules.

I waited until everyone left the room except one small boy. He was out of sight of the doorway and I knew my camera wouldn't pick him up. So, I stepped well outside the room and casually snapped my shot. Instantly, a tiny elderly woman whom I hadn't noticed rushed forward from the room's shadows, shouting at me. Her angry movements threatened to fling her tight little bun from her head. My camera's flash must have gone off, alerting her to my presence.

I'll never be sure of her precise complaint. She spoke a vituperative rush of Chinese, of which I only understood one phrase: *"Bu hao!"* ("Not good!" or, more to the point, "Very bad!") As she scolded me, she grabbed my elbow with one bony hand and smacked my arm with the other. When she propelled me down the walkway to an unknown destination, yelling and slapping my arm the entire way, I grew fearful. I was in a communist country. Evidently I'd broken a rule. But surely I wouldn't go to prison . . . would I? She was pretty old, her back hunched with osteoporosis, and I could have outrun her. But the temple was filled with young, fit Chinese who would surely side with one of their own. So I made no attempt to flee her grasp.

The little boy followed after us as the old woman pushed me into the office of an official in a green uniform. She kept pointing at the boy and pointing at my camera, screeching with even more emotion now that we had an audience. The man looked blankly from her to me. "Do you speak English?" I asked the man. He shook his head. So while the woman continued to shriek, I pointed at my camera, then at the little boy, and made negative gestures with my face and hands, indicating I'd taken no photos of the boy. In response, the man grabbed my arm and firmly guided me to another office where he presented me to two more officials: a young man and young woman. The grandmother followed, still gabbling.

I asked the female official, "Do you know English?"

"A litter," she said.

Oh God, I'm going to jail, I thought.

The young woman listened as Grandma continued her tirade. Even in my fear I was impressed at the old woman's lung capacity. After many minutes even the officials seemed to tire of her monologue. But they listened with exaggerated patience.

Finally I interjected, speaking slowly and distinctly: "I see the signs that say 'cameras forbidden' *inside* temple. I took no pictures inside. I stood *outside* and took a picture. My flash must have gone off. (Here I pointed at my flash.) I think this woman saw the flash and thought I took a photo of the boy. I did not. (Here I pointed at the boy, pointed at the camera, and shook my head.) I took no forbidden photos."

The old lady shook her head, stomped her foot, and made other gestures to indicate she didn't believe anything I said, whatever I said.

With deliberate calm, I gradually backed away. "I have done nothing wrong. I am sorry for the trouble. I will leave the temple now." I bowed and turned to leave. I tried this trick twice, and twice the officials blocked the doorway.

The young female official and the old woman began conferring and gesturing to my camera. "Please don't take my film. It will ruin my pictures. I have done nothing wrong." I was worried they wanted to do something worse than take my film, but thought it best to direct their attention to the most optimistic of potential punishments.

When I tried to leave a third time, the entourage shepherded me toward a desk where the young woman pulled out an official form. There was only one thing left to do. I thought, *Start crying, Cara. Now!* My nerves were already ragged, so it was easy to call forth some real tears. My lips trembled as I pleaded, "Please let me go! I've done nothing wrong. Please let me go!" That's when they did the most surprising thing of all. All three officials, and even the old woman, took one look at my face, shook their heads with pity, and more or less said, "Oh, no, no," in Chinese. The young female official and the old grandma gently shooed me out the door with a soft flutter of their hands. I turned and scurried out before they could change their minds. The problem was, once I started crying I couldn't stop. I found myself walking down a public street, weeping profusely before hordes of gaping Chinese, most of whom I towered over by several inches.

Through the water trebling my vision, I made out an old man smiling at me and holding out an ice cream bar. It took a moment for me to realize he was a street vendor. An Englishman who lives in China recently warned me, "Chinese ice cream can be a bit dodgy," but I bought one anyway. The old man patted my arm as if to comfort me. He kept smiling and asking questions in Chinese, even though I kept saying, *"Ting bu dong."* (I don't understand.)

By the time I walked away, slurping the watery-tasting ice cream, I was smiling. Then, as I recalled the tiny old grandmother dragging me and slapping me, I started to giggle. If anything, passersby stared even more than they had at my tears. But their eyes held no judgment, only barely suppressed mirth. Lack of understanding can carry a penalty, but it can also carry a reward: laughter, the trophy of escape artists and survivors.

DALI, CHINA

Today I spent Valentine's Day alone, in a land of 1.3 billion people. This morning I rented a bike for five yuan (about sixty-five cents) and rode from Dali to Xizhou, a village of Bai people, the local minority group. For twenty-five kilometers, I rode on a long ribbon of two-lane highway, passing acre after acre of flat farmland.

Along the way, I stopped in a hamlet to ask directions. The village looked deserted until I spotted an old woman standing next to a small temple. She smiled and beckoned. As I approached, she waved me into the temple. Curious, I bowed then stepped through the entry into a dirt courtyard. A small building stood along one of the four walls. There was nothing else except a palpable silence.

I crossed the courtyard to the building and took a few tentative steps into its single large room, which was barren of decoration. As my eyes adjusted to the dimness, I noticed the prayer rugs lined up before me and realized this was not a Buddhist temple. It was the prayer hall of an Islamic mosque. I remembered something and looked down. My shoes! I turned to walk back to the door and remove them. Too late.

Before I could exit, a girl of about ten appeared in the empty courtyard and rushed toward me, chattering. I didn't know what language she was speaking, but it was obvious she was scolding me. I quickly backed out of the building, bowing and apologizing in bad Chinese, *"Dui bu qi! Dui bu qi!"* (Excuse me! Excuse me!)

As I backed into the courtyard, the girl crawled partway into the temple on hands and knees, swatting and rubbing the floor. That's when I noticed the dirty footprints I'd left behind on the thin carpet. Even Buddhist temples often require people to remove their shoes and I should have erred on the side of caution in the first place, but in the profound silence I'd stopped thinking. The mosque was silent no more, and neither were my thoughts, as the little girl continued to pummel the floor. I wondered if this community frowned on women entering the prayer hall at all. The girl had entered, so maybe not. Still, I felt like an intruder.

I turned to leave and tripped over two more girls who'd followed the first into the courtyard. They stared at me as if I were naked. Self-conscious, I looked down again and saw my other mistake: I was wearing pants with zip-off legs, and I'd gotten so sweaty from bicycling in the heat that I'd zipped off the lower legs, converting the pants into shorts. They weren't all that short, but they showed my knees. I didn't need to be told that this was disrespectful to Islam. In fact, I haven't seen any women in China wearing shorts—Muslim, Buddhist, or otherwise. I gestured at my legs and repeated my apology, which sent all three girls into a fit of giggling.

It was obvious my pronunciation was gibberish to them. I still can't get the hang of the Chinese tones. Maybe these girls didn't even know Chinese. Nonetheless, I pulled out my phrasebook and riffled the pages until I hit on a word that seemed to fit the situation. Pointing at the prayer hall, I attempted to ask, "No women?" This only made them laugh harder.

Their laughter was cut off by a voice issuing from the mosque's humble minaret, a muezzin calling the men to prayer. Realizing that it was now too late to leave the mosque without being noticed by the men who were surely heading this way, I opened my fanny pack and found my pant legs. I frantically stuck a leg through one of them and began zipping it back on. I stopped in embarrassment when a man entered the courtyard, but he ignored me as if I were invisible, walked right past me, entered the hall, and knelt on a prayer rug.

While I pulled the second leg on, the scolding girl beckoned to an old man. He walked straight up to me with a questioning look. In my nervousness, I dropped the unzipped pant leg around my ankle as I again struggled to apologize. I repeated my rendition of, "I'm sorry. No women, only men?" as I pointed at the building. He looked even more baffled than the children.

Giving up, I hopped out of the courtyard, one leg off, one leg on, the three girls following at my heels. When I sat on the ground outside to finish re-assembling my pants, the scolding girl sat next to me and smiled. I smiled back and pulled out my phrasebook, hoping to find something new to say. She gestured that she wished to see the tiny book. I handed it to her, and she started reading some of the Chinese words aloud, unwittingly giving me a lesson in pronunciation. I looked over her shoulder and repeated some of the phrases. She smiled again and corrected me, this time squelching her obvious urge to giggle.

When I looked up from our lesson, I saw that we'd attracted a crowd of a dozen or so curious children and adults. Most of them were chuckling. I bowed and said, "*Ni hao!*" More chuckling. Then I asked the girl for the phrasebook, riffled the pages again, and haltingly asked the elders, "Please, how far to *Xizhou?*" Several of them pointed in the same direction. One white-haired man held up a single finger. I assumed he meant one kilometer, although he might have meant one minute. Maybe he was pointing to Allah. "*Xie xie ni! Zai jian!* (Thank you! Goodbye!)" I said, and mounted my bike. I turned to wave as I pedaled away. Several people smiled and waved back. That's when it became clear: I had not offended them, only surprised them. Their unreserved smiles made me wish I hadn't decided to leave so abruptly, but I could think of no excuse to stay now.

I rode one kilometer in the direction they'd pointed, and found Xizhou. When I arrived the market was in full swing and I had to walk my bike through the buzzing swarm of people. The Bai have dark, delicate, sweetly crinkled features reminiscent of Tibetans. Bai women wear either a multi-colored cloth wrapped around the head, or a flowery pink and blue fitted cap with a white tassel. The bright headdresses floated between vivid displays of vegetables, mandarin oranges, Popsicles, apples, and bananas. Slabs of fresh meat crawling with flies were thrown on bare folding tables. A butcher leaned over hunks of bloody meat, a cigarette bobbing up and down in his mouth as he haggled with customers. A dead rat lay stiff on the corner of the table, its eyes squeezed shut into little cartoon X's.

Ever since I arrived in China, I've mourned my lost eighteen inches of personal space. But it wasn't until I reached this rural village that the pressure of China's overpopulation felt physically dangerous. Bodies continued pouring into the market until I was wedged so tightly into a jostling line that the possibility of being trampled became quite real. It was frightening, but energizing. Being squashed in a crowd made me feel very Chinese—though the stares did not.

You'd think I'd be used to people staring at me. They've been doing it all my life. I both hate it and love it when people stare at my face and ask, "What are you?" Part of me wants to scream, "I'm an American!" or "I'm a human! What are you?" But another part of me loves being the melting pot personified, and watching their faces change as I share my story.

I'm not aware that any of my father's Mexican ancestors came to the U.S. by wading or swimming across the Rio Grande, just as none of his Chinese ancestors ever worked on a railroad. My Chinese great-grandfather was a restaurant owner in El Paso, where Mexicans have lived since long before the borders were drawn. My great-grandmother was Mexican, but I believe she and her family simply walked across the bridge from Juarez to El Paso.

On my mother's side, one of my Irish ancestors was a hillbilly. That great-grandmother was a poor girl from Appalachia, but she was lucky enough to be born with a pretty face. So when she was a teenager, she put on her best dress, came down from the mountains, went to the city, and caught herself a man. Then there were my English ancestors who lived in New England before the Revolutionary War, my Swiss ancestors who moved to the Midwest, and my French and Cherokee ancestors—I'm not sure I buy the bit about being descended from a Frenchman who married a chief's daughter, although that story has been passed down in my mother's family for years. According to another old family story, whispered for generations, one of our New England ancestors married a half-African woman. That makes me something like $1/2048^{th}$ African, completing the American mosaic, the torn bits and pieces that make up me.

Some people do recognize one of those torn pieces or another, and it seems that some don't like what they see. One tanned summer day when I was twelve, I was riding my bike through the white suburban neighborhood where I lived with my grandparents when a voice startled me from my daydreams. A little girl of about eight hollered, "Get out of my neighborhood, you dirty Mexican!"

Ever the optimist, I duck-walked over to her on my purple Schwinn with the banana seat to explain why it was wrong to call people things like that. I was sure that when she saw how friendly I was she would recognize her error and apologize. The pain didn't hit me until I saw the truth in that little girl's narrowed eyes, followed by her turned back and stomping feet: my friendly explanation only made her hate me more. I slowly pedaled away, thinking, *This can't be how most people are. This can't be how my life is going to be.*

I was right. Sure, a few store clerks have ignored me in favor of paler customers, and a few people who've heard both my last names have asked me questions like, "With a name like Lopez, why don't you speak better Spanish?" I wanted to ask that guy, "With a name like Mc-whatever, why don't you speak Gaelic?" Still, it's not how most people treat me. It's not how most of my life is.

Many men find my exotic blend intriguing. Then they discover I'm just another American woman who has spent half her life looking for an American man, often going to lengths that would shame the skeletons in my ancestral closet. They find me unusual, yes, but not in the ways they want.

Alaska taught me to embrace being different, to almost desire oddity. But the penetrating, sometimes hostile stares in this country are growing tiresome. Until now, I never really knew what it felt like to be a foreigner. Before China, the only foreign destinations I visited were Canada and Mexico. Because I'm 3/8ths Mexican, in Mexico I've sometimes been mistaken for a local. Because I'm 1/8th Chinese—as if a person could be broken down into a pie chart—Asians back in the U.S. sometimes study my eyes and ask, "Are you part Asian?" But here all they notice is my difference.

So when I returned to Dali this afternoon, I bought a new outfit: a pajama-like top and pants set, turquoise batik with tiny white flowers. While it's not traditional, it has an Asian feel that I hope will make me less conspicuous. I tried to buy a traditional *qipao* dress as well, but even the extra large was too tight to zip up. I'm barely five-foot-two and a size six, yet compared to the women of China I look like a Clydesdale clomping among ponies.

I returned to the courtyard of the Number 5 Guesthouse, where I'm staying, and a voice called out to me in a jovial accent, "You look amazing, like a China doll." I looked up to the second floor gallery to find the source of the voice: Rolf, a carelessly handsome young Dutchman with blond curly locks, a stubbly chin, and laughing green eyes. He was dangling his legs over the edge, grinning down at me, smoking a joint. He'd been sitting in that exact same place, joint in hand, when I'd arrived last night, and again when I'd left this morning.

I smiled flirtatiously, bowed deeply, and said, "*Xie xie*. Although I think I'm a little too big to fool the locals. Who would've thought I'd ever qualify as a giant?"

"In the Netherlands you will barely make the height requirement for the roller coasters."

Rolf's playfulness was an open invitation to conversation. We skipped right over the travelers' small talk—"Where've you been? Where're you going?"—questions that often start conversation but thwart communication as people exchange rote recitations of their travel resumes. Instead, I told him about my experience in the Islamic village, which tickled him.

"So, you have a dilemma," he said. "You wish to meet new people and learn about their culture, but you also wish to hide your own culture from them."

"No, I just want to hide my legs."

"And naked legs are not part of your culture?"

"Maybe . . ."

"I understand," he said. "It can be uncomfortable, people staring at you. I think they probably stare at me more than you, because my skin and my hair are more light. At first it seemed impolite. But I've been traveling in Asia for many months, and now I'm used to it."

Conscious that *I* had been staring at his light eyes, I looked away. He chuckled, and I wondered whether he was amused because he was used to women of any race staring at him, or just because he was high.

Rolf told me he and a few other Dutch travelers are going out tomorrow night to celebrate Chinese New Year's Eve and he invited me to join them.

"That'd be great, thanks," I said.

"Of course." He grinned and took another toke on his doobie.

* * *

The calligraphers have been busy for days, sitting in the street markets with little bowls of gold paint and broad red ribbons, creating messages of good luck, prosperity, and happiness. The red banners hang around doorways, bringing luck to each household for the coming year. The sweet, acrid smell of incense drifts from Buddhist temples and ancestral gravesites, invoking blessings from the spirit world. Long noodles slide from bowls to chopsticks to smiling mouths, imparting long life. These are the quiet signs of the Chinese New Year.

The rest is a deafening noise. By midnight last night, the celebration reached a thundering crescendo. Flowers of flame filled the night sky, and the air grew hazy with smoke. Firecrackers exploded up and down the streets. Many of them were more like small bombs, and the sudden booms, often just a few feet away, slammed my eardrums until I thought they might bleed. Surely I lost at least as much hearing in one night as a Dead Head ever lost in a year.

We foreigners have been swept into the happy maelstrom. Last night, Rolf, several other Dutch travelers, and I went to Café de Jack's to celebrate. At midnight, our group stood outside the café with dozens of other Westerners and blew up hundreds of yuan's worth of fireworks. A flaming ember flew off one string of firecrackers and landed in the fleshy web between my thumb and forefinger. I let out a yelp of surprised pain and shook it off. I was unscathed, but a few minutes later another burning piece of firecracker shrapnel smacked me in the cheek. I wondered aloud whether I might lose an eye, finger, or toe before this holiday was over. Rolf overheard me and chuckled in the slow way of the stoned.

We stayed at the café until well after three a.m. I tried to get drunk, but my friends from Holland outpaced me. Rolf observed the party with detached amusement as he lit a large joint and smoked it right at the table. A young woman in our party leaned toward me and whispered that she thought smoking pot in the middle of the restaurant a rude affront to the owner since it could get him in trouble. But Café de Jack's caters to backpackers, a group known to engage in fringe behavior, and I suspected that Jack, or whatever his real name was, wouldn't care.

I was glad to see Rolf misbehave so boldly. It put me on my guard. I have no intention of letting myself be charmed by another addict. Rolf made it even easier: he didn't appear at all interested in charming me.

As the hours burned to cinders, the beer-sodden party lapsed into Dutch. Rolf politely translated for me, when he thought of it. But the Dutch language has a friendly sound and I didn't mind not knowing the meaning. Besides, I couldn't hear a damned thing anyway.

★ ★ ★

When I woke around noon, my head still rang with beer and firecrackers. The screaming, hiccupping, bellowing holiday explosives had never ceased throughout the night. If possible, the celebration was even noisier today. The streets were packed with people in a festive mood.

Lunchtime was wrapping up when I walked into town for breakfast. I was just sitting down at an outdoor restaurant when a small lion pranced down the street. It was made up of two men festooned in yellow tassels: one man hidden beneath the red and gold lion's head, the other beneath the lion's yellow-draped rear. Together, they moved like a crazed cartoon character, gyrating to the drums, cymbals, and bells played by the colorfully dressed women behind them.

Unexpectedly, the golden lion frolicked right up to my table, and the guy in the rear stepped out and gestured to me to take his place. I smiled and gestured back: *Who, me?* He gestured again: *Yes, please, by all means.* I glanced uncertainly at the crowd of Europeans standing around the restaurant. "Go for it!" two people called out.

I grabbed the costume's rear flap, dove underneath, and rushed up the street, capering and dodging, hunched over, unable to see anything but the feet of the guy in front of me. I had to struggle to keep up with my quick and agile partner. I couldn't stop giggling, which made me all the more breathless. I danced halfway up the street before the other man took over again.

For the first time in China, I was more than just the observer, or the observed. Someone had invited me, if only for a moment, to play a part, even if that part was the butt of a beast.

YANGSHUO, CHINA

I can't stop wheezing and coughing, and every breath I take is an agony.

I'm not all that surprised to be sick, after three weeks of leaded gas fumes, factory smoke, cigarette smoke, filthy bathrooms, body-invading crowds, meals at which several of us dip our chopsticks into the same platters, and the universal Chinese practice of spitting into the street—everyone hawks loogies, I mean everyone, even well-to-do women in makeup and heels. The loogies alone are enough to explain why so many flu pandemics start in China.

I keep telling myself I'll be fine so long as I take my vitamins, drink water, and stay positive. After my communication problem in Yuantong Temple, I'm not about to set foot in a doctor's office. I'm liable to wake up in a hospital bed with hepatitis, or minus a lung. I'm a foreigner; would anybody care if I died? If I'm still sick by Thailand, I'll visit a doctor there.

Even as sick as I am, and as chilly and damp as the weather is, I couldn't stand the thought of staying cooped up in my dorm today. So I walked to the marketplace.

The town of Yangshuo was hunkered down like a criminal, concealed within low gray clouds and cold gloomy rain. The roads were pounded dirt turned to mud, lined with sorrowful wood buildings: dark little shops, cafés, and houses. The guesthouses have names like Micky Mao's and Hotel California. A fog-cloaked gang of rock formations surrounds the tattered edges of town; the mottled green karst limestone peaks rise abruptly, their tops unknowable portents swallowed by the mist. It's as if Yangshuo is the only place in the universe, and the rest of the world a hallucination based on memories of a life I've entirely imagined.

When I reached the market, I stopped at a butcher's table to stare at a dead dog. It was skinned, head intact, body and legs stretched out as if Rover had been killed while chasing a rabbit. Then, in a dark corner on the dusty ground, I spotted a woman selling unexpected sparkling treasure: sugar. I bought about half a cup, to go with the instant coffee and tea bags I carry in my pack—many guesthouses provide hot water in the mornings, but little else. Reluctant to sell me such a trifling amount, the woman grumbled as she poured the raw brown crystals into a cheap plastic bag, weighed it on her scale, and thrust the purchase at me with irritation.

After that, I stopped by an Internet café where I eagerly opened an email from Sean. His dad's doctor had confronted the family with a horror that I still associate with cheesy TV dramas and dark comedies. They were discussing whether or not to "pull the plug." His father had been on a breathing machine long enough to make his recovery appear unlikely. Sean wrote:

> *Next time you're at one of those temples, maybe you could light a candle for my dad. I don't know what we're going to do. It's not like he's a vegetable. I told him that I love him, and he squeezed my hand. Even though he couldn't talk, his eyes were open and he was looking right at me. I knew he wanted to tell me he loved me, too. I didn't know what else to say. I wish I could talk to you, you always know the right words to make me feel better. I hope you're safe, wherever you are.*
>
> *Whatever I leave unsaid in this life, there will always be just one thing left to say: I love you.*
> —Sean

With a sigh, I replied:

> *Dear Sean,*
> *I'm sorry you and your family are suffering. Of course I'll light a candle for your dad. I'll tell you more about my journey next email. For now I can't think of anything else to say except . . . I love you, too.*
> —Cara

After that, I came here to the Countryside Café to sit alone, cradling my hot milk-tea, raping the blank pages of my journal with an angry black pen, listening to the shuffling footsteps of the rain. I feel exquisitely sad, and tonight the emotion feels as sublime as a work of art, full of orgasmic pain and rage, tender longing and loneliness. I wanted to travel alone and unencumbered, to leave my past behind and find some peace. But peace is nowhere to be found.

THEY ONLY EAT THEIR HUSBANDS

THIRTY-FIVE YEARS OLD—PHUKET TOWN, THAILAND

Late last night, alone in my room in Phuket Town, I gave myself the first orgasm I've ever achieved on my own. It wasn't easy. Until now, I've always found masturbation to be an act of frustration, a way of reminding myself, "There's no one here to do this for you. You're all alone, so there, and there, and there!" I didn't expect it to work, and the climax came as a shock. Satisfaction lasted for one immeasurable moment, before time snapped back into its usual shape and I again felt my distance from the life I knew, and will never know again.

This morning when I went for a walk, the swollen Phuket sky released a sudden flood that filled every crevice of day with water. I saw no distinguishable raindrops, just one dense heaving mass of wet.

I rushed for cover in the Ranong Road Market, a hive of colorful, dirty, smelly, energetic life. The deluge threw itself against the motley collection of corrugated tin roofs and tarps, echoing throughout the market. Waterfalls gushed through breaks between the roofs, and shopkeepers caught the water in buckets to use later. The smell of the market was overpowering, heavy with the reek of fish bypassing their expiration date in sopping, 100-degree humidity. My stomach lurched, and I tried to breathe shallowly through my nose.

I peered through the curtain of water streaming off the roof and saw a silhouette against the sparkling rain: a black man raising a coconut overhead, tilting his head back to catch the clear juice in his mouth. He lowered the rough brown fruit and smiled my way. "Would you like to try some?" he asked, holding the coconut toward me. "It's wonderful."

"No, thank you," I said, smiling back. Then I moved on through the shadows under the thundering roof, happy to be alone.

When the rain ceased I walked out of the market to a sun still glistening, as if it, too, had been caught in the storm. As I strolled down the sidewalk, the stench of steaming human waste wafted up from the sewer. The smell was nothing compared to my joy at having this moment to myself. I may be lonely, but it's *my* loneliness, to share with whom I choose and no other.

A few days ago, I received an email from Sean, with answers to two questions I'd emailed him from Hong Kong: 1) although his father isn't out of danger, he's off the ventilator and still among the living (I'll never think of the whole "pull the plug" dilemma the same way again); 2) Sean is taking two weeks off work to join me, sometime in May, June, or July. That will put us together in Greece, Italy, or Spain.

He wrote: *I hope you don't meet the man of your dreams before I get there.*

I replied: *I met the man of my dreams seven years ago, although I didn't realize it then. Italy sounds almost sinfully romantic, don't you think?*

THE LAST FRONTIER
THIRTY-THREE YEARS OLD

The day after Chance dumped me and called me a "*Fatal Attraction* psycho bitch from hell," I called in psycho at work. Sick, that is. It wasn't a lie; I did feel nauseous.

Realizing I was in love with a man who despised me, I doubted the entire course of my life. Not that I thought his cruelty was my fault. I didn't have low self-esteem in the usual sense. I considered myself worthy of a good man. I knew I was an intelligent, attractive, loving woman with a sense of humor. I simply had no faith anyone besides me would ever see that. I believed that my compulsion to say out loud every thought in my head would drive most guys away.

But then, I felt reasonably certain that most male-female relationships were destined to disappoint, not just mine. So I'd always tried to make it work with whichever guy I was with—which was now nobody. In my opinion, this wasn't anyone's fault, just a fact of life. Yet this fact left me feeling copeless.

I spent that morning praying for catatonia. It would be so much easier to lose my mind. But I couldn't seem to lose consciousness of my own volition. So I decided that what I really needed was to smother myself in the sickeningly sweet syrup of self-pity. This required avoiding any efforts at bathing or grooming, and leaving the apartment just long enough to purchase a romantic novel and a pint of Ben & Jerry's. I put on my sweats, pulled a ball cap over my stringy hair, and drove to the bookstore.

As I walked through the arctic entry of the store, I almost barreled straight into him. No, not Chance. Sean, from aikido. I hadn't seen him since I'd stopped going to the dojo more than a year before, back when Chance used to be jealous of any time I spent without him.

Sean looked great. So did the tall blond woman with him. And here I was in my purple sweats, oh my God, with the . . . yes, with the food stain on the front! I stood there, wide-eyed, conducting an instant mental inventory: ball cap, greasy hair, unwashed face, tear-swollen eyes. A complete skank. And still no catatonia to save me.

But he'd always been friendly, and he was friendly now. His shockingly blue eyes flew wide and lit up with genuine delight.

"Cara!"

"Sean!"

I gave him a bear hug, as I'd always done. Once you've rolled around on a mat with someone in an aikido dojo, physical contact feels as natural as water flowing downhill. Yet when he put his arms around me, I felt my cheeks flush, reminded of the instant attraction I always felt for him. My other feeling caught me off guard: relief. It was the kind of relief I suspect a soldier might feel upon running into a close comrade after two years of combat.

"Wow, it's so good to see you!" he said.

"It's great to see you, too. Although it's kind of embarrassing to be seen. You've caught me playing hooky."

"Really?" he said, laughing. "I won't tell."

"I suddenly felt like I had to have a book. Well, that's dumb . . . I mean, you probably guessed that. This is a bookstore, after all. Anyway . . . how are you?"

"Great, and you?"

"I've been worse . . . It's so good to see you!" I said again.

"You, too. We miss you on the mat."

Looking as if he'd lapsed on her presence, he turned to the woman next to him and introduced her. Her name breezed past me, and I greeted her distractedly. Feeling awkward and unattractive, and surprised to find myself near tears, I said, "Well, I should let you go. But it was really nice to see you." (*Yes, Cara, I think he heard you the first two times.*) He gave me another hug and left.

I went inside and bought two Jane Austen novels. Then I stopped at 7-Eleven to buy a pint of chocolate chip cookie dough ice cream. For the rest of the day I flopped on my couch, disappeared into *Sense and Sensibility* and the comforting distance of the eighteenth century, and tried to forget about twentieth century men.

★ ★ ★

The next day, I returned to work. At lunchtime, I stopped at my favorite granola-head restaurant, The Middle Way Café. And there he was again. With the blonde.

I walked up to their table, grinning. "Stop following me," I said.

"We will if you will," Sean replied.

I turned to his friend. "I swear, until yesterday, I hadn't seen this guy in over a year. And now to run into him twice . . . This is so weird."

"She says that every time," he said.

Someone at the counter called out Sean's sandwich order. As he walked away to pick up his food, he turned to me and said, "Don't go away just yet."

While he was gone, the blonde explained that she was one of Sean's old high school friends, visiting from out of town; she overemphasized the word "friends." When he returned, we exchanged pleasantries. Not wanting to be a third wheel, I soon excused myself, saying I should get back to work. I was about to leave when his friend said, "This is too big a coincidence. You two should get together on purpose next time."

"We should," he said, and stared into my eyes for that second longer than you're supposed to, that extra second everyone recognizes but hardly anyone ever believes to be what they think it is.

"That'd be great," I said. "It's been great stalking you."

"I'll bet you say that to all the guys."

"No. Only the ones I chop into little pieces."

* * *

That night, Sean called, and I asked if he wanted to go with me to a seminar to learn about a "business opportunity." It was a multi-level marketing spiel I didn't give a shit about. I just wanted an excuse to see him, without putting myself in the vulnerable position of going on a date two days after being dumped. He laughed, though not unkindly, and agreed to go.

We spent an unbearable two hours in a crowded auditorium, pretending to listen to the speaker praise his new job for freeing him from the shackles of his old job. How had I let Chance sell me on this cult? Afterward, Sean suggested we stop for a late night snack at one of his favorite restaurants. It was an Italian place that also happened to be one of my favorites. "I love their breadsticks," we said in unison. He ordered a margarita and asked if I wanted one.

"No thanks!" I said, more forcefully than I intended. "I've decided to stay away from alcohol."

"Really? Why?"

What to say? "I've had some bad experiences with it. I never did like drinking much, anyway. I guess I just don't like altering my consciousness."

"It's just the opposite for me: I've had some bad experiences myself recently, and I've decided to give altering my consciousness a try."

"What kind of bad experiences?"

"The usual. A broken heart."

"Does the lady I saw you with have anything to do with that?"

"Julia? Nooo. She's just an old friend."

"I'm sorry. I don't mean to be nosy."

"No, no. I don't mind telling you, if you really want to know." So, while he tossed two margaritas down his throat, he poured his heart on the table. He'd met a married woman and she'd fallen in love with him. Without knowing if Sean would reciprocate, she'd separated from her husband to make herself available, then boldly told Sean how she felt. He was already attracted to her, and his ego could hardly fail to be moved by the lengths to which she'd gone. They soon began a romance disapproved of by all who knew them.

He was surprised to fall in love so hard. "Before her, I spent seven years on-again, off-again with Ann, and Ann never was all that excited about me. I guess I got used to that sort of lukewarm relationship. But Heather was

so open. She wanted to share everything with me. And she gave up everything for me: the security of her family life, her home, the approval of her
friends and family. She had these two little boys. They were great, and we
spent all kinds of time together. We became like this family. Heather even
told me she wanted to have another kid, with *me*. I'd never wanted kids
before, but I was ready to do it all."

It ended with a time-honored cliché: she went back to her husband. Sean
was devastated. "The thing is, I never allowed someone so deeply into my
life before. Then it was gone, just like that. And to all my friends I was
this home wrecker. I mean, they're still my friends, but . . . I don't know,
I guess I did it to myself, isolated myself, you know? And I haven't been
able to talk to anyone about it."

"When did all this happen?"

"Just a few weeks ago. Since then I've been hiding mostly. In fact, it's kind
of funny you saw me out. If Julia hadn't dropped into town, I probably
wouldn't have left my apartment."

Listening to his story, I was again surprised to feel relief. It wasn't just
that my misery loved his company. It was that he'd been so imprudent,
that he'd fucked up, and *been* fucked up, so completely. It was the look
on his face that said he thought he'd hit rock bottom before, but he was
wrong. Although we'd followed different paths, we'd both fallen into the
same pit. It was the world's oldest story, but both of us were discovering
it could still yield new pain.

When he was done spilling his guts, I jumped at the chance to spill mine.
I told him the whole sordid story about my misguided obsession with
Chance. Sean, too, looked relieved.

There was no judgment at this table, only acceptance—except when
he asked me to try his ceviche. The raw, lime-drenched fish was seasoned
with cilantro.

"I'm not a cilantro fan," I said. "I know, I know, it doesn't make sense—a
Mexican girl who doesn't like cilantro."

"What don't you like about it?"

"It has a sharp taste, like soap."

"Any other foods you don't like?"

"Raw tomatoes, except on sandwiches or hamburgers."

"What's wrong with them?"

"The texture. I don't like the slimy, gushy seeds."

"Anything else?"

"Birthday cake, the kind with the butter cream frosting? Too sweet. Blecchhh!"

"Has anyone ever told you, you have a lot of opinions?"

"You asked. What about you? Any foods you don't like?"

"I'll have to think about it. I mean, I try to be open to things."

"Oh, I see. You're, like, Mr. Enlightenment."

"Well, I like Buddhist philosophy. But if I was a true Buddhist I'd be a vegetarian. I'm not a vegetarian. Anyway, you say 'enlightenment' like it's a bad thing."

"I like enlightenment just fine, although I'm not big on the whole sitting still thing. But you're changing the subject—what don't you like?"

"Um . . . Okay, normally I don't like liver. But this one time I was at a friend's house and they made this liver, and I don't know if it was just that it was prepared in a different way, or if my taste had changed, but it was fantastic. So, you never know . . . "

* * *

Sean and I started spending most of our spare time together: meeting in coffee shops, going on hikes, and replaying our broken hearts like broken records. Winter came and buried the stink of death that loitered in the deep, damp piles of mulchy fall leaves. As the days grew shorter, the shadows of our carefully nurtured depressions grew longer. I worried when it seemed Sean grew more depressed than I.

"I've always known I'd die young," he said.

"If you think like that, you probably will."

"It's not necessarily a bad thing. Why is everyone so attached to the idea of living forever?"

"Doesn't the idea of not existing ever bother you?" I asked.

"I thought you believed in heaven," he said.

"I do. But *you* don't. Besides, what if I'm wrong? Doesn't it seem weird? I mean, here I am, this whole world unto myself, this consciousness full of thoughts and feelings and memories. Then all of a sudden, poof, one day it's gone."

"Sounds fine to me. My brain drives me nuts. I'm just a melancholy guy,

Cara, always dwelling on the past or worrying about the future. It's in the genes, man. My dad's suffered from depression for years. Once, when I was in high school, he went to API (the state mental hospital). At least I'm not *that* bad. I mostly feel this way in the winter, when it's dark."

I suggested he might have Seasonal Affective Disorder, or SAD, a kind of depression brought on by light deprivation—very common in Alaska. Sean had already accepted that possibility. He sometimes used a special lamp to simulate sunlight, often prescribed for SAD patients.

"Simulated sunlight," I said. "Now *that* is sad."

In spite of Sean's dark philosophical moods, or perhaps because of them, I was beginning to think I could fall for him.

Then one day, Chance came to my apartment to tell me he still wanted to be friends.

"That's ridiculous," I said. "You screw around on me, you break up with me, you call me a psycho, and now you want to be friends?"

"I'm sorry about all that. But we've shared a lot, and we've always been able to talk. I miss telling you what's going on in my life."

"I don't think it's a good idea," I said. "The relationship will be totally uneven. I'll always want something you can't give me."

"You mean sex?" he asked. "Is that all this relationship was about for you? You've always told me the most important part of any relationship is friendship."

"It's not about sex, it's about love. I want to join my life with yours, to be partners. You don't. And if we spend time together, I have less chance to find someone who does."

"You're friends with Kaitlin. That doesn't stop you from meeting people, does it?"

"What if I do fall in love with someone new? Will we still be friends?" I asked.

"I guess I'd have a hard time with that. But yeah, I think we'd still be friends."

As usual, I let him convince me. It must have been that voice, with its hypnotic Bene Gesserit spell. At first we just talked on the phone. Then, as time went by, we went out sometimes—platonically, of course. Yet I began to hope that by spending time with me he'd come to realize he was still in love with me.

When I started making less subtle sexual passes at him, like, "Wanna climb in the back seat with me?" he would say things like, "You should get out with other people, start dating."

"I do go out with other people," I said. I didn't specifically mention my platonic relationship with Sean. Two men, zero sex; I wondered how long I could keep it up.

Each time Chance and I spoke he said it again, as if he didn't hear me, or didn't believe me: "You should start seeing other people."

Each time, I replied: "Like I keep telling you, I am seeing someone. Would you like to hear about it?"

"No. I'd rather not. I just want to make sure you're not alone. It makes me feel guilty."

His condescension rankled, and it was only because I feared his jealous nature that I didn't scream, "I have someone else who gives me everything I need, so get over yourself!"

Strangely, my greatest ally in my efforts to win back Chance was Sean. I both appreciated and resented this. My ego couldn't help but wonder why Sean was so eager to get rid of me. Whether it was the kindness of a friend, or the self-preservation of another commitment-phobe, he regularly offered me relationship advice. Since he was a guy, I followed his pointers. But it seems all men are not alike; most of his advice never worked.

"What do you want from this guy?" Sean asked.

"What do you mean?"

"I mean bottom line: what do you want him to do?"

"I want him to marry me."

"Have you told him that?"

"Not in those words."

"I think you should tell him."

"But I wanted *him* to ask *me*."

"Has he?"

"No . . ."

"It seems to me that you know what you want. The only way you're going to find out if he wants the same thing is if you ask him."

"I think if he wanted the same thing he would have asked by now."

"I wouldn't be so sure," Sean said. "Asking someone to marry you is a pretty big step. Maybe he's just scared."

Once I decided to go for it, I felt an impending sense of release. Unhappy results seemed a foregone conclusion, but it would be good to get it over with and give up my hopeless fantasy. The next time I saw Chance, he made me lunch at his place, and I popped the question.

Maybe popped is the wrong word. As we cleared dishes, I looked across the counter at him and delivered what may be the stupidest proposal ever conceived: "Chance, I have this picture in my mind, of you as an old man. I can see you fixing stuff in the garage, and yelling at the neighborhood kids, 'Hey, you bums, get outta here!' Anyway, I kind of like that picture. What I'm getting at is, I'd like to get married. And I was wondering would you marry me?"

As if I'd sprung a hidden latch on a box, his face spontaneously opened into a broad smile. I grew hopeful, until he laughed and said, "Let me think about that for a minute . . . in the place where I do my best thinking." With that, he turned away, walked into the bathroom, and closed the door. It was a long time before he came out. He never answered the question.

When I told Sean the story, I started to laugh. He didn't laugh. Instead, he hugged me and said, "I'm sorry. That must've really hurt." My spastic laughter splintered into brittle tears.

"I wish someone loved me the way you love Chance," he said. "He has no idea how lucky he is to have someone like you care about him. I've never known anyone who was more honest than you are about your feelings, or more willing to take a risk."

"Maybe that's not such a good thing," I said. "It never gets me anywhere."

THEY ONLY EAT THEIR HUSBANDS
THIRTY-FIVE YEARS OLD—AO NANG, THAILAND

Maybe I was wrong, about risk-taking getting me nowhere. It brought me to Ao Nang, where I now sit staring at my freaky new roommate.

Each morning, I say hello to her, but she never replies. She just stares at me every time I enter or leave the bungalow, her head craning to follow my movements with her bulbous eyes. Until now, I'd never seen a praying mantis, except in a *National Geographic* special. The only thing I remembered from that show was a female biting the head off a male after sex.

While I've been privy to such urges myself on occasion, this struck me as a serious lack of boundaries.

Being ignorant of the praying mantis's disposition toward humans, I wasn't entirely comfortable falling asleep while my new companion clung to the light fixture next to my bed. Her obvious interest in my every move did little to put me at ease. So I did what I usually do when facing an unfamiliar situation: I asked a complete stranger for his opinion.

I ambled over to my neighbor's bungalow and called out:

"Hello? Hello?"

"Yes?" A young German man with an affable case of bed-head appeared on the porch.

"I'm sorry to bother you, but I was hoping you could answer a question."

"I will try."

"There's a praying mantis in my room, and it's probably no big deal. But I don't know much about them, and I'd hate to go to sleep and find out they're dangerous or poisonous or something. Do you know if they're safe?"

"You say something is in your room?"

"A praying mantis."

"I'm sorry, I do not know this word."

"It's an insect. I'm sure you'd know it if you saw it. Would you mind taking a look?"

"Yeah, sure. No problem. Now you're making me curious." As I expected, the moment he saw the creature, he recognized it. "Ah, yes. We call this one 'Gottesanbeterin.' In English I think this would be something like 'praying to God insect.'"

"That's almost the same thing we call it: praying mantis."

"Praying mantis . . . " he repeated, studying the tiny kung fu warrior. "Wow. It is very interesting, isn't it?"

"Yeah, it's really cool. But do you know if they bite people?"

"I'm not sure, but I don't think so. They only eat their husbands." I'm not sure if this struck him as funny as it struck me, or if he only laughed because I was laughing so hard.

A moment later he took his leave, saying, "I think you only need to close your mosquito net and she will not bother you."

I followed his advice and the mantis let me be. Nonetheless, I wasn't alone in my bed. Completely missing the purpose of a mosquito net, the resort's cleaning staff leaves a polite opening in my net each day to make it easier for me to climb into bed each night. This allows any number of tiny, unwanted, unidentifiable guests to crawl or fly into my bed every day while I'm gone. I scratched a lot and slept little.

Occasionally I stared up at the gauzy image of the praying mantis staring back at me through the mosquito net and chuckled, "They only eat their husbands." I wondered what this one would think if she knew how much time I'd wasted trying to catch one. She tilted her head at me and said nothing. A single female with no regrets, she was my new instructor in the art of silent observation.

* * *

With no one to talk to, I'm learning to listen. The sounds are what I'll remember most about Ao Nang: the croak of the geckos that live in the bungalows, calling their own names, "Geck-oh! Geck-oh!"; the vibrating crescendo of cicadas, like a space ship landing in a fifties sci-fi flick; the screech of the baby owl who lives at our resort, a sound more like the sad wail of a small child; thunder like the crack of doom and roaring waterfalls of rain, heralding yet another lightning show and power outage; the angry-bee drone of long-tail boats ferrying passengers to and from Railay Beach; the shouts of the touts and boat pilots pacing up and down Ao Nang Beach singing out for passengers, "Rai-lay-rai-lay-rai-lay!"

I shouted back, "Railay!" and a tout pointed me toward one of the boats bobbing in the surf. I took off my sandals, hitched my sarong up to my thighs, waded through the water, and tried to climb in. This was a challenge because the boat had high sides. I'm sure I looked like a beetle trying to climb into a bowl, legs flailing as I dropped over the side and tumbled in.

About ten minutes later, the boat passed around a tall, rocky headland, and my face stretched into a broad smile as Ao Railay was revealed. The small bay lay tucked between impressive cliffs, lofty Chia Pets of fluffy jungle greenery. The cliffs were dotted with climbers, the beach bars clotted with customers. The pretty little white sand beach sported a small collection of sunbathers, many of them young, topless European women.

Generally, Thais are modest Buddhists who'd never think of putting on a bikini, much less going topless. When visiting a beach, most Thai women wear shorts and t-shirts, and swim in those same clothes. But I could hardly judge the topless European sunbathers on their manners, since my bikini would also seem immodest by Thai standards.

I didn't strip down to my bikini right away. Instead, I went on a search. I'd heard the island had a trail to a beautiful lagoon trapped within a mountain.

At first, I missed the trail and found myself on Princess Cave Beach, at Outer Princess Cave. At the entrance to the shallow cave stands a libidinous little shrine to the Cave Goddess. Scattered around the shrine, stands what looks like a collection of wooden clubs, several of them two or three feet tall. They aren't clubs, but penises of outlandish sizes, monuments to man's self-delusion, painted lurid colors and draped with prayer scarves. Before the Cave Goddess statue sits a table filled with offerings, not only of flowers and incense, but beauty products like lipstick, perfume, and soap. A wooden plaque tells the story of a princess who fell in love against her father's wishes. One day she came to pray to the Cave Goddess, a deity of love and beauty. The princess ended up staying in the cave with the goddess, where she remains to this day. Assuming she came to pray for help with her love life, this sounds like poor service to me.

While the penises were diverting, they weren't what I was looking for. Determined to find the trail to the hidden lagoon, I asked around until I found an American who knew the way. He guided me back to the path I'd taken to the beach, and pointed up to a steep rocky slope alongside the path. A thick rope hung down from an unseen distance above. No one had mentioned that rope climbing would be involved.

I took a deep breath, grabbed the rope, braced my legs as if I knew exactly what I was about, and started climbing. I'm not a climber, and my intrepid progress up the rope was strictly Inspector Clouseau-school. The knotted ropes continued up the hill, stinking of body odor, sweat, and fear, and slick with slime that made my hands slip. I had an awkward time hauling myself up one protruding rock, and bounced into a jagged piece of limestone, punching a small but impressively bloody hole in my knee. Seeing this as a dare, I continued. Sean's voice spoke in my head: "When you get up in the morning, you never know what's going to happen."

Halfway up, I ran into two guys coming the other way, who warned, "You might want to know it's even steeper on the other side. You have to rappel straight down into the lagoon."

"Is there a rope on that side, too?"

"Yeah, the ropes go all the way. It's just steep—almost vertical."

"I'll be fine. Thanks."

After about ten minutes, I reached the top, and a minute later, hit the steep downhill descent. Those guys weren't exaggerating. This was one serious slope.

I looked up and spotted a young guy coming down behind me. He had the fit, at-ease look of someone who belonged on a cliff, and wore a t-shirt scribbled with the slogan, "NO FEAR." Must be an American.

"No fear?" I said. "But it wouldn't be any fun without *some* fear."

"Who're you trying to convince, me or you?"

Hearing a young woman's loud laugh, I looked higher. She might not have been a mountaineer, but her ponytail, muscular legs, and look of cheerful concentration all told me she was an avid athlete. The volume of her laugh told me she, too, was an American.

"Oh you laugh," I said. "But just wait until you get to this section." With that, I attempted to rappel down the steepest segment. Even if I'd been a trained climber, I had no harness or climbing gear. I was only hanging onto the rope, hoping that it was securely fastened to the rock above and that my hands wouldn't slip. I chose the wrong path down and hit a dead end. To rejoin the correct route, I had to pull myself partway back up, then swing across a gap. My first effort ended in a body-slam against the rocks.

"Shit!"

"Are you okay?" NO FEAR's voice floated down.

"Yeah. Just frustrated," I said, panting.

I tried again, this time leaning away from the wall and splaying my feet more firmly in front of me. I swung across and planted my feet on the rock.

"Very good!" the woman called down. "Thanks!" I called up, feeling like an idiot.

About half an hour later I reached the bottom. The lagoon was empty of water, except for a one-inch puddle with pathetic aspirations to become a pond. The rest was mud. I'd expected a large, sparkling pool, something that might invite a swim. But the lagoon is fed by seeping ocean water, and I hadn't thought about low tide. I smirked at yet another of my life's dramatically under-fulfilled expectations. "Well," I thought, "what else do you expect from expectations?"

Once I got over the missing water, it was quite beautiful: a deep circular hole in the mountain, surrounded by steep cliffs. Even in this hidden place, the fertile tropics exploded with the vivid greens of uncontrollable life. About a half-dozen people stood down there with me, pacing like animals in a cage. Our heads turned in unison as an echoing screech bounced off the walls. A large owl soared across the lagoon, landed in the large puddle, and stared at us. The owl circled and landed a few times, as if to let us know this was his territory.

I struck up a conversation with the two people who'd come down behind me. James is from Colorado, and Carly is from Boston. They're not a couple; they met on Railay. This climbing Mecca is overrun with Germans, Swiss, Swedes, and other Northern Europeans, but scant few Americans. So the discovery of compatriots was sufficient for the three of us to form an instant bond. Together, we climbed back the way we came. Afterward, they invited me to join them at the Sunset Bar to—what else?—watch the sunset.

First, I excused myself for an ocean dip to rid myself of sweat and grime. As I bounced through the water on the balls of my feet, a sudden sharp pain slapped my ankle. I instinctively grabbed my foot, and nearly did a face-plant into the water. I lurched back to shore, fell onto the sand, and examined my ankle. A tiny trail of welts wound around my limb. What to do? No clue. I wrapped my sarong around my waist and limped to the beach bar to join my new friends.

"What happened?" Carly asked.

"I have no idea." I lifted my sarong to show them the welts.

"You probably got stung by a jelly fish," James said. "You know, I've heard if you pee on it, it's like a natural painkiller."

Carly and I giggled at his earnest advice.

"I know it sounds gross," he said. "But hey, if it works . . . "

"Urine is acidic," I said. "So how would peeing on it make it sting less?"

"Yeah," Carly said. "This whole urine business sounds like shitty advice to me."

I declared that I had no intention of testing the medicinal benefits of peeing on myself, then closed the debate by lowering my sarong over the burning trail of pink circles. Carly complimented me on the sarong, a maroon print covered in small golden elephants.

I said I'd only bought it a few days ago and it was quickly proving to be my handiest multi-use item: "I've already used it as a dress, a skirt, a towel, a blanket, and a bathrobe."

Carly said, "It can also be used as a tote to carry things to the beach, a sling to carry a baby, a table cloth, a wall-hanging . . . I wish it was more acceptable to wear them in the U.S. I'd wear one all the time."

"No one would blink an eye in L.A.," I said.

"We must have something that versatile in the States," James said.

"Duct tape?" I suggested. "That's pretty versatile. I carry it in my pack."

"Why?" Carly asked.

"In case I rip my backpack or something. I've already torn the duffle that I use to carry my pack on planes and trains. Duct tape patched it right up."

"Yeah, but can you wear it like a skirt?" Carly said.

"Ouch," I said.

James chuckled, but Carly threw her head back and laughed with belly-busting abandon. She exuded intelligence, minus cynicism. I envied her rare blend of youth *and* self-confidence. I wondered what I would do with such incredible power. I wondered if she was even aware of it.

Our conversation was unabatedly pointless and, as three lone travelers high on unexpected companionship, we could care less. I ordered a fruit lassi—a Thai version of a smoothie, made with pineapple, orange, yoghurt, and ice—and talked animatedly with my friends of the moment, until the sunset whipped the sky into its own fruit froth.

I longed to stay, but the boats to Ao Nang don't run at night, and I had to return to my bungalow. As the sun slipped under the horizon, I left my friends and headed for the beach, where the few straggling boat pilots sang out, "Aonang-Aonang-Aonang!"

I lifted one lugubrious arm in reply. "Ao Nang."

As the boat skipped across the rising waves like a thrown rock, drenching me with spray, the sky turned to Hadean fire. I fell back into loneliness as one might fall into the arms of a vampire lover.

AYUTTHAYA, THAILAND

I arrived at Wat Phra Makathat as the sun bathed the crumbling temple ruins in the mellow, golden glow of afternoon—the color of memory. Numerous stone Buddhas sat in mute meditation. Most of them were missing their heads, as if they'd decided to finally remove, once and for all, the distraction of thoughts.

The conical towers of broken brick and stone reminded me that beauty is both timeless and ephemeral. They gave testament to the former splendor of Ayutthaya, Thailand's capital from the fourteenth to eighteenth centuries, a wondrous city of palaces and temples pointing to the sky. Most of Ayutthaya's graceful buildings were burned or toppled by the Burmese during one of that country's many attacks on Thailand.

Amid these broken pieces of Thailand's violent past, atop a low brick wall, silent and smiling, sat a young, shaven-headed monk. His saffron robes were a dazzling contrast against the backdrop of earthen red brick and blackened grey stone. He introduced himself as Wutthichai. His voice caught me by surprise; it hadn't occurred to me that a monk might speak to a woman. I knew he wasn't supposed to touch one.

I pressed my palms together to make a *wai* in his direction and said, "*Sa wat dee ka.*"

Smiling, he returned my greeting and asked where I was from.

"I'm from America."

"Oh, but this is good. If it's okay, I can practice my English with you?"

"I would enjoy that," I said, speaking slowly and distinctly. "Do you mind if I take your photo when we are done?"

"Okay."

I sat near him on the ruins, keeping a polite three-foot distance between us. As a woman in Thailand, I've fallen into an unconscious habit I call "monk awareness": that is, I always make note of whether any monks are in my vicinity, and when they are I give them a wide berth so they won't risk touching me.

Our conversation was rudimentary due to Wuttichai's limited English and my ignorance of Thai—beyond a few simple phrases, like "*Sa wat dee ka!*" (Hello) and "*Sa bai dee mai?*" (How are you?). He told me that he's studying humanities at a Buddhist University, and that he'll probably remain a monk for another two to four years. He's only twenty-one and not sure what he wants to do when he becomes a layman again. After four years of celibacy, that one would be a no-brainer for me, but I didn't dare make such a joke to a man I'd just met, much less a monk.

"What is your profession?" he asked.

"I do not have a job now. But I was a television reporter."

He drew himself up and widened his eyes into an exaggerated expression of surprise. "So, I know television. But what does a television operator do?"

"I am a television re-por-ter, not an operator. I tell stories for the news."

"You work as an operator for the news? And so you work with camera?"

I gave up trying to correct him, as he hammered me with questions about what an "operator" does and I tried my best to explain.

"You have much knowledge for someone who is so young," he said.

"I am not so young. I am thirty-five."

"Nooo! You seem much younger than that," he said.

This time *my* eyes widened with surprise as I thought, *This monk is flirting with me!* I know that Buddhist monks, unlike Catholic monks, don't have to take a permanent vow of celibacy. Yet I'd expected him to be as asexual as an amoeba.

As both our conversation and the daylight began to run out, I stood to take my leave.

"May I give you my information," he asked, "so we may write to each other and I may practice my English some more? We have talked and exchanged some ideas, so I think we are friends now."

"Yes, I'd be happy to write to you."

I'd never before exchanged contact info with someone while trying to avoid physical contact. I could swear the young monk was turning it into a game. First, I wrote my dad's address on a business card and, instead of handing it to Wuttichai, I set it down on the ruins so he could pick it up without touching me. I thought that was the end of it. Then he asked, "May I have your email address, please?" He set the card down on the bricks again. I picked up the card, wrote my email address on it, and set it back down. He picked it up again. "And will you write down the date you will return to the USA?" He set the card back down, and I picked it up again. This exchange went on until I was struggling to contain my laughter. All to avoid touching a woman. Gee, a girl could get a complex.

When he had all the information I could possibly fit on the back of a business card, he allowed me to take his photo.

"Thank you," I said. "It was nice to meet you." I made another wai in his direction, holding my hands near my forehead in a sign of respect.

"Thank you," he said. "I will send you an email when you return to the

USA. Take care of your heart while you are traveling. You are my friend now and I will worry about you."

The young monk's phrase stuck with me, as if I'd come to these ruins to hear it: "Take care of your heart." Looking around at the Buddhas, I saw that the war that had destroyed their heads had failed to reach their hearts. Maybe I've come to the right place to repair mine.

TRAIN FROM AYUTTHAYA TO CHIANG MAI

How am I supposed to take care of my heart when I can't even take care of my butt? I'm sitting on a hard wooden bench on the all-night train to Chiang Mai, and every rail in the tracks is sending a personal insult to my ass. Overhead, a few useless fans faintly stir the recalcitrant air. I'm surrounded by Thais and the musical chirping of Thai chatter and laughter. Apparently most foreigners just aren't up for an all night train-ride crammed into fourth class with wall-to-wall bodies and no air conditioning.

At nightfall, a pretty girl wearing a long ponytail and a ball cap sat across from me. She might have been anywhere from fifteen to twenty, but then most Thai people look young to me. We both gazed out the window into the darkness, which gave way to an intense orange glow as the night caught fire. Flames raced across open fields, and the smell of smoke drifted through the train's partially open windows. The ball cap girl confirmed my suspicion, leaning toward me to say, "Farmers. They burn old . . . plant, so they can make new one. This is normal. You don't worry."

After a pause she said, "You hear about big fire Kao San Road?"

"Yes, really terrible." It happened a few nights ago. While I was sleeping at Chai's place in Bangkok's backpacker ghetto, a Thai family was burning in their beds just a block or two away. An entire block of buildings burned down in the conflagration. I hadn't been able to bring myself to act the gruesome tourist and walk past the smoking ruins for a look.

"The newspaper say the owner did it on purpose, for the insurance." The girl shook her head, and her ponytail swished from side to side. "This man is a murderer. He want money, but his family now dead. What good his money now?"

As night wore on, the chatter and laughter ceased. Bodies sat, squatted, and curled in impossible positions as passengers tried to capture a few minutes of sleep on the tiny, hard benches. Some sat with their heads or feet in the laps of friends or family. The ball cap girl pulled the cap's brim low over her eyes, crossed her legs in the lotus position, and turned to lean her forehead against the window.

By midnight the fires had ceased and the night was black as pitch. The only evidence that we still moved was the feel of the train rocking beneath me and the sound of the wheels: allalone-allalone-allalone-allalone. I leaned my forehead against the window and caught the reflection of my eyes, where the fires of relentless memories continued to burn. Tears spilled down my cheeks. Wanting to avoid notice, I cried silently, not moving a hand to wipe my tears, tensing my muscles to keep my shoulders from shaking.

A voice broke through my thoughts, shy and tentative, the sweet hum of a small bird, "Excue me." I didn't move. Softly again, "Excue me." Another pause. Then, singing, "Hey-you."

I turned from the window, to the sympathetic face of the ball cap girl. I had thought her asleep, but she was sitting up, holding a tissue in her out-stretched hand. I gratefully accepted it, turned back to the window, and wiped my eyes. But her kindness only made me cry more.

Reaching across the empty space between me and other people is the way I broke my heart in the first place. The only way it will mend is if I allow people to reach back across the empty space to me. But that's become such a long distance to cross.

SHEER MADNESS

My screams were just a reflex. The corpulent, five-inch cockroach scuttling across the floor didn't scare me so much as surprise me. I've become quite used to burly bugs and rats and all creatures creepy crawly. My simple room at Pooja's Guesthouse is just two hundred rupees a night (about three bucks). At that price, insects are ambiance.

A moment later, the power went out in Kathmandu's Thamel district. Soon, candles were flickering in windows throughout the jumble of buildings crowded together like a child's building block city.

I escaped the dim indoors for a walk through the last smudge of dusk in this persistently rattling, honking, chattering town. Like a crying baby, the city demanded my full attention. Bicycle rickshaws, cars, pedestrians, motorcycles, and cows crowded together in narrow, dirt-paved streets without lanes or apparent rules. I've given up trying to figure out how to survive Asia's traffic, simply hoping fast reflexes and the odds will be in my favor. Although I didn't get hit, I soon got lost in Kathmandu's web of nameless roads. The strong air overwhelmed my nose: diesel and spices, dust and oils, animals and vegetables and deodorant-free humanity. Every second person wanted to sell me something: trinkets, tours, clothes. "Excuse me, madame, come inside, please. Only looking, no buying. Looking is free."

Young boys of eleven or twelve walked the streets hawking the same two wares: "Excuse me, madame, Tiger Balm? Pocketknife?" I thought, "What an odd combination." Then I realized these boys were canny little entrepreneurs: Kathmandu is trekker central, and they'd hit on two portable items that could come in handy on a trek. I already had a pocketknife, but I stopped the next boy and bought a tiny jar of Tiger Balm, legendary potion for aching joints.

Emboldened by that first purchase to take another risk, I walked into a store and bought a slice of yak cheese. The shopkeeper sliced it off a dusty cheese wheel that sat uncovered atop the counter. I shrugged, figuring half a dozen hungry flies couldn't all be wrong. It was delicious.

As I wandered farther from the touristy heart of Thamel, the hawkers and backpackers diminished, but the crowds remained thick. Women wearing the traditional *Kurta Surwal*—a long tunic over baggy pants—did chores, sold produce, or ran errands in groups of two or more. Men wearing close-fitting caps sat in small groups talking or ambled through the streets holding hands. Not because they were gay; it's just the Nepali way between friends of the same sex. Men and women don't walk together unless they're married, and even then they don't usually hold hands in public.

Shrines to the many Hindu deities were tucked into every conceivable corner. Children dressed in hand-me-down Western clothes played on and around the statues of their gods without deference or inhibition, and adults didn't seem to mind. In Nepal, secular life and religious life aren't segregated. Children playing atop shrines might give joy to the gods, or not—it isn't a matter for concern.

The power was still out when night fell with an almost audible clang, and the thousands of candle flames quivering in windows and doorways turned the streets into twisted braids of shifting shadows. A faint echo of exotic music drifted to me, weaving through the competing sounds of the city. I followed the sound to a small room with its wooden doors opened onto the street, revealing a tableau of men singing and playing drums and small instruments. I felt as if I'd wandered into an alternate dimension.

That was last night, when I was still in the honeymoon phase of my love affair with solitude. Today, Kathmandu let me know it didn't approve of my affair.

In the morning I guessed my way to Durbar Square, a major intersection of activity dominated by three temples—pagodas topped with triple-tiered roofs. The steps of each temple were dotted with locals and foreigners watching the world go by. A man walked past carrying a stand full of bamboo recorders, which jutted out like branches from a tree. I bought one, carried it to the top step of the largest temple, and began teaching myself to play. The instrument produced a mellow whistle, a sweet sound like the ghost of childhood happiness.

I'm not much of a musician, and soon I stopped playing so I could do my share of world watching like the others on the steps. The square was a happy maelstrom of human and animal traffic. Fake *sadhus* (Hindu ascetics) wearing dirty saffron robes offered to let tourists take their photos, then demanded donations. Non-payment could result in being followed by an outraged phony holy man for quite some time. In one corner, people on their way to and from daily routines passed a small shrine, brushing their hands along the little bells dangling from its eaves, sending the music of their prayers to the gods.

I stepped down from my perch to take photos, but soon found myself floundering in a steady stream of Nepalis, all of them insistent that I buy something:

"Excuse me madame, flute?"

"I have one."

"One for your father? Your sister? Your friend?"

"Excuse me madame, where you go?"

"I stay here."

"You have trekking guide?"

The worst tormentor was the man who dangled a pendant directly in front of my camera lens.

"No, thank you."

"It's very beautiful," he said, still blocking my lens with the pendant.

"*No*, thank you," I said.

He switched tactics: "Would you like to hear me play your flute?"

Before I could answer, he grabbed for the recorder. I beat him to it and held the instrument tightly, as I gritted my teeth and again said, "*No, thank you.*"

Now that he had my attention, he held up the pendant again. "You see? Very beautiful."

By now, several more salespeople had gathered to vie for my attention. I ignored them and lifted the camera to my eye to photograph a temple. The pendant man grabbed my recorder again and a tug of war ensued. "I'm not going to keep it," he said. "I am Sherpa. I know how to play." At this point about a dozen people surrounded me, all talking at once. Within seconds, I went from agoraphobic panic to tensely coiled rage. My voice resonated, strong, firm, and unrecognizable to me: "*I would like to be alone, please!"* No one moved. *"I'd really like to be alone please!"* No one moved. I cast an icy glare at all of them. "Then I will leave."

As I pushed through them and stalked away, the pendant man shouted after me in an imperious voice: *"You will spend your whole life alone!"* The effect of his words was stultifying. Minutes later I was still standing in the middle of the square holding my camera limply in my hands and staring into space. The man had voiced aloud the fear I carry with me everywhere I go.

I meandered back to the temple. An old man sitting on the steps smiled down at me and said, "You are welcome. Come and play." I complied, though I knew no real songs. I made up a tune, as my mind continued to turn. A young man sitting nearby asked if he could play my recorder. I handed it to him without hesitation, too tired to risk another confrontation. He played a beautiful melody, but the music seemed to float to me from far away.

"You will spend your whole life alone!" I couldn't shake the upsetting feeling that the pendant man had cast a curse on me, or perhaps, made a prediction.

THE LAST FRONTIER
THIRTY-FOUR YEARS OLD

I wish I'd understood long ago that love doesn't end loneliness. If I'd known that, I might not have struggled so hard to get it. If I'd known that, I might not have expected so much from it.

One day Sean and I went on a hike in Arctic Valley, just outside Anchorage. Early green struggled to push its way through thick, sloppy piles of melting snow. My feet were getting wet as they sank in the slush. We'd been lured outdoors by the false promise of a sunny morning, but the weather had turned and it was starting to sprinkle.

As we walked uphill, Sean asked, "What is the nature of rain?"

"Is this some sort of Zen koan or something?"

"No, it's just a question."

"The nature of rain . . . to be wet?" I offered. " . . . To fall?"

"There's no right answer," he said.

"All right, what do you think?"

"The nature of rain . . . is rain."

"That's a tautology," I said.

"A what?"

"A circular answer."

"Maybe that's life."

Our conversation wandered, the way conversation does when two people are trying to beat a path toward each other through a maze of internal obstacles. After six months commiserating with Sean over our failed relationships with other people, we'd become close friends. We talked for hours—over coffee, at bookstores, at his place, at my place. We hugged a lot. But neither of us had made any other move.

There was a long silence, filled only with the sound of heavy breathing and the weight of our thoughts, as we negotiated some thick piles of snow. Then Sean asked whether I was familiar with the Enneagram. I wasn't. He explained that it's a chart of personality types, based on ancient Sufi wisdom. The Enneagram breaks personalities down into nine basic types. Unlike astrology, these types are not dictated by external factors like the stars, but are revealed by observations of behavior.

According to Sean, I was a "Three," otherwise known as the "Performer," someone attached to image, achievement, and praise. He claimed to be a "Four," the "Tragic Romantic," someone who idealizes what he doesn't have, who romanticizes the past and yearns for the future, but has difficulty living in the moment. Sean theorized it was our unenlightened personality types that had damned our past relationships.

"That's why I can never get over Heather," he said. "Because I always want what I don't have. I'm not even sure if she really was the way I remember her, because everything I remember is always so much better than anything I ever have in the moment that I have it."

"That's kind of depressing," I said. "That means the only way any woman will ever be able to keep your interest is to leave you."

"God, I hope not," he said. "I mean, people do evolve."

Upon reaching the top, we sat on a tussock that was free of snow, and gazed down on a view of Cook Inlet and the City of Anchorage spread below. Sean was one of the few people I knew in Anchorage who grew up there, and he pointed out familiar landmarks that we could see from our vantage point: Ship Creek, his old high school, the neighborhood where he and some other boys once started a grass fire while playing with matches.

As we walked back downhill, my feet grew soaked and frozen from sloshing through the wet snow. I thought resentfully, *If Chance were here, he would have swept me onto his shoulders and said something about not letting his treasure get her feet wet.* Aloud, I joked about how numb my feet were.

Immediately Sean asked, "Would you like me to carry you on my back?"

"No. No, thank you."

Back at his apartment, he offered to make tea, and while we waited for the water to boil he asked, "Would you like me to warm you up with a foot massage?"

A strong, hot jolt shot through me. I mumbled that I remembered something I had to do, and while he rummaged in the cupboards for tea bags, I practically ran out the door. The way he expressed it later, "I turned around for a moment, and when I turned back you were gone."

The next afternoon we sat in his apartment on his bachelor-beige couch, talking nonstop as usual, yet still avoiding the subject that vibrated the air between us. I decided someone needed to say something. And it was going to be him.

"Sean, if you were going to tell me something that you'd normally be afraid to tell me, what would it be?"

As if we'd rehearsed this a hundred times and he'd only been waiting for me to give him his cue, he replied, "I'd say, 'You're a very attractive woman, I like you, and I'd really like to have sex with you.'"

I exhaled in relief and said, "I feel the same way. But I think we should talk about this. You realize I still have feelings for Chance."

"Yes, I know that. And I still have feelings for Heather."

"And I'm not ready to give up my friendship with him."

"I know."

"And I can't guarantee that, if the opportunity came up, I wouldn't go back to him."

"I know that, too."

"I like you very much."

"I like you very much, too."

"But I'm not sure if I can offer you any kind of long-term commitment," I said.

"I don't think I'm ready to do that again, either."

Then, without sparing a word on sentiment, I said, "I think we should have an affair."

"An affair?"

"A sexual relationship, but with no promises. I know this sounds . . . well, I don't know how this sounds, because I've never done this before. I consider you my friend. But I'm more comfortable being with you than I've ever been with anyone, and I feel like you understand me better than anyone. And . . . I want to have an affair with you."

"Okay," he said.

"There's only one condition I want us to agree to: neither of us can have sex with anyone else for the duration of this. If we want to have sex with someone else, we have to end it."

"Of course."

It was the first time I didn't try to tell myself I was in love with someone and intended to marry him, just so I wouldn't feel like a slut. Even the times I truly had been in love, I'd never been honest with myself; deep down I'd never trusted any guy to hold up his end of my commitment fantasy, yet I'd always pretended to believe he would. Look where that kind of thinking had gotten me. This time I fully intended to fornicate, and if that made me a slut, at least I'd be an honest slut.

So, for the first time, he kissed me, with six months' worth of longing, and we slowly went on from there. His every movement felt so gentle and generous, so impassioned and consuming that I forgot I was in love with someone else. I forgot everything except him and me. It was the first time I fully allowed someone to give to me, without feeling the guilty need to give a perfect performance in return. I told myself maybe it was because we were friends, or because we had no expectations, or because I didn't feel the need to impress him. I didn't consider that there might be no explanation at all, that we might simply be good together.

We talked into the silent hours when time holds its breath. "You . . . are . . . so . . . beautiful," he said, emphasizing each word and holding my gaze. His eyes told me he was simply saying what he'd been thinking. He'd taken out his contacts and his eyes were no longer the same impossible, Superman blue. They were the light but endless blue of a clear winter afternoon in the arctic.

"I like you better without the colored contacts," I said. "Your eyes are amazing. You shouldn't hide them."

"Isn't sex great?" he said. "It makes everything seem amazing."

"That's not it. Your eyes really are beautiful. This is not an opinion. It's a fact."

He smiled. "Do you remember the first day I met you?"

"You mean at the dojo?"

"Yeah. Well, that morning I had this dream. I didn't remember anything about the dream except these big brown eyes. That night, when I walked into the dojo, you turned around and I thought, 'There they are, those eyes from my dream.'"

"Yeah right."

"I knew you wouldn't believe me. But it's true. You know what else? Remember Julia, the woman I was with when I ran into you two days in a row?"

"Yeah . . . "

"Do you know what she told me after she met you? She said, 'You have unfinished business with that woman.'"

"Unfinished business . . . " I slowly rolled the words across my tongue. "So, are you through yet?"

"No. How about you?"

I turned to crouch over him, until my breasts grazed his chest. "I'll let you know."

★ ★ ★

For three weeks I abandoned myself to a liberating affair with Sean.

At first it was kind of embarrassing, because he lived in the downstairs apartment attached to his parent's house and the family business was attached to the front of the house—a small jewelry shop. They all worked together, designing, making, and selling jewelry: Sean, his father, sister, and mother. Each morning, Sean walked out his apartment door, stepped through another door, and voilà, he was at work. In such close quarters, discretion was impossible. I cringed that first morning when I left his place, sure that several pairs of eyes watched as I walked to my car out front.

The first time I visited him at the shop, I was surprised at how excited they all seemed to see me. I sensed that my presence in Sean's life was a source of relief to them, although I didn't know why. I felt guilty, knowing I had no intention of making a commitment.

Then, one afternoon, Sean took me for a drive down the Seward Highway to watch the sunset over Cook Inlet. He drove down Turnagain Arm until he spotted a rock looming over the mudflats and pulled over.

"I thought you weren't supposed to walk on the mudflats," I said. "I've heard stories about people who walked out on the mudflats and died. They got their feet stuck in the dense silt and drowned when the tide rushed in. I met a firefighter who says he held the hand of this one woman they tried to dig out. They gave her some sort of tube to breathe through, but she died of hypothermia *while he was holding her hand.*"

"Wow. Anything else?"

"So why are you taking me on the mudflats?"

"We're not going out that far. Trust me, this spot's solid. I've been here before."

"Ahhhh, so you bring all your women here."

"No. I usually come here by myself."

As we crossed the mud, I walked extremely slowly, planting each foot carefully, making sure it wouldn't sink before planting the next one. Sean turned to snicker at my progress.

"Shut up," I said, grinning.

We scrambled to the top of the rock, sat facing west down the arm, and silently waited for the sun to set. In summer, this is a long process. The sun tiptoed down the horizon, as if it were too timid to dive into the icy water of the inlet all at once.

When the final flame balanced itself precariously on the edge of the earth, I asked, "Hey, you know what time it is?" Sean looked at his watch as the last glint of sun vanished behind the horizon. "You missed it!" I said.

"What?" He looked up at the dark horizon, then gave me a reproachful grin. "Nice."

After we climbed back down to the mudflats, he said, "Here, get on my back. I'll carry you across. Then you don't have to get your feet muddy. And if we sink, you'll be on my shoulders and have more time to escape the tide." This time, I took him up on the offer.

Back at the highway, as we were about to get in the car, he said, "Wait a minute!" and ran across the street. He ran up and down the slope, picking wildflowers, most of them in variations of purple: violet larkspur, blue-bells, and indigo forget-me-nots. A warm ache spread through my chest. In that moment, I decided to give my heart to this man.

Out loud, I said, "Sean, I think it's illegal to pick the wildflowers."

"Oh my God! You think a trooper might catch me?" He rushed over to me and handed me the small bouquet. "Here, then. You better hang onto these. I don't want to go to jail."

"Thank you," I said. "Purple's my favorite color."

"I know."

I pressed them to my nose and inhaled. "This is the nicest thing anyone ever did for me."

"Gee, you're pretty easy."

"It's not that I'm so easy, it's that most people make things so hard." I cradled his cheek in my palm and kissed him gently.

As I held his gaze, he said, "Now don't go getting all serious on me." For a moment, I was deeply hurt. Then I realized that this was what I'd asked for.

Back at Sean's place, he brewed some hot tea and served mine in a mug imprinted with a martial artist wielding a sword. He glanced at the design and told me it reminded him of a funny story about a Zen master and his disciple.

As the story went, each morning the student served tea to his master in the master's favorite cup. One morning, before serving the tea, the student asked, "Master, why do we practice non-attachment?" The master explained that life is temporal, and that attachment only leads to suffering because in the end everyone dies. Then the master said to the student, "Why do you ask?" The student replied, "Because, master, this morning while I was preparing the tea, I killed your cup."

This cracked both of us up. It didn't occur to me that the story, or its punch line, might have anything to do with our affair.

★ ★ ★

"I never-lied-never-lied-never-lied." That was the mantra I repeated to myself all that spring. Chance knew that I was "seeing someone," and Sean knew that Chance and I were still "friends." Since I was honest with both of them, I believed that absolved me of responsibility for their feelings. I suppose I shouldn't have been surprised by what happened next.

But I was.

It started with Chance's phone call, offering to take me to dinner on my birthday. I felt a guilty pleasure in turning him down. "I'm sorry, but I can't. I'm going away for my birthday."

"Going away?" He sounded perplexed, like someone who's just gone to the store at the same time he always does, to pick up the same old thing, only to find the place closed. "Going away where?"

"To Kennecott, to ride that little pulley system across the river and see the old mine."

"With a *guy*?"

"Yes, with a *guy*," I said.

"When were you going to tell me you were seeing someone?"

"I've told you a bunch of times. You just never listen."

"So who is it?"

"Sean."

"Are you sleeping with him?"

"You're not my boyfriend anymore. That's none of your business."

"So you *are* sleeping with him. What do you mean it's none of my business?! All this time, I've been trying to decide whether to make a commitment to you and you've been telling me you still love me. I thought you were so honest and true-blue. I felt so guilty about how much I hurt you. And all the time you've been cheating on me?"

"It wasn't cheating!" I shouted.

"Okay. Maybe that's true. Maybe in a court of law you could get away with that. But you never listen to what I'm saying. I'm telling you how it feels to *me*, okay?" He began to cry, and his tears had unexpected powers of misdirection: I began to feel guilty for hurting him and to forget he'd ever hurt me. He said, "I can't believe I fell for all that crap about how you imagined growing old with me. How could you say that to me and go fuck someone else?"

"Look, you and I haven't slept together in months."

"So what? Were you afraid it would seal shut?"

"That's not fair. You know I wouldn't sleep with just anyone."

"And that's supposed to make me feel better?"

"When you and I split up, my heart was broken. He was my friend. We talked. We grew close. You kept telling me you didn't want a relationship.

You said we never *had* a relationship."

"You know that's just angry talk."

"Chance, you called me delusional! You called me a *Fatal Attraction* psycho."

"Did you tell *him* about that?"

I didn't respond.

"So you've told this guy everything about us, and I know nothing about him. That pretty much says it all, don't you think?"

I suppose it did. But at the time I didn't see that. I only knew, when he held up a mirror to my behavior, it looked wrong. The fact that it was not Chance, but Sean whom I'd wronged, didn't occur to me. Chance was the only indignant party, and the man I'd loved for more than two years. He was so angry I thought he must love me after all. Sean had never said he loved me. He'd only agreed to an affair. So it was to Chance that I gave an undeserved apology, and in one sobbing breath, cast Sean aside: "I'm sorry, I'm sorry. If you want me to, I won't see him anymore. I've always loved you. I didn't think you loved me anymore."

"I can't talk about this now," he said. "I have to think."

When he hung up, my pulse was still racing. I assumed this heart-thumping feeling was love, rather than the aftermath of adrenaline in the face of male rage—which has always terrified me. I knew if I wanted Chance back I had to say goodbye to Sean, for good.

So, still sobbing, I called Sean.

"Cara, are you okay?" he asked. When I heard his voice, my heart crumpled up like one of the tissues I used to find in the pockets of my grandmother's robe when I borrowed it.

Wanting to get it over with quickly, I blurted, "Chance found out about you and me and he got mad and he wants me back and I can't see you anymore."

There was a long silence. When Sean finally spoke, it was in that voice he usually reserved for long, dreary winter nights: "I knew this was going to happen."

"I'm sorry. But we did talk about this."

"I know, I know. So now we can't even be friends?"

"No. He's really mad."

"I don't see why. You didn't do anything wrong."

"That's not how he sees it. Anyway, I'm sorry. You've become my closest friend."

"I guess Chance will be your closest friend now."

This idea gave me pause. I found it hard to picture talking to Chance the way I talked to Sean. Chance and I hated each other's politics, he thought hiking was boring, I thought multi-level marketing was annoying. He told me I talked too much, but then a lot of people told me that. Except Sean—he always said, "You just have a busy mind. It's because you're so intelligent. I always learn something from you." That much acceptance was so foreign to me that I distrusted it like a ticking gift box. I was sure he was only being polite.

"I'm glad for you," Sean said. "I care about you a lot, and I want you to be happy."

I said, "I want you to know you've helped me a lot. You made a big difference in my life." I'd meant to say something profound, and was dismayed to hear my voice making sounds so shallow and trite.

For me, goodbye is never graceful, always a trip over a crack in the sidewalk.

* * *

When I broke up with Sean, I didn't know whether Chance would take me back. I believed this was the kind of sacrifice people made to prove their love: giving something up with no guarantee of receiving anything in return. I knew I ran the risk of ending up alone.

Two days later, Chance ended the suspense. "I'm sorry I said such hateful things to you. Jealousy is an ugly emotion."

I accepted his apology, but not his invitation to take me to dinner for my birthday. After all that had passed, I felt nervous about the pressure of an intimate evening for two. Instead, I invited him to come to a party with my coworkers. The two of us surrounded by reporters, people trained to be nosy—no pressure at all.

It wasn't planned as a birthday party, but my friends remembered my birthday and bought a small cake. They buried the frosting in thirty-four candles, and I obediently laughed as if it were the first joke in the world. As I leaned over the cake and felt the intense heat on my flushed cheeks, I glanced up at Chance and hesitated. I wondered what Sean was doing at that moment. Then, knowing my friends were waiting, I closed my eyes and, for the first time, blew out my birthday candles without making a wish. I had no idea what to wish for.

Throughout the evening, I caught several friends looking askance at my date. Though they didn't know every detail of my personal life, they knew this guy had been in the picture, then out of the picture—quite possibly "cut out," with scissors. But under the influence of wine he soon won the room. His trick was that it wasn't an act: he truly was a smart, friendly, funny guy. That just wasn't the entire picture. But for all I knew, everyone cropped their pictures, and the bits they left at home were just as ugly as ours.

At the end of the evening, came his husky whisper asking me to "come home," almost the way he used to say it: "Let's go home . . . back to our place . . . our house . . . Baby doll, when are you coming home?" Hoping to validate my choice, believing intimacy would further commit him to our reunion, yearning for home, I accepted.

Chance's body was familiar, but not comfortingly so. Sean was shorter, and I'd grown used to his more compact body wrapped around mine. If Chance and I were two spoons in a drawer, then I was a teaspoon accidentally placed with a soupspoon. I had the uneasy feeling I was cheating—strange, since I'd so readily accepted Chance's premise that Sean was the "other man." But this was the man I'd always wanted, and now he wanted me. So I finished what I started. He was a little rough, but that increased my excitement. We tore each other open like two colliding bombs and filled the open wounds with our bodies.

In the morning, he seemed distant. But then he'd run hot and cold ever since I'd known him. Not wanting to push things too fast—as if I hadn't already—I didn't press him for conversation, but simply left.

When I returned to my apartment, a small package was sitting in front of my door, a gift bag decorated with ribbons. I didn't realize what a miserable night and morning I'd spent until I felt the stretch of certain facial muscles signaling my first unforced smile in hours. I knew Sean had left this gift, cleverly keeping his promise not to see me without actually staying away. (Chance had given me nothing for my birthday.) With alacrity, I swept up my undeserved prize and greedily opened it. I pulled out a bag of chocolate drops, a videotape of The Joy Luck Club—one of my favorite movies—and a broken cup.

Sean had purposely broken a large latte cup into several pieces and glued it back together. The cracks blurred before my eyes as I sat down, cradling the cup in my lap, remembering our laughter over the Zen master and the student who had "killed" his master's cup. I thought about what the broken cup symbolized: non-attachment. The student had killed his master's favorite cup, and I had killed my favorite relationship. But there was forgiveness here, as well. Wisdom teaches us to practice non-attachment because life is transitory; yet, because life is transitory, wisdom also teaches us to treasure what we have. As brief as it was, Sean treasured what we had.

As I ran my finger over the cracks in the cup, the phone rang.

It was Chance. "Cara, I've been thinking, and I don't want to see you any more."

I grew livid. "So what was last night about?"

"Haven't you ever heard of a grudge fuck?"

"You were just using me for revenge? Revenge for what? I didn't do anything to you. You dumped me, and I went out with someone else. Then I left a perfectly kind and decent guy because you said you loved me and wanted me back."

"If he's such a great guy go back to him."

"So you're done, now that you've marked your territory like a dog?"

"Who are you now, Cara? The angry feminist who doesn't take shit from anyone? Next it'll be little miss sweet, innocent victim. Then it'll be the reasonable psychologist. Cara, I've seen all your personalities and I don't like any of them. Give it up. We're history." He hung up.

I felt the way Sean's gift looked. In a daze, I tried to glue myself back together, just enough so I could call Sean and thank him for the equally damaged cup.

"You should've seen me trying to break it," he said. "I bought two of them, just in case it didn't work the first time. A good thing, too, because I dropped the first one a couple of times, but nothing happened. So I threw it and it just exploded! There were shards everywhere."

Trying to maintain control of my emotions, I spoke slowly and deliberately: "The thing I've wanted most in life is for someone to understand me. And the gift you left me, it says you know who I am. Anyway, I certainly didn't expect it, after I cut you out of my life like that."

"Cara, you don't have to worry about that. I understand. So how'd it go, anyway?"

"He dumped me again."

"You're kidding."

"I think he just can't forgive me."

"Forgive you for what? What an idiot! Isn't he the one who slept around with other women and then broke up with you? I'm sorry, I know you love this guy, but I think he's an asshole."

Sean's empathetic hatred of someone he didn't know, on my behalf, was as romantic as a dozen roses. But I'd made my choice. And I'd lost. So I remained alone.

★ ★ ★

In my exile, I indulged in internal self-flagellation, mea culpa in the bathroom mirror to a streaked and swollen visage spookier than a heroin addict's. I frequently soothed my overheated psyche on the coolness of the bathroom floor, until guilt turned to self-pity and self-pity turned to nothing but the itchy imprint of vinyl on my cheek.

After two weeks passed, Sean called to lure me off the linoleum. "Some of my aunts and uncles are here from out of town," he said, "and I'm expected to do the family thing, and I was hoping you'd come rescue me. Every time they visit they tease me mercilessly about my love life: 'When're you gonna get a girl? So are you ever gonna get married or are you gay?' Anyway, I figured if you were here it'd shut 'em up. You just have to pretend to be my girlfriend for a few hours. Will you come?"

"That's a first," I said, laughing. "I don't know what to say."

"Say yes."

So I picked myself up, bathed and groomed until the vacant face in the mirror looked at least clean, picked a smile to wear that didn't look too overdone, and drove to his family's place.

I arrived to find Sean taking turns jumping on a trampoline with a boy and girl who lived next door. When he saw me he did a flip, and my heart skipped a beat when he almost went over the side. Instead, he landed on his face. Giggling, he jumped down to hug me.

We didn't act as if nothing had happened. We simply looked at each other, and in that look agreed this was the way friendship worked, just as it had when we were kids: knees got skinned, feelings got hurt, we said and did dumb stuff, then came back to play the next day.

"You look great! Thanks for coming. Hey, let me introduce you to everyone," he said, and shepherded me into his parent's place upstairs. "There's lots of food. My mother made this huge spread, and Grandma made her deviled eggs. They're my favorite."

I smiled prettily at everyone, ate too many deviled eggs, tried not to fart, and was pronounced charming by all. Sean winked at me, looking as proud as a kid who just brought home first prize from the science fair.

Afterward we stood outside, slurping up the last dregs of warmth from the late-setting summer sun.

"Thank you for bringing your pretty face over here and proving to my family that I'm not a loser."

"You're *not* a loser."

"I know. But you know how families are. Anyway, thanks. It meant a lot to me."

"We're friends now, right?" I asked.

"I hope so."

"Just friends?"

"That's up to you. I just like having you in my life, Cara."

Feeling no need to preserve a dignity I had yet to discover, I said, "I don't want to be just friends."

He embraced me as if I'd been resurrected from the dead.

Entering his bedroom, I heard a voice in my head, whispering the kind of words a schizophrenic might hear: "Used goods . . . Cheater . . . Liar." But when Sean made love to me that night, it was without any trace of a grudge. He did what he always did: gave and laughed and played without reservation. Afterward, I slipped into his welcoming shape, like a love letter into an envelope, and slid into the first relaxed sleep I'd had in weeks.

Surely I must have had a blinding insight after that. But I'll be damned if I remember what it was. For me, blinding insights, like happiness, are prone to fading. Blissful reconciliation was followed by the day after that, and the day after that.

One of the nights after that, while we were lying in bed, Sean gave me a warning sure to hurry the fading process along: "I care about you a lot, Cara, and I'm the kind of guy who likes being in a relationship. But I know you want marriage and kids and all that, and I don't really want those things. So, it's probably not a good idea to get too attached to me." I was so livid, if he'd just added the word "babe" he would have finished the conversation talking to a warm dent in the pillow next to him. I tuned out his words, though his voice continued to tickle my ear, the way Grampa's voice used to when I sat on his lap with my head on his chest

When my grandparents divorced, Grampa sat me down in the family room to talk—not on his lap, in a chair across from him. He talked for a long time, but I tuned out most of the words. The only ones I remembered were, "Cara, don't wear your heart on your sleeve like I have. You'll only get hurt." I was only twelve, but I knew what he meant. I set my jaw, and in my mind I replied, *Fine. If that's the way you want it.* From that moment on I acted like I didn't care, about any of it.

One night, Mom (my grandmother) sat in the living room crying in the dark, and I tried to sneak past her to my room without her noticing. But she called out, "Aren't you going to say anything? You're not even going to try to comfort me?"

I turned to her with a blank stare. "What do you want me to say?"

"You're cold, you know that?" she hissed.

I turned away silently, walked to my bedroom, opened the closet door, crawled inside, and cried, muffling my sobs in a pile of clothes until I fell asleep.

Likewise, when Sean told me, "It's probably not a good idea to get too attached to me," I set my jaw in that same firm line and thought, *Fine. If that's the way you want it.*

On one of the days after that, Chance returned. Sort of. I think. Like two balls of yarn pawed endlessly by kittens, at some point my dying relationship with Chance got tangled up in my growing relationship with Sean, until events got tied together in one confusing knot.

Sean never said he loved me, although he acted like he did. Chance often said he loved me, although he acted like he didn't. If this were about making a choice, none-of-the-above would seem the most reasonable option. But, in their best moments, the two choices before me seemed more reasonable than none at all. After years of failed relationships, I'd begun to believe that looking elsewhere would only land me in an equally humiliating predicament. After all, there was one thing all my relationships had in common: me. Maybe it wasn't the men I was choosing, but something else I was doing wrong. Surely there were no two people more different than

Chance and Sean. If I were missing some essential clue, I decided I'd prefer to figure it out now rather than go through it all again with someone new.

As a horny thirty-something woman sitting atop a biological time bomb, I was no longer willing to consider celibacy as an option.

So when Chance showed up on my doorstep, his eyes downcast, I invited him in. Though I opened the door wide, he seemed to squeeze himself through the gap like the final, reluctant dab of toothpaste that wanted to be sucked back into the tube. He sat on the couch arm closest to the door and said, "I've been miserable since the last time we talked. I can't eat. I can't sleep. I miss you. You were the one thing in my life I knew I could count on, and I blew it. I know this is my fault. I know you didn't cheat on me. I know I drove you out of this relationship. Just tell me what you want me to do, and I'll do it."

"I got back together with Sean."

He leapt to his feet, his eyes inflamed. "I knew it! You couldn't even wait two weeks for me?"

"I've already been waiting three years for you—waiting for you to stop being the guy who breaks up with me once a week. You want me on Monday, then dump me on Friday."

He continued as if I hadn't spoken, "I know you, Cara. Your problem is you can't spend five minutes alone. Well, you know what? That's why you're going to end up old and alone, just like your grandmother!"

"That's a terrible thing to say."

I'd never before seen Chance put the lid back on his self-control once he'd removed it. But this time he did. "Okay," he said. "You're right. I promised myself I wasn't going to get mad. I'm sure the only reason we keep hurting each other is because we love each other." This schizoid logic has been foisted on the world by romance novels, love songs, and wife beaters since long before I was born. But I was no longer buying it.

"I can't promise we'll get back together," I said. "But I'd be willing to go to counseling with you."

"That doesn't make any sense. You won't get back together, but you expect me to go to counseling? What's the point?"

"We've tried to be together and we've tried to split up. But we just keep ending up here, having this same conversation. Maybe a counselor will help us figure out how to get back together and stay together, or how to split up and stay split up."

* * *

We stayed split up and each found our own counselors. Mine was a diminutive, doughy, middle-aged woman with grey hair, a grandmother who seemed more like the kindly Hallmark variety than my own.

Each time she asked how something made me feel, I had ten answers: "I wasn't angry when he said that, just hurt. Okay, maybe I was angry . . . He reminded me of my dad. Well, at first he reminded me of my grandpa . . . It felt the way it did when my mother moved away . . . Come to think of it, it was more like the time my second step-mom told me I couldn't stay with my grandmother anymore, because she was going to be my mother now . . . Anyway, the weird thing is, no one in my family ever drank, so how come you think I keep ending up with alcoholics?"

The counselor had a few answers of her own, which always sounded logical but didn't feel like they had any bearing on the ambiguity of my experiences.

So, one weekend, I decided to stop my internal struggle and seek an external escape—no more analyzing old feelings, just breathing fresh air. I packed my car with camping gear and headed for a town called Hope. At first, the irony didn't occur to me. Hope was simply a place where I'd not yet been, just a couple of hours from Anchorage. As I traveled down the finger of Turnagain Arm, then hooked back up the other side, I decided hope was the bravest of emotions. It seemed fitting to travel alone as I tried to find it again.

You could say I grew up with hope: Hope was the name of the grandmother who raised me, though no one called her that. I just called her Mom. Right before I went camping, I phoned her to confess the triumvirate of doom I'd created.

"It's terrible having to choose between two men, isn't it?" she said.

"That's right—I forgot," I said. "You went through something similar, didn't you?"

At seventy-three, Mom was still an exotic beauty: half Mexican and half Chinese, with large, wintry brown eyes that slanted at the corners, and buttery skin that looked like it belonged to someone twenty years younger. Years ago, as a young woman in El Paso, she left a fiery wake wherever her high heels clicked, turning lovesick men into blackened cinders. She was oblivious to her effect on men, until years later, long after the flames had cooled. Years later, she often sighed over the beauty she once had, but never experienced. An orphan, she grew up among aunts and cousins who clucked in pity over the mixed heritage that made her singularly unattractive. Like the ugly duckling, having never seen anyone else who looked like her, she believed them.

Hope was born not of love, but of violence. Her Mexican mother was raped at fourteen, although some of the man's legitimate children later claimed she was only a victim of her own libido. The man was no stranger to the girl. He was her sister's husband, a Chinese man of thirty-five. She gave birth to Hope at fifteen, then died of tuberculosis at seventeen. For many years, the family told Hope her father was dead, too.

Hope was two years old when her grandparents took her with them from El Paso to East L.A.. Her grandmother died shortly after, and her loving "Papá" often left her at the mercy of aunts and uncles who only grudgingly accepted her, the family embarrassment. As soon as she was big enough to reach the stove, the sink, and the hamper, her aunts expected her to cook, clean, and take care of their children. In return, they shared a roof with her, for which she was expected to be grateful, regardless of the rats that lived in that roof—she woke one night to the tickle of whiskers on her neck, grabbed hold of the rat, and threw it across the room.

Feeling unwanted, except for the services she could provide, she withdrew into a persistent silence. Hope gave up on love.

When she got pregnant at seventeen, love had little to do with it, only loneliness. The father stayed around just long enough to pass on twenty-three chromosomes, then vanished. Hope gave birth to a son: my dad.

After she spent a few years as a factory seamstress, a sympathetic aunt told her she should ask her father for help. "Father?" Hope asked. "I have a father?" Her aunt confessed the family secret: Hope's father was not only alive, he was a man she'd always thought of as her uncle, and he owned a Chinese restaurant in El Paso. She sent him an angry letter, asking why he'd left her orphaned all those years. Though he never denied it, he sidestepped directly acknowledging she was his daughter. But he did offer her a job. In hope of starting a new life, she took her son on a train to El Paso, where she waited tables at her dad's restaurant, rented a one-room apartment, and went about the frightening task of raising a child alone.

When she was twenty-eight she met my grandfather, an army man seven years her junior who frequented the restaurant, one of the few men not intimidated by the hot blaze of her passing. Henry was a Korean American, but he'd grown up in Hawaii, and his unguarded nature must have thrown her off hers. At six feet tall, he had a laid back, swaying gait, as if he walked to the sound of internal island music. He was frequently surrounded by people, and his unhurried manner, his deep, ready laughter, his listening expression—even when he was the one doing the talking—all suggested he would always make time to visit with an old friend, or make a new one. It was a charisma that owed nothing to pretense.

When my grandmother started dating my grandfather, she was in love with someone else. But *that* man wasn't the marrying kind; Raúl only wanted an affair. In the 1950s, accepting such an indecent proposal wasn't the best way to impress family and friends. On the other hand, she was an unmarried mother whose family already believed her a fallen woman. She figured no one had to know what she and Raúl were up to in the wee hours after the night shift. For a time, she and the love of her life "lived in sin"—thrilling, heart-pounding, dizzyingly happy sin.

Then one night she told him that she needed "more," and that if he couldn't give her more he shouldn't come back. Tears streamed down his face, but he left without argument, or offer.

Shortly after that, Henry started taking her out: to the movies, to lunch, for long walks. Smitten by Hope's shy, though carefully tended, beauty, after just a few months he asked her to marry him. She liked Henry. Everybody did. But it wasn't love.

She told me, "You know how they say, 'When you're in love with someone, every day is like the Fourth of July'? Well, there were no fireworks."

"So what made you decide to marry him?"

"I asked your father who he'd prefer to live with, Henry or Raúl, and you know what he said? He said, 'I think you should marry Henry, because I think he'd treat you nice.'"

Just a week before she was to be married, Raúl showed up, looking as if he hadn't slept in months. He told her he loved her and missed her dreadfully, and he pleaded with her to marry him after all.

"So if you loved him why didn't you marry him?" I asked.

She paused. "I guess I didn't think he'd make a good husband. But for the first few years I was married to Henry, I still thought about him."

"Did Grampa know about this other guy?"

"I think he knew I'd been seeing someone else. And when I accepted his proposal I told him, 'I like you, but I'm not in love with you.' He said, 'That's okay, you'll learn to love me.' And you know what? I did."

Then, after twenty-three years of marriage, Grampa met someone else. He told his wife that she was "cold" and that he could no longer live with her distance. I don't know if he'd ever mentioned this to her *before* he decided to leave, but I got the feeling he was from the "if you loved me you'd know" school of thought. Although she'd grown to love him, perhaps she'd never stopped wondering if she'd settled for less, and perhaps he'd known it all along. Or perhaps her love-famished childhood had never given her an understanding of how to show love.

I often found her icy and forbidding myself. The frost deepened as she went through menopause and I entered puberty. Occasionally the ice thawed long enough for us to scream at each other, about how I was an inconsiderate slob and she was impossible to please.

One day she said to me in a fit of pique, "You know, I think part of the reason Grampa left was because of you. Because he couldn't stand all your arguing." Years later I told her how much that statement upset me. I expected her to cluck with remorse and explain that she'd only spoken in anger. Instead, she pondered for a moment before stating with conviction, "Yes. I think that was true. Part of the reason he left was because you lived with us. Raising another child at our age put a strain on our relationship."

When I was growing up, she wasn't the type to readily dispense hugs and kisses. By high school, I grew determined to change her. I took to randomly sneaking up on her and throwing my arms around her the way I used to when I was a little girl. She tried to find something to do with her arms in return, but they never rested comfortably anywhere. She usually settled on a chuckle and a pat on my arm.

As a young woman, whenever I told her about my hopes for my own life—the guys I was interested in, my college plans, my career opportunities, my dreams of travel—I was crushed by her apparent lack of interest. She seemed to stare right through me, as if she were consummately bored and merely waiting for me to finish. When I was done gushing about my latest plans, she would ask, "Have you seen any good movies lately?" Later

I wondered if, while I was speaking, her inward gaze was focused on the exotic destinations she never visited, the career she never had, the campus she never walked, the guy she never married.

The day before I drove to Hope, I asked her, "Did you make the right choice?"

"I don't know."

Her answer scared me. Seventy-three years old and she still didn't know?

★ ★ ★

I arrived in Hope at about five in the evening, quickly found a campsite, and started the hike to Gull Rock. I knew the walk would take three hours round-trip and I'd barely make it back before dark, but I couldn't resist the beckoning gleam of amber afternoon light. The trail rose along a ridge above Cook Inlet, thick with trees that seemed to brood over thoughts more troubling than mine. Their roots reached across the winding path like the bony fingers of old men, trying to trip me as a mean-spirited joke. Several waterfalls did trip over the old hands, but fell laughing down the mountainside as if, unlike me, they got the joke.

The further I moved up the trail, the fewer returning hikers I met. Fewer and fewer people foolish enough to push the daylight this far. About halfway down the trail, I met a young man coming the other way who warned me, "There's bear scat on the trail ahead, so be careful." I pictured a bear singing scat like Ella Fitzgerald, "Boppity-be-bop, be-bop, be-bear!" I kept walking, singing to make noise, until I spotted the bear scat lying in the middle of the trail. I stooped down to study it as if it might reveal something. Finding nothing about this particular bear turd that suggested an imminent attack, I looked around warily and continued.

A half-hour later, I broke free of the trees and stepped onto Gull Rock, a promontory that looked across the inlet at the great furrowed brow of the Chugach Range. I could hear the tide rushing in. The ocean stampeded the cliffs in a frenzy that would have been deadly to anyone ignorant enough about Alaska to stand on the rocks below. Within moments, massive boulders that had risen several feet above water were completely submerged.

Farther out, a small grayish-white shape rose from the inlet, sending up a spout of water. In a heartbeat, it happened again a few feet away. Then off to the front, then behind, again, again, again. Some twenty to thirty beluga whales glided by, surfacing and diving, surfacing and diving, riding the tide like surfers cruising an unseen wave, chasing the fish that were being swept up Turnagain Arm.

Surely this gathering of seafaring family and friends was repeating a pattern. If they hadn't been here before, their ancestors had. Likely none of them suffered any angst in knowing that this waterway would not take them anywhere new. I looked around the cliff. There was no one but me . . . and the whales. I drew in a deep breath and let it out in a sigh so loud it made me wonder when I'd stopped breathing. My mind was more silent than silence as I watched the last of the whales pass, their smooth backs glistening like pearls in the last of the day's sunshine.

Feeling that I'd seen what I'd come to see, I turned back down the trail. That's when I knew. I still had no idea which man to choose, but I was now sure there would be a moment when a choice would choose me. I would ride the tide in the direction it carried me. I would move in the direction where I was likely to be fed, and I would avoid the direction that led me into rough waters and struggle. Maybe, as long as we seek the truth, there are no right or wrong choices, only the choices we make and whatever comes after.

SHEER MADNESS
THIRTY-FIVE YEARS OLD—POKHARA, NEPAL

When I stepped onto the guesthouse roof in Pokhara's early morning sunshine and saw the snow-covered Himalayas for the first time, I felt like the first child seeing the first mountains that ever collided and thrust their way skyward. Unbelievable that these white-robed celestial giants sprang from the same planet as other mountains I've met, and there have been many.

I spent a good part of my five days in Kathmandu searching the backpacker message boards, checking online, and pumping everyone I met in an effort to find trekking partners. I've continued the search since I arrived in Pokhara last night. This is how things are done among lone travelers. That's not to say it works.

I could hire a guide or porter, but I've heard horror stories about trekkers who've been sexually harassed by porters on the prowl for "loose Western women," or swindled by porters who changed their fees halfway through a trek, or flat-out abandoned by porters who had no experience and no idea what they were getting themselves into.

I'm running out of time. The Annapurna trek could take up to three weeks. In three weeks the dry season will arrive and endless clouds of dust will engulf the mountain vistas I've traveled thousands of miles to see. This afternoon Pokhara's view of the mountains has disappeared in a dusty haze, making my choice clear: I can't wait any longer.

The Annapurna Circuit is popular with backpackers. Surely I won't be on the trail completely alone. Even if I am, it makes no difference. I won't let my solitary state dictate the pursuit of my dreams. Tomorrow I leave for Besisahar, the starting point of my trek.

"Never trek alone." That's the warning of every book and every expert on the Himalayas. At least, I think it is. I can't say I've read any of them.

THE MOUNTAINS ABOVE KALAMATI, NEPAL

Yesterday I woke up with good intentions at 6:45 a.m., but dawdled in denial. Maybe if I wasted time over breakfast in the guesthouse garden, or dilly-dallied around town buying supplies, a trekking partner would materialize. I finally gave up and walked to the bus station to take the 1:40 bus to Dumre, where I planned to catch a bus to Besisahar.

When I arrived in Dumre at four, I wondered if delaying my departure had been folly. I got to town just in time to buy a seat on the last bus to Besisahar, but the sun was beginning to set and I feared that the rusty old bus overflowing with Nepalis wouldn't make it up the mountain roads before dark.

As I boarded, my eyes fell on a beautiful young Nepali woman with high apple cheeks who sat in front breastfeeding her baby, one plump breast un-tucked from her bright pink sari. She dimpled sweetly at me and patted the seat next to her. I smiled back and took it.

During the interminable wait to depart, food vendors walked by with a variety of snacks. The young mother next to me selected a hunk of cucumber sprinkled with spices. I shook my head at the cucumber vendor, but my pretty young neighbor nudged me insistently. "You try!"

"No, thank you."

"Yes!"

I shrugged my shoulders and held up one finger to the vendor. I took my piece, paid the two rupees he asked, and couldn't figure out why he continued to wait. Then I realized my neighbor hadn't paid for hers. When I looked at her, she only smiled and tipped her head toward the vendor. So I paid for hers, too. What the heck? It was only two rupees.

Another vendor walked by selling nuts in little horns of paper. My pretty seatmate bought one, paid for it, and offered me some, temporarily restoring my faith that she wasn't playing me.

Then a third vendor came by selling sweets. My seatmate smiled at me and tipped her head again, indicating I should buy some. "No, I don't want any." At this she pouted, puffing out her lower lip like a small child. "Do *you* want some?" I asked. She brightened up and nodded. Another five rupees.

We waited on the hot bus for nearly an hour. Sweat dripped in earnest from my forehead, between my breasts, and down my back. My seatmate leaned toward me, pulled open the back of my collar, and blew on my neck. It did offer some relief, and I didn't object. I chuckled, wondering what would happen if someone did that for a stranger in the U.S. Here it seemed normal.

Finally, we started to move. The bus backed up two feet . . . and blew a tire. Moments later the fifty or so passengers were herded onto another, smaller bus. The young mother handed me her purse and shepherded me to another seat next to her. The benches were wedged so closely together that my knees were pressed firmly against the seat in front of me. The people who were forced to stand were packed so tightly that if one had fainted he or she would have remained standing. I wondered if I might faint at the unbearable stench of body odor. The young mother turned to me with a beaming smile, the picture of serenity.

It was well past five when we took off, and daylight was fading fast. I had serious doubts we'd *ever* make it to Besisahar. Not only did the bus's surfeit of passengers cause considerable drag on the steep hills, but a section of the bus siding next to the driver fell off several times. A man up front leaned out to tie the siding back on with heavy string.

As grey dusk blanketed the mountains, my seatmate gave me a knowing look, leaned toward my ear, and said, "This bus: no Besisahar tonight.

This bus: Bhote Odar. You come my house tonight. Besisahar tomorrow, okay?" At the word "okay" she bobbed her head from side to side like the wobbly head of a dashboard doll, neither nodding "yes" nor shaking her head "no." I wasn't sure how to respond to the head wobble, but I looked at the darkening sky and said, "Okay. Thank you." She introduced herself as Shyama.

I stepped off the now nearly empty bus at the small town of Kalamati, with Shyama, her baby Nirmala, and her father-in-law Narayan—one of the standees from the bus. The driver and his string-tying assistant urged me to stay on board, insisting the bus would make it to Besisahar. The girl and her father silently shook their heads at me. My mind was made up. Although I didn't know Shyama's intentions, she seemed a safer bet than continuing up the unlit, winding, rutted mountain road after dark.

After the bus drove off, we started to walk up the hill, using an uneven set of rock stairs. It took me a few minutes to grasp that we were not staying in Kalamati, but in a tiny mountain village high above the town.

As we walked, Shyama put a friendly hand on my arm, smiled, and said, "You, me, my father's house, eating rice—no money, okay?" There was that head-wobble again, signifying a question with the expectation of a yes. I thanked her. A few minutes later, she put a hand on my arm and said, "You my dear friend."

After we'd been walking about half an hour, I began to wonder just how far this village was, but I was afraid to ask.

Then Shyama turned to me and said: "Five minutes—"

Thank G—

"—resting."

Shit.

I threw down my backpack and flopped onto a rock. It was a good thing I'd shed about half the contents of my pack and left them at the guesthouse in Pokhara. But the pack was still heavy, and I was hot, hungry, and cranky. Shyama once again blew on the back of my sweaty neck, then handed me her baby and disappeared into the dark to pee.

After we walked at least another half hour, Shyama turned to me again and said: "Five minutes . . . resting."

By this time, night had filled every fold of the mountains. I turned on my headlamp for the rest of our uphill trudge. We passed several farms in the near distance, and the soft glow of candlelit homes dotted the blackness like distant constellations. I was impressed that neither Shyama nor her father seemed winded, nor did they ever indicate by word or facial expression that the steep climb was at all difficult. I knew they were used to it. But I also thought, "Bet that baby doesn't weigh as much as my pack."

After another half-hour we arrived at the home Shyama shared with her in-laws. I sat on the porch of the main house—a simple, one-room earthen hut—with Shyama and her sister-in-law, while her mother-in-law prepared dinner inside. The two young women chattered companionably in the candlelight. Every now and again Shyama stopped to quiz me on the names of her relatives, pointing at them and turning to me with questioning eyes.

"Baby?"

"Nirmala."

"Husband's sister?"

"Meena."

"And . . . "

"Shyama."

"Yes. Good."

Shyama was the village schoolteacher. I could picture her teaching-method: plenty of rote repetition, children's voices rising and falling in unison. Her sister-in-law, Meena, gazed at me shyly, but Shyama was the only one in the family who spoke any English. Shyama saw me writing in my journal and asked if I had another pen for Meena. I happily gave her one of my three spares, figuring it was the least I could do to thank them for their hospitality.

When dinner was ready, the silent but ever-smiling mother-in-law beckoned us inside where we sat in a circle on the smooth-swept dirt floor. Before each of us a metal plate sat heaped with Nepal's most common dish, *daal bhat*. *Daal* is a kind of lentil soup and *bhat* is rice. Both are usually served with curried vegetables or curried potatoes. This was my first time eating the stuff. I followed their lead, and when they picked up the food with their hands I did the same, swirling the rice in the *daal* and shoveling it into my mouth. Something in my manner must have given away that I wasn't used to eating this way because Mother looked as if she were holding back laughter as she handed me a large spoon. It looked like a serving spoon, probably their only one. I tried to indicate that I was perfectly happy eating the same way they did. But she continued to hold out the spoon, so I took it, though I felt self-conscious using it while they continued to shove handfuls of food into their mouths.

The rice was good, but the *daal* was too salty and the curry was bitter. I forced it all down with a smile. Such strict adherence to good manners might have been a mistake: Mother kept scooping more food onto my plate, over my polite but sincere protests. My guidebook suggests that, when staying in Himalayan guesthouses, it's more culturally and environmentally sensitive to order *daal bhat* because it's easy to prepare in large quantities. Many guesthouses along the trekking circuits offer their own versions of Western favorites, like pizza or spaghetti, but they're more difficult to make. The growing business of cooking for trekkers has caused many locals to cut down more trees for their cook-fires, leading to increased deforestation and erosion. But by the time I was finished with my first meal of *daal bhat*, I was pretty sure I'd never eat it again. Screw the forests.

After dinner, they gave me some sort of pickled vegetables, a special treat I suppose. I took a bite and it almost came right back up. It tasted like a cross between kimchi, dirty socks, and ripe armpits. Anxious to maintain my manners, I swallowed two bites whole, trying to avoid chewing. I couldn't keep up the ruse. "I'm sorry," I said, pushing the plate away. "It is too different from what I'm used to. My stomach won't let me eat it." They all smiled and didn't seem offended.

To show my gratitude for dinner, I pulled my best snacks out of my pack, walnuts and raisins, and presented them to Shyama's mother-in-law. She took a bunch in her hand and rocked back and forth, grinning at me and laughing. Shyama explained, "My mother very happy." But although Shyama, Meena, and I ate the goodies, Mother didn't take a bite. "My mother happy, but she will not eat." I suspect she wouldn't eat the nuts and raisins for the same reason I couldn't eat the pickled veggies.

After-dinner conversation was limited by my ignorance of Nepalese, while TV and radio were limited by their lack of either a TV or a radio. We went to bed at about nine. The elder couple stayed in the main house. The younger women and the baby slept in a separate hut, above the buffalo in the manger. Shyama had mentioned a husband, but he had yet to appear. I slept in the smaller hut with the young women.

As I prepared for bed, Shyama caught sight of the bar of soap in my pack. Her eyes narrowed on her target, then blinked wide and innocent as she looked up at me. "You give to me?"

"I'm sorry. No. It is my only one, and it must last for three weeks."

"Soap for baby?"

"No."

It seemed important to be firm, or this woman might try to cajole me out of everything. Instead, I offered her my cake of laundry detergent. I figured I could wash laundry with my bath soap, but not vice versa. Shyama wrinkled her nose at the inferior gift and again poked out her lower lip. Her disappointment didn't stop her from accepting the laundry soap, however.

After that, I crawled into bed with Meena while Shyama plopped down on the floor mat with her baby. I felt guilty, thinking I'd probably taken Shyama's spot in the bed. But the guilt didn't last: Meena stole the blankets in her sleep, so I was cold most of the night and slept fitfully.

* * *

I woke with the dawn as Shyama's village came to life, several dozen farms and perhaps five hundred people scattered across this shirttail of the Annapurnas. Everyone moved in a state of placid but constant busy-ness. I watched Shyama as she swept the floors and fed and clothed the baby.

I had to restrain the strong urge to intervene each time the baby cried, not because of the crying itself, but because of the way the family responded. One of them would put the baby in a small hammock on the porch and swing it back and forth so violently it's a wonder the motion didn't snap Nirmala's little neck, or at least make her throw up. I peeked in at her once while Shyama was rocking her and saw her tiny body rolling from side to side, her eyes wide, her face mashed into the sides of the hammock with each swing. The rocking did little to stop her tears. When she finally did stop crying, I assumed it was the result of minor shock.

After a bit of tea and toast, we were relaxing on the porch when Shyama's handsome young husband showed up, along with several neighbors and friends. Soon there was a gathering of nearly a dozen adults and children socializing on and around the porch. I don't know if this was part of the local routine, but as I was certainly the only foreigner on the mountain this morning, I deduced that I was the big draw. One young man began playing a lovely tune on my recorder and another asked me to dance for them. I smiled and shook my head.

Shyama asked me to take photos of her family and mail copies later. I'd already taken a few photos, catching the family in natural moments: doing chores, talking on the porch, shock-rocking the baby. In return I was happy to take a few posed portraits.

Eight a.m. came and went, the time Shyama had promised to walk me down the mountain to catch my bus to Besisahar. I reminded her it was time to go. In response, she said, "You, me, Besisahar tomorrow, okay?" There it was again, the question-mark head wobble. I told her I was grateful for the hospitality, but explained that my trekking permit only allowed me limited time on the Annapurna Circuit, so I must leave. She reacted with annoyance, "Yes, yes, okay!"

When I stood up to leave, Shyama announced that her mother-in-law had made more *daal bhat*, and she invited me inside to eat. "First eating, then walking, okay?" I raced through breakfast, which was pretty much the same as last night's dinner, with the added relief of sweet, creamy buffalo milk.

After breakfast, Shyama again smiled coyly and said, "You, me, Besisahar *tomorrow*, okay?" She tried this several times. Each time, I explained I must leave, and each time, she looked royally ticked off. In the end, she wiped the scowl off her face and said, "You still my very dear friend."

I went into the second hut to put on my pack, and while I was adjusting my shirt, Shyama caught sight of my bra strap. She walked up to me, pulled on the strap, and said, "You give me?"

"I only have enough for me," I said.

When she began her predictable pout, I said, "Besides, you see?"—I lifted my shirt up to point out my small breasts and thin sports bra, then gestured toward her much larger breasts—"It will not fit you." Two of my breasts squished together would not equal one of hers. She saw my point and giggled like a schoolgirl.

But a few minutes later, after going through the complicated process of wrapping herself in her sari, she strode up to me and demanded, "You give money, for eating rice."

Ah, friendship in Nepal is a fragile thing. For a moment I felt crushed.

But, though I was amazed at her audacity, I knew I must seem rich by her standards. Perhaps she thought asking for money from an American was no more pert than asking a friend for a tissue. I might never get used to the idea that, by the standards of most of the world, I am wealthy. For me, the realization is as embarrassing as passing a foul fart. Surely such a smell could not come from someone as well meaning as I.

Of course, I'd expected to pay *something* when she'd first asked me to stay with her. It was only her smiling "you, me, my father's house, eating rice— no money" that had thrown me off. The question now was how much to pay her. I mentally calculated all the things I'd already given her, which I wouldn't have given if she'd informed me upfront that I was a "customer" rather than a "guest": walnuts and raisins (more than 100 rupees), laundry soap (ten rupees), pen (twenty rupees). I subtracted my other losses from the estimated cost of a typical night's stay in a mountain guesthouse, and handed her twenty rupees.

She cast a dubious look at the coins in her hand and, now all-business, she protested, "Eating rice!"

"Last night you said, 'Eating rice, no money.'"

"More rice in morning, bread, milk."

I didn't bother mentioning that I hadn't asked for the breakfast, which was thrust upon me after I'd begged to leave. However, I listed the things I'd given her and pointed out that I was also giving her photos, which are expensive. As I spoke, I realized that it all amounted to less than three U.S. dollars, and that she had no way of knowing I'd ever send the photos. Suddenly I felt ashamed. I handed her fifty rupees.

As the money changed hands her father walked in, saw what we were doing, and scolded his daughter-in-law. He gestured to her to give the money back, but at this point I wasn't about to take it back. It was only fifty rupees. What was it to me? What was it to them?

"No, no. It's right I give money." I smiled at him. "You have been very kind and this is my way to say thank you." Then I turned to Shyama and said, "But maybe next time you make a new *friend*, you will tell them what you want first, so they understand they must pay."

Shyama then handed the money back to me and said gently, "You should give it to my mother (her mother-in-law)."

So I did. The older woman clasped both my hands in hers and smiled into my face, chuckling her gratitude.

That done, Shyama said her uncle would guide me down the hill because it was time for her to teach. She took my hand, said once again, "You my dear friend," and walked uphill to the school. In the end, I didn't know what to make of her, only that I felt relieved at my release. Anxious lest it be revoked, I immediately turned to follow her waiting uncle down the hill. He spoke no English, and we walked in silence. We'd traveled less than halfway down when we met up with a skinny old man holding an umbrella. The uncle left, indicating I should follow the man with the umbrella the rest of the way.

We were nearing the bottom when I saw a bus pulling out of town. The bus was so crowded that a number of people were sitting on the roof. One lanky white guy with blond hair sat among them, sticking out among the horde of Nepalis like a sugar cube floating in a pot of strong tea. I began running down the hill and waving my arms. Someone saw me, and the bus stopped.

As I reached the bottom I shouted, "Besisahar?"

"Besisahar!" a young male passenger shouted back, nodding.

I quickly pulled off my pack, threw it into the doorway of the bus, and jumped in after it.

* * *

When I stepped off the bus in Besisahar, I saw nothing but Nepali faces. The blond sugar cube from atop the bus had evaporated. I began to worry I would be even more alone on this trek than I'd expected. But I shrugged the feeling off. If I ended up walking alone, maybe it would be a profound mystical experience.

I found a rooftop restaurant, where I was the only customer for lunch. I was relaxing there in the warm sunshine, watching villagers come and go on the street below, when I heard footsteps on the stairs. It was the sugar cube. His surprise mirrored my own.

"Another white person!" he said in an unmistakably English accent. "You're the only other white person I've seen!"

"Me too!"

"I'm sorry. I don't mean to sound insane or anything. It's just that I came to Besisahar by myself, and I was hoping to find some people to trek with. But I haven't seen a bloody soul, except for Nepalis."

"Me too!"

"You're alone, too?"

"Yeah. And I'm looking for a trekking partner, too."

"I know I've probably blown it by sounding like an absolutely desperate madman, but I'll walk with you if you like."

"Absolutely. A desperate madman sounds perfect. I'm Cara."

"Nat." We shook hands and he sat down. "What a massive relief," he said. "When I got here and didn't see any Westerners—"

I interrupted. "Actually, I saw you earlier. I was on your bus. But when we got to town it was like you just vanished."

"On my bus? . . . Wait . . . Are you the one who was running down the mountain?"

"That was me."

"Bloody amazing! This I have to hear. Go on, then: what where you doing up there?"

I told him the whole story, which Nat punctuated with his amusing vocabulary of colorful exclamations, such as, "Bloody amazing!" "That's brilliant!" and "Fucking fantastic!" Later I dubbed him "Nat, The Constantly Amazed."

When I finished, he said, "I was pretty fucking astonished to see you come flying down that hill—out of bloody nowhere! I figured you must be some sort of social worker. I knew that wasn't part of the circuit, so it never occurred to me you might be a trekker. You know, you're very likely the only white person who's ever been in that village."

I thought about Shyama's shrewd bait and switch. Somehow I doubted I was the only foreigner who'd been there.

Nat and I hit it off so easily that I decided all my initial dallying had paid off. We began talking about the trek. He told me a friend had insisted he "must" look for a place on the trail where the friend had stayed on his trek: a combination bakery and guesthouse called The Braga Bakery, where the pastries were "absolutely amazing!"

"Speaking of sweets," Nat said, "I'd absolutely kill someone for a chocolate bar. Would you like to go for a walk through downtown Besisahar and see if we can find one?"

"Someone to kill?"

"If necessary."

We walked up and down the main street, a collection of small, unremarkable buildings that didn't look promising in terms of candy. We passed a gathering of about a hundred Nepalis singing and playing music. A local guesthouse owner explained that someone had died and they were celebrating that person's life. The mood was much more festive than any memorials or wakes I've ever attended. It truly sounded like a party. We also spotted a few other foreigners sitting at rooftop restaurants. The ones we spoke to were going rafting, not trekking, but it gave me hope that we wouldn't be alone on the trail.

"I'm not worried about it," Nat said. "I'll tell you what my problem is: there's no place to get a candy bar in this bloody village."

After dark the village's power went out. But life continued by candlelight, and children continued to play on the main street, running in and out of the flickering light.

Nat and I ate dinner on the roof of the Hotel Annapurna, where we're staying tonight, and agreed to depart by nine tomorrow morning. All our guidebooks and maps say it's about a six-hour walk to Bahun Danda. We figure, even if we take a two-hour lunch break, we'll still arrive with plenty of time before dark.

I know it will be physically demanding, hiking through high altitude mountains for three weeks. Yet it seems to me it will be mentally easy, knowing that all I have to do is get up each day and start walking.

BAHUN DANDA, ANNAPURNA CIRCUIT, NEPAL

At breakfast, Nat told me he'd heard a group of trekkers leave the hotel at 6:00 a.m. Under invisible peer pressure, we bumped our 9:00 a.m. departure to 8:30, which is to say we left at 8:45. Besisahar town, which had slowly filled with Westerners the night before, was quiet as a bar after hours when we walked out of town.

"Everyone's left except us," Nat said.

"Do you think they know something we don't?"

"Too late to bother about it now."

As we walked, we speculated about the Nepali people we passed. One small group of women walked by, all wearing identical pink and orange saris. Against the dull backdrop of the dusty town, they looked like spring flowers.

"Do you suppose it's some kind of uniform?" Nat said.

"Maybe it's like one of those embarrassing moments back home," I said. "You go to a party in a brand new sari and, damn, some other woman is wearing the exact same one!"

Further on, we spotted two small boys in school uniforms playing in the street until an old grandfather shouted at them. "They're dawdling on their way to school, and the old man's giving them hell," Nat said. As the old man approached, we exchanged greetings, *"Namaste!"* We exchanged this same greeting with everyone we passed.

The path remained more or less steady and obvious throughout the day. For two hours we walked through gentle green hills and alongside the rough, rushing beauty of the Marsyangdi River, until we came upon a suspension bridge leading into the Gurung village of Khudi. It was the first of many river crossings. The narrow bridge of thin, flimsy-looking bamboo strips felt dangerously pliable, a Wile E. Coyote deathtrap under my feet. I tried not to look down at the furious water and fat rocks far below.

After stopping to buy sodas and catch our breath, we pushed on for another hour to Bhulbhule. There, we ate lunch at an outdoor restaurant overlooking the river and watched two men try to coax a reluctant cow across another high, rickety bridge. The cow mooed pitifully, refusing to budge for some time. "I don't blame her," I said. We stayed in Bhulbhule for two hours, waiting out the worst heat of the day.

We walked nonstop from about two o'clock to five o'clock, before we spotted other trekkers ahead. It was almost dusk when we caught up to a group of seven people checking in at the first police checkpoint, just before the Brahmin village of Bahundanda. The first people we met were two young women bringing up the rear: Melanie, an American, and Lucy, a German.

"We started the day with that group over there," Melanie said, listlessly gesturing to the five trekkers gathered around the two checkpoint policemen. "But they're setting a very fast pace, and we decided there was no point in struggling to keep up with them."

"*Ja*, they act like this is a fucking race," Lucy said. The plump young blonde sat propped against her pack, red-faced and irritable. She went on to tell us her pack didn't fit right, this trek was already much harder than she expected, and she lost her camera in Besisahar. I wondered whether she'd give up and turn back.

While Nat and I sat around waiting for the police to check our permits, we also chatted with the other trekkers in their group: two other German women, a German guy, an Englishman, and an American guy. Everyone except the two other German women had started this trek alone. But, by unspoken agreement, we became a group of nine as we climbed the final steps to Bahundanda, which means "Hill of the Brahmins."

As we trudged over the next rise, we found ourselves in the midst of an all-male political rally. Several men carried white flags, each emblazoned with a red sun: symbol of the democratic communist party, known as the "Sun Party," which is rapidly gaining popularity in this country. Nepal still abides by a caste system. High castes, such as Brahmins, own land and live relatively well, while the lowest caste, the Dalits, receive little education and work as menial laborers. Under such a system, it's easy to understand why communism attracts followers. Graffiti painted on a nearby building said, "Vote for Sun . . . OK." I imagined Shyama saying "Okay?" with a hopeful wobble of her dashboard-doll head.

Our group bypassed the rally and moved en masse to a wooden lodge on the hill. The lodge gave us a CinemaScope view of the mountains, which hemmed in the village on all sides. Each room had two or more beds, but I scored a room alone. Each bed was nothing more than a thin mattress atop a wooden platform. Still, the beds seemed a luxury. After talking to people who'd done this trek years ago, I'd been prepared to throw my sleeping bag on the floor. The price was ridiculously low, just ten rupees per person (about fifteen cents U.S.).

Before dinner, I washed a few clothes in the bathroom sink and took a shower. The water was ice-cold, but after a long, hot day of walking in the sun it felt refreshing.

At dinner, all nine of us ate together. We ordered a variety of dishes that must have driven the few employees mad trying to keep up. It took about an hour and a half for them to start serving us, and then the food trickled out of the small kitchen in dribs and drabs. But it was a warm, breezy night, and we used the time to get acquainted, making a rambunctious job of it.

NOTES FROM LATER IN THE TREK

In social situations, I often see myself as the last planet in our solar system. Like the theoretical Planet X, I revolve around the periphery, I take

longer than anyone else to get around, and, even if I'm part of their system, no one else knows for certain whether I exist.

Yet for the first time in the company of others, I can feel the gravity that
has pulled us together. I have trouble thinking of us as anything other than
a group, even though none of us has ever met before, with the exception
of Charlie and Allison.

Intense experience often yields penetrating insights, but it would be arrogant to believe I see anyone in the group as they really are. I only recognize
them by the unique movements of their orbits. Nonetheless, here's the
way I saw them on our first evening together and in the days that followed:

Nat: About twenty-seven, with spiky blond hair, eyes of bad-boy blue,
and the grin of a good-natured jester. He's an Englishman who went to
law school, practiced law for two years, decided it wasn't for him, and
dropped everything to travel. He has traveled in Southeast Asia and lived
in Australia for a year.

When he arrived at the Kathmandu Airport and filled out his visa application, in the blank next to "occupation" he wrote "porridge tester." Much
to his embarrassment, as he left the crowded line with his visa an immi-
gration official waved his application in the air and yelled after him, "So,
Mr. Johnson, I see you're a porridge tester! We'll have great use for your
services here. We eat much porridge in Nepal!"

Nat is the madman.

Ron: Mid-twenties, with sympathetic blue eyes and the demeanor of
a sweet but sorrowful hound. He's another Englishman, and quite
a witty cut-up when paired with Nat. But catch him alone and he's a
thoughtful gentleman.

When I told him I brought my bamboo recorder just in case I find myself
alone on the trail, he looked truly delighted. "That's fantastic!" he said. "I
can just picture you playing your flute, dancing up the trail with a group
of children following behind you."

He works in computer programming or something of that sort. Or in
his ironic terms: "A truly exciting job that sends me traveling to amazing
places all over the world."

Ron is the amiable one. At six-foot-seven, he's also the tallest.

Melanie: Twenty-eight, an attractive woman who would never waste time fussing with her looks, and an intellectual dynamo. She's an American, but she has lived in England and Africa and has just completed two years teaching English in Japan. Melanie spends so much time considering everything that can go wrong, it makes me wonder how she ever convinced herself to leave home in the first place.

Although she's good-humored, she frequently comments that the group is moving too fast. "If you increase altitude too quickly, you can get altitude sickness. And you can't really experience the scenery because when you're walking fast you tend to look at the ground more to watch your footing. And if you walk fast and don't watch your footing, well, that's another risk." Before the trek she went to a lecture by an experienced trekker. She told us that he warned the audience to always pass mule trains on the side of the trail closest to the mountain, because a few pack animals have bumped people off the cliff-sides.

Melanie is the careful one.

Zack: Twenty-four, small and wiry, with an elvish face and rapidly receding dark hair. Zack is from South Carolina and speaks in a softly triangulated accent that drips with homemade biscuits, porch swings, and fireflies. He keeps asking Ron and Nat to supply him with British slang, and words like *bloody* and *wanker* sound particularly amusing in his Southern twang.

Zack is hiking through the Himalayas in a pair of cheap sneakers—I'd be hard-pressed to call them running shoes—but his choice of footwear seems to be more about sloughing off image and sticking to a budget rather than some awe-shucks pretension to being a simple country boy. He has a degree in microbiology but has never had a job in that field. Claims he's never held any job longer than a few months. In the summer he teaches water-skiing. He's traveled a bit and has spent much of the past year teaching English in Taiwan.

Zack says he can't stand "political correctness." He told us that, after his stint in Taiwan, "I'm sick and tired of rice, rice, rice, morning, noon and night."

Zack is the politically incorrect one.

Gunther: Early twenties. Pale and exceptionally slim with faint blue eyes and close-shorn hair, Gunther has the look of a monk. He doesn't say much. This might be partly because, of the four Germans in the group, he speaks the least English. On the other hand, even when he's speaking German with his three compatriots he still seems laconic and soft-spoken. Whenever my eyes touch upon him he seems to be intently observing someone or something. He has a sense of humor, but his laughter is as gentle as bits of goose down escaping a pillow. He exudes an almost ethereal glow.

Gunther is exceptionally kindhearted. Lucy told me that when he was in Kathmandu he met a Sherpa with a broken arm. She said, "Gunther gave him a ride to the hospital, but not only that: he also paid his bill. He told me he thinks anybody else would have done the same thing. But I think he's a very unusual person." As far as I know, Lucy is the only person with whom he has shared this story.

Gunther is the quiet one.

Lucy: At twenty-two, Lucy is the youngest. She's the only one in our group using walking poles. Although she's plump, her generous curves and alternately dimpled and pouting mouth promise the kind of passion that can entice observant men. She doesn't live in her homeland of Germany, but in London, where she works temporary jobs that allow her to travel frequently.

Lucy is both the best and worst companion on the trek. She's a study in annoyance and resentment: her pack is too heavy or the trail is too hard, people "can't even wait five minutes for her" or everyone is "just sitting around." Yet, as often as she complains, she's equally ready to laugh—including laughter at herself—and she has a dogged determination that's admirable.

Although her bottomless well of bitching can be irksome, its twin is her deep well of empathy. She's the first to defend someone else if she thinks they're being left in the dust; there's no sense pointing out to her that this group is a creature of happenstance, that none of us have formally agreed to travel together. I sense she's one of those people whose friends know they can always count on her, and whose habit of dumping all her troubles on the table is worth it to those who value her humor and loyalty.

Lucy is the devil's advocate.

Charlie: Mid-twenties. It's impossible to picture Charlie without Allison. The two are as inseparable as twins, at least on this trek. Both are tall, athletic women with the beautiful bone structure of fashion models, though they laughed when I told them so. They're both given to easy laughter.

When we met, I asked them how long they've known each other. They consulted in German for a moment.

"We've known each other eighteen years," Allison said.

"Wow!" I replied. "That's awesome. I don't think I have any friends that go so far back into my childhood."

"Oh, we didn't say we were friends . . . " Allison began.

"You only asked how long we *knew* each other," Charlie finished.

Though they're close friends, they're quite different. Where Allison tends to playfulness, Charlie tends to a take-no-crap attitude. As Charlie herself puts it, she's "very German." While the rest of us wait patiently for our meals—recognizing we're in the mountains of a third world country where things happen slowly—Charlie demands to know where her pizza is. Then again, like Lucy, she'll fiercely defend anyone in our group from even the most minor threat or injury.

I'm learning to appreciate her intellect and wit, although at first . . . she scared the hell out of me.

Charlie is the assertive one.

Allison: (Charlie calls her Allie.) Mid-twenties. Allison giggles more than she talks, and when she talks it's usually about something that leads to giggles. Her laughter is mischievous and infectious. One morning, Lucy blew her nose, I blew mine, and Allison blew hers, one after another, until we sounded like an orchestra of kazoos. Allison started giggling, and soon the three of us were leaning on each other, laughing helplessly. This is not unusual around Allison.

Allison is the laughing one.

Cara: At thirty-five, I'm the oldest. But who am I in this group? Do any of us ever see ourselves clearly? I can't even see my physical self: I left my mirror behind, and there are few of them in the teahouses along the way. This hike will take me about 250 kilometers (150 miles) in distance and up to 5,416 meters (17,769 feet) in altitude, the farthest and highest I've ever hiked in my life. But this is also spiritual terrain, where I find my soul reflected in the giant Himalayas and the diminutive Nepali people. A spiritual journey: unless we close our hearts and minds, is there any other kind?

Cara is the contemplative one. Also the chatterbox. A one-woman mismatched pair.

★　★　★

Just as we were all getting ready for bed tonight, terrified screams in the room next to mine sent the lodge into mayhem. Several of us ran to the source, where we found Charlie and Allison gripping each other and babbling as they backed away from the wall. Resting on the wall above their beds, apparently unperturbed by the commotion, was the largest spider I've ever seen. Including leg span, it was as big as my entire open hand, its body almost the size of a golf ball.

One by one, everybody came in to look, as fellow lodgers spread the word that it was, indeed, the biggest spider they'd ever seen. A few people started to look for something to trap the enormous creature without having to touch it. Melanie ran for her camera. When she returned, I said, "Wait! You'll never be able to tell how big it is. Here . . ." I stepped up to the wall and, to give her photo a size reference, splayed my hand out next to the spider. Okay, maybe I was showing off.

One of the Nepali lodge employees assured us this type of spider wasn't dangerous, and a few trekkers suggested it probably wouldn't bother anyone if left alone. This suggestion sent Charlie into a panic: "No! I am really afraid. I can't possibly sleep if that spider is in here. Someone must kill it."

The employee grinned and said, "I am brave. I will get the spider."

"Don't kill it," I said. "Just put it outside."

"No!" Charlie insisted. "You must kill it! I will not be satisfied until I see his dead body."

The young man only succeeded in chasing the spider through a crack in the wall, into my room next door, and back again. Then it disappeared completely. It took several of us to convince the arachnophobic Charlie that the creature was probably too terrified to come back out. The show over, we all retreated to our rooms.

Late last night, as the lodge drifted into a silence broken only by occasional snores, I was lying awake gazing into space, when I glanced up at the red night-light above my bed and saw the spider lurking there. I soon saw his purpose: a large moth fluttered around the glowing red bulb and was instantly devoured by the speedy predator. It was revolting to watch. Not wanting to turn the lodge into bedlam again, I said nothing. I simply pulled out my camera, snapped a photo, and tried to go to sleep.

Several times during the night I felt a tickling sensation and leapt out of bed in horror, certain the spider had jumped on me. But the tickling only came from the wings and legs of tiny insects and, once or twice, my imagination. When my eyes flew open for the hundredth time or so, I was dismayed to find that my eight-legged roommate had abandoned his post near the night-light. Where the hell did he go?! I barely slept the rest of the night.

I promised myself never to tell Charlie and Allison about the return of the gargantuan spider, or they might be afraid to ever again fall asleep on this trek.

Spiders don't frighten me as much as the thing I'm running around the world to escape: the slow death of my youth. I've come on this trek to drink the last few drops of that vanishing volition. From here, I can see the moment when wisdom will replace action, when acceptance will replace desperation. A college student who skips a semester and puts on a backpack is a traveler, a twenty-five-year-old who quits her job to put on the same backpack is an adventurer, at thirty-five she's a bohemian, at forty-five a drifter, at fifty-five a loser, at sixty-five a bum. However, those lines become blurry under the intoxicating influence of self-discovery or meaningful purpose.

Sometimes the lines blur enough to allow us to share each other's paths for a time: students hanging out with bohemians, drifters sightseeing with bums. For this trek, it's bohemian meets adventurers. The question is: will this bohemian be able to keep up? Especially after a sleepless night on spider watch.

CHAMJE, ANNAPURNA CIRCUIT, NEPAL

This morning, Nat and Zack led the charge up the mountain with the energy and competitiveness of teenage boys. Ron started the day in step with them, his long legs bringing to mind the deceptively lazy-looking gait of a camel. Shortly behind that trio, Charlie, Allison, and Gunther gamely kept up a steady clip. Melanie, Lucy, and I brought up the rear, and the gap soon widened until we lost sight of the rest of the group.

Mel and Lucy again questioned why the guys in front were rushing. I wondered, too, but the question didn't perturb me. By rejecting a fast pace, these young women were reaffirming the values that brought them here in the first place. But the guys in front might have been moving at a pace that felt equally relaxed to them. Even if they were pushing it, the choice was theirs. We're all independent trekkers, and although we appear to be on the same path, we're not.

The trail seesawed steeply: up . . . and down . . . up . . . and down. As I tried to ignore the pain in my calves and the twenty pounds on my back, I felt humbled by the sight of local men and women carrying astonishing loads up the mountain on their backs, the weight supported with the help of a strap across the forehead. Some carried entire wooden beds or sets of tables and chairs.

We were captivated by the giggling children who waved and called out, *"Namaste!"* and *"Hello!"* but we were disappointed when many followed their friendly greetings with unrelenting demands for candy and pens. Often they followed us for some way: "Hello-sweet! Hello-schoolpen! Hello-sweet! Hello-schoolpen!" Their persistence was so maddening we cursed the generous trekkers before us who'd given away those items. And where was the dentist to fill the resulting cavities? And who could carry enough pens in a backpack to stem this flood of harassment?

When we passed mule trains—bells jingling, plumes rising from harnesses, tassels swaying from colorful headdresses—I passed on the side of the trail nearest the mountain. On one narrow path, as I pressed myself against the hillside, an animal with a heavy load ground me into the rocks. I must admit, if I hadn't heeded Mel's advice that mule might have bumped me off the cliff.

I soon lost sight not only of the group ahead, but also of Mel and Lucy behind. Yet I didn't feel lonely. Instead, I treasured my private view of the world . . . like a secret. A wet, flowing, living secret.

Where there's life, there's water. Without it, there would be no Annapurna Circuit, no farms, no villages, no 250 kilometers of paths to link them all. Like most of the world's worthy hikes, this one embraces many waters and signs of water: contented streams gurgling in newborn wonder, garrulous waterfalls gushing headlong toward their destiny with gravity, vertiginous bridges swaying over adrenalizing contemplations of mortality, satiated crop-terraces surfing irrigated mountainsides, and, on this side of the pass, the constant company of the Marsyangdi River. The river is not a silent companion, but it is perhaps best appreciated in silence.

At lunchtime, I caught up with the main group in Jagat. Several people had decided to try their first *daal bhat*. Hoping that not all *daal bhat* is created equal, I ignored my post-traumatic taste disorder and ordered a plate. It was much better than the scary stuff I'd eaten at Shyama's place. As Nat put it, "I wouldn't serve it at a dinner party or anything, but it's not bad. One bowl of this and you could hike all day."

On the subject of hiking all day, I found myself defending my slow pace, although I don't recall anyone accusing me of anything. "I know I'm slower than all of you, but then my legs are shorter than everyone else's. I'm only five-two, the shortest one of you is about five-seven, and Nat and Ron are more than six feet tall. So, in actuality, I have to walk a lot farther than anyone else, relative to my size." Titters rose around the table.

Nat started to say, "Yeah, but taller people have more weight to carry—"

"Fuck that!" I interrupted, to an appreciative roar of laughter.

"Well, *that* ended that argument, didn't it?" Nat said. "There's nothing you can say to argue with 'Fuck that!' now is there?"

I left before everyone else did, hoping to get a head start. But the group quickly caught and passed me. Instead of speeding up to catch them, I slowed down. When I came to a waterfall overhung with leafy trees, I sat next to its small wooden bridge and played my recorder for a bit before moving on. When clouds began to gather and the afternoon sky grew prematurely dark, I picked up the pace and caught up with the main group at a lodge in Chamje. Within moments of my arrival, it began to rain.

As gathering trekkers wove the dining room into a noisy web of voices and laughter, several in our group voiced concerns about Mel and Lucy, who hadn't yet arrived. They showed up, weary and soaked, just as the wet gray sky became a black shout of water.

"The past two days have already been so much more strenuous than I expected," Mel said, with a look so downcast her face looked partially erased. "I just don't know how I'm going to get through three weeks of this."

"I'm just putting one foot in front of the other," I said.

"That's the only way to do it," Zack said, making me self-conscious about how banal I must have sounded. Yet the trite is often true: in any daunting undertaking, the only way I can cope is by focusing on the few steps directly ahead.

However, I share Mel's exhaustion. I can't keep my eyes open. It isn't yet nine, and I've already retreated to my room in the third floor loft. The voices murmuring below are rocking me to sleep, like a remembered sound from the happy moments of my childhood: grownups talking in the next room, a sound that tells me I'm safe and all's right with the world . . .

CHAME, ANNAPURNA CIRCUIT, NEPAL

Was it only four days ago that I told myself all I had to do was get up each day and start walking? Beware the simple idea. Today's leg was a long and difficult haul, and the realization that it's only going to get harder the higher I go is like that recurring nightmare: the one where I find myself at school taking an exam for which I've never studied. Dharapani sits at about 1890 meters, Chame at about 2680. That's an elevation gain of 800 meters (2600 feet) in five hours of walking. But it is, still, a simple idea: just . . . keep . . . walking.

We each fell into our own rhythm, and once again I found myself walking alone for most of the day. With no one else to distract me, each moment stood out in relief, the way I've heard moments do when you're on acid— or about to die.

Alone. If you say a word often enough it empties and expands, empties and expands with meaning until it is no longer one thing, but all things. Alone no longer means joy or pain, love or loss, good or bad. It is only the journey I walk through. Alone is inevitable, and if there were ever a place for inevitability it would be the Himalayas. These mountains know what it is to be beyond loneliness, to simply sift the sun and snow for evidence of time and signs of life.

In Bagarchhap, I bought a small loaf of bread from a tiny bakery. A handful of children began following me, their eyes keeping time with the hard, dark little loaf swinging from my hand. I gave them each a piece, and their grins made the remaining heel of bread more enjoyable, although no less tough and chewy.

As I pushed on to Danaque, I heard bells jingling and was flabbergasted to see two men on horseback appear out of nowhere, bearing down on me at a gallop. I've become used to goats, cows, and pack animals, but this was new. It was the first sign that I was truly moving high up into the Himalayas and the villages of Nepal's ethnic Tibetans.

In Danaque, I passed a whitewashed stone Mani Wall in the middle of the path, lined with a row of metal prayer wheels on either side. In a Mani Wall, each cylindrical wheel is inscribed with the Tibetan Buddhist mantra, *"Om Mani Padme Hum,"* and each wheel is stuffed with paper scrolls inscribed with the same mantra. An old woman was circling the wall counterclockwise, spinning the wheels—passing her hand along them the way a child might pass her hand along a chain link fence to set the metal vibrating—sending hundreds of mantras spinning to the heavens. I had the strange impression she had been walking around that wall, spinning those wheels, since the beginning of time, and would still be circling there at the end, when the universe stops circling and collapses inward on itself.

Leaving the old devotee to her loop, I continued moving forward to Chame, to meet the moment I've been waiting for: my first glimpse of Annapurna II, a true behemoth of the Annapurna Range. How do you describe the way your heart feels when you first fall in love? The way your body feels when you have your first orgasm? The way your mind feels when it first understands that everyone and everything will die, and in the next moment grasps the pure dumb miraculous luck of being alive? It is no wonder that great masters have wandered into the mountains and found enlightenment. Here enlightenment is not only something within, it is something external—so for even the most foolish among us there must be hope to find it.

As evening came, I spotted fresh snow falling on the distant peak of Annapurna II (8000 meters, or 26,000 feet) and the closer Lamjung Himal

(6900 meters, or 22,700 feet). With the first sight of snow, came the first night of bone-aching cold.

Before dinner, I showered under a slender strand of lukewarm water so spare it only warmed one body part at a time, leaving the rest of my body a map of gooseflesh in the rapidly cooling high-altitude air. I made the mistake of washing my hair. It refused to dry and I shivered through dinner, even though I wrapped in several layers of clothing and pulled a wool cap over my wet head. Every few minutes, I left the dining area to stand by the kitchen woodstove with my cap off, trying in vain to dry my hair and warm up.

Several porters sat around the stove and we swapped pleasantries. Alan, a dark, compact porter with a wide, white grin, taught me several Nepali phrases, including the common greeting, *"Kosta cha?"* (How's it going?), and the standard reply, *"Ramro cha!"* (It's going great!).

After dinner, Nat philosophized about the spirituality and simplicity of Nepal's mountain cultures. "The people who live in these mountains don't stress over all the crap that drives the rest of us mad: getting ahead, buying a better house or car, working more to get more. They don't concern themselves about acquiring things or attaining wealth the way Westerners do. As long as they have enough food to eat and a home to sleep in, they're happy."

Zack's response was, "Yeah? Well if they're so satisfied with what they have, why do their kids keep asking for my fucking pens?"

Seems to me we're climbing to a place where both happiness and madness are beside the point.

PISANG, ANNAPURNA CIRCUIT, NEPAL

This morning I set out early and on my own, beholden only to my path. Beyond the brilliant white, muscular peaks of Annapurna II and Lamjung, the immense shoulders of Annapurna IV slowly revealed themselves. The mountains continued to astonish me, although to look at the pine forest around me I might easily have been in the high country of California or Colorado.

I was resting on the sundeck of a lodge in Barathang, turning my grateful face up to the fleeting heat of the intense mountain sun, when up walked the rest of the nine. We all ordered *daal bhat*. An hour later my friends were grumbling about the long wait for our meal. I dryly observed, "I never thought I'd be waiting so impatiently for *daal bhat*."

Mel looked unhappier than the mere wait for food could explain. I asked her if she was all right. "No," she said. "I have a terrible headache and I felt nauseous all last night. I'm afraid it's altitude sickness. A couple of the others said it's too early, that it's just my imagination. But Chame's above ten thousand feet, and people get symptoms at even lower altitudes. Do you think I'm overreacting?"

Since I'd met her, Mel had been talking about, worrying about, and planning for altitude sickness, a.k.a. Acute Mountain Sickness, caused by lower oxygen levels at high altitude. I half-suspected her symptoms were psychosomatic. On the other hand, she was right: people do get AMS at altitudes even lower than 10,000 feet. So I said, "You could be overreacting, or you really could be sick. No one knows how you feel except you, so only you can decide."

"What would you do?"

"You may just need more time to acclimatize. You know what the saying is: climb high, sleep low. You've already climbed higher today than you spent last night. So you could go back to Chame, spend another night, and if you feel better, continue up. If you don't feel better, descend to a lower altitude. It'd be a bummer, but it's not worth risking your life."

Mel seemed relieved to hear advice that supported doing what she wanted to do anyway. "You're right. I hate to do it, but I'm going back to Chame."

The group suggested she could catch up with us in Pisang, where we planned to spend a rest day. Hugs went around. And then we were eight.

When she left, Nat said, "It's all psychosomatic, if you ask me. She's been talking herself into altitude sickness since we started."

"Yeah. I think it's all in her mind," Zack said.

"What do you think, Cara?" Ron asked.

"It may very well be 'all in her mind.' But that phrase is kind of tricky, isn't it? I mean, everything we experience we experience in our minds, whether it's real or not."

"Yeah. If she's a wimp in her mind, she's probably a wimp in real life," Zack said.

But Ron said he thought my comment "made a lot of sense."

Back in Chame, Ron had complained of tingling in his fingers, worried he might have AMS. I asked him if the tingling was gone.

"It's not so bad. But now I have a headache." Seeing my concern, he added, "It's okay. I think all this dust is mucking up my sinuses. Anyway, if it gets worse I'll turn back. I don't have a death wish or anything."

If I had a death wish, I could think of no place more sublime to fulfill it: fatal beauty rushing toward me, my mouth exhaling a final "oh" of unfinished wonder.

★　★　★

Pushing ever higher into the unrelenting Himalayas, I feel as if I've returned to my body after a long absence. The past is a mythology of memories, a collection of stories arranged to support my view of the world. The future is a fantasy I can forever move toward but never reach. What is the point of trying to live in those places, or anywhere but now, and now, and now?

We crossed the Marsyangdi at a point where the river had built up a good head of steam, roaring over boulders worn smooth by the pressures of water, glaciers, and time. Without command, comment, or consent, our entire group halted on the bridge, a dumbfounded huddle of Lilliputians overmastered by the land of the Brobdingnag: in one direction, our view of Annapurna IV expanded all out of proportion; in the other, a stupendous wall of sheer dirt and rock, called the Paungda Danda rock face, rose like a warning. The wall looked like the end of the planet, its upper half attempting to summit the sky, its lower half rushing toward us like a giant child's slide. A glacier had scooped out its smooth face eons ago.

Nat stood slump-shouldered and gape-mouthed, and said, "It's sheer madness, isn't it?!"

It took something infinitesimally small to steal our attention from something so shamelessly large. Ron groaned with a revulsion that drew us all to gather around and join him in staring at the water bottle he held up against the blue sky. We've all been drinking the local water, purified with iodine tablets. So we all shared his stomach-churning disgust at discovering two tiny shrimp-like organisms floating in his bottle of light-tan, cloudy water. Though Ron allowed that, indeed, the creatures were fascinating and the situation amusing, he also expressed the sincere conviction that he might vomit.

"At least they're dead," someone offered.

"That's not comforting," he said.

We all agreed it was best not to think about it, as we had little choice but to continue filling our bottles with river water.

Further on, at a lodge staked out in the middle of no man's land, Nat and I sought forgetfulness in our daily candy bars, Western luxuries carried to this outpost on the backs of enterprising locals. Nat pretends to panic whenever he can't find a Snickers bar, and Zack teases me whenever I buy a Mars bar "for the hike": "'For the hike' . . . right. You know it'll be gone before you even hit the trail."

This time I was distracted from the pursuit of chocolate. The woman who ran the place was tending a quiet but unhappy little girl who was lying under a blanket on the dusty ground in the sun. Although the mother's anxious face made the answer obvious, I asked anyway, "Is she sick?" The mother nodded and pointed out an infected sore or cut on the girl's cheek, the original injury nearly obscured by an angry red swelling and a white glob of some sort of lotion. She touched the girl's forehead and gave me a distressed look to indicate the child was feverish.

"Do you have medicine to put on it?"

She looked puzzled.

"Med-i-cine?" I repeated slowly.

She shook her head.

I pulled out my first-aid kit and gave her a small packet of antibiotic cream, pantomiming that she should apply half now and half tomorrow. I felt the unhappy certainty that it wouldn't be enough. Yet she looked relieved and thanked me.

As I moved on with the group, I realized I hadn't suggested to the mother to wash the child's cheek first. I wondered if I should have given her Band-Aids to keep the cream from rubbing off. I wondered if I should have searched my first-aid kit for more remedies. I couldn't get the pair out of my mind. With an infected cut, the child could either be up and about in no time, or the infection could spread and make her seriously ill. This was the risk of getting "involved," a slippery slope that took me spiraling downward from curiosity to worry to guilt. All without benefit of knowing so much as their names.

But I'm no Gunther. I didn't turn back and offer to carry the girl down the mountain to a doctor. I continued uphill and saved my candy bar for later. We climbed the trail to Pisang, which is divided into two neighboring settlements in a small, dust-swaddled river valley. Lower Pisang (3200 meters) sits on the lower side of the river. Upper Pisang (3,300 meters) sits across the river on a hill. Each is a cluster of medieval-looking stone buildings. We decided to stay in Lower Pisang. It felt as if we were walking into a ghost town. As the sun gave up the last of its warmth, few people remained outside in the dust-blown cold. A sorrowful wind blew through the narrow spaces between homes, the warning of another ice age awaiting its time.

In contrast, the dining hall of our wooden lodge was a warm invitation, floating in a haze of eye-stinging smoke from the woodstove in the center of the room. Trekkers and porters gathered around the fire to eat and talk, half-visible in the wafting smoke, like the last laughing ghosts of Pisang. One German trekker lit a joint and passed it around. As usual, I declined.

Alan and a couple of other porters sang a Nepali song, creating a convivial harmony. I asked the meaning of the words. Alan said it was about a scarf blowing in the wind. The lyrics seemed to be based on images, rather than a story or message. Maybe the images told their own story, one that could only be understood by giving up the effort to understand. I floated inside the music until my eyelids grew heavy. Then I went to my room.

All the rooms in this lodge are coated in a thick layer of brown dust: the same dust we've been breathing, coughing, and blowing into our tissues on the trail, the same dust that's been obscuring the Himalayas each time it fails to rain of an afternoon. As always, I've spread my sleeping bag atop a wooden bed with a thin mattress. But this time, as I settle in, the mattress and sheets beneath me release a visible cloud of dirt that sets me sneezing.

BRAGA, ANNAPURNA CIRCUIT, NEPAL

I awoke to the pressure of dirt-clotted sinuses. I wasn't the only one. After a night of dust-shrouded sleep, half our group came to breakfast clutching tattered tissues and aching heads. Ron sneezed his way through breakfast, and lamented in an Elmer Fudd voice, "I cambe on this trek to be filled with the power of the Himbalayas, but all I'mb getting filled with is bloody dust."

I took an allergy tablet. This later turned out to be a dangerous move. Last night we'd all agreed to take a rest day in Pisang or I wouldn't have taken a pill known to cause drowsiness. But, by the end of breakfast our sniffling contingent agreed: Pisang's restorative powers were suspect. Several people declared we should press on to the legendary Braga Bakery and hope for a more restful day tomorrow in cleaner digs.

Lucy was outraged. "This is absolute crap! What about Mel? We told Mel we'd wait for her in Pisang. We said, 'See you in Pisang.' We'll be going back on our word."

I, too, was disconcerted by what seemed like a decision to desert Mel. But, seized by a sudden paroxysm of sneezing and coughing, I conceded, "When Mel experiences this dustbin for herself, she'll understand why we had to leave."

"We don't even know if she's going to show up," Nat said.

"And there are other trekkers who'll be walking with her from Chame," Ron said.

Lucy surrendered. However, she grumbled throughout the day about how "it seems like nobody in this world ever keeps their word."

On our way out of town, we passed a Mani wall. In silent, single-file procession, we set the squeaky prayer wheels spinning. We do this in every village, never asking each other whether we do it to pray, or for fun, or just because the walls are there. I do it for all three reasons.

For me, a prayer is a kind of focused thought. This is no minor thing. If thought is energy, and if energy and matter are made of the same stuff, then prayers must have power. Each Mani Wall reminds me of the opportunity to transform the energy of my prayers into the energy of action. These days my prayer rarely varies: "God, please help me discover the purpose of my life and help me fulfill it."

Zack confessed he just prayed for less dust in Braga.

As we climbed the northern route out of town, the Himalayas seemed to surge in size. Their white peaks touched the ceiling of the sky until they appeared as if they were forced to bend and lean over me, threatening to crush me with their overwhelming weight. In the thinning air, it's increasingly difficult to perceive the distance that separates me from the scenery.

If the switchback trail that led uphill to Ghyaru had been a ski run, it would have been a double black diamond. Everyone's stride shrank and slowed to that of eighty-five-year-old wheezers in need of walkers. My breathing sounded like that of an emphysema patient. As the leaders neared the top, a voice called down from above, "You're almost there!" To which Zack responded, "That's it! I can't take it anymore," and started to run. He ran five steps, then slowed to a near halt as he gasped for air.

I was second to last to reach the top of the rise, where a teahouse came into view, along with the group sitting around a picnic table grinning at me. "We ordered *daal bhat* for you, Cara," Ron said. I thanked them, relieved that this would reduce my waiting time for food.

Lucy arrived a few minutes later and was informed that they'd ordered *daal bhat* for her, too. "But I don't want *daal bhat*," she said.

"You might try saying thank you," Nat said. Instead, Lucy threw herself down on a bench, red-faced and scowling.

As we dug into our meals, the guys suggested we should have a *daal bhat* eating contest sometime, which I knew would never happen. This macho discussion ended when everyone turned to stare at my plate. I'd completely cleaned up a substantial pile of the food while everyone else's plate remained half-full. The table burst into laughter.

"That's bloody-fucking amazing!" said Nat, The Constantly Amazed. "You're, like, the tiniest person here. Where do you put it all?"

Ron came to my defense. "They say a hearty appetite is a good sign that you're acclimatizing to the altitude."

"So, Cara, you must be way acclimatized," said Zack.

Although I ate much, I said little. The allergy tablet had made me drowsy, the hill had taken everything I had, and we still had a long way to go. I crossed my arms on the table and rested my head. Charlie said it wasn't like me to stop chattering. I smiled, but said nothing.

After lunch, my exhaustion became dangerous as I somnambulated along the high, narrow mountain paths. My eyes began to close. Several times my head nodded and jerked me awake. When I dreamily pictured myself sleepwalking off the side of the mountain, the image jolted me sufficiently out of my daze to realize my danger. I decided to take a break at the next town, regardless of the plans of the others.

The stone village of Nagwal was even dustier than Pisang, and spookier. Soon several in our group were murmuring that this town made them uneasy. Even though we saw people working and talking and children playing, a peculiar silence enveloped the village. Sound doesn't carry well through thin mountain air, but this silence went beyond that. I wouldn't have been surprised to discover that the villagers were aliens who communicated by telepathy.

We threaded our way through a narrow cobblestone maze flanked by grey stone walls to a small guesthouse where we ducked under a tiny doorway into a dirt courtyard. The courtyard was empty, so we climbed a makeshift wooden ladder to a rooftop terrace where a befuddled man of about fifty greeted us with a blank stare. He seemed confused by our presence, despite the sign outside that announced the place as a guesthouse. The imagery of gothic horror was now complete. Our unnerved group stopped just long enough for Ron to refill his water bottle.

More afraid of falling off the mountain in a doze than facing the supernatural or inhospitable, I stayed an extra twenty minutes to drink hot tea, eat a couple of stale cookies from my pack, and shake the cobwebs from my head.

I chatted, in a very limited fashion, with the innkeeper and another local. They perked up when they discovered I knew three or four Nepali words, and some of the eeriness of the place fled at the sight of their smiles. I didn't understand the conversation they directed my way, but it didn't matter. I've spent my life engaged in endless chatter, while other people have waited their turn to speak. I wonder if we ever really hear the individual words anyway. The smile, the laugh, the touch, the bow or handshake or embrace: aren't these the things we truly ask for with all the words we say?

Revived by the exchange, I moved on to Braga alone, but awake. The trail traversed rolling desert, flecked with sparse alpine shrubs, stunted pines, and trickling streams. I passed several Mani walls that had no prayer wheels. Instead, the low walls were topped with haphazardly broken tablets of stone. The tablets were carved with gracefully inscribed prayers, or Mani, each including some variation of *"Om Mani Padme Hum."* There was nothing to spin, so I brushed a finger over the indentations in the sun-warmed stone.

When the legendary Braga Bakery appeared, it looked as isolated and out of place as a mirage in the desert. Although in another part of the world such a building might appear plain and unremarkable, here it seemed a truly pretty place: a two-story cottage of grey stone and blond unfinished wood. The Marsyangdi River flowed behind the lodge, and

Annapurna III and Gangapurna rose to fill the sky beyond.

A bacchanalian nirvana, the Braga Bakery lives up to its legend, at least in terms of a mountain trek. The spicy homemade veggie-burger is the best I've eaten anywhere, and the apple pie is the best yet on the trail. For reasons obvious to any Westerner who has ever spent extended time far from home, many optimistic trekkers keep ordering apple pie from the catch-as-catch-can guesthouse menus, knowing full well that this dish remains a misinterpreted mystery to many of these mountain people—most of whom only have a vague impression that it has something to do with apples and dough. But this time, if the apple pie is not just like Mom's, it's close enough to rouse the memory of Mom. There is power in that image. The scent alone is a mantra sending up the love of home, however imperfect or broken.

The prices at Braga are high, but we don't care. Walking on the Annapurna Circuit is like working out on a stair climber for four to six hours a day—while suffering oxygen deprivation. After six straight days of torturing our legs and lungs, we're ready to be pampered.

At sunset, I washed a few clothes in a freezing cold bucket of water behind the lodge. As I wrung out my last shirt, my hands red and raw, Zack stepped onto the back deck to gaze at the Annapurna Range. He remarked how beautiful the snow looked in the setting sun. "That rose color on the snow?" I said. "In Alaska they call that alpenglow." In response he put an arm around my shoulder and gave it a brotherly squeeze. I leaned there for a moment as we admired the deepening ruby and indigo of snow and sky.

Then he glanced at his arm on my shoulder and said, "That's something I missed in Taiwan: affectionate people." His words broke the spell. There was an ineffable idea that separated us, a worldview thrust upon us by memories we could not erase. As close as we stood, there was no way I could explain the gap he'd exposed. I silently moved away, turned to hang my clothes on the line, and went to my room.

I'm sharing a room with the girls, and as we climbed into bed they all exclaimed at the blessed lack of dust. In spite of myself, I gave silent thanks to Zack, who had prayed for something practical.

I suppose praying for more oxygen would be too much to ask.

MANANG, ANNAPURNA CIRCUIT, NEPAL

We arrived in Manang just in time for the daily altitude scare. Just a half-hour walk from Braga, Manang is the last sizeable village before the push over the pass: Thorung La. At 3,540 meters (11,600 feet), Manang is also the last chance for the Himalayan Rescue Association to frighten the piss out of everyone with a free lecture on altitude sickness.

Several in our group are already suffering minor symptoms: mild headaches, loss of appetite, and sluggishness. My only complaint is sluggishness, but then that's been my family's complaint about me for as long as I can remember.

Some two-dozen trekkers gathered outdoors to listen to an AMS expert, who, with very little effort, convinced several bug-eyed listeners that their lives were in imminent peril. The doctor explained that high altitude headaches are caused by swelling of the brain. He warned us that puking one's guts out is definitely a bad sign, as is becoming dizzy and disoriented, or losing coordination: someone who continues to climb higher with those symptoms might lose consciousness, go into a coma, or die. I could swear one guy wasn't just taking notes, but hastily scribbling his last will and testament into his travel journal.

Another young man said, "I was told I could keep going as long as I don't pass out."

The doctor's response: "Well, and you can keep living as long as you don't die."

As for preventative remedies: the locals swear by garlic soup; spiritually inclined trekkers get a blessing from a lama who, no kidding, lives high atop a nearby mountain; and the doctor recommends a pill called Diamox (acetazolamide). Diamox helps people acclimatize if they're suffering mild symptoms. One unfortunate side effect is a constant and voracious need to urinate. But our group was sufficiently freaked out by words like "coma" and "die" to line up for free pills after the lecture—everyone but me. I've been peeing up a storm for days, and I'm just relieved to learn that this freakish change only means I'm acclimatizing normally.

The doctor gave us his conservative strategy for our trip over Thorung La: take one rest day in Manang, then make our way to the pass in four stages, instead of the three we planned. The idea is not to gain much more than three hundred meters (or one thousand feet) of altitude a day. This idea will insure the further fracturing of our group as we each decide whether or not to follow the doctor's advice. Ron is leading the campaign for the four-day plan, and the women agree with him. Nat and Zack have voted to stick to three. After the lecture, they teased Ron about "being a man."

"I won't seem like much of a man if I die on the way over the pass, either," Ron said.

Nat has dubbed the contagious fear of AMS "altitude madness." In our group, Gunther alone seems immune. That may be because Gunther, who's rooming with me, has been stuck in our room with a horrendous case of diarrhea and therefore missed the death lecture.

★ ★ ★

Manang isn't much higher than Braga, which means that, technically, yesterday was our acclimatization day. However, poised on the edge of the big moment, no one seems ready to leap. With little discussion about either manhood or altitude madness, today we all agreed to remain and put off facing our dharma until tomorrow.

Lucy hoped this would give Mel a chance to catch up, but she never showed. Later, Lucy found out from a trekker who'd met Mel in Chame that she'd turned back. "So it's a good job we didn't wait for her," Lucy admitted.

Gunther spent a second day lying in bed, dehydrated, weak, and pale (even for him). Alarmed, I insisted he drink some water. Ron offered some of his rehydration salts. Gunther politely turned him down. "Don't be stupid," Ron said. "You can die from dehydration. It's not as if we're close to a hospital if you get into any trouble, you know." Gunther acquiesced.

The higher we've climbed, the more scrupulous Ron has become about health and safety. Yesterday, when several of us teased him about how frequently he washes his hands, he explained that he didn't want to risk contracting some virulent disease. After Ron gave Gunther his morbid lecture on dehydration, Nat declared, "Once again Dr. Death gives his prognosis, which is, as usual: death." The nickname stuck, although the women cut him some slack and gave him the gentler appellation of Dr. Ron.

Confident we couldn't prevent Gunther's death by remaining at his bedside, most of us, including Dr. Ron, decided to go on an acclimatization hike.

Lucy, who had a severe headache, remained behind, saying, "I know it's bloody altitude sickness. I'm really worried."

"Imagine that," Nat said. "Ms. Whine-er-schnitzel has come down with altitude madness."

"I may be a whiner, but at least I'm not a wiener. You're not that funny anymore, you know. Now you're just rude."

"Wait, let me try to wrinkle my forehead with concern!"

Between her grousing and his teasing, Nat and Lucy have developed a mutual animosity so strong it threatens to destroy five decades of peaceful Anglo-German relations. She eyed him with disdain and then conferred with the more sympathetic among us.

"Why don't you take some Diamox?" Dr. Ron suggested.

"And get some rest," I said.

"*Ja*, but what if I fall asleep and go into a coma?"

I told her that was unlikely, but she was not to be mollified. We gave up and left her to dream of her doom while the rest of us hiked to a high ridge some 500 meters above town.

As we started up the slope, we skirted a glacier-fed lake below. Across the lake, the Gangapurna Glacier loomed, a colossal waterfall frozen in motion.

While the glacier left us awestruck, after a week of trekking we've become somewhat complacent about sheer drop-offs. Then Charlie woke us up. She took one tiny misstep and started to slide off the loose dirt of the narrow ridge. My heart lurched as she pinwheeled her arms for balance. She righted herself, turned to Allison with her hand to her chest, and said, "I have looked in the face of death." Allison giggled, but we all slowed our pace.

We reached a point well above town for a magic-carpet view of the pale brown valley and its matching stone buildings. Manang looked like a settlement in a North African desert, yet it had a desolate beauty set against the backdrop of the indomitable Himalayas to the south.

When we returned to the lodge, a creeping mountain malaise seized control of our wills. We retreated to our beds for what was supposed to be a nap. Instead, we passed out for several hours.

The late afternoon sun chastised my lazy eyelids, waking me to a guest-house so quiet it seemed to have fallen under a Sleeping Beauty spell. In a trance, I walked away from the hotel with the hypnotic conviction that I'd "see" something. I did. But first I heard it: the steady, insistent drumming, a sound that brought to mind a Native American ceremony.

I followed the sound until I reached an open area where dozens of local men and women were gathered for a ceremonial sporting competition. Two young men were beating large drums, while a group of men armed with bows shot arrows into two large wooden targets. Cheers periodically went up and a holiday mood prevailed. I climbed atop the roof of the community lodge, where a group of locals and trekkers were standing for a better vantage. A local explained to me that this event was part of the *Meta* Festival (*meta* means archery). As the sun cast its final, red, Svengali gaze over the town, the arrows continued to fly.

One by one, most of the fellowship awoke and followed the sound of the drums to join me on the roof. Ron said, "I was nearly killed on the way here. There are little boys running all over town shooting arrows, *real* arrows. For pity's sake! What do these people think they're doing arming ten-year-old boys with live ammunition?"

Only one person failed to show. "Where's Lucy?" I asked.

"In a coma," Nat said. Only he and Zack laughed, but everyone else's mouths twitched with suppressed grins.

We watched the archers until it grew too dark to see. Then we returned to the guesthouse to eat dinner, and to listen to the miraculously recovered Lucy extol the merits of Diamox. Her headache was cured, and her transformation to a cheerful human being—a side of her we'd rarely seen—convinced most of the others to begin popping their stash.

After two days of so-called rest, tonight everyone was in high spirits. After dinner, several people started a card game, during which Nat took up the sophomoric habit of asking people to pull his finger and then cutting loose a trumpeting fart. The "pull my finger" prank was better received than the joke he tried on Allison: with his limited German vocabulary, he constructed the ridiculous phrase, "Would you accept a sperm donation?" The joke received a smattering of polite chuckles, which encouraged him to repeat the foul remark, until Lucy said in a voice foamy with sarcasm, "*Ja*, and I'm sure every woman would die for this opportunity."

Everyone burst into laughter, even Nat.

The sperm joke marked the only time I've seen Allison irritated, although she kept her cool as she explained that it didn't make sense in German anyway. Charlie, less subtly, told Nat he was acting like an ass and began swearing at him in German. The only word I recognized was *scheizer* (shit), but it all sounded as deliciously vitriolic as acid spit.

I tried to diffuse the tension by remarking to Charlie, "I love listening to you swear. Anger just sounds so much better in German."

"*ACCCH!*" she shouted. "Will no one ever let us forget World War Two?! *Still* everyone insists on thinking we're all Nazis!"

"No, no! That's not what I was thinking at all. Nazis never even occurred to me. I just like the way the words sound."

Charlie took one look at my earnest face and her anger dissolved into giggles. She said she knew that wasn't what I meant and apologized for her knee-jerk reaction. She explained that she's met a lot of people who still cling to old stereotypes gleaned from Hollywood movies. The passage of more than fifty years has not been sufficient to erase the images, or the scars on the German psyche, even for Charlie's generation. I fell into an embarrassed silence.

Clearly, it's time for all of us to stop talking and resume walking.

YAK KHARKA, ANNAPURNA CIRCUIT, NEPAL

As we started day one of our long-awaited approach to Thorung La, our group splintered into four acclimatization factions:

- Nat and Zack decided to push for Letdar. Ron, in an apparent fit of male bonding, set out with them despite his misgivings.

- Allison, Charlie, and Lucy, opting for a cautious advance, decided to head to the lower-lying village of Gunsang.

- My plan was part aggressive, part conservative: I would spend the morning climbing the hill to visit the lama for a blessing, then hike to the village of Yak Kharka. This would put me ahead of the girls, but behind the boys.

- Gunther was feeling better this morning, but still a bit pokey. He decided to go with me to see the lama, then spend another night resting in Manang.

The lama was supposed to bless Gunther and me for safe passage over Thorung La. Yet our climb to the centuries-old monastery filled me with as much foreboding as Thorung La itself.

At first it seemed simple: a sign pointed out the path to Praken Gompa. But after five to ten minutes, the path petered out. When we lost the trail we were at the level of the high farm terraces, so we guessed it was necessary to climb the terraces like giant steps until we found the trail again. Then the terraces ran out, and there was still no path in sight.

At that point, we chose to follow a narrow gully. We could see the *gompa*, or monastery, above and we could see where the gully passed it, but as we continued upward, the cleft filled with dense, prickly brush until it became impassable. This forced us to climb out of the gully and scramble straight up the sheer slope on hands and feet. Loose dirt continually gave way beneath us. I looked down and saw that we were poised at such a severe angle that if I were to wind up in an uncontrolled slide it might be a few hundred meters before a thorn bush stopped my fall.

My foot started to skid downhill. I quickly drew it back and tried to back up the way I'd come, but that move started a small rockslide. Paralyzed with anxiety, I clung to the side of the mountain like a panicked cat. "Gunther! I'm stuck!" I yelled. There was no answer. Shit. "Gunther?" I twisted my neck to look around and saw nothing but a desiccated slope of dirt, rock, and brush. *And you can keep living, as long as you don't die,* I thought.

After an eternity of seconds, I lifted my foot and tested the earth with one cautious toe until it hit a firm foothold. Then I backtracked to look for Gunther, but he'd vanished into some unseen fold in the mountainside. The monastery was still in sight and, not knowing if Gunther was above or below, I decided to continue upward.

Finally, I spotted prayer flags ahead. As I moved toward their fluttering colors, an old woman wearing a green apron over thick layers of clothing stepped onto the balcony of the monastery and silently beckoned me. She looked like a Native American, with dark coppery skin and white hair tied in braids. Her expression held the kind of blank serenity one might expect from Prozac. "Which way?" I called out. She said nothing, just beckoned. I pointed left. No response. I pointed right. Nothing. "Fat lot of help you are," I muttered.

I was startled by a gentle voice behind me, "Hi, Cara." It was Gunther. "Am I glad to see you! I was beginning to worry."

When we reached the monastery, we'd been walking for about an hour and a half, but it felt like hours. We collapsed near the entry, next to a small white *stupa*, a dome-shaped Buddhist shrine. The old woman appeared again, smiled, and pointed toward the building. We followed her through the entry and down a long hall to a small doorway.

Hesitating to pass within, we peered into a tiny, dark room lined with cloths: sacred hangings of red and gold, layered over second-hand bed-sheets with pink roses. On the floor behind a low table sat an old, bald man with a scraggly beard and a forehead as furrowed as the monastery's stone masonry. He's known as Lama Deshi. *"Namaste,"* Gunther and I said, bowing with palms pressed together. The lama beckoned us to duck through the low doorway and sit on a low bench across from him. His small, bright eyes moved from one to the other of us, and he nodded, chuckling as if we'd just told a joke, though we'd said nothing after our initial *"Namaste."* Loosely translated, *namaste* means: "The divine spirit within me honors the divine spirit within you." I don't think that was the source of his amusement.

"What country?" he asked.

"U.S.A."

"Germany."

These neutral responses seemed to amuse him even more than our entrance, and he chuckled and nodded with increasing enthusiasm.

"Married?"

"No."

"Friends."

More chuckling.

It seemed to me his soft laughter was simply a way of smiling out loud. Maybe it encompassed all that he guessed about us: our clumsy climb to see him, our inexplicable desire to cross over Thorung La, our unspoken quest for meaning. How often have I made the offhand remark, "Life is funny"? Maybe that's the ultimate truth. Maybe enlightenment renders everything into comedy, which is, after all, merely tragedy set on its head.

Lama Deshi stopped laughing, donned his tall, red gnome's hat, and gestured for me to come forward for the *Puja* ceremony. He poured oil into his palm, sipped some of it, and smoothed the rest into the sparse hair over his forehead. He then indicated I should do the same. As he began chanting, he picked up a book of Buddhist scripture and held it over my head.

He then chanted over a bit of yellow ribbon and tied it around my neck. He smiled at me, pointed at the ribbon, and said, "Good luck." Then he pointed at his flexed bicep and said, "Strength for Thorung La."

He repeated the ritual for Gunther. Then he asked us each for 100 rupees.

Afterward, he chatted with us for a few minutes, in his limited fashion, while the old woman brought us hot tea and a handful of tiny boiled potatoes, which we ate with our fingers. He pointed at himself, smiled, and said, "Eighty-three." Then he pointed at the woman and said, "Eighty-two." He chuckled again and told the woman that Gunther and I weren't married. Intimidated by his holy status, I refrained from asking whether he and the old woman were married.

He gestured at the tiny passport photos that wallpapered one wall of the little room and told us he'd blessed trekkers from many countries. Then he began to list the countries, carefully enunciating each one: "U-S-A, Eng-land, Ger-ma-ny, Aus-tra-lia, Is-ra-el . . . " I reached into my money belt and offered him one of my spare passport photos to add to his collection. With an air of reverent ceremony, the old priest opened a container of paste, applied it to the photo, and indicated I should place it in an empty space on the wall.

Before we left, I asked Gunther to take a photo of me with the lama and the old woman, for which Lama Deshi once again beamed his Nirvanic amusement. As I stuffed my camera back into my bum bag, the woman spotted the Mars bar I'd packed "for the hike."

She pointed and asked, "Chocolate?" with a hopeful look.

"For strength on the way down," I said, and closed the bag.

She only smiled.

We left amid warm goodbyes and mutual thanks. I sat outside by the stupa and took a bite of my candy bar. As I chewed, I thought about the tea and tiny potatoes the old woman had given us. My throat constricted. I wrapped up the rest of the candy bar, walked back into the building and, as reluctantly as Amy March giving up her Christmas dollar, handed it to the woman. She smiled broadly and thanked me, chuckling like the lama.

Gunther and I returned down the correct path—the obvious path, now that we'd found it. Breathing was easier on the descent, and we took the opportunity to talk. It was the first time we'd ever had a private conversation. Gunther explained that Lama Deshi is of the Nyingma sect of Buddhism, a different sect than the Dalai Lama, who is of the Gelugpa Sect.

"Have you studied a lot about Buddhism?" I asked.

"Yes. I like Buddhism very much."

"What is it you like so much?"

"In Buddhism, enlightenment is attainable for everyone. And we all have it, inside us. It is something you can do yourself. You don't need a priest or someone else to do it for you, or to tell you how to do it."

A vulture chose that moment to fly overhead, so close we could hear its wings straining against the thin mountain air. We stopped to watch in silence. To me, until that moment, vultures had always symbolized death. Some Buddhists still invite vultures to eat their dead, in the high country of Tibet and Nepal where trees for cremation are scarce. The ceremony is called a sky burial, or *jhator*, which literally means "giving alms to the birds." Yet here in the east, death leads to rebirth. I saw this vulture not as an omen of danger, but as a harbinger of renewal.

As if the bird had put him in mind of it, Gunther told me about a dream he had last night. "I don't have all the words in English to tell you, but the dream made me wake up, and it made me think . . . made me ponder? . . . the most important question: the purpose of my life."

"And what is that?"

"I don't know." He smiled. "I said it made me think about it. I didn't say I had the answer. Maybe I will think of an answer, maybe I won't. But I believe it is a good question to think about."

I had to laugh. I'd been holding my breath, expecting at least a clue to my own unanswered question, expecting someone else to do it for me.

★　★　★

The teahouse in Manang has a mirror, and before I left I looked into it for the first time. What I saw struck me with an emotional force I didn't expect: my face was grimy, my hair oily, my clothes mismatched, yet I looked more beautiful than I ever would have believed possible. This woman, I thought with wonder, who is she?

Outside the lodge, I gave Gunther a hug goodbye, trying not to squeeze too hard; he felt so fragile, like a skeleton wrapped in fleece. There were dark circles under his eyes. It was obvious the hike to visit Lama Deshi had taken all his strength.

"Take care of yourself," I said, "and don't hike any higher until you feel better."

"Don't worry. I'm going to take a nap, then go to the altitude lecture. So you see, I'll be going to the doctor today. You be careful, walking alone."

It was a three-hour slog to Yak Kharka. The stone settlements grew sparser the higher I climbed. Gunsang's only purpose seemed to be providing two or three teahouses for trekkers. As I approached one of them, I spotted Lucy sitting alone on its upper terrace, scowling. She forced a smile and waved me up.

While I drank tea, she explained that Charlie and Allison had left a couple of hours earlier for an acclimatization hike to Yak Kharka and had not returned as they'd "promised." "I've never known so many people to constantly go back on their word," she said. I said nothing. When I finished my tea and rose to move on, she stood and declared she would join me. "I'm not about to stay here by myself."

In Yak Kharka, we found Charlie, Allison, and Ron lounging at a picnic table in a guesthouse courtyard. All three looked half-asleep.

Ron had decided not to push on to Letdar with Nat and Zack, saying he didn't want to risk altitude problems. Letdar is only half an hour away, but it's 650 meters higher than our last overnight stop, while Yak Kharka is only 450 meters higher. The Himalayan Rescue Association's expert fearmonger had suggested only 300 meters a day. "Nat and Zack are determined to run all the way to Thorung La," Charlie sniffed. "Well, they can kill themselves if they want. I'm not moving one more step today."

I wasn't worried about AMS, but after my trip to the lama's perch, another half-hour of walking sounded like an eternity, especially to join people I wouldn't be able to keep up with anyway. I stuck with my original plan and stayed put.

As night fell, the lodge pulsed with the pent-up energy of dozens of trekkers: eager to just get there already, bored by our plodding pace, nervous about the obstacles that could still rob us of our goal. From day one, we've encountered trekkers returning from the pass, turned back by altitude, by snow, by injury, by illness. In the absence of firsthand experience, Thorung La has begun to take on mythical proportions.

Frank, a Californian in his mid-thirties, arrived here with his group yesterday. Last night he started throwing up. When his friends took off this morning, he stayed behind. Frank described his plan to catch up: "I know it's cheating, but I'm going to rent a horse tomorrow and ride it over the pass to Muktinath. Can you imagine their faces when I pull into town on horseback?"

"I think they'll be jealous," I said. "And it may be the only way for old folks like us to keep pace with these youngsters."

"We're not old. We're just mature."

"You might have something there," Ron said. "Cara's one of the few people who hasn't had any real altitude problems. I think it's because she *is* more mature. She's not one to go charging up the mountain too quickly and get sick."

I smiled. "Sounds like a polite way of saying old people are slow."

"Yes, Mama Cara, you are old. But you are also wise," Charlie said.

The girls laughed.

We whiled away the evening playing cards until another trekker provided a new distraction. He'd packed a telescope all this way just for the pleasure of viewing the moon through the clear, undistorted air of the Himalayas. He set it up outside and called out an invitation to anyone who wanted a look. As I looked through the scope at the cold, white, unconcerned orb hanging above us, it occurred to me that the moon will have the same craters and markings a thousand years from now, while in a few days I'll come down from these mountains marked a different person, even if it's only my belief that makes it so. This is as it should be; unlike the moon, I don't have millions of years to play with.

LETDAR, ANNAPURNA CIRCUIT, NEPAL

It's not just the walking and the altitude that exhaust us; it's the nightly slumber party. At bedtime last night, we couldn't stop giggling, as five people are liable to do when crowded into one small room.

I was fighting a tug of war with the contents of my backpack, and when I started to curse, Allison, who was taking off her shoes, asked, "What's wrong? It's not my socks is it?" That started the first wave of giggles.

We all smell as pungent as an unwashed, incontinent old dog left in the rain. None of us have showered since the Braga Bakery and we've all agreed it will be too cold to do so until we reach Muktinath, on the other side of the pass. Charlie said, "It's like 'No sex before marriage'—'No shower before Muktinath.'" This prompted the next wave of giggles.

Not only are we all pretty ripe, as we've climbed higher, the entire group has fallen victim to a farting epidemic. So when I lit a candle, Allison said, "Better not. One candle and we might explode." Another wave.

We settled into our beds to sleep, and the sudden silence was so profound my ears rang. That was when something small and furry tickled my face. I leapt up from my mattress and shrieked, causing a chain reaction of yelling as everyone else was startled from near-sleep. "What?! What?!"

"Something was crawling on me!" I turned on a flashlight and discovered it was only a moth, prompting helpless giggles of relief.

"Thank God," Charlie said, wiping her eyes. "I thought it was another spider."

I opened the door and flung the moth outside. After that, I almost got a decent night's sleep . . . except that Allison snored, Lucy kept calling out, "Stop Snoring!" and Ron talked incessantly in his sleep. On top of all that, everyone except me was taking Diamox and they were all stricken with a constant need to pee. During the night, all four of my roommates tripped over my mattress or stepped on me several times each as they made their way to the outhouse.

Luckily, it was only a half-hour's sleepwalk to today's stop in Letdar, altitude 4200 meters (about 13,800 feet). Ron, Charlie, Allison, and I decided to go on another acclimatization hike. Once again, Lucy opted out: "I want to get some rest, not go on a bloody acclimatization hike. What do you think I'm taking Diamox for?" The rest of us walked up into the rolling green hills behind the lodge for a couple of hours.

After that, we spent the rest of the afternoon sitting outside the lodge and watching the yaks graze. Acclimatizing is mostly about waiting, and even in the Himalayas this can be dull work. My companions and I fell into the near-catatonic silence I've come to call the "Annapurna daze."

When I pulled out my journal and started writing, a Nepali porter wandered up and looked over my shoulder, his eyes following the progress of my pen.

Charlie admonished him in an acerbic tone, "Excuse me! She is writing in her diary. Hello! Yes, you. She is writing in her diary. That means it is private."

"It's okay," I muttered. "I don't think he can read English."

"That's not the point," Charlie said. "It's rude!"

The porter backed away, looking as frightened as I'd felt when I'd first met her. No one fucks with Charlie.

I felt sorry for the porter but smiled to myself, realizing that, somewhere along the way, I'd passed an invisible boundary, past Charlie's defenses into her circle of trust. During the long afternoon of breathless waiting, she and I began an arrhythmic conversation—full of sleepy stops and starts—about growing up in dysfunctional families. Is there any other kind? We discovered that we both had the same authoritarian, distant father. At this revelation, a bond of understanding began to weave its way through the ever-shrinking space between us.

A late afternoon chill drove us back to the lodge, where our languor was overtaken by a new spate of fear. An agitated young woman was careening from table to table, talking in earnest, forehead creased with worry. When she reached our table she explained that her boyfriend had disappeared some-where in the hills where we'd been hiking. They'd set out together, but he'd wandered off without her. Had we seen him? No, we were sorry, we hadn't.

As dusk fell and the temperature plummeted, a palpable anxiety took hold of the lodge. Nervous glances skittered toward the girlfriend, then away. People began debating the merits of a search. Someone said there was no point in risking more people for a guy who had willfully wandered off alone. Wasn't there a rescue group who handled this sort of thing?

The philosophical among us considered our mortality. The pragmatic saw it as a reminder of the serious nature of our undertaking. The compassion-ate pitied the girlfriend. One or two dared to feel sorry for the missing guy.

Just before Letdar was mantled in total blackness, just when I began to think no one at this lodge was going to get any sleep, the young man returned. He muttered some excuse about trying to see the glacier and walking farther than he'd realized. The five of us exchanged a silent look that made our feelings clear: we all secretly hated him.

THORUNG PHEDI, ANNAPURNA CIRCUIT, NEPAL

If we simply keep moving in the direction to which we've committed, we have little choice now but to reach our goal, whether it unnerves us or not. Today we reached Thorung Phedi, final stop before the push over the pass.

There's no traditional village here, just one lodge. If it weren't for trekkers, this inhospitable, sere rock would suffer the blasting of wind, snow, and sun without any company to share its brutal loneliness. The lone lodge is a place to fuel up and to wait, to gather courage and to celebrate the coming day of truth.

Inside: while the lodge's kitchen staff pounds out homemade pasta for the evening meal, trekkers arrive in a steady stream and the tense excitement notches up to an insuperable pitch. If an outsider were to walk into this setting without knowing what it was, that person might assume it was a reunion of fifty or so longtime friends.

Outside: the lodge is surrounded by peaks so brown and stark they're an extreme beyond beauty or ugliness. To one side of us stands a mountain peak topped by a fall of ice, glacier, and snow. To the other side, a fold, a crease, a promise of the unseen pass hidden above.

When we arrived, Dr. Ron asked if I thought we needed an acclimatization hike. My firm opinion was "no," even when he pointed out other people heading uphill for that purpose. The benefits seemed outweighed by the benefits of resting and gathering strength for tomorrow.

Ron nodded as if in grave deference to authority. "Well said. That sounds very sensible."

"Of course it is. She's Mama Cara," Charlie said, and gave me a look of fond respect.

Ever since Manang, the group has increasingly sought my input in decisions. I get the impression they're not just being polite, that they honestly value my opinion. Among these people thrown together by chance, I feel a sense of belonging I've never felt before. This is no minor hike. It's a full-on trek, with all the dangers that implies. Trust means a lot. Our lives are in each other's hands.

This afternoon, when I rushed out of the main lodge and across the windy compound to grab something from our dorm room, I received a small shock: when I stopped running, my heart started to flutter like that of a small, frightened bird. Soon the flutter began to happen every time I made a sudden move. A couple of times it was so startling I hyperventilated. I asked Charlie, who I'd also seen gasping for air, if she'd noticed a heart flutter. "Yes. It's terrifying. My pulse is so fast. I'm beginning to think this is crazy to be up here."

Then came another, more pleasant shock: Gunther showed up, looking

much better. He accepted our exuberant hugs with a pleased but diffident smile. He still wore the lama's yellow ribbon around his neck, and he
remarked that I still wore mine.

"I'm not taking it off until after the trek," I said.

"Yes, me too, although it's already very dirty."

As if the ribbons were symbols of a bond between us, he gave me a
more unguarded smile than I'd yet seen. I called him my "soul brother"
and he blushed.

After he and the group caught up, Gunther and I talked for a long time.
I mostly listened as he shared his life goals and plans. He's studying to be a
teacher, but he loves music and would rather make guitars for a living. He
said he wants a life of simple harmony, much like the life of the mountain
people we've seen.

"Yes, but we only see the surface," I said. "We don't really know what their
lives are. To us it looks like harmony, but if you lived it every day it might
seem more like hardship."

"Of course. That is true. But I will not be living in a country as poor as
this. I think it's possible to have balance without being so . . . so . . . ."

"Deprived?"

"Yes."

Gunther made it clear that this was an ideal he'd long held, not some
romantic whim inspired by his surroundings, only to be forgotten upon
his departure.

Because we'll have an early start tomorrow, tonight our group went to bed
at eight. Once again I stare into the dark, listening to everyone's snoring and
dreaming and tossing. Dave, the girls, and I all lie squeezed into five narrow
beds butted more tightly together than our beds in Yak Kharka, not an inch
between them; there's no way in or out without crawling over someone.

When we shut off our flashlights, Charlie's voice probed the darkness,
uncharacteristically soft and tentative: "Last night I dreamed about the pass.
It was a terrible nightmare. I could not reach the top, no matter how I tried.
My father was there and he was very angry with me."

Funny. When I dream on this trek, my dreams are invariably about the
past: I've seen Sean and Chance, I've talked with my grandmother and my
father, I've seen old friends and those people in dreams who you seem to
know even though they don't look familiar at all. But, although it's very
much on my mind, I never dream about the pass.

MUKTINATH, ANNAPURNA CIRCUIT, NEPAL

Lucy's travel alarm started beeping at four a.m. Lucy, Ron, and I groaned. Allison laughed. Next to me, Charlie was so silent I knew she was pretending she hadn't heard. I felt neither excitement nor dread, just exhaustion. After lying in denial in the dark for ten minutes, we rushed to dress and pack by the inadequate light of candles and flashlights. Murmuring voices broke the morning stillness as trekkers throughout the compound did the same.

In contrast, the main lodge sounded like a high school cafeteria. The race was on: fifty or so people all wanted to eat breakfast, pay their bills, and be first up the trail. Nobody really knew how long it would take to reach Thorung La: four hours? five? six? Nor did we know how difficult it would be. Nor how long it would take to get down the other side. We'd only heard secondhand accounts, all of them wildly different.

At six a.m. we were the last group to head up the slope in the amorphous glow of dawn. "Goodbye *didi!*" a lodge worker called to Lucy. "Goodbye *dai!*" she replied. (*Didi* means sister, *dai* means brother.) Lucy's trekking poles clattered across the courtyard cobblestones, until they met dirt and fell as silent as the rest of us.

The mountain had a look of expectation in the growing light. Each day the pass is renewed, virginal and pure, and each day another group of trekkers enters her folds, ending that momentary innocence. I looked up to see several groups ahead of us, snaking up the trail slowly.

So slowly.

I led the way. We agreed last night that the slowest person should walk in front and set the pace, to ensure no one would get left behind. Ron and I read a horror story posted on the wall of the lodge, about a young man who died on the pass a few years ago: he suffered severe AMS, got separated from his group, became disoriented, wandered off the path, and fell. A snowstorm buried his body, which wasn't found for weeks. Humbled, the six of us swore to stick together.

As we began the steep ascent, Charlie, usually feisty and full of laughter, looked worried and miserable. Her eyes rolled like those of a spooked horse. For the first fifteen minutes several of us repetitively asked how she was doing, until she snapped that she was fine and to stop asking.

There wasn't much talking after that. All our energy was focused on the next step upward . . . and the next.

Each time I stopped to catch my breath, I turned to watch the dawn break. The sun's rays crept over the snow-and-ice covered ridge behind us, turning its jagged edge to cold fire, until the sun leapt from its hiding place, shattering the morning with its brilliance.

Then I took another step . . . then another.

In the lead, I pressured myself to increase my usual effort, so the others wouldn't feel frustrated with my pace—this on the hardest day of all. The lanky Dr. Ron was always on my heels. A few times, I felt that scary rapid flutter in my heart and my lungs seemed empty of air. Each time, I'd stop and hunch over my thighs, gasping until I felt my breathing become even. Then I'd continue. Whenever we stopped to rest I didn't bother to remove my backpack, just dropped where I stood, falling backward onto my pack like a helpless turtle. I lay there in a half-stupor, eyes closed, denying the moment when I'd have to rise again. Each time, Ron asked, "Cara, you okay?" Each time, I smiled, nodded, and gave a silent thumbs-up or okay sign. I really was okay, just stretched to the limit of endurance.

I was better off than some: Ron had a pounding headache, Charlie had a headache *and* a racing pulse, Lucy was recovering from diarrhea. Only Gunther and Allison seemed to be a hundred percent, but who knows? It's their nature to be quiet and uncomplaining.

As we climbed, several of the highest peaks of the Himalayas encircled us, like high lamas gathered for a secret meeting, wearing their ceremonial pointed hats. Snow, ice, and glaciers rose behind us, beside us, before us. What was not white or glacial blue was brown or gray, severe and harsh against the clear sky. We'd left the roaring Marsyangdi River behind to follow a smaller, whispering tributary as it tiptoed through this land of titans. We reached several false summits. We'd been warned about them, but knowing didn't make me feel better. Each step forced me to question whether I could take another. I was exhausted nearly to tears, then beyond that to numb acceptance.

It was not fun. Yet I was deeply moved. These mountains. This suspended moment. This sense of the temporal confronting the eternal. As we rose, my soul swelled outward from some deep place, as if trying to merge with the strange beauty surrounding me.

Just before eleven, nearly five hours after setting out, we spotted a mass of multicolored prayer flags strung in several lines radiating outward from a post, like the dusty, ragged remains of a circus tent. At the sight, tears of joy swam in my eyes. We had reached the high point of the pass: 5416 meters (17, 769 feet). Looking around, I realized we'd truly arrived between a rock and a hard place: to one side, soaring brown rock, to the other, a soaring white hard place.

Like a bunch of high school seniors on graduation day, we rushed to the high point, where we hugged and jumped up-and-down and took photos. Faces that just a few minutes before had been grimacing in agony were now beaming with self-congratulations.

The celebration lasted fewer than five minutes. The wind whipped us with stinging nettles of freezing cold, and my bladder hit me with a blinding need to pee. There was no possibility of privacy in this barren, wind-blasted saddle. I rushed down-slope and behind the low-lying teahouse to squat with relief, still visible to anyone upslope who cared to look.

No, the teahouse was not a delusion brought on by exhaustion. A true entrepreneur knows no bounds. I bought a Mars bar and a cup of tea from the Tibetan who told us he lives at the Thorung La Teahouse for two weeks at a time, before trading shifts with someone else. He was a distinguished fellow, fortyish, wearing a fur cap and fleece jacket. The candy bar cost an exorbitant 110 rupees. That's about $1.50, more than twice what it would cost in the States. But I figured I'd earned the chocolate and the Tibetan had earned the cash. He had to drag candy bars, biscuits, and tea up the mountain, then live at this frozen outpost for days on end—all to sell snacks and drinks to foreigners between the hours of nine and noon each day. *Thorung La* means "hearth god pass." It is a bizarre place for a hearth, and a lonely existence for the one who keeps it.

After about fifteen minutes, we got ready to leave. Lucy and I were still putting on our packs when our companions tore downhill at full throttle. "I really hate that!" I shouted after them. "Can't they wait thirty seconds?" No response. "Yeah? Fuck you too!" I don't think they heard me. Then, while I was still buckling my straps, Lucy, who'd complained all along about people rushing off without her, tore after them without a word. I guess the whole "all for one" bit only applied to the way up, not the way down.

Yet the way down had some dangerous pitfalls. We had gained about 900 meters (nearly 3,000 feet) climbing from Thorung Phedi to Thorung La, but we would lose about 1,600 meters (more than five thousand feet) on our way down from Thorung La to Muktinath. The going was so steep it was hard to keep from pitching forward into an uncontrolled, breakneck rush. And there was quite a scary drop alongside the narrow path.

The terrain was a tilting moonscape of rock, with few changing sights to distract me from my anger at being deserted. Having eaten nothing since breakfast but a candy bar and tea, I was so ravenous I developed my first headache of the trek. This did little to improve my mood.

I didn't catch up with my friends until the next teahouse, and by then I was in such a snit I couldn't speak. I let them assume I was too worn out for words. Deep down I knew I was being petty. The only risk we'd discussed when we'd planned to stick together was AMS. We were on our way out of that danger, and it was presumptuous, I suppose, to expect anything we hadn't specifically agreed upon. Some silent time with a bowl of noodle soup improved my point of view considerably.

As the hours of downhill pounding went on, my boots pulverized my toes into a mashed clump of tenderized meat. My legs felt like spaghetti. Once, my foot gave way, twisting my ankle into a tuning fork of pain. Then I fell on my ass for no apparent reason.

I walked the final stretch with Lucy, both of us lagging well behind the others. As we wobbled down the final rocky stairway into the village, we were taken aback by a seeming mirage: a patch of luminescent green farmland in the center of the valley. After hours of stone and dust, ice and snow, we could hardly have been more surprised to see a chlorine-blue swimming pool full of bikini-clad women.

The others had stopped at the first guesthouse they saw, too exhausted to investigate further, and Lucy and I arrived to discover they'd reserved a room for us. This time Lucy didn't complain that she wasn't consulted. It was about four in the afternoon, ten hours since we'd set out. It felt like days. For a time, I wandered about the lodge in a stupor.

One by one, we gathered in the dining room, slumped in our chairs, and fell into an inexorable Annapurna daze. Then Nat entered in a Tazmanian Devil whirl, as loud, charming, and obnoxious as ever, and we couldn't help but laugh. He looked different, and it took me several minutes to realize it was because he'd shaved and showered. He'd arrived in Muktinath yesterday. Zack had moved on.

When I came to my senses, I took my first shower since Manang, four days ago, and washed my hair for the first time since Chame, eight days ago. It was a relief to feel clean again. But the glow of accomplishment I'd felt atop Thorung La was gone, replaced by an anticlimactic weariness that penetrated every last nerve, from my outermost skin to the bottom of my soul.

★ ★ ★

This time Charlie's rant was about religion. "Before I came to India and Nepal, I heard about the devotion of the people to their Hindu religion. I'm not impressed," she blew the words out in a disdainful huff of air. "I think this idea of reincarnation is nothing but an excuse to accept fate and do nothing to improve life, just throwing your hands up and saying it's your karma, waiting for the next life to make things better. The caste system is disgusting, this idea that the poor deserve their fate. This system only helps the higher castes keep their privileges."

I considered arguing that the fallibility of human institutions didn't disprove the existence of the divine, but disagreeing with Charlie is an invitation to apoplexy. While she derided the beliefs of Hindu people, I knew that her opinion was born of compassion. Charlie wants all the disenfranchised people of the world to be as strong as she is, to learn to say "no."

An equal-opportunity humanistic atheist, she doesn't like Christianity either, or any religion, "Although, at least Christians only have one God—or maybe three, I still can't figure that out. Well, do you know the Hindus have 3000 gods and goddesses? That is ridiculous. Just imagine how long it would take to study them all! And how can you decide which god you want to pray to? I mean it's a logistical nightmare, isn't it?"

We were walking to the nearby holy site of Muktinath. For the six of us—the girls, Gunther, and Ron—it was an intriguing way to mark our completion of the passage over Thorung La. But for Hindus and Tibetan Buddhists, Muktinath is the final destination of a sacred pilgrimage. *Muktinath* means "Lord of Salvation," another name for the Hindu god Vishnu. The site also goes by the name *Chumig Gyatsa*, a Tibetan phrase meaning "A Hundred Waters." People come from all over the world to bathe in Vishnu's sacred waters and see his sacred flame. Many of the faithful are Indians who walk hundreds of miles to get here.

At first glance, Muktinath is a humble collection of temples, shrines, and gardens, remarkable mostly for its location. Its strings of prayer flags—red, green, white, yellow, and blue—look festive against the brown and white rain shadow of the Annapurnas. When we entered, I walked up to one of the pagodas and rang the small bells that dangled before the shrines. As I passed into a temple courtyard, I met a venerable sadhu in saffron robes. He told me he spent 180 days walking here from India. His English was limited, but I learned that he was a true sadhu who had renounced all worldly things, not one of those fake sadhus who hand out wildflowers to surprised tourists then demand money from the befuddled recipients.

As we walked on, Gunther told me the well-known story of another sadhu, known as Lotan Baba, "The Rolling Saint." A few years ago Lotan Baba spent six months rolling 2500 miles across India to reach a shrine in the foothills of the Himalayas.

"Rolling?" I said, "You mean like doing somersaults, head over heels?"

"No, he rolled while lying down," Gunther said. "They say his body was covered with blisters when he arrived."

"And this was supposed to prove what?"

"It was his way of showing his humility and dedication."

"But what benefit is it? Does rolling lead to enlightenment?"

"I think it depends on your intention. It's like chanting a mantra—"

"Or kneeling to repeat prayers with rosary beads, or sitting in Buddhist meditation. I think I get it. It still sounds weird."

"Yes, it is weird. But I also think it's very impressive."

"I guess it's no weirder than doing anything else. I mean, what's the point of walking for three weeks through the Himalayas?"

"Riiight," he said with a gratified nod, as if pleased to be understood.

Leaving the sadhu and Gunther behind, I wandered into the outer courtyard with Ron. There stood a stone wall with 108 spigots shaped like the heads of boars, all pouring water from their mouths. Hence the name *Chumig Gyatsa*, "A Hundred Waters." The water originates from a mountain spring. According to tradition: once upon a time, a guru came here with 84 siddhas, holy men with special powers. Each siddha made a hole in the ground with a stick, and water appeared in all eighty-four holes. Today, it's considered a blessing to bathe underneath all 108 of the fountains fed by the holy spring.

When we entered, a woman wearing a bathing sari was standing at one end of the wall, steeling herself for the shock of cold water. She then rushed along the wall with mincing steps, passing under every spout, shivering. At the end she turned my way, and when our eyes met we both laughed. As she bent over to wring the icy water from her long dark hair, Ron and I moved on in search of the other element that makes Muktinath holy: fire.

At the Temple of Jwala Mai, the Temple of Miraculous Fire, there burns an "eternal" flame. The flame is fed by a natural gas source in the mountain, and it floats atop the spring at a place where the water rises through the earth. That flame, combined with the spring, is what makes Muktinath so uniquely holy, because it combines all four sacred elements: earth, water, air, and fire.

We asked several people where we could find the fire, but some didn't understand what we were talking about, and others said it wasn't possible to see the sacred flame. It became clear that our problem was the language barrier. I felt a stab of regret, knowing that language is a key to culture and I was standing at a locked door.

Ron and I gave up on finding the miraculous fire. As we started to leave, I spotted a long procession of mani walls lined with prayer wheels. I told him to go on without me, while I stayed to spin the wheels. When I reached the end, I spotted a plain, whitewashed building inside a courtyard. Just as I decided there was nothing much to the place, a young woman sitting on the balcony of another structure told me to step inside the unremarkable building. So I opened the door and walked in.

It took my eyes a moment to adjust to the darkness. The nearly empty room was just as humble inside as out. Several candles burned before an altar. A few fresh candles sat nearby, so I donated a coin and lit one. As I stared at the flames and tried to let my mind go, the young woman from the balcony entered. She pointed out a box near the floor, just under the altar. Its opening was covered with a mesh screen. She indicated I should look inside. And there it was: a pale blue flame hovering above unseen shadows.

In response to my excited spluttering, the woman verified that I was, indeed, looking at the holy fire that "never goes out." Like the men who expected the Holy Grail to be made of gold and precious jewels, Ron and I had made the mistake of trying to find the flame in a place of auspicious appearance. Now that I'd found it, I was both awed and amused. Awed because, well, here it was, the thing all these Hindus and Buddhists trudged hundreds and thousands of miles to see. Amused because, as I told the group when I caught up with them, "It looked about as awe-inspiring as a pilot light for a gas stove. The Eternal Pilot Light of Muktinath."

Unlike a climb up Mount Everest, a trek around the Annapurna Circuit does not lead to a single, ultimate destination, but instead takes people in a circle. In a circle, beginning, middle, and end are arbitrary designations. We merely pass through various points and let them mean whatever we want. Even if we want to forget that it's not about the destination but the journey, the circle won't let us. Whether we're on a spiritual quest or simply crave new experiences, here we discover that everything we seek is only part of a journey without end.

POKHARA, NEPAL

After eighteen days, today all of us were ready to quit walking, maybe for the rest of our lives. So, with dogged purpose, we booked downhill toward Birethanti, a nearly 1700-meter (5600-foot) plummet in altitude in just four hours.

The terrain was radically different from everything we'd seen since the first day. It was a superfluity of tropical madness: Tarzan jungle, monumental trees, and careless mosses, all bisected and re-bisected by waterfalls. The forest hemmed us in like a shadowy, wet, green cocoon.

Then came the extreme downhill push. The pull of gravity was intense. My left foot twisted out from under me no fewer than four times, wrenching my ankle until I feared one more twist would sprain it. A Spanish trekker came by and walked backwards for a few steps, just for a change in the muscle strain.

"*Muchas escaleras!*" he said, grinning up at us.

"What did he say?" Gunther asked me.

"Many stairs."

Lucy and I soon fell far behind the group . When we reached Birethanti, she was like a horse that's smelled the barn, swinging her walking poles like tiny galloping hooves, clack-clack-clack-clack. As I chased Lucy down the long cobblestone street, the large village of Birethanti flew past me in a blur of cookie-cutter stone houses, cafés, and souvenir shops.

We found the gang waiting for us at a café above the river. Our final stop. There were uncontainable grins and irrepressible laughter and a flurry of congratulations. "You did it, Cara!" Nat said, slapping me on the back so hard I almost tripped.

Gunther sat on a bench nursing his ankle. The thing I'd feared would happen to me had happened to him: he'd fallen on the unforgiving rock stairs and sprained his ankle. It was already swollen. I offered him the instant cold pack I carried in my first aid kit, but he turned it down, insisting the pain wasn't that bad. He wasn't convincing. As we rushed to catch the bus on the edge of town, Gunther limped to keep up.

At its edge, the pretty town of Birethanti unraveled like the ends of a cheaply made skirt, giving way to pitiful hovels made of wood, tin, and paper. Women wearing stained dresses and long hair-scarves held babies with wide, staring, liquid brown eyes.

A stairway up a dirt slope led to the bus stop. As I climbed the steps, a tiny girl, maybe two years old, smiled down at the passing trekkers from the window of a wooden shack and shouted in a voice twice the size of her tiny frame: *"Namaste! Namaste! Namaste!"*

I shouted back, *"Namaste!"*

So she shouted louder, *"Namaste!"*

So I shouted louder, *"Namaste!"*

So she shouted at the top of her lungs, *"NAMASTE! NAMASTE!"*

We exchanged silly grins.

When I reached the top and saw the bus, I felt the disorientation of culture shock—experienced in reverse. It was the first motorized vehicle I'd seen since Besisahar three weeks ago. Part of me wanted to shrink back from its imposing metal and rubber, its smell of petrol and hubbub of activity.

The bus was pretty full, so about half our group climbed onto the roof. The three German girls and I squeezed inside with dozens of Nepalis, a handful of other trekkers, and a baby goat. The German girls and their packs sat wedged into the back seat, next to an old woman who was falling-down drunk. The old woman was also nursing a rattling cough, which prompted all three young women to lean as far away from her as possible, pressing together into a tighter clutch.

The smelly, crowded, coughing bus could not check our high spirits. We couldn't stop grinning at each other. Even Lucy was infected by the same exuberant cheerfulness as the rest of us. However, when she attempted to lead a sing-along, Charlie kindly browbeat her until she gave up.

Halfway through the ride the rain started, then the lightning, then the wind. The bus stopped, and the driver and his assistants hustled everyone off the roof and into the standing-room-only bus. I offered Gunther my seat, deferring to his injured foot. Ever gallant, he refused.

Nat complained, "I wish they'd let us stay up top. It's the dog's ballocks up there! I don't know what all the fuss is about. It's just a bit of rain." In response, one of the Nepalis pointed at the wall of darkness closing in on us and said two words: "Tropical storm." Those words had barely left his mouth when the storm unleashed its full force with a sudden hammer blow of thunder, a blinding flash of lightning, and a deluge of water.

★   ★   ★

It was as if the storm began to wash our trek away. When we arrived back in Pokhara the group split up. We resettled into the separate guesthouses where we had each started a solo trek three weeks ago, and showered off the last traces of our journey together. Then we gathered to celebrate at the Everest Steak House. When we arrived, we gawked at each other in dumb surprise. None of us had ever seen each other looking quite so clean, or wearing anything other than two changes of clothes. Charlie and Allie wore skirts, and I wore my Chinese batik outfit; nothing fancy, but compared to what we'd trekked in, we might as well have been wearing the latest in haute couture.

During dinner, Lucy caught my eye and nodded in Gunther's direction. He was slumped in his chair, slack-jawed and fast asleep. He'd given in and taken me up on the ice pack, though my guess was it was too late to do much good.

Nat and Ron shared a Chateaubriand for dinner, a hunk of steak so shamelessly huge it could easily have choked Shyama's entire family. Quite a switch from *daal bhat*. I thought Charlie, a dedicated vegetarian, might make a derisive comment, but she took it in stride.

I said, "I feel like I could eat a steak, but I don't dare. Do you know my stomach is actually bigger than when I started the trek?"

"Me too!" Charlie said. "I thought I could eat anything because I was getting so much exercise."

"I've *definitely* lost weight," Nat said in a girlish falsetto. "What about you, Ron?"

"Yes, I feel like a positive feather! I think I've lost just enough weight to fit into that cute little outfit in my closet."

"All right, all right," Charlie said with a crooked smile, as we all laughed.

I want to hold onto these people forever. But even if I could suspend time, all that would do is stop the very ebb and flow that brought us together. Without separation there can be no joining. After a couple of rest days in Pokhara, most of us are moving on.

After dinner, the boys walked with me part of the way back to my guest-house. When we reached their guesthouses, I gave hugs all around and we parted company. The trek was over.

Walking the final blocks alone in the dark, I turned on my flashlight. As I passed one house, I noticed a dog perched on the fence. This didn't alarm me. The dog started growling and barking. This didn't alarm me, either. I figured that he was simply guarding his owner's property, like any dog, and that as long as I didn't make eye contact he'd leave me alone. Then, in my peripheral vision, I saw his lip pull back in an increasing snarl. Behind him on the lawn, another dog joined the chorus. Suddenly the dog on the fence leapt off, the other dog fast behind. Both charged straight for me.

I kept walking, a litany repeating in my head, "Don't run, don't run, dontrundontrundontrun!" I hoped they were bluffing, and I thought running would only make me appear more like prey, encouraging an attack. But in an instant they were at my heels, showing no signs of slowing. When the lead dog was close enough to take a chunk out of my leg, I whirled around and, without forethought, thrust my flashlight in his face and shouted: "Stop right there!"

And they did.

Although I walked back to my guesthouse with a pounding heart, a small self-satisfied smile began to assert itself on my face. In the guesthouse courtyard, I brushed my teeth at the outdoor basin. A small mirror hung above the basin, but I didn't bother to look. For the first time, I didn't feel the need. I just shook the water from my toothbrush and went up to my room, where I fell asleep to the scuttling sound of rats on the roof.

I'm still a Western woman, and I'll never feel completely at home in the East. But I no longer feel lost. I only hope my new internal compass still works when I point it west.

FLYPAPER FOR FREAKS

As my ferry sailed into the crater of Santorini Volcano, I felt the awe of the tiny and insignificant when faced with unfathomable power. The crater was created in about 1650 B.C. by the deadliest volcanic eruption in human history.

Before the eruption, the volcano rose from the green and purple peace of the Aegean Sea in a single hill known as Round Island. Then the mountain exploded, spewing some seven cubic miles of molten rock from its magma chamber and creating a column of ash up to twenty-three miles high. Either moments or years later, the center of the island collapsed and filled with water, setting off at least one deadly tsunami. That titanic wave likely destroyed the entire Minoan civilization. The capacious bowl of water that remains is about thirty-two square miles wide and one or two thousand feet deep.

Today, three slender islands draw a sketchy circle around the caldera and the steamy, dark cone at its center. The longest cliff, shaped like a crescent moon, is the main island, known locally as Thira. Its cliff-side is striated in reds and yellows and earth's other searing colors. Its top is crowned with breezy whitewash and flowers and tourists. In the main village of Fira, a slender tangle of footpaths teeters about 250 meters (some 800 feet) above the abyss, seducing visitors with an Olympian view of the caldron where Vulcan lies hidden beneath the sea.

To save money, I decided not to stay in Fira, instead heading to the beachside town of Perissa, an hour bus ride away. Perissa's main draw is an attractive but scalding black sand beach. I found a cheap room just off the beach and immediately fell into a deep sleep, though the sun was high. It was full dark when I was awakened by the persistent drone of motorbikes passing on the street below and the insistent bass line of bad disco blasting from the bar next door.

Ravenous, I walked to a nearby restaurant, the Bella Aurora. I had no idea what time it was. So I was surprised when, before I finished my moussaka, the young Australian waitress began turning chairs upside down on the tables around me, imprisoning me with chair legs. Through those legs, I glimpsed the waitress sitting at a table with the owner and another man, all of them eating spaghetti. Not wanting to keep the staff waiting, I rose to slink out.

"Don't worry, ah?" the owner called out. "Please! Sit, sit! Relax! We will be here for a while and there's no rush, ah?" He waved his hands at me and spoke in a gruff manner that would have frightened me when I first arrived in this country two weeks ago. Now I realize Greeks use nearly the same tone to express friendliness as they do for anger. As it was, I felt intimidated enough to sit back down, lest I face his friendly wrath.

I started writing in my journal. A few minutes later the second man, the owner's uncle, came over to my table. He was in his early fifties, but looked much older with unkempt gray hair, the deeply creased face of hard living, and a slight stoop to his walk. He sat across from me uninvited, and as he opened his mouth to speak several black teeth flashed into view.

Without preamble, he said, "There are two things I like to see: a young woman putting on makeup and a young woman writing in her diary."

I smiled, but said nothing. While I like meeting new people, Greece had taught me to be on my guard against sexual harassment.

"So, what do you write in your diary?"

I told him I was writing about my trip. I tried to be vague, but he questioned me until I gave away enough information for him to understand I was on an extensive journey. This prompted him to tell me about his own travels: he was born in Greece, used to live in Canada, currently lives in Rome, has traveled in the U.S. and Europe, and visited Nepal ten years ago. He gave me tips on things to see when I reach Rome. His name was Zephyros.

"But you call me Zeph. This is what my friends call me, right Susie?"

The Aussie waitress looked up from her pasta and laughed. "Yes, Uncle Zeph." To me she said, "Be careful with him . . . No, don't worry—he's a perfect gentleman, but he'll talk your ear off."

This was true, but not in an annoying way. Finding a fellow wanderer in an unfamiliar place felt like drifting alone in uncharted waters and find-ing the only castaway who spoke my language—not English, but the true language of my secret self. Zeph and I talked until two a.m., long after the place was locked and empty. On her way out, Susie admonished him to see me back to my hotel.

After sharing our stories, Zeph observed, "You are someone who becomes lost among familiar things and can only find your way among unfamiliar things. I know. I have felt this way all my life. It is difficult for people like us to say this place is home or that place is home. It is difficult to stay in one place. You always make new friends, yet it is lonely."

"Exactly. But the loneliness can be beautiful, in its own way."

"Just be careful or you may wind up alone, like me. Then this loneliness will not seem so beautiful. I have seen many amazing things, but that is not enough. You must have someone to see those things with you. If you cannot stop wandering, then you must find someone who will wander with you."

"My boyfriend's meeting me in Italy."

"Why did he not come with you?"

"He said he couldn't afford it."

"Ah, but this is no excuse. If he loves you, it should not be so easy to let you go away without him."

"I think he regrets that now. That's why he's coming."

"Do you love him?"

"Yes."

"Does he love you?"

"Yes . . ."

"Then you should get married! What are you waiting for?"

"I don't know. For a while I thought I loved someone else. But I was wrong."

"When he comes to Italy, you tell him you were wrong and you marry him. Then you can wander *together*."

"What if he doesn't want to get married?"

"Then you tell him 'get lost!'" He gave me a knowing smile. "Don't worry, he will marry you. A man never wants to get married. It is the woman who decides."

"But will marriage make a difference? Sean likes to repeat this saying that 'everyone sleeps alone.' Do you know what I mean?"

"Yes, of course, I see. But when a man and a woman are in love, sometimes we find someone who understands our loneliness, and there are moments when you are like one person. You can live much life in these moments."

"Maybe. To me, being with Sean has always felt like being at home. So, if I marry him, he'll become my home, and maybe I won't feel the need to wander anymore."

"No, I don't think so," Zeph said. "People like you and me, rarely do we change."

* * *

When I emailed Sean to tell him I was *relaxing* on the islands, he wrote back to accuse me: *I don't believe it. You'll never relax, Cara. That's not you.* I think he finds comfort in the idea that some things about me won't ever change. Maybe he's right, about my never relaxing: I feel lost when I don't have at least the illusion of a purpose.

So although this is the laziest part of my journey, each day I create one goal. Today the challenge was six hundred marble stairs leading from the cliff-top town of Fira to the tiny port below. I shared the stairway with hundreds of cruise ship passengers walking downhill and about fifty mules carrying tourists both uphill and downhill. The already-slick steps were slimed with mule shit, and I slipped, skidded, and swore my way to the bottom.

The mule drivers insistently called out to me, trying to sell me a mule ride. One of them refused to take no for an answer. As I rounded a switchback, the driver led his mount toward me and boxed me into a corner, repeating, "Why do you walk? It is better you ride!" I dodged to the left. He cut off my retreat. I dodged to the right. He cut me off again. All the while he insisted that I was foolish to walk in the heat. I refused to answer him, or look at him, just stood stubbornly silent in my corner until he backed off. A male tourist astride a mule gave me a sympathetic look and said, "Persistent, aren't they?"

By the time I reached the bottom, my clothes were pasted to me with sweat. I noticed a German couple swimming near the dock. It wasn't a proper beach and I didn't have a proper bathing suit. No matter—I didn't have any shame, either. I stripped down to my bra and panties and hopped in, which amused the Germans. The water was chilly but refreshed me for the climb back up the beshitted stairs in the pitiless sun.

Most people take the cable car to the top, and I hadn't seen anyone hoofing it *up* the stairs, except the mules. This time the mule drivers were even more insistent and shook their heads at my incomprehensible desire to walk. Several tourists coming down the stairs gawked at me, a few laughed, a very few smiled encouragement.

I couldn't explain to them my compulsion to complete this Sisyphean task. To me the steps represented something on which I could concentrate my attention and will, and that was enough. The steps were part of the Santorini experience, and I wanted to experience them. If I chose not to ride a mule, it was because I wanted the exercise, it was because I didn't want to shirk a challenge when I had nothing better to do, it was because I refused to pay money to men who would publicly corner me rather than let me do as I wished.

But it was draining and disgusting. With a chagrined smile, I grumbled to myself, "Six Hundred Steps Through the Shit of Santorini."

Back at the top, I lost myself in the cobblestone labyrinth of Fira. The maze of walkways was originally meant to confuse pirates. Now it just confuses tourists. I didn't mind being lost, beguiled by the virgin white buildings and promiscuous magenta bougainvillea—tiny, nattily dressed pirates who had found a way to politely plunder the village.

I came upon an Orthodox Church and the sound of a priest singing prayers lured me inside. I stood among a handful of worshippers, most of them elderly women whose black dresses and black kerchiefs made them nearly invisible in the dimness of the church. Gold icons gleamed in the darkness. The priest walked around swinging a censer on a chain, trailing white smoke, the acridly sweet smell of incense, and the gentle jingle of tiny bells. I couldn't understand what he was saying, but his singing carried me far away, to a place where I met the quiet part of myself I sometimes forget is there.

I again asked God to help me discover my purpose in life and fulfill it. A voice echoed in my mind, "Six Hundred Steps Through the Shit of Santorini." God, please tell me that's not the answer.

TURNING THIRTY-SIX YEARS OLD – SANTORINI, GREECE

Red sand is beautiful, but it burns. "Ooh, ooh, aaa, aaa, ouch!" I yelped as I ran across the beach to jump into the water, its soothing aqua a sharp contrast to the feverish red sand and scorching white cliffs of Akrotiri. Floating effortlessly on my back in the buoyant, salt-saturated sea, I remembered today was May 30, the day before my birthday.

I've reached that awkward age when the life ahead is almost as daunting as death, when the excuse, "I'm still young, there's plenty of time to decide," becomes less and less convincing. Tomorrow I turn thirty-six.

It's been nearly nine months since I left Alaska, and I'm tired in a way I never knew I could be without a job to blame. But like a whiny kid up past her bedtime, I don't want to stop. There's still so much to see. Besides, I have no real home to return to. All I know is that I carry with me a ticket for a flight from London to New York in August, which I'll probably change to September. Sometimes I try to see past that, but I stop myself before anything comes to me. I'm just not ready to look.

At sunset, I wandered to Perissa's black sand beach where a full moon emerged blood red from a sea the color of lava. On the sand in front of one of the popular beach bars, a lone man fed tree branches into a fledgling bonfire.

After sunset, I started to walk back to my hotel but ran into Uncle Zeph at the Bella Aurora. "Ah, so there you are!" he called through the open door. "Why have you not come back to see us?" I sauntered over and sat to talk with him while he drank a couple of glasses of wine.

Slowly, a noisy crowd gathered around the nearby bonfire. Two young men filled their mouths with beer, flicked their lighters, and spit impressive jets of flame into the night. As each new flash burst from the young firedrakes, several dogs barked wildly.

I asked Zeph, "Is it like this all the time?"

"No, it's the Full Moon Party. They have it every month. Would you like to go over there and have a drink?"

"Why not?" I smiled and shrugged. "At midnight it'll be my birthday."

"It is your birthday?" he shouted. "Then you must let me buy!"

We walked to the open-air bar, where Zeph was the oldest patron in a place hopping with young tourists and blaring with young music. In spite of his fish-out-of-water appearance, he was obviously a regular; the bartender and cocktail waitresses knew him by name. We sat at the bar, and I got tipsy on two glasses of wine while Zeph plowed through two more drinks. He'd switched to vodka on the rocks.

He asked me whether I was engaged yet.

"You mean since we talked two days ago? No. How about you?"

"Me? Nooo!" he said. "I have been married twice already. A gypsy for-tune-teller once told me I would have three wives, but I don't believe in that stuff. And I don't want another wife. You tell me one thing I can-not do by myself!"

I thought of several smart-aleck answers, including the fact that this seemed a hypocritical position to take given his advice the other night, but I kept those thoughts to myself. Instead, I watched the people gath-ered around the bonfire, whooping and hollering like victorious warriors. Without taking my eyes off them, I said, "Did you ever notice that even if you're part of a group, *you* are always the *one* person you can never see in the scene? I mean, you never really see yourself, your whole self, except in a mirror. You can see all the people around you, but never you. No wonder so many people never feel like they belong. They can't see the evidence. It's like . . . the opposite of solipsism."

"I do not know this word, but for your birthday you must give yourself a present: to not think so hard. Sometimes it is time for asking questions, sometimes life should just be enjoyed."

"You're right," I said, and raised my glass to his. "Yassas!" We both shouted the traditional Greek toast and tossed back our drinks.

He asked me if I'd like another.

"No, thank you. I've already had enough."

"You don't like to drink?"

"Not much. I used to hang around people who drank all the time, and some of their problems had a bad effect on me. So I don't like to drink too much."

"I don't drink very much either. Some people, they drink a lot. But I always limit my number of drinks," he said. Then he ordered another. Maybe five is his limit.

At about two a.m. I took my leave of Zeph. He gave me a fatherly kiss goodbye on both cheeks.

I took off my shoes and walked down the beach until the shouts of the partiers fell to a distant murmur. The full moon, now radiant white, laid a long finger of silver light from the horizon to the surf, pointing to the place where I stood alone. "Fuck introspection!" I shouted at the moon, as my toes curled like tiny question marks in the nighttime coolness of the sand.

* * *

Last night I dreamt about Chance again. In the dream, he held me in his arms and promised he'd never again let me go. I felt a confusing mix of passion and sorrow. Then I heard Autumn, the other woman, in the next room laughing. Overcome by a terrifying feeling of suffocation, I jolted myself awake.

Many nights on this journey, I've fought my way to Morpheus through a miasma of loss and regret. Chance's face often floats through these end-of-day vapors, which morph into bad dreams. I've worried that such dreams meant I was still in love with him. But I'm starting to think that's not it. This wasn't a dream; it was a nightmare. The reason I keep thinking about him isn't that I still love him: it's that I still suffer from the cruelty he inflicted, the love I wasted, and the fear that no amount of experience can ever protect an open heart.

Then again, maybe I *am* still in love, with the dream of who I believed he could be, instead of who he really was when he was with me. It's not love that hurts, it's loving people in parts, because there are some pieces we never want to throw away, even when the rest must go.

THE LAST FRONTIER
THIRTY-FOUR YEARS OLD

The second time I broke up with Sean I wasn't planning to go back to Chance again. I just wanted to forestall the ineluctable pain of another relationship with another guy who didn't want what I wanted. I wanted a commitment, Sean didn't. Put more bluntly: I was falling in love, he wasn't.

One day, I asked him to come over to my apartment after his aikido class to "talk about something." I planned to break it off then. A few hours before Sean and I were scheduled to meet, Chance invited me to meet him for dinner, also to "talk about something."

At dinner, Chance told me he wanted to thank me. He said his counselor had helped him a lot. "I owe that to you, because I never would've gone to counseling if you hadn't suggested it. I realize you were right: a lot of the problems we had were probably because of my drinking."

We talked about our relationship, what went wrong, what went right, what we missed. He missed the way I let toothpaste suds run down my arm when I brushed my teeth and the way I ran out of a room when I got embarrassed. I missed the way he used to grab my hand and lead me around his condo to show off the improvements he built—doing chin-ups from his shelves to prove how sturdy they were. We didn't decide to reconcile, but agreed to talk again soon.

After dinner, I drove home for my dreaded appointment with Sean.

When he showed up, he was obviously nervous. "I think I know why I'm here. You never invite me to your place."

"I thought it would be easier to talk here. At your place we always end up making love." I explained that our relationship wasn't enough for me anymore, that I needed to be free to find someone who could offer me more than just friendship with sex.

He looked at his hands. When he spoke, his voice shook, "I know this is happening because I held back. But I do love you, Cara. I tried to stick to what we said: have an affair, no attachments. I tried to have sex without falling in love. But I couldn't."

Before I could absorb this new information, the phone rang. I debated letting it keep ringing, but I knew who it was. I didn't want to sit on the couch with Sean while we both listened to my ex-boyfriend leave some sweet-talking message on the answering machine. Worse, I feared if I didn't answer, Chance might decide to show up at my door. So I picked up the phone.

Chance said he was just calling to tell me how much he'd enjoyed dinner and how hopeful he was about working things out. I kept my responses vague, things like, "That's nice, but let's not get ahead of ourselves."

I glanced nervously at Sean. I could feel the comedy of errors rushing toward me, and I wasn't laughing. Sean paced the room, acting as if he'd developed a sudden interest in the artwork on my walls. He soon gave up the pretense at art appreciation, shuffled into the bathroom, and shut the door.

Chance's voice buzzed enthusiasm in my ear, but I was distracted by the dawning realization that just a moment ago, for the first time, Sean had told me he loved me. In the sane life I sometimes imagined for myself, I would have evaluated my feelings while gazing into the eyes of the man who'd just declared his love, instead of listening to my ex talk about . . . whatever the hell he was talking about . . . while trying to calculate which guy was worth the risk.

Then I realized Chance had fallen silent. "Cara . . . is someone else there?"

"Hmm? What? Why?"

"Is someone else there?"

I looked at the closed bathroom door and considered my answer: Well, Sean would be gone soon enough, since I was breaking up with him, and it wasn't Chance's business at this point anyway. I knew if I admitted someone was with me, Chance would throw a fit. So I said, "No, no one's here."

"You sound funny . . ."

"That's probably because this subject makes me uncomfortable. We already talked at dinner. Let's not spoil the progress we made. Let's just take some time to think things over."

"Okay. You're probably right. I'll talk to you later."

When I hung up, I began to panic. Chance was suspicious, and I was gripped with the conviction that he must be on his way to my apartment to spy on me.

Sean emerged from the bathroom but said nothing. Our eyes refused to meet.

"I told you I still talk to him," I said, and immediately felt contrite. "I'm sorry. Maybe we should talk this over. You know . . . we've always been more comfortable at your place. Let's go over there and talk."

Either ignoring or not understanding my transparent attempts to flee my apartment, Sean said, "No, I don't want to go to my place. Here is just fine. Besides, what else is there to say?"

"I don't know. You told me you loved me. You never said that before."

"I haven't had much chance. You've always been in love with someone else."

"So have you," I accused.

This was perhaps the wrong subject to broach if my object was to wrap this up in the fifteen minutes it would take Chance to drive from his place to mine. As Sean and I talked, I repeatedly leapt up to pace the room, casting surreptitious glances out the window, fearful of spotting a familiar SUV. I sensed my ex-lover charging toward me like a tsunami. The anxiety was so intense it became impossible to continue a coherent discussion about the relationship in front of me, which now seemed worth saving.

"I don't know what to do," I said. "You're my best friend."

"But you don't love me."

"I *do* love you." I was only slightly surprised by my feelings. I was more surprised by how painful it was to admit them.

"But you loved him first. I get it."

"Tell me you're not still in love with Heather," I said, with a bitterness I hadn't known I felt. "You talk about her all the time. Tell me you wouldn't want to get back together with her if she showed up."

"Cara, that's *never* going to happen. But that's not the issue. You just need someone who can make you happy, and I don't think I can do that. I can be a real dick. You just haven't had a chance to find out yet. You're probably making the right choice."

"I don't even think Chance and I are going to get back together. I'm just confused and I need time to think." I walked over to the window again.

"Why do you keep going to the window? You think he's going to show up?"

"I don't know. Maybe."

"Are you going to be okay?" By this he clearly meant to ask whether I was in danger.

"Yeah."

"I'm going to go then."

"But . . ."

"Look, we can still talk later. But I'm going to cry now and I don't want to do that in front of you. You've got to let me go."

As I watched him drive away, I exhaled in relief that we'd gotten through it all without Chance showing up. Then the phone rang again. It was Chance calling from his cell phone; I could hear his car humming in the background.

"Cara, why'd you lie to me?" he asked, in that quiet but trembling voice that everyone knows men use before they chop entire families into bite-size pieces with a meat cleaver.

"I was going to tell you—" was all I managed to squeak, before he cut me off.

"You lying little slut. I knew someone was there. I just had to see for myself."

"You never let me explain."

"Fine. Explain."

"I invited him here to break up with him. I figured there was no point telling you he was here, because I was breaking up with him anyway, and because I knew you'd react like this."

"You have an explanation for everything. You think all that matters is that you had good reasons. You never think about how it makes me feel. All that bullshit you gave me about not wanting to 'get ahead of ourselves'—for a minute I thought, 'Oh, she's so wise.' *But you're just another fucking cunt!*"

In that moment, I found the eye of the storm and felt instantly immersed in a deep calm. My voice softened. "What did you call me?"

"I called you a fucking cunt."

"So let me see if I understand you: you think I'm a 'fucking cunt'?" I didn't flinch from speaking the odious words, hoping he'd see them for the ugly emotional weapons they were.

But all he said was, "That's right."

"A 'fucking cunt'? Are you sure those are the words you want to use to describe me?"

"Yup."

I repeated the phrase until it sounded silly: fucking cunt . . . fucking cunt . . . fucking cunt. Then I said, "And you don't think you'll regret it later?"

"No way."

"I see," I said, and quietly hung up.

He called back and started yelling. I hung up again. He called again and, in a voice so reasonable it made me twitch, said, "Cara, let's not argue anymore. I think we should just be friends."

I screamed into the phone, "I don't want to be your friend! My friends don't treat me this way! I can't take this anymore! Leave me alone! Leave-me-alone! Leavemealone!" I was lying on the floor, and I ended each exclamation by kicking the wall for emphasis. On the third kick, my foot disappeared in a puff of plaster. I yanked it back with a yelp of surprise.

"Cara? Are you okay?"

I spoke through clenched teeth, "Don't . . . *ever* . . . call me or come over here again."

After I hung up the third time, there was a long and blessed silence as I studied the hole my foot had made.

The next time the phone rang it was Sean. He said Chance called him.

"Oh my God! This is just too much," I said. "I'm so sorry. What happened?"

"Nothing. Really. He told me you were upset and said I should call to make sure you were okay."

"That manipulative snake," I said. "Can't you see what he's doing?"

"Of course. I'm not stupid, Cara. That's why I wanted to make sure you were okay."

"I'm fine." I took a breath and told him everything that had happened.

An astonished gust of breath crackled through the phone. "So now he's *stalking* you?"

"Technically, I don't think it qualifies as stalking."

"Cara, I think you should stay away from him."

"So do I. I'm so sorry I got you into this."

"There's nothing to be sorry about. I knew what I was getting into. You've always been honest with me. I know you're just a human being who's doing the best she can. You have a good heart, even if he can't see that."

"You think so? I kicked a hole in my wall."

"You did? Awesome."

"I'm serious," I said, trying not to laugh.

"Cara, have you ever seen those three holes in the wall at my apartment? Where do you think those came from? I practically broke my hand putting my fist in the wall. I mean, it's not the smartest thing you can do, but you didn't hurt anybody did you?"

"No."

"And your hand's okay?"

"It was my foot," I said, laughing.

As usual he made me feel better, mostly because he knew everything about me, understood, forgave, and loved me anyway. In my life before Alaska, I'd often been teased about being a Miss Goody Two-Shoes, Little Mary Sunshine, Pollyanna, or any number of irksomely nice girls. That night, I knew I could no longer play any of those roles. I'd finally discovered what it was like to do everything absolutely wrong. Maybe I had to do something unforgivable and be forgiven for it, before I could understand the true nature of love.

Although Sean still loved me, our relationship remained a casualty of my war with Chance. The war was over, but the wounds ran deep. I told Sean I couldn't see him for a while. Speaking psychobabble so perfectly that even I couldn't detect my lack of conviction, I explained, "I need time to just be with myself and no one else. If we've really got something here, surely it can wait a month or so?"

I knew he would wait. He'd confessed many times that he was the type who felt attracted to whatever seemed most difficult to obtain. Convincing him to wait for me would be the easy part. The difficult part, once he had me, would be convincing him I was still hard to get.

Chance did what I asked and left me in peace. He didn't try to see me again—although I did see *him*, a few months later when I was covering a news story. A construction worker was crushed when a piece of equipment fell on him. When I arrived, a paramedic was on his knees trying to revive the victim. The paramedic was Chance. One of the victim's friends yelled at the photographer and me for videotaping the rescue effort: he called us "vultures." But Chance never saw me. He was completely focused on the unresponsive body before him.

The man died. It wasn't Chance's fault; the guy was dead when medics arrived. But Chance wouldn't give up until he had to. He was always sober and professional on the job, and at his best in a crisis. He truly was a hero. Just not mine.

Without a man in my life, at least for the moment, I took the next step in my personal sexual revolution: I patched the hole in the apartment wall by myself. Performing a home repair with actual tools, without male assistance or advice, might have been a simple act of self-sufficiency, but it was also a start at repairing my damaged self-esteem. I could fix a wall; maybe, just maybe, I could fix myself.

FLYPAPER FOR FREAKS
THIRTY-SIX YEARS OLD—XANIA, CRETE

It seems to me a woman who travels alone is automatically an object of suspicion. What could she possibly be up to, *all by herself?* A woman who travels alone must be looking for trouble, or at least . . . a man.

One afternoon in the National Garden in Athens, I stopped at a long and lovely arbor of overarching vines, sat on a bench in the green tunnel of sun-freckled shade, and began writing in my journal. I was lost in my own world until I looked up to see a man in the shrubbery across from me, staring directly into my eyes as he pulled his private weapon out of his pants and started playing with it. People continued walking up and down the path, oblivious to the sexual assault taking place on either side of them: masturbating pervert to the left, eye-rolling victim to the right. If Kaitlin were here she'd say, "Face it, you're flypaper for freaks." I sighed in disgust, closed my journal, and moved to another bench.

One day on Naxos Island, I was dozing atop my sarong on a nearly empty beach when I heard shuffling footsteps in the sand. I opened my eyes to a pair of hairy legs. I tilted my face up to a dark, bare-chested, curly-headed young Greek man with a towel draped over his arm. He gave me an oafish grin and asked, "Ameriga?"

I closed my eyes, pressed my face into my sarong and, in a voice muffled by sand, replied, "No. Canada."

"Ameriga!" he repeated, still grinning. He laid down his towel just a foot above my head, turning my sarong and his towel into a capital "T" in the sand. Then he lay down.

In disbelief, I propped myself up, pointedly looked around me at the acres of vacant sand, and turned a disgusted look at this man invading my personal space. "No!" I bellowed. "I'm not looking for a boyfriend. I have a boyfriend. Goodbye!"

"*Ameriga!*"

"No! I don't want to talk. Go away! Goodbye! Goodbye!"

"*AMERIGA!*"

I had two options left: leave or ignore him. I wasn't about to let him chase me away. So I ignored him. A few minutes later he silently picked up his towel and walked away.

Another time, I was walking along a waterfront when I ran into a Greek waiter from a café where I'd stopped earlier. A walking cliché, the barrel-chested, beer-bellied man wore a loud orange shirt open in front, a fluorescent blue tank-top underneath, and a huge gold medallion resting on a fluffy bed of Chewbacca chest hair.

"*Yassas!*" he said.

"*Yassas,*" I replied politely. I tried to keep walking, but he stepped in front of me, blocking my path, leaning so close I could smell the meat on his breath.

"Would you like to come out with me for a drink?" he asked, rubbing his chest hair and dipping his hand under his tank top. I guess this was supposed to make me weak with desire.

"No, thank you," I said, and darted around him before he could cut me off.

Such men apparently presume female travelers are sexual adventurers who would naturally find it exciting to be stalked by rapacious predators.

Today I arrived on the island of Crete, where the people have a reputation for being religious, old-fashioned, and mistrustful of foreigners. I hoped that meant I'd be left alone. So when I explored the town of Xania this afternoon, I let down my guard.

I started along the waterfront: a horseshoe with a stone fortress at one end, a lighthouse at the other, and in the middle a lineup of wish-you-were-here cafés where outdoor tables yawned with boredom as they waited for the summer crowds. As sunset approached, I wandered into the town's old neighborhoods, down narrow cobblestone walkways lined with narrow Venetian buildings. Xania still looks the part it once played as an outpost of the Venetian Empire. With peeling plaster and paint, crumbling brick and stone, colorful shutters and black iron balconies, the slender homes are dying the slow, romantic deaths of a Shakespearean drama.

I crossed paths with a tiny old woman carrying groceries. She wore a black dress and a black kerchief over white hair. Her short legs moved with nimble energy, though her progress was slow.

"*Kalispera!*" I said. ("Good evening!")

Her eyes widened with surprise. She walked up to me and patted my cheek, chuckling. "*Orea,*" she said. ("Beautiful.")

"*Efharisto.*" (Thank you)

As I continued deeper into her neighborhood, I saw more grandmothers dressed in black, sitting in kitchen doorways—knitting, chatting with neighbors, and keeping small children in line as they played in the walkways. Entranced, I sighed and relaxed my guard another notch.

"*Yassas,*" a few of the women said to me, smiling and nodding as I passed.

"*Yassas!*" I smiled and nodded back.

So it was that I thought little of making the same exchange with a pot-bellied grandfather standing at his kitchen door. Liver spots filled in the blank left behind by his receding hairline.

"Where you from, my dear?" His tone labeled him a perfect gentleman.

"Alaska."

"Ah, an American. Welcome to *Creta*. You are in a hurry?"

"Why?"

"If you are not in a hurry, maybe you will like to come in to drink coffee with my family?"

As I considered his question, I cautiously surveyed the street: an old lady sitting across the way nodded in my direction, another woman down the street talked to a male neighbor. The neighborhood seemed safe enough, and I was excited at the prospect of enjoying the hospitality of a Greek family in their home, so I said, "Thank you. I'd be honored."

"You're welcome, my dear."

He introduced himself as Constantino, "but you may call me Costas, my dear." Costas shook my hand, opened his kitchen door, and bowed as he made a sweeping invitation with his arm, indicating I should precede him inside. He guided me through a messy kitchen, then upstairs through two stories of cheerful clutter, to the roof where he had a small garden of flowers and herbs. I saw no family members along the way.

"It's a beautiful garden," I said.

"Thank you, my dear." He said "my dear" a lot. "You would like a soda?"

"No, thank you. I'll wait to take coffee with your family."

"They will be here soon. Until then you must have a soda." He scurried downstairs and returned with a soda. Then he went into the next room and returned with three coffee table books. "Here are beautiful pictures of my country. You look. I've been fishing and I need to wash. I will return." He left, and a moment later I heard a shower running inside.

Suspicious, I decided to leave while he was in the shower. But first, I couldn't resist walking to the edge of the roof for a quick peek at the view. A patch of ocean blue peered at me from a distance. On the street below, several more neighbors arrived as the workday ended, gathering in small clutches of casual conversation. This lent credence to his story that his family would arrive soon, so I relaxed and sat down.

A few minutes later he returned, his damp hair slicked back, a dollop of brown hair grease still on the edge of his hand—the quivering ooze slid off as he reached into a shelf and pulled out two scrap albums. He showed me old photos and newspaper clippings from the sixties and seventies, all featuring him, while he explained in halting English that he used to be an important politician. After listening to a rambling, incomprehensible discourse on Greek politics, I deliberately asked him to tell me about his family.

He spoke vaguely of adult sons and daughters who were very accomplished and made him quite proud, but who didn't live here.

"So you live here with your wife?"

"No, I live alone. I'm about to go out to have coffee with my friends. Would you like to come?"

Annoyed at his subterfuge, I began considering how best to extricate myself from this situation: should I politely take my leave, or run down the stairs without another word? He was at least sixty-five—not a hearty sixty-five, but a rotund, out-of-shape, slow-moving sixty-five, maybe even seventy or more—and if things turned weird I could easily knock him down and out-run him. Old and alone, maybe he was just lonely for company. I decided to bow out politely. He'd said he was about to leave anyway, so I took that as my cue to move toward the stairs.

"So, you meet these friends every day?" I asked.

"Sometimes. We play cards. You know cards?"

"Yes. I also see many Greek men playing backgammon in the cafés. Do you play backgammon?"

"Excuse me?"

"Backgammon? Do you play backgammon?"

"I don't know this word."

"It's a good game."

"And you, my dear, you are a good person." He kissed both my cheeks. By Greek standards this was still within bounds.

Nonetheless, I said, "I'm sorry, I won't have time to meet your friends. I'm meeting my own friends." I couldn't resist adding, with lifted brow, "It's too bad I didn't get to have coffee with your *family*."

He didn't respond.

I was relieved when we returned to the ground-floor kitchen, where my eyes fastened on the door. It was just two feet away. Before I could reach it, he leaned over and opened the refrigerator, right next to the door, blocking my way to salvation.

His eyes scanned the refrigerator's meager contents. "Would you like anything, my dear?" he said—leering, I now thought.

"No, thank you."

"I have some very nice fruit. You must allow me to give you something. Here!" He thrust a peach in one of my hands and a pear in the other.

"Thank you," I said, staring stupidly at the fruit.

"You're welcome, my dear." He leaned forward as if to kiss me on the cheek again, but this time he managed to crash wetly into my lips.

I pulled back in dismay and looked in confusion from his face to the fruit to the door.

As I was calculating how to take him down with a simple aikido move if he tried to block my escape, he said, "You can stay here with me and sleep with me, my dear."

My face must have registered the dumbest of dumbfounded looks. "Oh . . . n-no . . . I, I cannot . . . " I stammered.

Before I could say or do anything more, he opened the kitchen door, said, "Well, thank you, my dear, have a nice holiday," grabbed me by the elbow, shoved me outside, and slammed the door in my face.

In a daze, I stumbled away, staring at the two pieces of fruit in my hands. Hoping to soothe my nerves with something sweet, I took a bite of the peach. It was hard and sour. I switched to the pear. It tasted fine, but my stomach began to sink and roll, and I felt the urge to vomit. Nauseous, I threw the fruit in the trash.

I felt like a little girl who's been attacked by the local child molester, a grandfatherly neighbor no parent would ever suspect. I'd been thrown off my guard by the friendly neighbors and by my memory of the guileless, avuncular kindness of Zeph. But it's not as if Costas were the first sex-addled skirt-chaser I'd ever encountered, only the oldest. I had recognized the risk. It's just that keeping my guard up is fatiguing and the temptation of apparent kindness is great.

I suppose any woman who travels alone is flypaper for freaks. Which makes me even more eager to see Sean, not only because he's not a freak, but also because his presence by my side might keep them away—and because I'm hungry for a taste of kindness that I know is real.

EN ROUTE FROM PATRAS, GREECE TO BRINDISI, ITALY

I was supposed to leave Greece yesterday and head to Rome to meet Sean. But the day before that I endured a fourteen-hour nightmare of buses and trains, missed connections and ridiculous layovers just to get to Olympia for the express purpose of visiting the site of the original Olympic Games.

When I arrived I discovered the site would be closed until the next day—today. I refused to leave without seeing the Olympic Ruins. I'd worked so hard to get there and I might never get another chance. So I sent Sean an e-mail saying I'd arrive in Rome a day late.

This morning, I visited the Olympic Ruins with an Englishwoman from my hostel. We felt fortunate to see the site, considering it was once off-limits to people like us: women, that is. "Get this," Julie said, referring to her guidebook, "women were not only forbidden to participate in the original Olympic Games, they were not even allowed to watch. It says here, 'Women who tried to sneak in to see the games used to be thrown from a nearby rock.'" The greatest pleasure our day afforded was guessing which rock was used for this misogynistic tradition.

"Maybe that one?" Julie suggested.

"No, not big enough. They'd only break an arm or a leg."

"Maybe that was the idea."

"Nah, I'm sure they meant to kill 'em."

It took a lot of imagination to make the site interesting. We spent fifteen confounding minutes just trying to figure out how the perfect little squares and circles on my tour map related to the tumbled, crumbled rocks and columns scattered around us. The gymnasium and the wrestling school, the Temples to Zeus and Hera: they were all in utter . . . well . . . ruins.

Among the sights we could find, our favorite was the one with no columns, walls, or foundations, ruined or otherwise. It was little more than an arched entry, leading to a dirt field surrounded by grassy slopes. This was the stadium where the Ancient Greeks held the first Olympic footrace: the 200-yard dash, known as a *stadium*. For more than three hundred years the *stadium* was the only athletic event at the Olympics. The starting and finish lines are still there: two long lines of stone embedded in the dirt. We giggled as several tourists sprinted down the track.

"It's much too hot to bother," I said, as if I were above such ridiculous behavior. However, I did ask Julie to take a photo of me posed in the "ready" position at the starting line.

"It's best you don't run," Julie said. "You wouldn't want to be thrown from a rock."

She was right, about it being best I didn't run. I needed to save my strength for the Olympian challenge to come. I didn't know it, but I was about to run an unexpected footrace.

* * *

I left Olympia yesterday afternoon, taking a bus and a train to the port town of Patras. From Patras, I planned to catch the overnight ferry to Brindisi, Italy, and from there a train to Rome. But when I arrived at a travel agency in Patras, a man informed me, rather rudely I thought, that I was two hours late for the last ferry to Italy. My eyes filled with tears. This might seem an overreaction, but my delay at the Olympic Ruins had already pushed my thirteen days with Sean down to twelve. Missing the ferry would knock that down to eleven.

"But I called ahead and they told me the ferry to Brindisi leaves at ten," I said.

"That's every second day," the travel agent said with a pompous show of indifference. "*Tomorrow* there is a ferry at ten."

"Is there no other ferry to Brindisi tonight?"

"No. There is one, but it's leaving now."

"Maybe I could still make it."

"No. There are procedures. There is paperwork. You will never make it. That ferry leaves now, and it is never late."

Dejected, I sank into the nearest chair. "Are there any other options?"

He shrugged in that now-familiar Greek way: shoulders near the ears, elbows akimbo, hands palms up, lips pressed into a grimace. The Greek shrug has dozens of meanings based on the shape of the grimace and how emphatic the gesture. It can be used to show indifference, acceptance, confusion, anger, disdain . . . This guy was giving me the disdainful one.

"Thank you," I said stonily, and walked out.

After nine months of traveling, I've learned never to trust anyone who says, "It's not possible." I walked a few doors down to the next travel agency and straight toward the first person who smiled at me. A woman. I wiped all traces of desperation from my face, figuring the key was to calmly declare what I wanted as if it were the simplest of requests.

"May I help you?"

"Yes, I'd like to take the next ferry to Brindisi," I said, smiling serenely.

"Tonight?" she asked.

"Tonight," I echoed.

She made a quick phone call, hung up, and explained, rapid-fire, that I might be able to catch the last ferry if I hurried. "But you must buy your ticket quickly!"

"How much?"

"Ten thousand drachma."

I slapped ten thousand drachma on the counter. She slapped down a form to fill out. I slapped down my passport. Then, with the speed of a stock show auctioneer, she gave me complicated directions to the ferry, which I rattled back verbatim: "Left out the front door, to the train station, through the gate to the dock, turn left, go just past the duty free shop to the port police, give them this ticket with the passport, then ask which way to the ferry?"

"Yes. And you must run!"

I flung on my hefty pack, rushed out the door, and started to run—possibly faster than I've ever run in my life—with a thirty-five-pound load bouncing up and down on my back. People gaped as I ran past. Sweat poured down my back and chest, my calves and lungs burned. I grew dizzy and spots jumped across my vision. This was no short sprint, and I was no Olympic athlete. I was surprised at the immensity of the ferry terminal. More than half a dozen mega-ferries and a number of other boats lined the long docks. *Don't slow down! I know it hurts, but don't slow down!* I thought. *You'll suffer even more if you miss the ferry. Sean's waiting for you.*

I flew through the port gate, darted left, wove in and out of people and port vehicles, shot past the "Duty Free" sign to the port police desk, where I waved my ticket and passport at . . . no one. The police weren't there. I rushed across the building to a small bar and shouted hysterically at the two or three bewildered people standing there, "Port police? Where are the port police? I will miss my ferry!" My eyes were wide with panic and oxygen deprivation. The middle-aged bartender said, "Port police, six hundred meters, that way!" He pointed in the direction from which I'd run. I would have to backtrack. "Drop your pack here. You'll kill yourself."

Afraid to lose the time it would take to remove the pack, I simply turned tail and kept running. My ferry sat a tantalizing fifty meters away. Workers were loading trucks into the gaping aft-end, and the line of waiting trucks was rapidly shrinking. I pumped my legs harder.

Suddenly I realized I hadn't asked the bartender what kind of sign to look for. I tried to run into the grocery store next door to ask directions again, but the glass doors wouldn't open. It must have been the exit, but I couldn't see any other doors, so I banged on the glass, startling a lineup of cashiers and customers. The closest cashier rushed toward me and opened the door.

"Port police?" I frantically waved my passport at her and pointed at the nearby ship. "I will miss my ferry!" She pointed at the building I'd just left, the building with the empty police desk and the bartender who'd told me to head the other way. "There's no one there!" I moaned.

She shook her head insistently, took me by the elbow, and guided me back to the building, where the bartender heaved a sigh and said, "The police are not here. I told her to leave her pack! It's six hundred meters *that way.*"

He then rushed past me, through the front door, and urged me to follow. He jumped on a motorbike parked just outside and started the engine. I unbuckled my pack and, without pausing, let it fall from my shoulders to the ground as I leapt onto the back of the scooter. I grabbed the bartender's waist and we took off, speeding down the docks, dodging passengers and vehicles from another boat. "I'm afraid I'll miss my ferry!" I shouted merrily and giggled, picturing how we must look.

We stopped at the little window of a small building, where a policeman started from his seat in surprise. The bartender shouted something in Greek as I handed the policeman my documents. He scribbled on them and handed them back. Then I jumped back on the bike, and we were off again at high speed. It was like a James Bond chase scene—no bad guys, but plenty of near misses, fleeing pedestrians, and brake-squealing trucks.

"What's your name?" I shouted over the bartender's shoulder.

The unfamiliar Greek syllables he shouted back got lost in the din of the motorbike's engine.

"I'll tell this story to my grandchildren!" I said.

"It is a good story," he agreed.

"I guess I'll either make my ferry or I won't."

"Don't worry. You will make it for sure."

"*Efharisto,*" I told him as we approached a small group of people gathered around my backpack.

"*Parakalo* (You're welcome)," he replied as I leapt off the bike.

I hauled on my pack with help from a couple of bystanders. I bowed deeply but quickly to the entire group, said another "*Efharisto!*" and started to run.

"*Siga! Siga!*" they shouted after me. "Slowly! Slowly!"

The cashier from the grocery store rushed forward and yelled, "I ran to the ferry to tell them you are coming. They will wait for you!"

I halted and turned an incredulous face on the small clutch of half a dozen Greek strangers on the dock. I smiled, pressed my hands together in a prayerful clasp, and shook my joined hands toward them, a supplicant thanking the saints who've interceded on her behalf: the bartender, the grocery clerk, the cop, and the dock workers. *Brava!* Thank you." I turned and walked away.

When the purser took my ticket, he said, "So you are the one they told me about."

"Yes, that's me!" I said, with a self-effacing grin.

It was 8:30 when I boarded the eight o'clock ferry, which the first agent had told me was "never late." It left five minutes later.

Still dizzy, I made my unsteady way to the Pullman deck: this ship's version of steerage, minus the partying and dancing promised by James Cameron's *Titanic*. I was one of five backpackers flopped amid dozens of uncomfortable seats. After stepping outside to watch the sunset, I showered and found a spot to sleep on the floor, wedged between chairs, my sleeping bag pulled indifferently over me. The floor was hard, but I slept even harder, exhausted from my much more than 200-yard dash through the obstacle course of the ferry terminal.

During the Ancient Olympic Games, the city-states of Ancient Greece—Athens, Sparta, Mycenae, and the rest—would declare a truce, setting aside war for peaceful competition. In the modern Olympics, that's what people call "the spirit of the Games." Some American travelers have told me they think Greeks are rude. Judging by the angry graffiti and shouts I've endured, many Greeks don't think much of Americans, either. Not to mention the perverts, pick-up artists, and psychos who've had a go at me. Yet my last thought before drifting off to sleep last night was of the small group of Greeks who, although they had nothing to gain, pulled out all the stops to help a complete stranger, a foreigner, an *American*, make her boat on time.

This morning, as the ferry runs from the Ionian Sea into the Adriatic, fleeing the sunrise, I feel as if my heart is spreading throughout my body and trying to escape through my pores. I don't know whether this stinging, tingling surge is about Italy or Sean, whether I'm excited or terrified. It's been almost a year since Sean and I last saw each other, and there's no denying I've changed, but that no longer frightens me. I guess I'm just afraid he hasn't.

Or maybe I just haven't recovered from running.

IL DOLCE FAR NIENTE

I spent thirty-eight hours working my way to Sean—ten months and thirty-eight hours—but when the train pulled into Roma Termini, I still had no idea how I felt about seeing him. I walked up and down the platform looking for him. Twice I paced up the *binario* and back again, but no Sean.

Then there he was. He later told me he'd been standing there all along, but at first he hadn't recognized me. We walked toward each other, quickly but not running. I felt excited but nervous. I also felt the irrational anxiety that even as I walked toward him we were already running out of time.

As I reached my arms around him, I registered that he'd gained a little weight. Then I registered that something was flooding through me. Love? Confusion? Adrenaline? I squeezed him tighter, then we both moved in for a clumsy kiss and half-missed each other's mouths, noses clashing, lips mashing, hitting more cheek than mouth. I want to explain how I felt at that moment, because surely that information must be important. But even once I saw him and held him, I didn't know how I felt.

I still don't know.

The farther I travel, the less certain I feel about anything. There are moments when I begin to know who I am, but those moments have yet to reveal my relationship to the people, places, and events surrounding me. Who is Sean to me? I have no idea. Maybe God just plants people in my life and I must simply accept that they're there and move toward them or away from them as the truth of who I am pushes or pulls me.

Sean spent his first night in Rome in a hotel room that cost 125,000 lire (seventy bucks), a bit rich for my shoestring budget, although we've agreed to split costs. So today we moved around the corner into an airy room in a wistful saffron paint-peeler with creaking wood floors. It cost half what Sean paid last night for a tiny bourgeois cupboard with showy sheets and shiny faucets.

"Wow, this is so much bigger," Sean said.

"And it has more character."

"So, this character, is he the one making the creaking noise?"

"Watch it, or you can forget finding out if the bed squeaks."

No, the bed doesn't squeak, but the headboard does bang against the wall. After ten months of separation, waiting, and doubt, in the end it was as easy to abandon myself with Sean as it has always been. Maybe that's because there are no secrets between us; or maybe it's because the last time either of us had sex—with a partner—was with each other, ten months ago.

"So, was it worth flying thousands of miles just to get laid?" I asked.

"Absolutely."

We lay in bed for hours, watching the afternoon sun glide across the room until day was gone, as stories of my journey tumbled onto the crumpled sheets in a silken skein of murmurs.

By the time we dressed for dinner it was 9:30 and Sean suggested we eat nearby. But I insisted we catch a bus to the lively nightlife of Trastevere. Three buses and four helpful Italians later—the people in this city really are friendly—we still had no idea where Trastevere was.

At eleven we gave up and got off our third bus, near a restaurant where the kitchen had stopped serving everything but pizza. I ordered one with flaked salmon and praised the delicate crust. Sean smiled, but said nothing. When we finished it was past midnight. Most buses had stopped running and no taxi would pick us up from an undesignated stop so late. We had to walk about two miles back to the hotel.

On the way, we passed the Roman Coliseum, glowing in its nightly bath of lights, the last remaining luminance of the Roman Empire, a colossus of forgotten pain and remembered beauty. "Isn't it beautiful?" I asked.

"Beautiful," Sean parroted in a weary voice.

"They probably thought it would last forever."

"I feel like this walk is gonna last forever."

We arrived at the hotel at 1:30. As we crawled into bed, Sean said, "You know, all the time we were walking tonight? I just wanted to sit down on a curb and cry."

I wanted to tell him it was better than all the endless, exhausting walks

I've taken *alone*. But I knew it would only make him feel worse. All I said was, "I'm sorry. You were right, we should've eaten near the hotel."

"That's okay," he said, laughing. "That's just you, Cara. You never want to take a chance of missing something."

"Maybe that's how I miss *everything*."

"No. Even when you miss something, you don't miss anything."

"I missed you."

"With a whole world of new sights and sounds to keep you occupied?"

"Especially then."

Sean fell asleep before I did, as he always has. And the night slipped away, as everything between us always has, leaving only forgotten pain and remembered beauty.

THE LAST FRONTIER
THIRTY-FOUR YEARS OLD

"So, what now?" I used to ask Sean with impish impatience. I was always excited about what we were going to do next, where we were going to go, what we were going to see. He always laughed, tickled by my desire to experience everything. He wanted to discover Alaska's treasures as much as I did. More than that, he wanted to share with me the treasures he'd already dug up and watch my reaction.

One summer day in Anchorage, we rode our bikes to a place he knew: Ship Creek. Not the busy banks near the inlet, where hundreds of people lined up for combat fishing, but further upstream at a serene little pause where salmon jumped up an old fish ladder. As fish leapt up the humble manmade falls, their scales flashed silver in the sunshine. Downstream from the watery stairway, we spotted a salmon swimming against the current without making any headway, just maintaining his position like someone running on a treadmill.

"Maybe he knows the destiny that awaits him and he's in no hurry to get there," I said. "Imagine only getting one chance to have sex and then you die."

"Do you think if they *really* knew what was going to happen to them afterward they'd turn around and go the other way?"

"Nah. Think about it. Even humans aren't smart enough to do that," I said. Then, as usual, I turned to him with a grin and asked, "So, what now?"

We hopped back on our bikes and continued on to the Coastal Trail, where we stopped to walk along a silty, rocky beach near downtown. The beach was decorated with a collection of rock cairns like a display of featureless totem poles. The cairns weren't intended to delineate a trail, but purely to give bored beachcombers something to do. Sean picked up the tiniest rock he could find and balanced it on the most precarious tower, where large boulders teetered atop small rocks, triangular stones atop oval. It looked as if each person who added to this particular pile had dreamt of a life as a circus performer.

When I pointed out my observation, Sean said, "You know, I used to want to be a magician. I bought magic kits and books, and studied and everything. I juggled, too. I actually performed in a few high school shows. I wasn't bad."

"Will you show me?"

"Sure. I'll show you when we get back to my place."

I picked up a rock to place on the cairn, but hesitated, a sly grin tugging at my lips.

Sean looked at me quizzically. "What?"

"When I see a tower like this, I have a wicked desire to kick it over."

"That's because you're an artist."

"I want to destroy something other people created, and that makes me an *artist*?"

"Of course," he said. "You want to make your own statement. The only way to create something new is to destroy something."

"Matter can neither be created nor destroyed, it can only change form."

"That's what I mean. To create a painting, you change a blank piece of paper, so it's no longer what it was. To create a sculpture, you cut stone or carve wood or dig up clay. You're destroying 'what was' to create 'what will be.'"

"Okay, so to create a relationship, what do you destroy?"

"Wow. I don't know," he said. "Your mind never stops does it?"

"No. Neither does yours." I turned to face him, arms akimbo, and said, "So, what now?"

We rode on to Kincaid Park. At the park chalet, we climbed a metal stairway to the rooftop, for a view of Cook Inlet and Mount Susitna, otherwise known as Sleeping Lady.

"That mountain does not look like a woman," I said.

"Sure it does." He traced an outline in the air with his hand. "See: she's lying on her side with her hair flowing around, and there's her breasts . . ."

"*That* does not look like breasts. Men just see breasts everywhere."

"Only if we're lucky."

The wind picked up and we heard an unearthly sound, like dozens of ghosts sighing into great silver flutes, evoking an elegiac music. We traded puzzled glances, wordlessly questioning what could be haunting us. As we descended the stairway, the sound increased. Together we stopped and looked down at the stairs, a metal lacework of diamond shapes, and realized that the music was created by wind passing through the grating. Listening, we exchanged smiles of wonder and kissed, as the mystical sound wafted around us.

I whispered, "What do you think it is that keeps people together?"

"Great sex?"

"I think what binds people together are the secrets they share."

Back at Sean's apartment, he made me dinner. After he slid two pieces of nut-encrusted halibut into the oven, he poured two glasses of wine.

I raised my glass in a toast. "To us and the music of the wind in the stairs." I took a sip, then remembered, "Hey, you were going to show me your juggling."

"I'll warn you, it's not that impressive," he said. But he disappeared into his bedroom and reappeared with a set of colorful cloth balls. He started with three, then added a fourth.

I clapped my hands with delight. "Wow! Can you do five?"

He shook his head and chuckled. "I used to. It's funny you ask. I used to practice and practice until I could juggle three. Then someone asked, 'Can you do four?' So I learned four. Then someone asked, 'Can you do five?' So I got up to five. Then someone asked, 'Can you do six?' And I realized: this'll never end. So I stopped at five."

For the moment, he stopped altogether; a strange sight outside the window had caught our eyes. As the summer night gradually insinuated itself across the sky, an orgy of clouds rapidly multiplied on the glowing horizon. We opened the window and stared out. "That looks so bizarre," Sean said. We heard a single clap of thunder and exchanged a look almost as puzzled as when we'd heard the wind in the stairs. Thunder was uncommon in Anchorage; in my eight years there, I only heard that sound about half a dozen times. A few raindrops began to fall, but the air was so dry each drop disappeared before it hit the ground.

I left the window to pour myself another glass of wine and was surprised to find the bottle empty. My brow furrowed as I calculated how quickly Sean had finished three glasses. I told myself not to jump to conclusions. But as I put the bottle down and walked back to his side to watch the reticently falling rain, I couldn't help wondering, "So, what now?"

★ ★ ★

I worked the evening shift, from 1:30 to 10:30, producing and anchoring the late news, or reporting and doing live shots. After work each night, I went to Sean's, where he waited up for me . . . at first.

One night he wasn't waiting. I opened the apartment door with a quiet click, and heard an abrupt stumble-thump as he leapt from his bed and lurched down the hall, his hair standing up in odd spikes. He had the pop-eyed look of someone trying to pretend "No, you didn't disturb me at all!"

"I fell assseep," he slurred. "I'm sssorry. I tried to zzztay awake. I wanted to give you a s-prise." He glanced behind me at the kitchen counter where several small, gooey brown blobs sat on a plate. Closer inspection revealed them to be chocolate-dipped strawberries. "You told me it waszh your favorite." He chewed his thumb like a nervous child bringing home a bad report card.

I hugged him and said, "That's so sweet. Thank you. Nobody ever did this for me before." I picked one up and popped it in my mouth.

He tried to stop me. "I don't know if you should eat 'em. I sssscrewd-emup. The shocolate was hot when I dipped it and it kind of cooked the sssstrawberries to muszh."

That was an understatement. But I felt touched that he'd remembered my favorite treat. The slurred speech I put down to the fact that he'd just woken from a dead sleep.

As time went by, he waited up less often. I frequently arrived to the sound of thunderous snores blowing down the hall from his bedroom. Alone, I sat up late, watched TV, and raided the fridge. When I threw away trash, I usually noticed one or two bottles of wine in the trashcan. I thought nothing of it. Rather, I kept thinking about it and telling myself there was nothing to it.

One night when I got off work early, Sean cooked dinner and rented a movie. When I arrived, he'd already worked his way through a bottle of wine. His kiss tasted like vinegar. At dinner, we opened another bottle. He drank most of it. Fifteen minutes into the movie, he fell asleep and started snoring. Frustrated, I elbowed him in the side, hard. He grunted, rolled over, and recommenced snoring.

But he was never mean. He never yelled. If he fell into dark, philosophical moods, that was just his personality. If he was often depressed, that was just seasonal affective disorder.

Then, one chilly evening when I was alone at his place, I decided to borrow a sweatshirt. As I pulled the sweatshirt down from his closet shelf, two tiny, airline-size liquor bottles tumbled onto the carpet. I stared at them, stunned, rooted to the spot as blood hammered my eardrums.

The next night I confronted him. I sat next to him on his couch, took his hands in mine, and said, "I have something I need to tell you." I looked straight into his eyes and forced the words out in a rush, "I'm worried because it seems to me that you drink a lot."

"And you're wondering if I'm an alcoholic?"

"Yes," I exhaled. It was such a relief to hear him say it that I was sure the answer must be no. He was always so kind. His apartment was scattered with dog-eared books on philosophy and Eastern religion. His father had gone through A.A. Sean couldn't be an alcoholic.

But he said, "I'm not going to answer that question. That's something you'll have to decide for yourself. But you know what I think? I think you need to be with someone who doesn't drink."

"But can't we talk about this? I mean, I'm not saying you are. I know a lot of people drink wine, and that doesn't make them all alcoholics."

"Okay, then tell me what you think. Like, what's too much to you?"

"Well . . . every time I come over here I see bottles of wine in the trash."

"You've been digging through my trash?!"

"No, Sean." I was growing impatient. "I throw things in the trash and the bottles are just there."

"And . . . ? It's not like I hide them or anything."

"Nooo . . . But it seems to me . . . it seems to me that two bottles of wine a night is a lot."

"What else?"

"I grabbed a sweatshirt from your closet last night and . . ."

"And you found some little bottles of alcohol?"

"Yes."

"I think you should leave."

"What?"

"Look, I don't have a problem with how much I drink, I'm not going to go to A.A., and I'm not going to quit. So if it's an issue for you, you should leave."

"Do you *want* me to go?" I began to cry.

"No, wait. You know what? You stay here and decide what you want and *I'll* go!" In a sudden fury, he grabbed his coat off the rack and headed for the door.

For the first time, it occurred to me to ask, "Have you been drinking?"

"Of course. Don't you know I'm a drunk?"

I looked at his eyes and saw the telltale lack of focus. Why hadn't I noticed before? With fierce determination, I said, "If you drive off right now, I'll call the cops and give them your plate number and tell them you're driving drunk."

He clenched his jaw. "What right do you have?"

"What right do *you* have to get in a car and endanger *my* community? I think it's only right for me to try to protect the people you might kill. I'm certainly not going to try to protect you from the consequences of your actions."

"You mean you won't be an *en-ab-ler,*" he said. "Don't feed me that twelve-step crap. I've been through it all with my dad. I know all the big words. I don't need you to explain it to me."

"Why are you doing this? Do you really want to destroy what we have?"

"It's already destroyed. I told you not to get attached to me. I told you that you just didn't know yet what an asshole I could be."

"Yeah, you were a real hero, the way you tried to save me."

Without another word, I walked out the door. As I made my way through the arctic entry, the hatred I'd long denied began to choke me. I don't know whom I hated, or what, but the feeling was palpable, as if it were a parasite that had been lying within me for years, growing undetected as it fed on my humanity without my knowledge or consent.

I'd run from Denver to Alaska, from Joe to anyone else, from Chance to Sean, all to avoid this feeling. But no matter how far I ran, I kept walking out the same door.

IL DOLCE FAR NIENTE
THIRTY-SIX YEARS OLD—ROME, ITALY

Rome and romance might sound as if they were made for each other, but that doesn't mean Rome is a good place for estranged lovers to start over. In this city of impetuous romantics and wine, Catholic rules and wine, summer heat and wine, everyone seems relaxed, and everyone seems ready to blow their tops. Sean wasn't the first to unscrew the lid on his latent anger, and neither was I.

I blame the tour guide.

Even before we met the angry American ex-pat, my trust in tour guides was not high. I suspect many of them fall into this line of work because they never got that history degree they always wanted. While there are some good guides who know their stuff, there is no archaeological site, old building, or cultural phenomenon that can be described with one unarguable explanation. I've taken tours from different guides in the same country and heard conflicting interpretations of the past. And that's with the licensed guides. With the unlicensed guides I wonder: are they making this stuff up just to mess with us, and how would we know the difference?

Some fellow travelers I met on the train to Rome arranged today's walking tour at a bargain basement price, with an *unlicensed* guide. When Sean and I arrived, our new friends were nowhere in sight. Our guide was the only person there.

Susan the Angry American Ex-pat was a fast-talking, fidgety young woman, her lank hair impatiently knotted in a plastic clip, her brow creased in permanent irritation. Susan hated us before she met us. We were cutting into her exciting life as an ex-pat. Sure, our under-the-table tour would help pay for that life, but we weren't paying enough to earn her gratitude.

"Hello. You're a little late," she accused.

Sean frowned and looked at his watch. "You said to be here at nine. It's nine-o-two."

When four more people arrived between 9:05 and 9:10, she sighed heavily and scolded them for their tardiness. Our friends still hadn't arrived; we later found out they'd been at a pub until three a.m. and were sleeping off a drunk.

"Should we wait?" Susan asked.

I gave her a measuring look. "Why don't we give 'em five minutes?" She heaved another explosive sigh, threw herself onto a bench, tapped her foot, shook her head, leapt up, and barked, "Let's just go! Now that we're running late we're already going to have to eliminate the first sight from our itinerary." It was all of 9:15. Sean and I exchanged a look and jogged to catch up with Susan, whose punishing stride quickly put her well ahead of us.

The pace never changed. On this walking tour we didn't walk, we ran, or faced the wrath of the shouting Susan: "Pick it up guys, we're running behind!"

I muttered to Sean, "She probably moved to Italy after she lost her job as a prison guard."

Oddly, even though we only spent five minutes at most sights, the fact that we were behind schedule never changed. Maybe she shouldn't have crammed fifteen sights into four hours.

At the Trevi fountain we barely had time to toss coins over our shoulders to ensure our return to Rome, before Susan barked at us to "get moving!" At the *Bocca della Verità*, or "Mouth of Truth," we each swiftly stuck our hands into the mouth of the beast to prove our honesty, while Susan looked at her watch with exaggerated patience. I whispered in Sean's ear, "Do you think that mouth only bites the hands off liars, or assholes, too?"

At Circus Maximus, she asked us to gather around. As she began to talk, she cut herself off and abruptly insisted, "Would you all *please* stand on one side of me instead of scattered around, so I don't have to keep turning my head!" Half the group scurried to obey. She then told us about Ancient Roman events at Circus Maximus, such as chariot races and feeding Christians to lions. She said the Romans used to put the heads of Christians on poles and set them on fire to use as torches for evening events. Sean whispered in my ear, "That'd be another way to keep her from having to turn her head."

As the group started moving again, I hung back and told Sean, "I just want to stick with her long enough to see the Mammertine Prison, because I don't know how to find it on my own. Then let's ditch 'er."

"Deal."

This brief exchange put us some twenty feet behind the group, so we sprinted to catch up.

Susan shot us a baleful glare. "You guys, you really have to keep up!"

"Lighten up!" Sean growled.

Mammertine Prison was where Saints Peter and Paul each spent their final days, surrounded by thirty to fifty prisoners, chained in a tiny dungeon that felt crowded with just ten tourists. Susan explained that, in addition to other tortures, the guards used to dump urine and excrement on the prisoners through an opening in the low ceiling. She showed us a place on that ceiling that's been rubbed smooth by the touch of thousands of human hands, the place where, according to legend, Peter once bumped his head.

"How did Saint Peter die?" one woman asked.

"He was crucified," Susan replied.

"Many people believe he was crucified upside down," I added, with a sardonic glance at Susan. "According to tradition, he said he didn't deserve to be crucified in the same manner as Jesus."

"What about Paul?" someone asked. "How did he die?"

Susan raised her voice so that it filled the cramped space, "Does anyone here know how Paul died?"

An American tourist frowned at her and quietly informed our group, "He was beheaded."

At the Roman Forum, Sean and I made up some excuse about being tired, and dumped Susan.

I'll give her credit for one thing: our freedom felt so much sweeter after she'd taken it away. In the afternoon, we paid for a tour of the Coliseum with a licensed guide. After that, free of Susan's clutches, we climbed up to the cheap seats to relax and neck a little. I sighed blissfully and said, "There's nothing to stir romance quite like a place where men and beasts used to kill each other in front of huge audiences for entertainment."

But Susan had infected our mood. Or maybe, once Sean and I were alone together, it was only a matter of time before our past caught up with us.

On the way back to our hotel, we started to cross a busy street near Piazza Venezia when I saw an oncoming car speeding toward us just fifty meters away. I grabbed Sean's arm and pulled him back toward the curb as I gasped, "Look out!"

He stumbled, then wheeled to face me, red with fury. "What the hell are you doing?!"

I stepped back in surprise. "I'm sorry. I was afraid that car was going to hit you."

"I saw it, Cara! I would've made it!"

"Okay, maybe. But I wouldn't have. I wasn't just afraid you'd get hit, I was also afraid of getting separated and losing you in the crowd. You have no idea how afraid I am of getting left behind."

"Don't ever do that again! If anything, you put me in more danger."

"It was a reflex. I said I was sorry. Why are you so angry?"

"Look, I don't want to have a fight here on the street." He shot an embarrassed glance at the crowd of pedestrians sharing our curb, but they seemed too busy looking for an opening in traffic to notice us.

I lowered my voice anyway. "I'm not trying to fight. I'm just trying to explain—"

"Okay, okay, I get it! Can we drop it now?"

We walked in silence until we reached a quiet, unfamiliar intersection, where we realized we were lost. There were no people in sight. We stopped to stare at my map, then stare at our surroundings, then the map again, unable to find any clues to our whereabouts.

"I think I see some familiar buildings that way," I said, pointing down one street.

"I think it's this way," Sean said, pointing down another.

"Okay." I followed him. But when we reached the next intersection, I said, "This feels even less familiar. I think it's back that way."

"All right!" He threw up his arms. "So I'm wrong again, as usual."

"I never said that." I was near tears. "I said 'I think it's back that way.' Why can't we just discuss our options, together, like partners?"

"What's to discuss? Nothing looks familiar to me. So let's go your way." He turned down the street I'd suggested, with angry-tour-guide strides.

I followed after him, silent, sad. I felt like a child. I didn't understand how to make this spiral of anger stop. Although we were walking down the street I'd suggested, I felt that I was being dragged down a street neither of us had chosen.

A moment later, Sean's pace slowed as he looked around with an expression of dawning recognition. "You know, I have to apologize, because you're right. I recognize this street now."

Tears overflowed from my eyes and dripped onto the street as I shook my head. "Don't you see? It's not about being right. What hurts me is that you misunderstand my motives. You always think I'm trying to tell you you're wrong, or tell you what to do, or trying to hurt you. It makes me feel like you don't know me."

At that moment I felt lonelier and more invisible than I had in all my months alone. I thought, *If Sean doesn't know me, who can?* We fell silent again until our hotel was in sight.

Sean stopped and turned to me, startling me out of my thoughts. "I *am* sorry," he said. "Not just because you were right, but because I know the fear of being wrong is something in me. I know it's not you that makes me feel that way."

He held me and pressed his forehead to mine. I imagined the romantic picture we must appear to passersby. They couldn't know how my heart ached. We'd only had a typical argument any couple might have, lost in a foreign city. Yet I feared that his wild-eyed anger, and my equally wild panic, presaged our doom.

In the past couple of days we've bonded over our hunger for sex after a lengthy celibacy, our awe at the aged splendor of Rome, and our dislike of Susan the Angry American Ex-pat. But standing on that forgettable street, with nothing to occupy us except the connection between us, I began to wonder if that connection was made up of nothing but memories. Perhaps, together, we *are* going in the wrong direction. Maybe that's why Sean pulled away when I pulled him back toward the curb.

At dinner, he ordered a Coke and I ordered a carafe of wine—cheaper than a Coke. I thought about how he had seemed drunk with rage today on the streets of Rome and wondered if it had anything to do with drinking Coca Cola instead of wine. His volatility is that of a man on edge. We joked about our megalomaniacal guide and excitedly made plans for tomorrow. But I could feel the jack-in-the-box crouching inside each of us, waiting for the windup.

LUCCA, ITALY

Il Dolce Far Niente (The Sweetness of Doing Nothing): the byword of Italy, the antithesis of my life.

We missed the fast train from Florence to Lucca by mere seconds, running to the platform just in time to see the caboose diminish to a disappointing silver dot. Twenty minutes later, we caught the next train, a clattering old bucket of bolts dragging a string of colorful boxcars. We were on the milk run, which stopped at every tiny Tuscan village along the way.

I sulked. "I want to explore Lucca with you, not spend all day on a train."

Sean smiled. "I don't care, Cara. Don't you understand? I just want to make love to you in Italy, in every town we go to. In the meantime, isn't this what *il dolce far niente* is all about? Taking it slow?"

He was right. Caught up in the anxiety of fishing in the wastebasket to retrieve the relationship I'd thrown away, I'd forgotten that I was on a journey, and that the journey itself was the destination. I took a deep breath, exhaled, and looked around. Our car was nearly empty, except for a man who sat in the far corner with his back to us. Outside our open window the countryside breathed soft and warm, its chest rising and falling with fecund desire, down into tame green rows of vineyards and olive groves, up into wild green hills and stone cottages.

As the heat rose, we moved to the open passage between the cars and stood in the warm breeze. Standing behind me, Sean reached around me and laid a bold but gentle hand on the curve of my breast. A slow smile rose from my belly, although I darted a pointed glance over my shoulder at the man in the corner. "No one can see us, Cara," Sean breathed, tickling my ear. He kissed me deeply, until we melted back into our seats, talking and laughing and kissing in slow motion, as time stretched into a new shape.

When we arrived in Lucca, we walked through its arched gates into a time that surely never existed. In reality, medieval times could never have been this idyllic or the people wouldn't have felt the need to build the high walls of earth and stone that encircle this city. Then again, in Lucca the walls have never been breached. Today, only locals are allowed to drive cars through the city gates, and only on a few select roads near the city walls. It's a town of pedestrians and bicycles, heels and wheels stuttering across uneven stones. Whatever the time in the actual world, ever since we've arrived within this bewitched circle, the clock that ticks away the moments of our lives has stopped.

Awakening here this morning I felt clarified, returned to an atavistic sense of self: my feet down to earth, my soul connected to the people around me, my thoughts open to the heavens. We woke when we felt like it and slid into a nearby piazza to drink cappuccinos, sitting at a little metal table under a great spreading tree dripping with white blossoms. We ate crème-filled croissants, and Sean laughed as mine oozed all over my hands.

I read aloud from my journal about the Annapurna Circuit while he listened with rapt attention. After spending much of the past few months in solitude, in the company of others I'm more of a twittering clown than ever. The compulsion to explain my life feels as difficult to ignore as a persistent itch, and the results are as painful as scratching that itch until I bleed. While I was reading, I became aware of the inexhaustible sound of my own voice and felt the blood rise to my cheeks in patches of shame. Sean saved me from myself by touching my arm and pointing behind me.

I stopped in mid-sentence and followed the direction of his finger to a Siberian husky drinking from a public water spigot. The insatiable dog lapped at the everlasting stream of water as if quaffing a canine elixir, while his patient master waited, and waited. Smiling, we both fell silent, watching people pass through the piazza and listening to the rise and fall of friendly, angry, happy, melancholy, flirtatious Italian voices. Could life really be this simple?

Not for everyone. Our eyes were drawn to a shop across the piazza, where human limbs hung in the display window: prosthetic legs, arms, and hands of various sizes. "An Italian deli for cannibals?" Sean suggested. The disconcerting deli motivated us to move our own limbs while we still could.

As we got ready to leave, Sean teased me with my old phrase, "So, what now?"

"I have no idea," I said, jumping up from the table. "Let's go find out."

In each piazza, stout marble churches posed proudly for pictures, and I stopped to photograph each one. In Italy, this kind of behavior is beyond obsessive, like taking a photo of every Starbucks in Seattle.

At the *Chiesa di San Michele*, the white and green wedding cake tiers and Gothic columns drew noisy praise from the gathered tourists—except Sean, who stood transfixed by death. No, not by the bronze-winged Archangel

Michael spearing the small harmless-looking dragon atop the church, but by another sight below that.

"My God, those spider webs are huge," Sean muttered. "I think that's a bird wrapped up in there . . . and over there, too."

"You're kidding! Where?" I asked.

"In those recesses behind the columns."

I squinted for a moment, until I saw a silk-wrapped bulge in the shadows. "Ewww! That's disgusting. Actually, I think they're rats."

"Either way we're talking some big spiders."

The church stood in solid splendor, not crumbling ruins. Yet after Sean's morbid observation, the building called to mind Miss Havisham's wedding cake in *Great Expectations*, rotting and cobwebbed and overrun with spiders.

A real wedding party gathered on the steps, waiting for a bride and groom to emerge from the aged cake. The couple's family and friends threw their arms around each other and exchanged kisses, *"Ciao . . . Ciao . . . Ciao bella!"* Then the bride and groom appeared, young faces glowing with a belief Sean and I have never known, their open smiles free of cynicism or doubt. Wedding guests threw rice at the pair as they floated down the steps, and the pigeons prevalent in every piazza scuttled forward to peck at the tiny white good wishes.

After the couple rode off in their flower-decked car, we walked into the empty church. The pews were adorned with red roses. At the last wedding Sean and I had attended in Alaska, I'd caught the bouquet. Sean had teased me about not getting "any ideas." I'd felt degraded and we'd fought. Today neither of us hinted about our connubial surroundings. We simply agreed that the ordinary interior of the church was anticlimactic after the luscious layers of frosting on the outside.

At the *Cattedrale di San Martino*, scaffolding covered the façade, which is undergoing a facelift. But we weren't as interested in the church's outside as we were in what was inside: the *Volto Santo*, or Holy Face. The *Volto Santo* is a thirteen-foot crucifix of dark cedar which Catholics believe was carved by Nicodemus. According to biblical tradition, Nicodemus was a member of the Sanhedrin who knew Jesus during his lifetime, came to his defense, witnessed his crucifixion, and bought precious oils for his burial. The carving is simple, but believers consider the plain, passive, bearded face of this particular crucifix to be the "true likeness" of Jesus.

Its very simplicity appealed to me more than the vestments we later saw on display: clothes used to dress up the *Volto Santo* for an annual procession. The garments included a jeweled gold belt, gold crown, gold shoes, and other glittering accessories.

"I understand that Jesus sits on a throne at the right hand of God and the royal clothes are symbolic," I whispered. "But I can't help thinking it's like playing *Volto Santo* Barbie."

"Me, I just look at it as a jeweler," Sean said. "This is amazing work."

I preferred to see Jesus dressed down, like a "man of the people," like someone I could talk to—which I did. Standing in the church before the unadorned *Volto Santo*, I closed my eyes and asked Jesus to show me the purpose of my life and help me fulfill it.

Surely there wasn't any connection between my prayer and our next stop in the small room next door? The Tomb of Ilaria del Carreto. Ilaria, the wife of a thirteenth century nobleman, died in her early twenties. She would have had no visitors some seven hundred years after her death, if not for her glorious casket. While Ilaria's bones moldered below, her fair and youthful likeness lay on the lid of her casket in lovely white marble sleep, immortalized by Lucca's famous sculptor Jacopo della Quercia. It took one to three years to finish the piece. Her widower, Paul Guinigi, remarried before the sculpture was finished. So much for the eternal beauty of a dead woman.

Looking at the marble woman lying atop the casket in her high-necked gown, I saw my stepmother lying in the ICU in her hospital gown. Dad recently emailed to announce he's getting married again, to the woman he met before I left. I'm not surprised. I'm happy for him. It's not death that's disconcerting so much as the relentlessness of the world revolving past it.

In this village, time has only stopped for the buildings. For people, the time between youth and death has sped up to a blur. Here, dozens of generations have left the path of time, leaving behind nothing but stone to mark their passing. Ilaria's immortal beauty is an illusion. No artist, however great, can hold back the rot that will soon sweep us all off the path.

Feeling churched-out, we left the dark sanctuaries of the past for the light of the present. We strolled atop the city wall, a wide pedestrian avenue lined with trees. Day and night, locals and tourists walk or jog around the wall's four-kilometer circumference and picnic in its grassy parks.

We found an empty park and spread out a deli lunch on my sarong—panini, marinated mushrooms, and strawberries—which we cheerfully defended from a surprise assault by party-crashing ants. Then we took part in another traditional pastime on the wall: making out.

Sean's hand had just snuck under my skirt and started plundering the territory beneath, when a guy on a bike pulled over at a nearby tree to do some sort of repair. Sean, an avid cyclist, puzzled over the guy's aimless movements—which didn't appear to be fixing anything—until he theorized there might be a local Petting Patrol, undercover bicycle cops who make sure no one has sex atop Lucca's wall. Either way, our picnic was over. We resumed our walk until the sky threatened us with grey clouds and rain.

"You wanna go back to the room and finish our picnic?" I asked.

"Yes I do."

We reached our upstairs room, with its dark wood floors and dark antique furniture, just as a violent thunderstorm burst outside. Trapped in the storm's dark center, we reflected its fervor with our own answer to each burning white flash and deafening explosion. Never before had we been so uninhibited with each other.

After the rain stopped and nighttime fell, we left our room to walk atop the nearly empty wall in the dark, listening to each other breathe into the quiet night as time continued to hold its breath. When we came down from the wall, we followed a narrow canal, where we came upon a group of boys playing soccer in the street. A young man on a motorcycle drove through the middle of the game, and the ball hit his front tire and bounced away. Sean and I exchanged a look. We'd shared the same illusion: that the motorbike had playfully kicked the ball.

In this place, with this man, I'm beginning to feel a tranquility that has eluded me most of my life, minus the restlessness and ennui that I feared would accompany it. My soul is pulsing in rhythm with *Italia*, in synchronicity with Sean. Yet we cannot stay behind these timeless walls forever. Even here, the church bells toll the hours, though we ignore them.

CORNIGLIA, CINQUE TERRE, ITALY

A beautiful beginning, full of anticipation; a painful ending, marked by the probing of deep wounds: that's the *Via dell'Amore*, the Way of Love. Today Sean and I walked the path of the same name.

The *Via dell'Amore* follows the cliffs of the rugged Ligurian coast. It starts as a paved path, but turns into a rugged trail of steep ups and downs, linking the five villages known collectively as *Le Cinque Terre*, "The Five Lands": Riomaggiore, Manarola, Corniglia, Vernazza, Monterosso. In the five villages, merrily painted boxes cling to each other atop steep cliffs and along rocky shores: homes and *pensiones* laced with intimate mazes of walkways, stairs, and passages. Up the steep hills above the towns climb groves of twisted olive trees and vineyards dotted with clusters of tiny, green early grapes. Far below the towns, the aquamarine of the Ligurian Sea explodes against the rough coastline in an ecstatic frenzy of white froth.

Suspended between those highs and lows, the *Via dell'Amore* comes alive each day with an antlike procession of hikers, mostly foreigners, mostly Americans. According to Sean's guidebook, the entire walk usually takes four to six hours, but . . . something about best-laid plans, good intentions, mice, and the road to hell . . . or whatever.

At ten this morning, at the paved trailhead in Riomaggiore, a wiry old man leaned one arm against the railing and spoke to a handful of Italian tourists. His bent frame lifted and his shriveled voice swelled with pride, as one thickly veined hand pointed at the meeting place of land and sea. Though we couldn't understand what he said, his voice and arms and bushy eyebrows rose and fell in a passionate upwelling of love for his home.

Along the rocky shoreline of the first four villages, locals and tourists have created four makeshift beaches, each one little more than a tongue of concrete boat launch and a lick of ocean. In Manarola, the natural rocks have arranged themselves into two pools. We paused our hike to join the two-dozen people sunning and swimming in the miniature cove.

It was a challenge timing the bobbing swells so that I could launch myself into the water without getting thrown back into the rocks. When Sean shoved off the rocks, a mean bully of a swell shoved him back, threw him into a boulder, then ground him back and forth across the stones. He hauled himself out of the water in frustration, his knees dripping blood. I rushed ashore and grabbed my first-aid kit. As I bandaged his knees, I told him I was excited at this rare opportunity to use my kit. He ruefully responded that he was happy to make me feel useful.

In the middle village, Corniglia, we climbed a trail into the vineyards to eat our lunch of focaccia while overlooking the cliff-top houses and the surf far below. We were quite alone on our high perch.

After lunch, I looked at Sean's watch—it was just past noon—and said, "We have time to neck for five minutes, then go."

"Five minutes?" He made a show of disappointment.

"Okay, make it ten."

By the time we started the rugged hour-and-a-half hike to Vernazza, most of the other hikers were either well ahead of us or done, so we almost had the trail to ourselves. The air was hot and syrupy. Sean was deep red. "Let me know if you need to slow down," I warned playfully. "Remember, you're in your heart attack years." After that, whenever he fell behind, he mimicked me, "Remember, I'm in my heart attack years."

At about 3:30, we arrived at Vernazza's castle tower, where men once kept a lookout for enemies and pirates. I wasn't content until we climbed to the top of the tower and then explored every nook of the village: up and down stairs, under archways, past green wine jugs glistening in the sun. Most locals were indoors hiding from the heat, while on the stoop in front of the *farmacia* a group of panting young hikers leaned back on their elbows and licked lackadaisical cones of melting gelato. In a girlish, wheedling voice, I suggested we stop to buy one.

Much to Sean's amusement, I've yet to miss a day of gelato consumption: tiramisu, *niccola, fragoli,* pine nut, chocolate mixed with candy . . . licking a scoop, swinging my feet, and humming a made-up tune, as blissful as a child answering the calliope call of the ice cream man.

It took another hour and a half to reach Monterosso, via a trail so precipitous and narrow it felt more like "Lover's Leap" than "The Way of Love." Then, gravity dragged us down a steep stairway to the last of the five lands. We arrived at about 6:30, faces burning, skin dripping, feet dragging. The piazza was nearly empty, the day-trippers gone. The beach—the only one in Cinque Terre with a resort-like stretch of sand and a line of colorful umbrellas—was also empty.

Eager to cool off, I challenged Sean to a swimming race, to the breakwater and back. He turned his bloodshot eyes and mottled purple-and-white face toward the breakwater, about fifty meters away, and said, "I don't think so. I've already been beaten up by the sea once today. Besides, don't forget, I'm in my heart attack years." But I teased him until he relented.

I arrived at the breakwater just one stroke ahead of Sean, and reached out a hand to grab hold of a rock. As I drew my feet up to rest them on the rocks below, I looked down to check for sea urchins. A needle had stabbed my foot in Greece and I wasn't interested in repeating the experience. I spotted several of the black, spiny maces lurking among the rocks and turned to warn Sean, "Be careful where you put your f—" Before I could finish my sentence, he yelped and grabbed his foot.

We swam back to the beach to inspect his injuries, which were worse than I expected. Both heels were shot through with deeply imbedded spines. Out came the first-aid kit again. For fifteen minutes, I tried to prod out the spines and splinters with tweezers. But I made no headway.

"We should probably head back so we can take care of this properly," I said, allowing childish disappointment to creep into my voice.

"No," Sean said, kissing my forehead. "I know you want to see the town, and we're never going to get all these spines out. Let's just walk."

A girlfriend once told me there's always one jerk in every relationship. If that's true, then this time it must be me. Why else would I have taken Sean up on his offer when he was in obvious pain? Why else would I have taken Sean up on so many of the offers he's made since I've known him, when it was obvious I was causing him pain?

I walked and Sean limped—wincing with each step—as the promenade filled with lovers out for the evening *passeggiata*, shadows moving through the chiaroscuro of a summer sunset. Although Monterosso is the most commercial-looking town of the five, the waning sun turned it into a mellow dreamscape, from the house overrun by purple bougainvillea to the male giant carved into the rock of a beachside cliff. The stone giant's face strained as his back bent under the weight of a building. The sculpture was an anomaly; there were no others like him in sight.

At a small restaurant overlooking the beach, we ate dinner, a spicy seafood linguini dish for two. Sean plucked out the choicest morsels and placed them on my plate. Although the Cinque Terre vineyards are famous for their wines, I didn't order any. After our first couple of nights in Rome, I decided to abstain for the rest of Sean's visit. It seems rude to drink wine in front of a man who I once walked out on because of his drinking.

So it wasn't wine that made me bold. Maybe it was the chivalry Sean had shown throughout the day that gave me the courage to tell him my fantasy: "Wouldn't this be a perfect spot to get married? I wonder, if we wanted to elope tomorrow, how hard it would be?"

Sean chuckled, but said nothing.

Now I felt foolish. "I don't mean to be . . . I won't talk about it anymore."

His eyes filled with concern. "No, don't stop talking about it. I just laugh because I get embarrassed. But I like it when you talk about it."

If anything, this response only made me more nervous. I smiled, but dropped the subject.

We took the train back to Corniglia, where we're staying. From the train station we had to walk—or in Sean's case, hobble—up three hundred seventy steps to reach the cliff-top town. In the piazza, local men had gathered, as they do every evening, to harangue each other about terribly important issues or outrageously funny nonsense, or both. We exchanged a polite *"Bona sera"* with them, then returned to our *pensione* so I could perform surgery.

For the next hour, in our tiny room overlooking the sea, Sean lay splayed out on the bed while I crouched at his feet digging out urchin spines, first with tweezers, then a needle. He repeatedly twitched his leg like a wounded dog and gasped in pain. I asked if he wanted me to stop, but he insisted I continue. Frustrated by the deepest splinters, I started flaying away bits of skin, creating small bleeding holes all over his heel. I started to cry.

He asked, "Are you okay?"

"Yes, I'm fine. I just hate hurting you."

I pried out about ten pieces. A couple of spines had worked their way in too deep for me to dig out without the risk of seriously hurting him. After I bandaged his heel, which looked as if it had been shredded with a cheese grater, he kissed me tenderly. "Thank you. That's the nicest thing anyone's ever done for me."

"It is? Then you need to hang out with a better class of people."

"Cara, I'd rather be with you, suffering and in pain, than anywhere else."

It was such a corny thing to say that I gave him a doubtful look. But his eyes told me he spoke the truth. That's when I knew: I love him more deeply than I've ever realized, this man who would walk on swords for me. The realization is as comforting as coming home and as unnerving as waking up in a strange land. Until tonight, I always felt guilty because I believed Sean loved me more than I loved him. If that's not true, I need no longer worry about Sean. But what about me?

We cuddled up to sleep, my body in a fetal position, his wrapped around mine in placental protectiveness. I knew he was still in pain. But instead of falling asleep, he grew increasingly amorous, until I said, "Well, if I'd known flaying the skin off of you would turn you on so much, I would have tried it a long time ago."

Maybe I had.

FLORENCE, ITALY

For our final two days together, Sean and I have come to Florence to finish painting the renaissance of our relationship in the summer-drenched colors I most want to remember. I don't know if this revisionist work of art will survive our next separation. But in my memory it will remain imperishable, ever fixed in the frame of *Firenze*, the flower of Italy.

We were equal parts entranced and appalled as we gaped at the Duomo, a pixilated neo-gothic bombardment of Florentine pink, white, and green marble. The overdressed façade of *La Cattedrale di Santa Maria del Fiore* is enough to make a religious person say, "There really is a God," or inspire an atheist to say, "Oh my God!" Or, as Sean put it, "Holy shit! I feel motion sick just looking at it."

Tonight, a festival atmosphere took over the pedestrian-only streets of Florence's historic city center: tourists and locals alike circling endlessly on a hot summer night, coalescing around street performers from all over the world, revolving through the gelato shops where soft, cold delectation was piled in great humps of glistening colors more distracting than the Duomo.

After dark, we stopped to admire the work of the street artists, some of whom were still hunched over their tasks, drawing amazing chalk artwork on the walkways. Next to each drawing sat tip jars filled with money. Some drawings were clever copies of Renaissance paintings, like Botticelli's *Birth of Venus*. Others were original works of imagination, like the nude gazing at her reflection in a pool. All of it was temporary. "Now there's an exercise in non-attachment," Sean said. "By tomorrow these drawings will be all stepped on and smeared and faded."

Now, lying in our hot, stuffy attic room, we're exercising our own non-attachment. It's too hot to make love, so we've been trying to sleep, arching and stretching our sticky bodies away from each other in the narrow twin bed. Arriving in Florence late on a Saturday afternoon at the height of the tourist season, the only room we could find was this tiny attic cubbyhole. I call it our "Room Without a View." It has no air conditioning, no fan, no windows, and no oxygen. It must be more than 30° in here (around 90° F). After I shifted so far away from Sean that I fell off the bed, I gave up on sleep and pulled out my journal. Sean is still tossing and turning.

I suppose I should at least try closing my eyes. Tomorrow is our last day together, and already I feel stepped on and smeared and faded.

★   ★   ★

My last day with Sean was as perfect as Michelangelo's *David*. That's what made it so awful.

At the *Galleria dell'Accademia* I circled the *David* for at least half an hour, staring at the fiercely concentrating eyes and the overlarge hands holding the tools of his destiny. Although the *David* is perfect, perhaps because the *David* is perfect, I felt more affinity for Michelangelo's four unfinished *Prisoners*. Here was something familiar: the soul trapped inside the body. They're muscular men, but unable to break free of the marble blocks in which they're trapped, imprisoned by the very stuff of which they're made. Art historians disagree whether the artist truly didn't finish the sculptures or intentionally left them that way. Either way, the message was complete. The *Prisoners* asked me just one question: how can any of us break free of our own natures?

After the *Galleria*, we returned to the Duomo to see the inside. There was a long line to get in, which gave us time to watch the unending slapstick routine of the *Piazza del Duomo*. Every day, dozens of illegal street vendors from Africa and Asia set up shop on blankets and cardboard stands in front of the cathedral. Every half hour or so the police cruise through, prompting the vendors to fold up their blankets and stands, with their wares stashed inside, and meander away, pretending they're up to nothing. Meanwhile, the police pretend to patrol the area, somehow failing to notice the obvious vendors. The moment the cops leave, the souvenir stands reappear.

"It's like a game," Sean said.

"Who's winning?"

"I don't know. The rules aren't very clear."

In between rounds, we spotted two Gypsy children passing through the line to the Duomo and dipping their hands into the pockets of an oblivious American couple. Before we could shout a warning, before the tiny fingers reached anything, a young African vendor abandoned his stand to chase the children off, shouting in Italian and waving his fist. The couple looked up in alarm as the tall, dark man bolted past, and they grumbled at his suspicious behavior, never noticing the criminal cherubs who had darted away.

After we toured the Duomo, we wanted to climb to Brunelleschi's Dome for a commanding view of *Firenze*, but the Dome was closed. We climbed the bell tower instead.

Following the cavernous expanse of the Duomo, the skinny tower was a shock to the senses. Its spiral staircase was nearly as narrow as a coffin: the tower's wall hemming us in on one side, the axis of the stairway swirling like a chambered nautilus up the other, people one step ahead and one step behind. Sean and I giggled and made nervous jokes about claustrophobia, but the young man walking just ahead of us with his girlfriend came completely unglued.

The man kept babbling: "This is crazy! The walls are too close. Stay off our heels, will you? Back off!" When the entire line was forced to stop and allow people coming down the stairs to squeeze past, his panic increased. "Jesus, I feel like I can't breathe!" When we continued upward he stopped so suddenly I almost fell into him. He crossed his wrists and made a violent slicing motion of denial, barking, "I've gotta get out of here! Move out of the way!" He shook his head at Sean, his white-circled corneas jittering madly as he forced his way past us. His receding voice floated up to us, "I'm outta here!" along with the grunts of people he stepped on and pushed in his frantic scramble down the stairs.

It reminded me of the time my birth mother took me to Disneyland when I was eleven. She was fine on the first few rides. Then we boarded Pirates of the Caribbean, a water ride that, at one point, took us floating through a pitch-black tunnel. In the tunnel, my mother started a litany similar to that of the man on the stairs, her voice rising in pitch, "Cara, I can't do this! You don't understand. *I really can't deal with this! I have to get out!"* I felt her body shaking next to mine and I feared she would either jump out of the boat or faint. I thought I should do something but had no idea what. Her helplessness frightened me. More than that, it made me angry. I was the child; she was the adult. I didn't want to take care of her; she was supposed to take care of me.

Luckily, our boat floated into an open cavern before she grew any worse. I turned and saw the beads of sweat on my mother's forehead, and the whites of her eyes.

When I used to visit her in Arizona, on the last day of every visit I always stood before her sobbing and begging, "Mommy, why can't I live with you?" But that day in the dark, as Animatronic pirates fired fake cannons over our heads, I felt grateful that this terrifyingly terrified woman had the wisdom not to try raising me on her own.

I never knew what dark tunnel in her life had left her that way. I only knew that her father had been so traumatized by World War Two he used to leap into the air screaming whenever his four daughters accidentally ran into him in the halls of their home, that he stuck knives in the walls to threaten them when he was angry, that once he shoved the head of his youngest daughter through a wall. "Monica used to be such a sweet, smart little thing," my mother said. "She was never the same after that." My dad once told me that my mother was often hungry as a girl, but never dared fetch food from the refrigerator without asking, because her father had threatened to cut off her hands if she did. My mother never told me that story.

Did she panic in that small, dark tunnel because her father once locked her in some small, dark place? Or did the stifling darkness simply remind her of what she saw whenever she closed her eyes and tried to look within herself?

I've never had claustrophobia in the true sense. Still, I felt relieved when Sean and I reached the top of the bell tower. We broke free into a dazzling view of *Firenze*: sun-blasted whitewash and terra cotta, heat-shimmering marble and cobblestone, the coruscating River Arno and its bridges, all laid out like a 1000-piece jigsaw puzzle. It was the sort of puzzle that families might put together at a kitchen table as they try to dream their way out of the dark.

In the early evening, we walked to the Ponte Vecchio. The fourteenth century stone bridge was the only bridge in Florence to survive the German bombs of World War Two. There—amid the tiny twentieth century shops of gold jewelers and silversmiths, the crowd of lovers out for an evening *passeggiata*, the street musicians playing guitars and singing with humble talent but great gusto—we watched the sunset turn the River Arno to liquid gold.

I opened my guidebook, looked up the Ponte Vecchio, and played tour guide for Sean: "It says here the bridge used to be lined with butcher shops, and the butchers used to throw animal parts and rotting meat into the river. It also says some Florentines used to piss into the river, knowing it would flow downriver to the towns of their enemies."

"I wonder how many of them fell in," he said.

I sat atop one of the walls, while Sean stood next to me on the bridge, gingerly holding my waist. I gave him a knowing grin. "Are you trying to protect me from falling in?"

"Something like that."

"Is that why you're not sitting up here?"

"Yes," he confessed with a laugh. "You know I'm afraid of heights."

Leaning back on the wall to tease him, I felt grateful to have no phobias. Or do I? How deep does a fear have to go before we name it a phobia? I keep moving forward through life, facing new people, new places, and new situations with an attitude some call courage. But maybe that's an illusion. Maybe what scares me is to stand still, in one place, holding onto one person. "Let's live in Florence," I said. "I'll become a photographer and you can be a jeweler on the Ponte Vecchio."

"When I can't even stand on the bridge without feeling sick to my stomach?"

"Okay. Let's live in Cinque Terre."

"Same problem."

"Lucca?"

"Okay."

I closed my eyes in contentment, to watch the warm red coals of day's end play against my eyelids and memorize the feeling of Sean's fingertips lightly trailing over my hip.

After dark, we walked back through the pedestrian center of old Florence and slowed to survey the wreckage of last night's fleeting art. As Sean had predicted, the intricate chalk drawings of the night before were already smeared with the passage of indifferent feet.

★ ★ ★

Last night, we made careful, sweaty, uncomfortable love in our Room Without a View. This morning, as the first hint of dawn troubled the dark, we walked to the train station. It had rained in the night, and the streets shimmered wet and yearning in the glow of the streetlights. Sean was catching the six a.m. train to Rome.

As we walked down the platform, he said, "I've spent the past two days trying to think of what to say to you at the train station. I know I might not see you again for a long time, so I wanted to say something special. But it was too much pressure. I never thought of anything."

"Sincerity is more important than originality," I said.

"I had fun. I'll miss you. I love you, Cara."

"I love you, too. It'll be lonely traveling without you."

"But you'll still have fun."

"Well, *ye-ah!*" I said. "*Of course* I'll still have fun."

"Of course. I don't know what I was thinking." He laughed, but tears were in his eyes.

"I'm sorry . . . I didn't mean . . . I mean, I *will* miss you . . . I just don't want you to think I'm all needy and . . . you know what I mean."

"I know."

We lingered, kissing and embracing as awkwardly as we had when I'd arrived in Rome—as if, instead of our time together coming to a close, it was unraveling. When we couldn't put it off any longer, he turned to board the train. As he looked for a seat, we saw each other through the window and I waved, flapping my hand energetically like a child, trying to overcome sentimentality with silliness. He grinned and waved back. I wonder when we'll see each other again.

It's probably best we didn't elope in Italy. I could hardly have married him only to send him home alone while I continued traveling for another two months or so. No, I would have had to leave with him, and I'm not yet ready to end this journey. And although we've rekindled our romance, so far it has all been in the context of Italy, country of romance. I'm not ready to trust him in the emotional minefield of life's ordinary routines. Come to that, I'm not ready to trust myself, either. Making a commitment to this relationship was easier for me when there seemed little likelihood it might be reciprocated.

He's only been gone a few hours and already his time with me feels like the distant past. In a few minutes I'll catch a train south. To stay in Florence would only depress me now.

Alone, I took one more walk through the *Piazza del Duomo*, and stopped to watch the African street vendors and the cops play their "game" one last time. This time I found out who was winning, or rather, who was losing. After the vendors concluded one of their disappearing acts, one lone cop returned to their midst unnoticed. He walked up to a surprised African man who was overseeing a blanket lined with handmade wooden trains, planes, and cars. The policeman shouted at the man and kicked his display, scattering the toys.

The frightened African protested plaintively, *"Far Niente! Far Niente!"* (Doing Nothing! Doing Nothing!) as his shaking hands pulled some paperwork from his pocket. Another cop walked up, and when the two officers bent their heads together to talk, the African made a run for it. The cops ran after him. A third cop cut him off at the edge of the piazza. *"Far Niente! Far Niente!"* the man cried as they dragged him away, his feet bouncing along like a rag doll, heels skittering across one of the chalk drawings that were, by now, almost entirely faded.

"Doing nothing! Doing nothing!" he continued to cry in Italian as he was dragged one way and I walked the other. I turned to look over my shoulder at him, my eyes filled with tears of pity: pity for the African, likely to be deported back to a hungry land and cruel life that he'd probably fled for good reason; tears for myself, alone again and still running for no clear reason.

Far niente no longer sounded so *dolce*.

AEOLI ISLANDS, SICILY

Stromboli is me: a restless volcanic island, out-of-place in a sea of "doing nothing." The most active volcano in Europe, Stromboli raises hell in the vacation paradise of Sicily's Aeoli Islands. The mountain rises from the sea to vent its fury in constant explosions of viscous lava, volcanic bombs, steam clouds, and ash. It erupts several times an hour, creating flashes in the sky like a beacon in the night, earning Stromboli the nickname "Lighthouse of the Mediterranean."

The volcano has been erupting like that for at least 2000 years. In 1919, during one of its more violent tantrums, the giant threw multi-ton blocks at the villages of Stromboli and Ginostra, killing four people and destroying a dozen homes.

By contrast, the island of Lipari is sweet, hot, breezy lassitude. That's where I'm staying, behind the walls of a rambling, grey stone castle. I've been delayed here four days, waiting for stormy, threatening weather to clear so I can hike up Stromboli. The volcano's eruptions tend to be small, and seeing them is unlikely without climbing the mountain itself for a closer look. That is my purpose in coming to these islands.

I've spent most of my long wait sitting at this café overlooking the tiny harbor, reading a paperback copy of *Moby Dick* and drinking granita di caffè. The frozen blend of coffee and sugar sets my leg and mind tapping, so I have to reread sentences. Who cares how to properly coil a rope on the deck of an eighteenth century whaler? *Moby Dick* in the summer heat; I must be mad.

By this morning, I grew stir-crazy and went to an Internet café to check my email. There were three from Sean. In the first, he'd written: "It's been one week since I've been back and all my dreams are of looking for you in small towns, on winding stone-lined streets. I feel like a mouse looking for the prize at the end of the maze. I miss you."

In the second e-mail, he'd inserted a freehand drawing of a heart with the words "I love you" in the center.

In the third, he'd written only three words, "Marry me, soon."

When I read that one, my hands flew to my suddenly warm cheeks, even though there was no one else in the café except the young woman who ran the place. But my reaction soon changed from excitement, to puzzlement, to disappointment. Was it a proposal, or a mere test of the waters? I've never given much thought to how I'd want a man to propose, but I'm sure "via email" would never have occurred to me.

I've sent no reply . . . yet. I want him to ask me face-to-face. I want to be sure it wasn't the ease of pushing the "send" button that prompted him to write those words. I want to be sure our two-week reunion was long enough to tell me all I need to know. Will I ever learn all I need to know?

So it is that everything inside me is threatening to erupt, as I prepare to hike up Stromboli tonight.

* * *

A small pleasure boat took us to Stromboli Island. The little island is only the 900-meter-high tip of the volcano, which rises more than 2000 meters from the floor of the Tyrrhenian Sea.

Our tour group was three Italian couples of various ages, and me. I sat alone and silent in the bow, sprayed mercilessly with water and the colorful confetti of Italian conversation. I assumed none of them spoke English, until a blond woman who looked as if she'd stepped out of a sailing brochure turned amused blue eyes my way and said, "You are really wet!" The boat had churned up enough spray to turn me into a sparkling pillar of saltwater. I laughed politely, an awkward seal-like cough. I could think of nothing to say. I felt so conspicuously single.

As we approached the island, we were escorted by a cheerful contingent of leaping dolphins, but my attention was on the swirling white clouds circling the bald upper reaches of the green-flanked volcano. There was something odd about those clouds; the rest of the illimitable sky was a spotless azure. It took me a moment to realize the clouds were not the aftermath of yesterday's storm, but the result of heat rising from the craters hidden in their midst.

I blurted, *"Che bella vulcano! Il . . . il . . . nubes suben la caldera!"* in a muddy blend of Italian and Spanish that probably meant nothing, but got everyone's attention.

"Oh!" exclaimed Mrs. Blond Sailing Brochure. She tapped her blond brochure husband on the arm, pointed, and said, "I think she's saying those are clouds from the volcano!"

The captain nodded and said something in Italian that prompted everyone to point at the mountain and chatter. Unable to understand them, I smiled blankly. A young black-haired goddess with skin tanned the deep bronze of endless summer put a sympathetic hand on my arm and explained, "The captain said the same thing you said, more or less."

At the island, the captain turned us over to a hiking guide: a short, barefooted man covered in wild curls from the top of his head to his muscular calves. He spoke no English, so I'd be learning little about the volcano. Before we started up Stromboli, we walked to the guide's house in the village, where he put on hiking boots and kissed his wife and children goodbye.

I was surprised there was a village on the narrow grass skirt of the volcano. Hadn't these people learned anything from Pompeii, where the villas and bathhouses and temples of a once-thriving civilization still wait for masters who will never return, where hundreds of suffocated victims left their imprints in pumice, where plaster casts of the dead still huddle in agony around the bones within?

So, if I was so smart, what was I doing here?

We started the hike just before sunset so we'd arrive at the top after dark, when it's easier to see the fireworks. For the first hour, we walked single-file through the grasses of the lower slope. The sun began to bleed, then drowned in an indigo sea. During the second hour, the group fell quiet as the terrain changed to a steep rise strewn with sharp rocks. Soon, deep volcanic ash sucked at our shoes. During the third hour, the sky turned black and the group pulled out flashlights. I donned my headlamp.

We were resting among a clump of rocks when I saw it: a shower of flaming red pyrotechnics sprayed from one of the mountain's three craters and flew high into the dark sky. The volcano's thunder was distant and faint. I had no clue how to say "look!" in Italian, but grunted loudly, "Ag-g-g-b-b-b . . . !" and flapped my hand in the direction of the explosion. The exclamations and sighs of the group were equally inarticulate, as they turned just in time to see the glowing rocks fall earthward and float ever so slowly down a collapsed segment of the cone, called the *Sciara del Fuoco*, the "Stream of Fire." I wished Sean were here to see it.

"Okay, I'm satisfied. I have seen it and I can turn back now," the Bronze Goddess of Endless Summer muttered. She leaned against a rock and rubbed her calves. "Not that I'm afraid. Just exhausted. Walking through this ash is like walking across the sands of the Sahara!"

When we continued upward, I chuckled. Mr. Blond Brochure turned and asked, "What's up?" This American euphemism sounded new and charming in his Italian accent. I answered, "I was just thinking, we're going the wrong direction. I'm sure if you told most people, 'You see that mountain there? It's ex-*plo*-ding,' they'd run the other way." The Blond Brochures and the Bronze Goddess laughed and passed a translation down the line to the non-bilingual Italians. Delayed laughter floated back to me in a slow wave.

The guide took us to the ridge and then up into the sulfur-stinking cloud of steam that rose from the craters. Then we came down out of the cloud to sit in the ash and eat. As I ate my panini, I stared unblinking at the craters below, waiting for the next thunderous expletive.

Twice more the volcano bellowed and sent up salacious spouts of lava, fragmented into fiery red blobs. We were closer this time and the loud booms gave several people a start, followed by nervous laughter. The third time, the fireworks disappeared momentarily into the cloud overhead before returning to sear the mountaintop. The radiant red cinders crept down the black void, and we could hear them crepitating like dozens of distant campfires as they flared and dimmed into a sizzling after-glow of gold embers. We stared in awe, pre-hominid children from the primordial sea witnessing the violent dawn of creation.

Creation: an act of violence. I remember Sean standing on the sand of Cook Inlet, among the rock cairns, telling me that the only way to create something is to destroy something else. Maybe that's why I'm not ready to answer his near-proposal: I'm not yet sure that we've destroyed *what was* to create *what will be.*

While our group waited for another blast, Mr. Blond Brochure told us he'd just had a discussion with the guide about how safe we were. The guide had told him only two hikers had ever been burned while standing in this spot. "He said they got hit with the sciora, the hot rocks, and one of them got hit in the head. But they didn't die," Mr. Blond Brochure reported. "A man was killed once, but only because he walked too close to the crater."

Mrs. Blond Brochure elbowed him. "You could not wait to tell us until later?"

The Bronze Goddess lifted an eyebrow at me and said, "So, we did come the wrong direction."

TRAIN FROM MILAN, ITALY TO PORT BOU, FRANCE

The volcano didn't burn me. It took people to do that. I'll never know who they were. I never saw their faces. I'll never know exactly what happened. The most disturbing thing of all is the absence of memory, the dreamless three hours or so between "before" and "after" that are forever lost to me.

On my way out of Italy, I stopped in *Milano* to see Leonardo de Vinci's *Last Supper.* I could think of no other inducements to stay in such a homogenous, city-like city. So after the *Last Supper,* I caught an all-night train to Port Bou, France. From there, it would be a quick hop to Barcelona. That meant breaking a vow I'd made to myself for my own protection: "Never take an overnight train."

Rather, I wasn't breaking my vow, only amending it, to: "Never take an overnight train *alone*." I walked through the passenger cars until I found a compartment with three female travelers who spoke English. I asked if I could join them, and explained that I was nervous about traveling alone. They were very obliging. I never thought to ask, and they never thought to tell me, whether they were taking the train all the way to Port Bou.

The first two women got off the train somewhere on the coast of France. The other woman left a couple of stops later. With that, I was alone.

The hour was late. I looked up at my heavy pack on the overhead shelf; I would have to don it again if I wanted to search for new companions. And, I knew by the murmurs and snores sneaking through the walls from neighboring compartments that many people had already gone to sleep. I decided to stay put.

If one must take an all-night train alone, the travelers' grapevine offers the following advice: don't fall asleep; don't put your bag near the door where someone can quickly reach in and grab it; don't lie with your head near the door, because some robbers chloroform travelers to knock them out before fleecing them of their belongings.

It wasn't possible to lock the couchette. So I slid my pack away from the door, then I lay on the bench with my feet propped against the door so I'd feel it move if someone tried to open it. I was determined not to fall asleep. I read *Moby Dick*. Not the best reading material to keep me alert after 2:00 a.m., but it was all I had. At about 3:15, I glanced at the tiny travel-clock I carry in my pocket. Then I lay on my side to continue reading. A few minutes later someone opened the door. That's the last thing I remember.

The next thing I knew, I woke up from a strange blankness and again checked my little clock. It was 6:30, more than three hours later. Odd, never on a train had I slept for more than an hour. But then, I didn't feel as if I'd been asleep. I felt as if it had been 3:15 a moment ago and now it was 6:30 and the time between had vanished. I felt disoriented, my thoughts gummy and knotted. There was a funny taste at the back of my throat and a strange chemical smell in my nose, which I felt a strong urge to blow.

I walked down the hall to the toilet, where I grabbed copious streamers of toilet paper and repeatedly blew my nose. But the odd smell didn't go away. It dawned on me that the train had stopped. Concerned that maybe we'd reached my stop, I wandered into the next car.

When a young woman stepped out of her couchette, I asked, "Y'know where we arrrrr?"

Her eyes studied mine for a moment before she asked, "Have you been robbed?"

"No. Juz' worried thiz may be my . . . ztop." To my own ears I sounded quite normal.

She gave me an odd look. "Do you know where your stop is?"

"Yeah, wrote on a 'lil peez of paperrrrr . . . " I was about to take out the slip of paper, which was in my pocketbook, when I realized I didn't have my pocketbook. "Thaz ztrange, I muz've lef' it in the couzhette."

She put a hand on my shoulder, looked me in the eyes, and over-enunciated her next words, as if she were talking to someone deaf and wanted to make sure I could read her lips: "Are you sure you weren't robbed?"

"I don' thing-zo," I said. Why did she keep asking me that?

"Why don't you show me that little piece of paper?"

She followed me to my couchette. I was puzzled to see that I'd left my pack behind, too. Anyone could've taken it. What was I thinking? My pocketbook with the neck strap was lying on the bench. Picking it up, I said, "I pud the peez of paperr righd here. Thaz funny . . . " All the pocketbook's compartments were unzipped, the money I'd carried in it gone. "Oh my God . . . " I said, instantly alert. "I *was* robbed." I reached down to feel the many zippered pockets of my travel pants. "Jesus! He must've had his hands all over me. All my pockets are unzipped." How could I have slept through that? I looked at the girl, puzzled. "How'd you know?"

"You weren't the only one." Her accent was American. "Another woman came to our compartment a few minutes ago looking confused, like you. But she *knew* what had happened to her. She said she was scared because she'd just been gassed and robbed, and she asked if she could stay with us."

"Gassed?!"

"Yeah. She said someone sprayed something in her face and when she woke up later her money was gone. My friends and I heard about this kind of thing. We promised to keep each other awake all night because we were scared it might happen to us. So did they get a lot?"

"No, it was just thirty-five bucks. I carry the rest of my money somewhere else . . . Oh my God!" I reached into the waist of my pants for my money belt, yanked it out, and tore it open.

"Is everything still there?"

"Yeah, it's all here."

"That makes sense. I hear these thieves move fast, hop on at one stop, get off at the next. You know, I think we saw the guys who did it, too. A few hours ago the door to our compartment opened and these two guys were standing there. They looked surprised to see the three of us sitting up, wide awake, just staring at them. They muttered some excuse and took off. And that girl who came to our car? She met another girl in the hall who it happened to. They must've hit a bunch of people."

I kept looking through my pocketbook in the compulsive way a hungry person will keep staring into an empty refrigerator. I thought back to when I'd first woken from my drugged sleep. The sarong I'd pulled over myself had still been draped over me. Rather, it had been neatly put back over me after someone had removed it, taken my pocketbook from around my neck, and rummaged through my pants. I pictured some man looming over me while I lay there helpless. With a train full of loot to plunder, the thieves wouldn't have taken time to molest me, but the thought that they could have without me being any the wiser . . . A chill shook my body.

The girl put a sympathetic hand on my shoulder. "You can come sit with us if you want."

"Thank you. That's very kind of you. But I think I'm going to go sit in the coach."

Still a little out of it, but no longer the clueless zombie I'd been when I'd first woken up, I put on my pack and walked through the train in search of the conductor. I told him simply that I'd been robbed, that I knew he probably couldn't do anything, but that I thought he should know. He shrugged with such elaborate unconcern it bordered on malice. He acted as if he was enjoying my misfortune, and I wondered why. After that, I walked to a nearly empty coach and sat down with my pack by my side, draping my arm across the seat behind it like a lover.

Now I'm on a different train, to Barcelona. But as this train fills with morning light and sleepless travelers, I keep trying to piece together what happened to me on that other train in the dark. I can still see the door opening . . . then nothing. It's what I do when things go wrong: I go back and back and back, trying to figure out how I could have changed what cannot be changed.

Looking back, it occurs to me I've been dazed and confused for a long time, long before I was drugged and robbed last night. I've spent too much of my life unconscious while men have taken what they wanted from me, leaving me with little but my next destination. Luckily, this time they didn't get much. Anyway, that's all behind me now. It's a new morning in a new country and another chance to start again.

Shit! I just realized. I left *Moby Dick* on the train to Port Bou.

ACROSS THE ABYSS

It was after ten tonight when my train arrived in the small Spanish town of Cuenca, and I'd just missed the last bus up the hill. I shouldered my pack with a sigh and started walking.

Two men stood on the corner talking and I asked them, in Spanish, for directions to my *pensión*. One of them—a portly man of about sixty-five with thinning white hair, straightforward eyes, and a brow creased with years of patience—explained that my *pensión* was at the top of the hill, too far to walk with such a large pack. He offered me a ride. I said I didn't want to trouble him. No trouble, only five minutes by car. When I still demurred, the other man, sensing my unspoken concern, told me not to worry: Eduardo was a respectable gentleman and only wished to help. My pack was heavy and I was ready to be convinced, so I followed Eduardo to his car.

He drove a tiny beige vehicle that looked like a Volvo, although I can't readily identify the various motorized toys Europeans drive in lieu of the super-sized beasts so popular in the States. I explained this as we motored uphill, and he chuckled. His smile was kind, although the corners of his mouth moved only slightly, as if the muscles were stiff. I remarked that the cliffs of Cuenca looked pretty, lit up at night. Then, embarrassed by my rusty Spanish, I fell silent. Eduardo didn't speak English.

Even wedged in a clown car, Eduardo maintained the proud, erect bearing of an old *caballero* as he pointed out the landmarks we passed: the *Plaza Mayor* and its gothic cathedral, the medieval convent, the old prison that once housed prisoners of the Spanish Inquisition. We passed through an arched entry in the old castle wall into the *Barrio del Castillo* (Castle Neighborhood). There, atop the hill where a castle once stood, my humble *pensión* now sits among a handful of bars, restaurants, and lovely but faded dowager homes.

Eduardo insisted on carrying my pack to the door, where he waited until the owner answered the bell, a woman about his age named Maria. They greeted each other by name. I thanked Eduardo and offered to buy him a coffee if I saw him in town. My offer was genuine, but I was surprised when he replied, with courtly dignity, that he would come this way tomorrow evening at six to pick me up. Recalling the old man in Crete who'd slobbered on me and shoved me out of his kitchen, I tried to think of a way to amend my offer, but Eduardo left before I could reply.

When he was gone, I asked Maria if she thought it was a good idea to let Eduardo pick me up in his car. She replied that he was a good man from a good family and said it was fortunate I'd found a friend who knew the town. With that, I relaxed. Now, sitting alone in my room, I'm beginning to feel excited at the prospect of making a Spanish friend.

* * *

Cuenca climbs up a narrow hill poised between two gorges. It's a plank tilted between two great rifts in the parched summer earth. This morning I walked downhill on a path that follows Cuenca's eastern cliffs. Those cliffs line the Río Huécar Gorge, a slender drink of water poured down a long rippling throat.

In the *Ciudad Antigua*, or Old Town, three fourteenth-century homes cling to bulging, uneven rocks on the edge of the cliffs, their balconies hanging over a gut-wrenching drop. It's believed the *Casas Colgadas*, or Hanging Houses, were once summer homes for Arab royalty. Two of the *Casas Colgadas* are linked together to house the *Museo de Arte Abstracto Español*. I wasn't as interested in abstract art as I was in the renovated medieval homes and the blood-percolating sensation of standing balanced over a precipice. The homes were a capricious gambol of multi-level spaces, conforming to the uneven rock below. A series of windows each picked up a different aspect of the gorge, creating stop-motion frames of art.

After exploring the museum, I walked back uphill to take a nap before Eduardo arrived. On the way, I passed a group of children on a dirt playground, hanging upside down on monkey bars and chasing each other in the games-without-rules of the very young.

One girl of about eight played by herself, and I imagined her an outcast.

She wore thick glasses and her hair was cut in a bookish pageboy. When she stepped up to an old stone fountain to drink, I snapped a photo. She strode up to me and commanded me to take her photo again. Anticipating a request for money, I declined.

To soften the blow, I told her she could take a photo with my camera if she liked. She nodded vigorously, and her whole body vibrated with excitement as I showed her how to snap a shot. She asked me what to shoot and I told her she could decide. She turned in a slow circle, reconsidering her familiar world through the viewfinder. *"El Corazon de Jesús!"* she squealed, as she pointed the camera across the gorge to a towering white statue of Jesus that looked down at us from the opposite hill. Then she took a few more photos of sights invisible to my adult eyes before I rescued my camera from her random exposé.

"¿Cómo te llamas?" I asked. ("What's your name?")

"Monica. ¿Cómo te llamas?"

"Cara."

Soon, all of the half-dozen children had gathered around me. They chattered away in Spanish while I nodded and smiled at the half of their words I understood, and nodded and smiled even harder at the half I didn't.

When the others tired of me and left Monica alone with her pet foreigner, she insisted I must mail her the photos she and I took, as a birthday present. I agreed. Also, a birthday card. Okay. And some makeup.

"Si yo puedo," I said. ("If I can.")

Not giving up, she listed her demands: makeup, card, photos. *"Me prometes!"* she insisted. ("Promise me!")

I made no promises, but as I left, Monica's shouts of "Don't forget!" followed me up the hill. I thought about my sister, only two and a half when I left L.A., an age when most conscious memories are soon forgotten. Has Iliana forgotten me? Worse, does she think I've forgotten her?

As promised, Eduardo showed up at my *pensión* at six. With an air of ceremony, he opened the passenger door of his car and handed me in. Although my original offer was simply to buy him a coffee, he took me for a long drive over a bridge to the other side of the Huécar Gorge. We drove to the top of a pine-forested hill across from Cuenca to visit *El Corazon de Jesús*.

Eduardo barely looked at the statue, instead shaking his head sadly at the surrounding mountains. He said they were once blanketed in endless pines. To me they still looked plentiful, but he said it was nothing compared to before. Cuenca was once the center of a booming timber industry that deforested his home. As a teenager, he had worked on a reforestation project and planted many of the trees now standing, but they were never enough to replace those that were cut down. The pines around us whispered in the breeze, as if they, too, mourned their brethren.

I asked Eduardo if I could take his photo. He drew himself up in a formal pose, arms behind his back, chest and nose thrust forward. He didn't smile, but stared down the camera with a look of gravitas.

On the way back, he stopped at a resort on the outskirts of town, a place of flowered linens, stiff waiters, and high-priced views. We were the only people in the bar besides the bartender. I ordered a *café con leche* and Eduardo ordered a soda.

He told me he's lived in Cuenca his entire life. "I still live in the house where I was born." He held up one declarative finger. "It is the same house where my father was born, and his father before him." He spoke of his family, extolling his wife's delicious cooking, his two sons' successful careers, and his grandchildren's beauty.

I told him I had a *novio*, a fiancé. This was more or less true, since I'd finally responded to Sean's e-mail, "Marry me, soon," with an equally short answer, "Okay, when?" Yet I felt as if I were lying.

I expected this gentleman, with his old-fashioned manners, to be surprised that I was traveling alone, without family, friends, or fiancé. Instead, he commended me on seeing the world and broadening my mind before settling down. "I think it would be a better world if everyone spent some time visiting another culture," he said. "It's important to see the world from someone else's point of view. If everyone did this, maybe we would all understand each other more and not fight so much."

The moment we finished our drinks, he said, "Shall we go now?" and handed me down from the barstool. He kept a prim distance between us, and I realized with increasing joy that he had no ulterior motives. He honestly wanted to show hospitality to a visitor, someone who might be lonely and in need of a respectable chaperone.

When he dropped me off he said he would stop by at the same time tomorrow and show me more sights if I was interested. "You don't need to decide now. You're on my way home. It's easy for me to stop here. Then, if you'd like to go, we can go."

★ ★ ★

Today I climbed down into the other gorge, on the western side of Cuenca. That deep swath is cut by the *Río Júcar,* a loping jade mystery where weeping willows mourn the seepage of time through futilely grasping fingers. I crossed a low wooden bridge over the sun and shadow of the river. Then I climbed a hot and panting path up a rocky slope to the small hermitage of *San Julian el Tranquilo,* which overlooks the gorge from the opposite side.

Just above the stone chapel stands an arbor, its wooden trellis laced with grapevines. There, I lay on a stone bench staring up at clusters of green grapes and diamonds of white sun until that place's living poetry and killing heat sent me helplessly into a long siesta.

A couple of hours later, as I crossed a different bridge on my way back to Cuenca, I spotted a lone instance of graffiti scrawled on a large rock: "GLORIA: FÁCIL DE QUERER, DIFÍCIL DE OLVIDAR." (Gloria: Easy to love, difficult to forget.) I thought of Sean, easy to love, and of Chance, difficult to forget. It made me wonder if Sean has forgotten Heather. Sometimes I wish he'd never met Heather and I'd never met Chance—the interim lovers who cut such deep, hemophiliac paths through our hearts, forever changing the landscape of our lives.

Maybe things could've happened differently. But have you noticed? They never do.

THE LAST FRONTIER
THIRTY-FOUR YEARS OLD

I admonished myself that just because I'd seen Sean drunk didn't mean he was *a* drunk. I was probably just paranoid because Chance had a drinking problem. But where Chance had been cruel and irrational, Sean was kind and philosophical. I couldn't bring myself to believe that anyone as evolved as Sean could be an alcoholic.

Instead, I decided that our real problem was his obsession with his ex-girlfriend.

I was growing tired of Sean's stories about Heather. For months, I'd listened with compassion, then patience, thinking it would be unfair to stop him. After all, no subject had been taboo back when we were *just friends*, and we'd formed our initial bond while commiserating over our lost loves. How often had I bored him with stories about my ex? But over time I stopped talking about Chance, and I hoped Sean would follow suit and shut up about Heather already.

He once told me, "Heather was always doing thoughtful things for people. She was a Two."

"A wha . . . Oh, the Enneagram." I sighed, not trying to hide my irritation. "Which one is the Two?"

He either ignored or mistook my sigh and answered, "Two is The Giver. Heather was the most generous person I ever met. Like, if a friend of hers was feeling depressed she'd buy them flowers. This one time when I was sick she brought me homemade soup."

"A lot of people do stuff like that. You're not trying to tell me they're all Twos?"

"No, it was more than that. It's hard to explain . . . Okay, for example, her sister committed suicide—she shot herself. And afterward, Heather was the one who went into that apartment all by herself and cleaned up the mess. I asked her why she didn't ask someone to help her. She said she was the only one in the family who could handle it and she didn't want anyone else to see it." He went on, "And then there was the time I got arrested for drunk driving . . . "

"You got arrested for drunk driving?!"

"Yeah, I was out late one night and I had a few drinks and I got a DWI. Anyway, I had to spend three days in a halfway house, and while I was there Heather came to see me every day. She brought me groceries and even made me dinner one night and brought it over. Definitely a Two."

These stories pissed me off. What made Heather so much more giving than I was? She was a wife and mother, responsible for two small children, yet she dumped her husband on the hope that Sean *might* go out with her. Then, after he did fall for her, she dumped him. So what if she cleaned up some blood and brain and pieces of skull? If I had a sister who blew her brains out, I'd be in there scrubbing, too. So she did nice things for Sean after he got a DWI—he might have killed someone, and she brought him dinner? Why did she rate such a great personality type? *The Giver!* It sounded so sweet and kind. Not like me, *The Performer,* which sounded so self-centered and egotistical. Hadn't I given plenty? Men had treated me like shit for years, but I kept on giving and *forgiving.* I worked hard. I volunteered in the community. I was a good friend. But Heather got to be *The Giver* and all I rated was *The fucking Performer!*

I said none of this, just nodded, trying to look sympathetic. But I've never been good at hiding my feelings, and Sean easily read my mind. "You know, one personality type isn't better or worse than any of the others," he said. "Being a Giver's not always a good thing. Givers can be generous, but they can also be manipulative, or co-dependent."

"Yeah, but co-dependent just sounds like another word for victim, like someone you should feel sorry for."

"Don't you believe it! Givers can be aggressive, too. And Performers can be very generous."

"Only 'cause we want to look good," I said.

"Well, isn't that what it all boils down to in the end? We all want to be loved."

His understanding only made me more keenly aware of my pettiness, which made me feel unlovable, which made me even more anxious to exorcise Heather. Yes, we all want to be loved. Some more than others.

★ ★ ★

One dark, snowy afternoon, Sean and I sat in my apartment with the lights off, gazing out the window at the falling flakes, two tiny figures in the bottom of a snow globe. At 3:30 it was already dusk. Low clouds wrapped the city like a cocoon. The city lights reflected between snow and clouds, creating an effulgence that seemed separate from the objects it touched.

"Everything looks so clean," I said. "The city looks happier when it's covered in white."

"You know what Heather used to say when it snowed like this?"

That's when the storm erupted, there at the bottom of the snow globe. "You know what? *I don't want to know!*" I snapped. With difficulty, I lowered my voice, "I know when we were just friends we used to talk about our exes all the time. And I don't want you to feel like you can't talk about her if you need to, but . . . "

"I was just . . . "

"Let me finish!" I was close to shouting again. "I think it's time we stopped constantly inserting our old lovers into our everyday conversation. You still talk about Heather so much it's as if she's still your girlfriend. It hurts my feelings."

Sean's breathing was fast and shallow as he stood up and began to pace, clenching and unclenching his fists. "I have to listen to you talk and talk, until you say everything you want to say. And if I don't, it's 'let me finish!'" He began to shout, "But I don't ever get to finish! I don't even get to start! Heather and me, we made a choice, and you don't care. We made a fucking choice, and we knew we'd have to live with the consequences. So fuck you if you don't understand! Fuck you!"

I was shocked. Sean wasn't acting like himself at all. He was acting like . . . Chance. Although my insides began to seethe with rage and fear, I didn't let my emotions take over the way I used to with Chance. Instead, I maintained an external calm. "If you insist on screaming swear words at me you're going to have to leave."

But he continued to shout, "So now you're gonna kick me out 'cause you don't like what I have to say? You can say whatever you want to me, but I don't get to speak?"

"You're putting words in my mouth. I'm not kicking you out unless you scream and swear at me. I'm a nice person and I don't deserve it. Nobody talks to me that way anymore. Nobody. You understand?"

" . . . made a choice . . . " he mumbled.

Suspicious, I tilted my head to study him. "Are you drunk?"

"So now we're back to that!" he exploded. "This is not about being drunk. You don't know anything about it. I made a choice . . . and . . . and *fuck you!*"

"Look, you're not even making sense. This is why I refuse to get involved in arguments with drunks anymore—it always turns weird. So you should just leave, because I'm not participating in this conversation anymore." I turned and stared into space with fierce, silent determination, while Sean stood over me breathing heavily, staring at me in mute frustration.

Then his expression slowly changed and his stare turned inward. Several minutes passed before he spoke again, in the gentle, compassionate voice I'd come to know so well: "Cara, I know you're just trying to protect yourself. I know if you'd been in a relationship where you were abused you'd try to prevent being in a situation where you could get beaten up again. In your case, you've been with alcoholics and you don't want to deal with that again. I get it."

I'd expected him to leave, or yell some more. His acknowledgment took me by surprise, deflating my anger and leaving me defenseless. I curled up on the couch and cried.

He knelt in front of me and said, "You *are* a nice person. You're also a very intuitive person. You *have* found another one." He choked on his next words. "I *am* an alcoholic, and I know I need to fix me. I know I'm dysfunctional and my communication is dysfunctional."

I saw the tears swimming in his arctic blue eyes, and my own tears ceased. My finger traced the damp trail on his cheek, and a chuckle bubbled up from my throat. "This may sound strange," I said, "but that's the nicest thing anyone's ever said to me."

We both laughed. I hugged him close, and he clung to me like a child.

I knew awareness wasn't the same as action. Just because he admitted he was an alcoholic was no guarantee he would stop drinking. Nonetheless, in that moment I loved him with such bleeding empathy it felt as painful as loving myself.

When the storm passed, he said, "Isn't it good to have a friend you can be honest with and tell the truth?"

"Yes. It is."

But the truest things are the things we never say.

ACROSS THE ABYSS
THIRTY-SIX YEARS OLD—CUENCA, SPAIN

It might be safer to never trust another man. But I can't bring myself to judge billions of people based on the sins of a few. And I can't stop believing in redemption. Where would that leave me? Not only do we all deserve a second chance, we all deserve a first chance. Every person, place, and situation I meet on my journey might hold the key to my purpose, or I might hold the key to theirs.

I don't know why Eduardo has chosen to befriend me. We have nothing in common. I suppose friendship itself is reason enough. This afternoon, he took me on our longest drive yet, through the mountains to the *Nacimiento del Río Cuervo*, the Birthplace (or Source) of the Crow River. He mentioned again how many more trees there used to be in these mountains when he was a boy. He's always careful not to show strong emotion; I sense he would consider such a thing an imposition on me. Yet I heard in his voice the sadness that comes with the realization that time not only changes a place, but completely replaces it with another place. Then, memory becomes a graveyard for the people we once were and all we once knew.

We stopped at the edge of a forest and walked down a short path to a mountain spring. The *Nacimiento del Río Cuervo* looked like one of the wet, green, shadowy dells of the Tongass Rainforest, another gathering place for fairies and elves. The only sound was the dulcimer chiming of water. It dripped in narrow rivulets, slipped down curtains of deep green moss over a rambling wall of rocks, then freefell into a shallow pool. Behind the sparkling curtain, shadows led to a shallow cavern. Somewhere outside the forest, the sun was setting, and a reverie of tawny light flowed over the watery place where the river is continually reborn.

Over the quiet trickling, Eduardo's gravelly voice startled me. "Many years ago this was a great waterfall. Even now, there's a lot of water in the spring. And in the winter, ice."

"It's perfect," I said. "It's a magical place."

"I knew you would like it. You should take my photo here, for a memento (*un recuerdo*) of your trip." He spoke in a tone of command and struck a dignified pose.

I dutifully snapped a shot.

We shared the dusky daydream of water for some minutes, until several Spanish tourists appeared. They smiled and greeted us, but exchanged sidelong glances with each other as if they suspected us of something.

We then drove to a nearby village, where we stopped at a small bar for *tapas* and Cokes. As at some of the other places we've visited, Eduardo knew several people. He paused to say a friendly hello to a few before we stopped to stand at a small table in the middle of the room. A couple of times, I looked up to see someone staring at me with obvious reproach. Then I overheard several whispered exclamations of disapproval over Eduardo keeping company with a younger woman—and flaunting it in public, too!

One middle-aged couple carried their drinks to our table and came straight to the point.

"Eduardo!" the woman scolded. "Where is Gloria? And what are you doing here with this young woman?"

Her husband lifted a suggestive eyebrow at me and said, "Although if you are going to play with a younger woman you certainly have good taste."

The woman looked me up and down, snorted her disapproval, then said, "I never saw anything." She exaggerated averting her eyes, miming that she'd seen an assignation and would pretend to ignore it. My face flushed. Perhaps she thought I was a whore.

Eduardo scowled. "It's not what you're thinking. This young lady is a foreigner from Alaska. She has a fiancé, but he couldn't come with her. So she's alone. She doesn't know anybody here and I'm showing her around. I wanted to show her the *hospitality* of Cuenca."

The woman's face twitched with embarrassment. "I am sorry," she said to me, placing a gentle hand on my shoulder. Then she slapped Eduardo's shoulder. "But what was I supposed to think, seeing you out with such an attractive young lady?"

Eduardo formally introduced us, and we all had a friendly conversation until he and I left fifteen minutes later. I still felt embarrassed, although I could hardly blame them for sharing the same suspicion I had when I first met their friend. Eduardo treats me with the same joviality with which he treats everyone, yet the conjecture that rippled through the bar tonight made me realize that, although we've acted with propriety, the appearance of impropriety still exists.

As we left the bar, Eduardo asked me about my plans for tomorrow. I told him I planned to see the *Torcas y Lagunas*, and he offered to take me. I didn't want to hurt his feelings, but I'd been looking forward to spending an entire day alone. The moment in the bar had only strengthened that desire. I could imagine how much worse the whispers and stares would be if people saw an older Spanish man visit a swimming hole with an American woman half his age, especially if I were to go for a swim in my bikini as I hoped to do. I sat in silence, trying to figure out how to tell him I didn't want company.

"You seem very serious and quiet," Eduardo said.

"I'm sorry. I respect you very much and you have been a real gentleman. But I'm uncomfortable with the attitude of the people tonight. I'm worried that in Spain it may not be right for a young, single woman to enjoy the company of an older, married man."

"You shouldn't worry," Eduardo said, with the unflinching directness of a man who knows who he is and never worries about the opinions of others. "We're only friends. We're doing nothing wrong and I have no bad intentions. What other people think is not our problem."

"This is true, in theory. But in reality, what other people think can be our problem. They can make me uncomfortable. They can say something to your wife and make her think something is wrong. They can be unfriendly to you."

"My true friends would not act that way."

"No, but you live in a community, with other people besides your friends, people that you must see every day. And when I'm visiting your country, in some way I'm representing my country. I don't want to give my country a bad reputation." I'm sure that, in Spanish, my grammar was much worse than I've expressed it here, but the meaning was there. I took a deep breath and got to the point: "I think of you as a friend and I'm grateful to you for showing me your city. But I'm thinking maybe I should go alone tomorrow."

Eduardo looked crestfallen, but there was no resentment in his voice when he said, "I understand. You should do whatever makes you feel comfortable." I looked at him and thought about the grandfather who was once a father to me. I remembered the silliest thing: After my grandfather divorced my grandmother when I was twelve, he kept promising to take me to Six Flags Magic Mountain. But we never went. I never got over the disappointment. Now here was a kind, harmless man nearly my grandfather's age, who never had a daughter, who wanted to take me somewhere that I wanted to go.

I felt foolish. Had I come so far down an unconventional path, abandoning society's notions of "normal" and "acceptable," only to break down at the first real sign of peer pressure? I might fear the disapproval of others, but what was the point of acting on that fear? In any life, rejection is inevitable. Trying to avoid it by rejecting myself is irrational. Trying to avoid it by rejecting another is cowardly.

Still, I did want time alone. So I said, "If you would still like to take me, I would like to see some of the sights with you. But I would like to spend part of the day alone, to write and to be alone with my . . . " What was the Spanish word for thoughts? " . . . to be alone in my mind."

Eduardo cheered up a little. He said that would be best, after all, because his son was coming to town and he would have to end our day before two.

He dropped me off at my *pensión* and watched from the car to make sure I made it inside safely. When I reached the front door, Maria was already opening it, as if she'd been waiting. She waved at Eduardo as he drove away, then she gave me a saccharin smile and said it looked like I'd made a good friend. But a sly gleam stole the sweetness from her eyes as a pointed question tumbled out of her mouth: "Eduardo is married, isn't he?"

"Yes, he is," I said tersely. Then I switched to exaggerated politeness. "He's treated me like a daughter. At first I was worried, because I had a bad experience with an old man in Greece. But when you told me he was a good man from a good family, I decided to trust him. He has shown me much of Cuenca. Someday I want to return with my *novio* and show it all to him."

Her look changed to relief. It took me several minutes to extricate myself from her many questions about how I'd met my *novio*, how he'd courted me, and how he'd proposed. A likely reader of romance novels, she seemed carried away with the idea of a lone woman traveler who had a fiancé waiting at home. I finally pled exhaustion. She apologized, patted my cheek, and shooed me off to my room, insisting that I did too much and should get more rest.

Now I lie here "alone in my mind," as I described it to Eduardo. Tomorrow is the last time we'll see each other. Why couldn't I have kept my mouth shut for one more day? I fear our friendship is now marred, not by the ill opinion of others, but by my inability to hold onto my own truth in the face of a cynical world that can more easily understand a lie.

★ ★ ★

Today the only faces that stared at Eduardo and me were the faces of the *girasoles*: field after field of sunflowers standing in unified attention as we drove past, each and every face turned to the sun.

We stopped at a spot in the woods that gave little indication it hid anything unusual until we reached the startling edge of one of *Las Torcas de los Palancares*. The *torcas* are thirty giant, circular holes scattered through the pine forest of the *Monte de los Palancares*. The abrupt holes range from fifty to seven hundred meters wide, and as much as ninety meters deep. Sean would have suffered vertigo if he'd been with us, standing atop a vertical, rippling cliff, looking down into the crater.

Eduardo told me he's taken part in several rescues of climbers who've underestimated the *torcas*. Some have died.

The *torcas* were created millennia ago when an ancient sea receded from these mountains, leaving behind just enough water to slowly eat away the rock. The erosion turned the mountains into Swiss cheese. To me, the round chasms represented tremendous symbolic power, because the circle embodies one of the unifying mathematic principles of all the spinning, revolving energy in the universe.

The craters were scattered with greenery. Along their upper edges, pine trees jutted from the walls, starting out horizontally, then stretching vertically toward the sun. Some of the trees were stunted dwarves, their shapes twisted into nature's own bonsai.

The *Torca del Lobo* was arguably the most beautiful *torca*. It's named for the many wolves, or *lobos*, that once roamed the area, until shepherds killed most of them to protect their flocks. But I was partial to the small, relatively plain *Torca de la Novia*, because of its haunting legend. Eduardo told me it was named for a sad, true story that took place when he was young.

As the story goes, a young woman's family betrothed her to a young man she didn't love. Perhaps she was in love with another man; Eduardo didn't know. She and her family lived in a village near Cuenca. One day, the girl and her family went into Cuenca to buy the traditional dowry items the couple would need, such as a bed and other furniture. I suspect they rode in a carriage. Cars have only been in use here for a few decades. On their way home, as they rode past the *Torcas y Lagunas*, the girl asked her father to stop so she could relieve herself. She needed more relief than her family realized. She walked into the woods and never returned. The family later found her at the bottom of this *torca*, where she'd jumped to her death.

"How sad," I said, scanning the crater as if she might still be there.

"Yes. It is sad. It's not good for parents to force children to do something when they are that unhappy, even if they think it is the right thing. What good is it to force a child to do what you think is right, if you lose that child?" I sensed that Eduardo spoke from personal experience, but I didn't ask.

We drove on to *Las Lagunas de Cañada del Hoyo*. In these mountains, a *laguna* is basically a *torca* filled with spring water. We stopped at three. One small lagoon was murky and shallow and blanketed with algae, but two craters were filled with freshwater of an intense aquamarine, too deep to be limpid, yet pure and clean as the beginning of time. A cliff rose above the water line, tracing the circumference. Pines and lush greenery clung to the lip.

At the edge of one of those pools, in the rippling August air, Eduardo and I said farewell. A few people were swimming and picnicking nearby, but no one looked at us with judgment or surprise. Perhaps they took us for father and daughter. I told him, *"Siempre te recuerdo"* ("I'll always remember you," or in my creative grammar, "I always remember you"). He said he felt the same. I gave him a kiss on both cheeks and took his right hand formally but fondly in both of mine. Then he drove away.

At that moment, I missed my grandfather. I remembered a day when I was eleven, when Grampa took me on a drive high up into the California mountains, just him and me. We drove for hours and just talked. It was the first time in my life anyone talked to me like an adult. Having yearned since I was five to be taken seriously by one of the unpredictable giants who ruled my world, I drank up his show of respect like a thirsty desert traveler who's discovered a well. The words in my crowded brain tumbled over each other in their mad rush to get out and be heard.

Grampa and I talked about the role of politics in social change, the importance of loyalty in friendship, the nature of romantic love, the mystery of God, even the meaning of life. He obviously had something on his mind and he was unusually disposed to listen. I distinctly remember him remarking that he was surprised an eleven-year-old had spent time considering life's big questions. I knew that was partly because I spent so much time alone, but I kept that thought to myself. There have been few times since that I've felt so visible to another.

After Eduardo left I became invisible again. But only for a moment. Then the *laguna* stared at me with its single, fathomless eye and dared me.

I walked down the rocky slope to the *laguna's* edge. A young German couple were pulling themselves out of the water, hugging their shivering, goose-bumped bodies. They laughed heartily when a Spanish man jumped in, shouting expletives at the chilling shock. His wife and son stood at the edge, laughing too. The son, a boy of about thirteen, leapt in after him while the wife watched, her eyes round with amusement and worry. I found a spot where I could wade in and called out to the wide-eyed wife, *"Venga!"* (Come on!) She grinned but shook her head firmly: no way!

Because there were three small groups of people standing and swimming around the edges of the pool, I decided it would be safe to swim across the center to the other side and back. I wouldn't have done it if the place were deserted; I could picture getting a cramp in the middle of the icy pool and sinking to the bottom.

It was an arbitrary goal, perversely inspired by fear. I had no clue how deep the water was and this gave the idea a creepy thrill. The opposite side was a sheer cliff with no shallow place to put my feet down. There were some limbs to grab onto over there, but I wouldn't be able to touch bottom until I returned to this side.

I'm not a particularly strong swimmer, and this was not the salty Mediterranean Sea to which I've become accustomed. It took a lot of work to stay afloat. I swam for about five minutes to reach the center, where I told myself, "Okay, now all you have to do is do that again." About two minutes later, I felt a wave of panic as my limbs began to scream at me: in reaction to the intense cold, my muscles were stiffening, my skin burning. I feared that I wouldn't make it after all and that the people on the opposite shore would never reach me before I sank to oblivion.

Then I reached the large tree limb that forked out into the *laguna*, grabbed it like a drowning woman, and held on as if my life depended on it. I felt that everyone along the distant edges of the lagoon must be able to hear my sobbing, gasping breaths.

When my breathing returned to normal, I looked back at the water I'd just crossed and realized that, in spite of my panic, I'd been well within my range of ability. I'd been frightened only by the idea of it, by the inscrutable depth of the water beneath me.

On the way back, my fear departed. When I grew tired I simply rolled over and did a lazy backstroke until I felt ready to continue. It took longer than ten minutes to get back, but I was a lot more relaxed. Still, when I reached a spot where my feet could touch bottom, I exhaled with relief. A small group of Spanish teenagers stared at me wordlessly as I rose from the icy water back into the searing hot air. Unable to repress a grin of victory, I winked at one of the girls and she gave me a congratulatory smile.

I dried off and sat on a ledge, looking out over that water which appeared clear even though it was opaque. With a new clarity of mind, I knew that the mystical green circle below had imparted to me some of its power. As much as I've gained from the friendship of others, this is one of the gifts I've received from friendship with myself, as I've swum out of my depth, across the circle, over the abyss.

Invisible power is the perfect gift for a lone traveler, because the unseen void can open beneath us at any time.

I'VE BEEN DINGLED

The wood floor nagged so loudly beneath my feet, the old girl sounded ready to give way. The three-hundred-year-old Ballintaggart Manor has been converted into a hostel, but it feels like a home, the kind you might find in the pages of a cozy fireside mystery. Sunlight poured into my dorm room through two picture windows, and the view made me laugh out loud; if I'd seen a painting of the Irish countryside that looked like this, I would have accused the artist of nostalgic exaggeration. Outside the windows, black-and-white cows and roly-poly white sheep munched on grass, which grew in overzealous green pastures. The gentle pastures rolled down, down, down to the lovely puddle of Dingle Bay, where one long, low cloud skimmed the water. An old stone watchtower watched over it all. Everything was silent, save the occasional moo of a cow.

I was quietly unpacking yesterday when Jukka and Janet noised in, discussing their plans for the afternoon. Jukka, a young man from Finland with a contagious good humor, asked for my input, as if we were old friends and it was understood that I'd join them. Janet is a lively, up-for-whatever, recent college grad from Texas. I declined to join them for a hike, wanting some time alone to explore the town. However, I agreed to meet them later to go to a small concert.

I whiled away the afternoon with a stroll into town, just a mile away. Dingle's diminutive waterfront is lined with boxy shops and pubs, each painted a different color. Small fishing boats bob in the bay. The town is surrounded by green hills that disappear into low clouds, but I sense promise hidden there. The scenery reminds me of Juneau, making me homesick for a place that was never really home.

On my journey, internal peace has come and gone, and come again.

But there's an external peace to this place, which is settling into me with every breath of the breezy sea air. Instinct tells me that the two worlds through which I've been traveling for nearly a year—the internal and the external—have found their harmonic meeting place in Dingle. I'd planned to visit a couple of other towns in Ireland, but I know now that I'll never see them, not on this journey. I might not have a home anymore in the traditional sense. But if a wanderer can experience anything like home—a place where she sighs with the comforting feeling that she has returned to a place where she belongs—then for me surely Dingle is it.

In the evening, Janet, Jukka, and I took the hostel van into town. We were joined by Gareth, a soft-spoken Englishman with dark good looks and a serious air. The van dropped us off on the waterfront, and from there we walked to a little bit of a church, the venue for the concert.

The bill featured an eclectic handful of musicians: an American harpist, a Northern Irish folk guitarist, a German violinist, and a local bagpiper named Owen. While all of them were talented, Owen's slow airs reached into my soul and found my Celtic ancestors weeping there, while his jigs found them dancing and laughing until I felt possessed and nearly leapt to my feet.

Jukka, who'd been to a concert at the same church last week, regularly leaned toward the rest of us with a grin to say, "I love this song" or "This is the one I was telling you about" or "Do you like it?" It was slightly annoying to be interrupted in my enjoyment of the concert so often, just to be told how enjoyable the concert was. But Jukka's enthusiasm was hard to resist.

In between comments, he pointed out the tall window behind the altar. Sparrows darted back and forth across the pale evening sky. They kept changing direction, like auguries unsure of their message: time to go home; not done flying; no, time to go home; no, not done flying.

After the concert, as we walked out of the church, Jukka suggested we go pub hopping.

"Definitely. I can't wait to have my first pint of Irish ale," Janet said.

"I don't know if I can finish a whole pint," I said. "I'm not much of a beer drinker."

To which Jukka loudly replied, "Don't lie to me. I'm tired of you stumbling home drunk every night, staying in the pubs until all hours, leaving me with the children!" A middle-aged woman who was also leaving the concert turned to stare. Jukka leaned toward her and spoke in a confiding tone, "I've been putting up with this for nine years because I promised to stay with her for better or worse." He threw a devoted arm over my shoulder and squeezed.

Rolling her eyes, the woman asked me, "Is this your first date?"

"I barely know him."

"How can you say that, after all we've been through together?!"

The woman pursed disapproving lips and hurried off while I doubled over with laughter.

The four of us then laughed our way down the street, debating which pub to visit. It wasn't a simple choice: there are more than four-dozen pubs in Dingle, even though there are fewer than 1500 residents. We decided to start at An Conair (pronounced "On Conner").

Because this is Ireland, I ordered a pint. I could only finish half of the dark amber ale, which prompted my companions to start calling me Half-Pint.

"Great," I said. "I'm going to get laughed out of Ireland."

"No, no," Gareth said. "In Ireland the people laugh with you, not at you."

"It's no wonder they laugh so much," I said. "When I got off the ferry in Cork, the pubs were full of people drinking pints—at nine a.m.! Beer for breakfast? What's up with that?"

"But this is quite normal in Ireland," Jukka said. "A full Irish breakfast can include eggs, beans, sausage, bacon, toast, and a pint of ale, maybe two."

No wonder I feel so at home here, I thought, once again surrounded by heavy drinkers.

After everyone finished their pints—except me—we walked to another pub called "The Little Bridge." (More accurately, it's called "The Little Bridge" *in Gaelic*, but I can neither pronounce nor remember how to spell it.) It's named for the little bridge across the street, which crosses the stream that runs through town. When we arrived Owen was there, playing the bagpipes again, along with a backup guitarist and accordionist.

Gareth suggested we sit so close to the band that I worried the musicians would ask us to back off, but he laid a staying hand on my arm and said, "Just wait, you'll thank me in an hour." He was right. As music filled the pub, so did people, until we were so hemmed in I couldn't shift from one butt cheek to the other without bumping into someone, who bumped into someone else, who knocked over a drink.

Gareth bought us all a round. I ordered a Bailey's Irish Cream, forced to admit that Irish ale was too rich for my blood. When I thanked him for the drink, he said, "A friend once told me giving is like a river: you dip in when you need something, then put something back later so someone else can dip in downstream."

"So you're saying I owe someone *else* a drink?" I asked.

"Did I hear ye say you're buyin', then?" an elfin-faced Irish girl asked me.

"Aw, you're scarin' her, Maureen," shouted the plump young woman next to her. "Don't mind her, she's jest TEE-zin ye!"

With that, the pair joined our group. Both of them became quite drunk, but rather than making them annoying and unruly, each drink only enhanced their friendliness. The elfin Maureen apologized several times for being "so pissed." She and her friend are from Cork, where they're studying for their teaching certificates. Maureen knows five languages: "English, Gaelic, French, German, and Japanese. I'm very excited to learn Spanish next."

"I'm surprised you want to be a schoolteacher. You sound like you should be a translator, or a linguistics professor."

"Nah, I love children. And if I teach, I'll have summers off for what I love to do best: travelin'. That's where I want to use m' languages."

Between sets, she leaned over to light a cigarette for Owen. When she was out of earshot, Gareth leaned my way and pronounced her "really sweet." He looked half in love, and I was mildly surprised: she was so chattie and chirpie, while he was so quiet and serious. I suppose opposites attract, but only Jane Austen has ever made me consider that a sensible thing.

Maureen asked Owen if she could sing "Black is the Color." This is the way of pubs in Dingle, where there's not a strict division between performer and audience, and anyone game enough to join in is welcome. Maureen sang the traditional Celtic ballad with tear-jerking feeling: "Black is the color of my true love's hair . . . His lips are like some roses fair . . . He has the sweetest smile and the gentlest hands . . . I love the ground whereon he stands." It was a song about romantic love, yet she was clearly singing about her love for Ireland. Do I love my own country with such passion? I feel so adrift it's hard to say anymore.

As the evening went on, the room turned into a roller coaster, a Tilt-a-Whirl, a Bouncy House of human joy, everyone clapping and laughing, stomping and swaying. I leaned toward Gareth's ear and shouted to be heard, "One thing I love about Irish music: no other music can make me feel so happy and so melancholy at the same time, no matter what the song is."

He nodded with enthusiasm. "I know just what you mean. I call Irish music 'my blues.'"

Then the band invited an American musician to join them, a blues singer from New Jersey who's come to Dingle for the upcoming Irish Music Festival. The crowd parted to create a wide berth for the morbidly obese man, who made his way to the front with the help of a burled wood cane. As the band switched to playing backup for the ballsy, bad-ass singer of American blues, the crowd sang along with new energy. It was your basic blues: someone done him wrong, and all he wanted to know was "woman, why you treat me so bad?"

I told Gareth, "And this is *my* blues!" The song reminded me that American culture is more than fast food and skyscrapers, suburban malls and pre-fabricated housing. It's the home of jazz and rock, Ernest Hemingway and Jack Kerouac, hippy counterculture and hip hop rebellion. Americans don't just dream. We rebel, we confront, we expect. The world thinks us mad, and maybe we are, but it's a divine madness. Like the blues, sometimes we're at our best when we're being bad.

I *am* an American. No matter how long or how far I wander, there's no escaping the influence of the places I come from. Nor would I care to. I may think I have no home, but America is the home that lives within me. Much as I might resist belonging to anything, I do belong to that.

That doesn't mean I'm ready to go back. I still don't know when, where, or how to end my long escape. Maybe Dingle knows. This town of mist and music feels alive with portents.

* * *

Jukka had hiked up to Conair Pass before and he was excited to show us the killer view. So today Janet, Gareth, and I followed him into the hills, hoping the mists would clear.

When we began walking uphill from The Little Bridge, the morning was foggy and wet. My feet throbbed with the memory of months of mountains, stairs, cobblestones, and city streets. But the countryside took my mind off the pain: more of my green Irish fantasy trimmed with tiny flowers, rock fences, and a jolly, rocky stream. All of which Jukka pointed out the entire way: "Isn't this great . . . This is the stream I told you about . . . Isn't this scenery fantastic?"

"What scenery?" Janet asked. "I can't see a damn thing." As we'd climbed higher, the hills had disappeared in a dense cloud bank, which now rained on us in quiet but steady earnest.

The hill we walked on was a series of spongy, boggy hillocks, and our feet were occasionally sucked ankle-deep into the mud. After we crossed a small waterfall—"Isn't it wonderful?!" Jukka enthused—we quickly lost the trail.

Two confused hours later, we reached the parking lot at the saddle of the pass. The views Jukka had raved about—Dingle Bay below us to the south, Tralee Bay below us to the north—were completely obscured. I peered down through the heavy white mist until I could make out the faint outlines of some nearby lakes, and said, "I can tell there's a great view. I just can't see it." This prompted gales of laughter all around.

Although there was no view at Conair Pass, there was free, if dangerous, entertainment. I had just sat down atop a steep slope to pull my lunch out of my bum bag when a rock pressed against my back and shoved, nearly knocking me downhill. I turned to see what had pushed me.

It wasn't a rock, but the horns of the Killer Goat of Conair Pass. The goat clearly intended to send me off the cliff and inherit my lunch. He's taken up panhandling at the pass after discovering that some tourists have yet to learn you should never feed a strange animal. As I stood up to move away, the goat ran at me and butted me again, harder this time, nearly sending me over the edge. A few feet down the slope stood a small fence, which would have halted my fall but would have mangled me in the process. My companions backed away, laughing.

"Oh my God!" Janet said.

"Oh sure, it's easy for you to laugh. You haven't been targeted for"—here I dodged a third butting—"termination!"

We moved away from the slope to eat, each keeping a wary eye on the killer goat. Tourists trickled in by car, and several people approached the goat before we could warn them. One woman walked toward the animal, cooing and reaching out a hand to pet him, when Janet cried, "Look out, he'll charge you!" This prompted the alarmed woman to turn tail and

sprint back to her car. One man stood next to the goat, prepping his camera to take a scenic photo, when the animal swung its head sideways and
bashed him in the chest with its impressive horns, nearly goring him. The
man retreated to his car, hand pressed to his chest as if it hurt to breathe.

The climax came when a middle-aged German couple showed up in a
red, pint-size rental car. The woman rolled down her window and started
to feed the goat. Not only did the beast stick his head through the window,
horns and all, but he also proceeded to climb halfway into the passenger
seat, forelegs in, hind legs out, hooves scrambling in her lap as he tried to
launch his entire body into the tiny vehicle. The man and woman both
retreated to the driver's seat, as they tried to shove the animal out of the
car. They honked the horn, but this had no effect on the goat. Then the
husband tried to be a hero, leaping out of the car and rushing to his wife's
side, where he pushed and prodded the back end of the goat, and finally
gave it a swift kick in the rear.

Hint: never kick an animal with horns. The goat did jump back out of
the car, all right: it ran at the man, ducked its head, and butted him, hard,
horns first, right in the groin. The man yelled and scrambled backward,
losing a shoe in the process. Somehow, he escaped emasculation, retrieved
his shoe, and jumped back into the car, where he and his wife rolled up the
windows and stayed put. They didn't bother trying to step out to enjoy the
view, which, as I've explained, couldn't be seen anyway.

As we started back downhill, the last thing I saw was the goat standing
in front of that tiny red compact, pressing its chest against the grill, staring
the car down like a bull facing down a matador, as if he dared this pusil-
lanimous red pipsqueak to take him on. Who needs a killer view? Tourists
see them every day. But a killer goat? Now we're talkin'.

Janet said the thing that got to her was the way the goat's expression
never wavered. As she put it, "That blank yellow stare seemed sort of . . .
I don't know . . . evil, somehow." I wonder if the beast even wanted our
food. Maybe he just wanted us to get the hell off his pass.

★ ★ ★

Slender strands of rain and sun string together to make up the days in
Dingle. The rainy days are a relief because they expect nothing of me.
On those days, I lie in bed late and listen to the rain pattering outside the

window. The world's cares are kept out by Dingle's green hills and white clouds, making me feel safe, like a child tucked into a magical green and white quilt.

On rainy days, I spend hours wandering from pub to café, café to pub. At some point most days, I settle into the warm embrace of An Café Liteartha, known by locals as the Café Lit. It's part café, part bookstore. The tiny bookshop out front is filled with Irish literature, while the café in back is filled with wayward tables and locals, expansive conversationalists and intellectual recluses, and always at least two people working on the day's crossword puzzle.

We're all waited on by one of the women travelers who've come to Dingle for a visit and decided to stay, or by the owner's son, a good-looking Irish lad who wears his hair in a polite ponytail. The young man is always apologetic when the place is busy and he can't get to everyone right away, but no one really cares; no one's in a hurry. Me? I'm just happy to be in this place that smells of books and tea. A pot of hot tea with cream and honey and a fudge biscuit-cake buy me a seat that stops time as I write and read and chat with the locals.

On my first day at the Café Lit, a senior gentleman with a grizzled beard handed me a newspaper article about a local girl who'd scored ridiculously high on her college entrance exam. "She was home-schooled," he said with an approving nod. "We grow 'em smart in Dingle." It seems the Irish take deep pride in each other's achievements. When I browsed through the bookshop out front, the owner informed me that Ireland has turned out more world-renowned writers than many much larger countries. He reminded me of some of their names: James Joyce, C.S. Lewis, Jonathan Swift, Oscar Wilde, William Butler Yeats, and several others I'd never heard of, though I nodded and smiled, not wishing to appear illiterate.

The owner is an oldish gent with bushy gray sideburns and long crusts of gray hair emerging from a jaunty tweed hat. Saoirse (Sorshya) is his name—a Gaelic name, so at first I wasn't sure how to spell it. He speaks Gaelic, too, and, like Irish music, the sound makes my heart ache with a pleasant yearning. He always smiles cheerfully, though his voice is gruff, as if Dingle's sunny and stormy days have both woven their way into his personality. Each time I tell Saoirse I'm ready to pay my bill, he asks what I ate, then questions me: "Did y' sit or stand? Did y' have milk or sugar?"

as if he might charge extra for those things.

Like that, with a devilish wink, Dingle's quiet days end, and its rollicking evenings begin.

⋆　⋆　⋆

Whether the days are cloudy or sunny, each night I make my way to the Ballintaggart hostel's music room. There, a big bay window frames a perfect view of Dingle Bay, a fire often crackles in the grate, and the mood constantly shifts with the people who come and go at all hours.

First, there are the Irish hostel workers: the laughing Irish sisters Eileen and Wendy, and the moody Rory—the Irish Sisters have pinned up a note at the front desk advertising Rory for sale. Next, there's Joe, the young tour guide from Belfast, Northern Ireland, who looks more like a member of the IRA—he brings a different group through each week. Then, there's the revolving door of backpackers: Vicki the Scottish siren, the Argentinian man with the didgeridoo, the self-conscious American guy whose name I can't remember, the pair of smirking Englishmen whose names I *don't care* to remember, and an ever-changing cast of characters. By midnight, the music room is usually full with a dozen to two dozen people.

One early evening, I was sitting by the window, half-writing and half-listening to the conversations that wandered in and out. The Irish Sisters were sitting on one of the couches chattering. The American whose name I can't remember walked in, wearing his usual painstaking smile, and shrugged himself into a corner of the second couch. He kept working his mouth like a beached fish, as if he were about to say something to the Sisters. He seems never able to decide whether to jump into a conversation or press himself into the woodwork, always ending up in the uncomfortable middle.

The two Englishmen whose names I *don't care* to remember walked in next and made a noisy, intoxicated production of sitting down in the murmuring room. The noisier of the two, with thick dark brow and storm cloud eyes, dramatically flung himself into a chair, while the quieter, fairer of the two flopped onto the second couch, prompting the Nameless American to shrink further into his corner. The Englishmen were in mid-conversation, and the noisy one was saying something about having "offended again." Then he announced loudly to the rest of us, "But I don't believe in all this being polite. I'd rather be honest."

I looked up from my journal and smiled. "I believe it's possible to be both."

"That's ri—" Wendy began to agree from the couch.

Her voice was drowned out with Mr. Honesty's reply of, "Oh, ballocks to that!"

This prompted a discussion of the difference between honesty and rudeness. The debate featured Mr. Honesty and his friend versus the Irish Sisters, whose feminine attention the men had surely hoped to rouse in the first place. Having quickly read the danger signs—namely, the nearly empty bottle of wine Mr. Honesty had placed between his knees—I lowered my head and resumed writing. The Nameless American tried to interject with trite one-liners like, "If you don't have anything nice to say, don't say anything at all," which drew guffaws from Mr. Honesty. The Nameless American stood up, declared, "I'm sorry, I didn't mean to be boring," and left. The Irish Sisters left a moment later, waving to me in sympathy.

"Well, we certainly cleared the room in a hurry," Mr. Honesty said to his less talkative but equally sneering friend. His tone, and his friend's snort of laughter, indicated they were quite proud of this achievement.

Then, in walked Joe, the tour guide from Belfast who looks more like an IRA guerilla: thin and proudly slouching, with angry dark stubble poking through his shaved head. A member of his tour group followed, a young American with a boy-next-door face. They sat at a far table, intent on some deep discussion. Mr. Honesty interrupted them several times, trying to muscle into the conversation, but they barely glanced at him. Mr. H managed to squeeze out of Joe a confirmation that he was, indeed, from Northern Ireland, but when Mr. H asked whether Joe was Catholic or Protestant, Joe said he didn't want to talk about it.

"So you're Catholic then," Mr. H concluded. Joe refused to respond. Undeterred, Mr. H blurted, "So, do you know anyone personally who's been killed?"

My heart skipped a beat. Not metaphorically—I actually felt it. I kept my head down, but my pen stopped moving as I listened.

With an infuriated sigh, Joe addressed Mr. H, "That's my business and I don't have to tell anybody! But just think about what you're asking." He paused. "There are some things a person should be able to keep to himself."

"All right. That's fair. Fair enough. That's . . . that's very fair," said Mr. H, abashed for the first time since he'd walked in. After an awkward interval, he then tried to draw *me* out, "So, where are *you* from?"

I dragged my head upward and answered, "The States."

"Really? But you don't look American . . . " He studied my face so insinuatingly that I felt molested. "You have a different coloring . . . darker . . . like you might be Latin maybe, or . . . "

I replied with scorn, "I'm part Mexican."

"That's it!" he said.

Then I added, speaking slowly and underlining each word with sarcasm, "Yes . . . We have black people, too." I was startled by Joe's roar of laughter behind me.

Mr. H dropped his shoulders and said, "All right, all right, I get it. I'm sorry."

I replied with a silent smile of forgiveness but said nothing. Joe left the room.

"I didn't mean to offend," Mr. H said to The Boy Next Door, "but how am I supposed to learn anything about other people if I don't ask questions?"

"You could try visiting the places those people come from," the Boy Next Door said.

"Visit Northern Ireland. Are you mad?"

"No. Really, you should go sometime. It opened my eyes."

"What do you mean?"

"Well, I've always lived in a country that's been at peace. I'd never been in a country before while it was at war, and . . . that's all I'm going to say. You should just go."

Mr. H's silent partner finally piped up, "Go to a war-torn country just for the educational experience? Not bloody likely! I like to learn and all that, but I don't have a death wish."

"Me either." Mr. H took a swig from his bottle of wine, stared at the bottle thoughtfully, and said, "Although I may drink myself to death."

"A fuck of a lot better than getting blown up," his friend suggested.

"I'll drink to that," Mr. H said. He raised his bottle, his friend raised his plastic cup, and they both took a swig.

The Boy Next Door shrugged in surrender to the pointlessness of a conversation with two pissed troglodytes, sat at my table, and talked to me instead. He told me about his tour of Europe, which is coming to an end so he can start college next week. I asked what he plans to study. He said the world was so full of possibilities he had no idea how he was ever going to pick a major. I asked what possibilities he was passionate about. Everything: travel, history, social anthropology, environmentalism, film, art, writing.

He gushed about his dream of becoming the next Ernest Hemingway. "He's why today anyone can pick up a book and just read it, because he wrote so simply."

"What's your name?" I asked.

"John."

"John what?"

"Turner."

"So instead of trying to be the next Ernest Hemingway, why not try to be the first John Turner? I mean, lean, straightforward prose is a great thing to strive for. But Hemingway became a great writer by being unique."

"Right. Of course," he said, nodding, receptive to my hackneyed advice.

Thus encouraged, for the next hour John Turner poured out his fascination with the world, until the light outside faded. Then someone lit a fire in the fireplace, the room slowly filled with people, and John and I fell silent as we wrote in our journals.

I again felt compelled to put down my pen when Vicki the wine-soaked Scottish siren made her grand entrance. A young woman with luminous hazel eyes, bright auburn hair, and a curvaceous figure, Vicki is clearly used to commanding attention, male or female, with her witty, seductive allure. She started telling Wendy, and everyone else in earshot, about a hosteller she was hiding from, whose excessive attention made her feel stalked. Though I didn't ask, I knew she was talking about the Nameless American. She explained, "I figured out why he makes me so nerrrvous. It's because he's sooshly eenept. (The term "socially inept" sounded reinvented in her thick Scottish accent.) But it's hard to get awee from 'im, because I feel so sorrry for 'im."

It wasn't just Vicki's own drama that interested her. When she caught sight of my journal she laughed with delight, "All you Americans are alwees carrying journals. Bring that over here." She patted the couch next to her. "I want to see what you people write in those things."

Laughing, I said, "I'm not showing you my journal. It's full of my private thoughts."

"That's exactly why I want to rrread it. You're spoilin' the fun." When I wouldn't give in to her wheedling, she asked, "Did ye' write anything in there about the ghost of Ballintaggart?"

"This place is haunted?" asked Janet, her eyes shining. Janet had been talking to someone else, but Vicki's strong personality has its own gravitational pull. A couple of other women also leaned forward.

Surrounded by an audience, Vicki was in her element. Lifting an eyebrow and slowly scanning our faces, she dramatically pointed at a portrait on the mantel, a painting of a young woman with strawberry blond hair piled on her head, wearing what appeared to be a nineteenth century dress. "That's Lady Ventry, the ghost of Ballintaggart," she whispered, as if not wanting the ghost to hear. She told the tale in a husky murmur while light from the fireplace danced across our faces, turning us into the picture of young girls telling ghost stories around a campfire. Long ago, the English Lord Ventry owned most of the land on the Dingle Peninsula. According to Vicki, Lord and Lady Ventry were staying at Ballintaggart Manor "when it happened . . .

"Her husband thought she was fooolin' around with a servant. He was very jealous. So he hired someone to kill 'errr. The killer thrrrottled her and threw 'er down the stairrrs!" She said the murder took place, at least as far as the throttling went, in Room F. "And sooometimes," she paused for effect, "people still hear 'er walking around that rrroom, or see 'er at the window looking ooot. Some people have even heard 'er getting thrrrown down the stairrrs."

I'm staying in Room D, where, so far, I haven't heard any ghosts, just creaking floorboards. "But," I said, "if I were going to see spirits, I'm sure it would be here in Dingle. I can't explain it, but it's like this town talks to me on some deep ancestral level."

"I know exactly what you mean," Vicki said. "This town has put you under a spell: you've been Dingled!"

It's not any one thing that casts the Dingle spell, but if I were to blame just one thing, it would be the music—in the pubs, in the streets, and at Ballintaggart. Each night in the music room, two or three guitars appear. Often there are drums. Sometimes there are harmonicas or other instruments.

That night, Gareth was the first to bring in his guitar. After he plucked a few folk tunes, I overheard him tell someone that he used to give guitar lessons to prisoners. He declined to elaborate. Although he's a serious man, he's not a brooding one, and he didn't just play for himself; mostly he played requests, so other people could sing along.

Gareth's inner schoolboy came out when he discovered he could drive the Irish Sisters up the wall by playing "More than Words," the popular ballad by Extreme. He's taken to poking out his tongue and playing that song every time the Sisters walk into the room, knowing full well he'll never get through the first verse before they start throwing things at him, punching his arms, and shrieking protests until they drown him out: "Stop, stop . . . you're killin' us! Every bloke with a guitar who passes through Dingle plays that shite song!"

Eileen, the bolder sister, strummed tunes by Sarah McLaughlin and Jewel. Rory played traditional Irish ballads and songs from slightly more recent Irish artists like Van Morrison and Crowded House. All three played folk, rock, and blues: Bob Dylan, Tom Petty, Tracy Chapman . . .

Under the spell of music, hours melted like Salvador Dali clocks. Wine spilled on the rug and cigarette smoke hung in the air. The smoke would have driven me out of any other room, but here it seemed necessary, part of a ritual intended to transport us on a collective vision quest. The mood shifted as the room filled with nothing but the primitive sounds of two hand-drums and a didgeridoo, rivaling the story of Lady Ventry for thrilling spookiness. I got so lost in the mantra of the drums that I disappeared. I might have been sitting there for minutes, hours, or days.

I felt high. If I'd ever taken a drug that made me feel that way, I would have become an addict long ago. Was this why they seemed to vanish before my eyes, all those addicts I've loved? Was this the elusive escape they kept chasing, but never seemed to find?

I stayed until I could no longer hold my eyes open.

After I crawled into bed, I heard John (The Boy Next Door) and another young guy enter the co-ed dorm. They went into the bathroom, whispering about how great Ballintaggart is. I heard John say, "Did you meet that Cara? She was really cool." Smiling in the darkness, I wondered what made him think I was "cool." Looking back on the evening, I realized I hadn't said much. I'd mostly asked questions, watched, and listened. I hadn't been trying to get people to like me; if I had, I would more likely have talked up a storm. The simple wisdom this implied was nothing new, but it was a new way for me to experience myself.

I drifted off to sleep filled with wonder, as I have been ever since. For the first time in my life, if I could change anything about myself, I wouldn't. I want to hold onto this feeling. I don't want to let go of this place.

* * *

I've asked Saoirse for a job at his little café that smells of books and tea. I've decided to try to stay in Dingle for the winter.

So what about Sean?

What *about* Sean? After I replied to his email, "Marry me, soon," with my answer, "Okay, when?" I received no response. In Spain, I emailed my reply again, just in case he didn't receive the first one: "Okay, when?" No response again. In France, I sent the same two words: "Okay, when?" Here in Dingle, I checked my email at the town library. Still no reply.

I have no fiancé. I have no home. No job waits for me in the States. Although my flight from London to New York is in eleven days, I've never planned on New York as my final destination. I've always planned to decide that later. Later is almost here, and I still have no idea where to go. How can I go home when I don't have one?

As Vicki said, I've been Dingled. So for now, I've decided to stay under this town's spell, if I can. But I'm running out of cash, which means I'll need a job.

When I asked Saoirse if he'd hire me, he gave me a measuring look and pulled on his chin. He asked about my experience. I told him I spent several years as a waitress in college.

"We'd expect y' to do some of the bakin' and the food preparation. Do y' have kitchen experience?"

"Well, I've never baked for a restaurant . . . but I'm a pretty good baker at home when I put my mind to it . . . and I'm a fast learner." God, I must have sounded pathetic.

He told me he'd think about it.

This evening I told Janet and Gareth about my plan. (Jukka left a few days ago.)

Janet said, "Sounds like that's the end of your guy back home."

"Not necessarily. I'm just not going to plan a life with him until he asks me to." I shook my head. "You know, this whole trip I've been asking God to show me the purpose of my life. I don't know the whole answer yet, but I've discovered one thing: The purpose of my life is not to get what I *want*. The purpose of my life is to become who I *am*."

Gareth looked skeptical. "You're telling me you'd be happy even if you never got anything you wanted?"

"I'm telling you I'll never be happy if getting what I want means giving up who I am." I've spent a lot of my life talking, usually about myself, but, for the first time, I listened to myself as if I might have something useful to say. "That's what this journey is all about. It's not about *finding* something, it's about *becoming* something."

Janet stared at me with fierce concentration as if I were a Rubik's Cube and my words were a disordered jumble of colors. "That's what your journey around the world is about?"

"Not just *that* journey. My life. How I live it. Me. When I die, that's all I'll have to show for everything: just me."

"I agree with all that," Gareth said. "But as for your feller, I have to say, I'm with Janet. You don't really expect him to wait for you, do you?"

"You don't understand. I know it doesn't look like it, but I'm the one who's waiting."

THE LAST FRONTIER
THIRTY-FIVE YEARS OLD

Last year, Sean was the one waiting. But it wasn't me he was waiting for. His whole family was waiting, for life to either get better or unravel.

Sean's dad, Stuart, was an entrepreneur and, in the way of the Alaskan frontiersman, his dreams became subject to boom and bust. When the oil boom came, his little jewelry shop had its own boom. When the oil bust followed, the shop continued to thrive as more expensive stores left town. Then the retail boom came, filling the city with big boxy superstores and little discount outlets. Stu's neighborhood store just wasn't a convenient place to shop anymore. The business started to tailspin, and so did Sean's dad.

The first sign of Stu's decline was his greenhouse. He used to grow gorgeous red tomatoes. He once gave me a few to take home. He was so proud, I didn't have the heart to tell him I didn't like tomatoes. But last year he let the tomato plants go, along with the other fruits and vegetables, and the flowers that used to cheer him in winter.

Stu had given up drinking years before. I remember he once pulled Sean and me aside and drew something out of his pocket to show us. It was a gift from a fellow member of Alcoholics Anonymous: a coin emblazoned with the number thirty. "Thirty years of sobriety," he confided. Then he gave us an impish grin. "And it only took thirty pounds of marijuana to get through it." Last year, instead of planting tomatoes in the greenhouse, Stu grew pot.

As Stu spent more time getting high, he spent more time sleeping upstairs in his recliner. He left the running of the shop to Sean's sister. Sean's mom, Tess, set her mouth in that funny little line that was her way of tolerating her husband's foolishness without stooping to approval.

Tess's mother lived with them. Grandma Mae was a tough, broad-shouldered old gal from Montana's Bitterroot Mountains. She held onto the no-nonsense attitude of the Great Depression—and anything else she could still use. Forced to slow down by poor health, she spent her days in the matching recliner across from Stu's, knitting dishcloths. She'd knitted me a set the previous Christmas, and everyone had stared in surprise as she accepted a hug from me without fuss, chuckled, and patted my arm—an uncommon honor. The only thing she knitted last year were disapproving brows, aimed at her son-in-law. "You should get off your rear and stop feeling sorry for yourself," she said. In response, he got off his recliner and went to bed.

He stayed there for months.

That Christmas, Sean and I spent as little time as possible at his family's house. On Christmas Eve, he escaped to my place and watched me decorate a tree. I asked him to help me.

"I'm just not into the tree decorating thing," he replied. "But you're doing a great job."

"What *are* you into?" I asked. He rarely wanted to go skiing any more, or to the movies, or to the dojo, or anywhere. I looked at Sean sitting listless on my couch staring out at the snow and pictured his dad sitting on his recliner staring into space.

He shook his head and said, "I'm sorry you got stuck with such a Scrooge. What you need is someone more cheerful than me, someone who'll do things with you."

"I hate when you do that."

"Do what?"

"Tell me I need someone different from you. Why don't you be that guy, instead of trying to pass me off on someone else? Or why don't you just tell me you don't want to be with me? Why doesn't anybody ever want to take responsibility?"

Although the days grew longer, Sean's winter blues held onto internal night. His sense of humor remained, but it was dark humor. He made fun of himself for being over-thirty and living at home.

I argued against his self-indictment. "But you live in your own apartment. You pay rent."

"Cara, my parents live upstairs, I live downstairs. I pay rent, but it's ridiculously cheap. I live at home."

"Okay. But it's not as if you're a mama's boy. You're very independent."

"Maybe that's the problem. I mean, my dad expects me to take over the business, but I don't want to. I hate it. I mean I like making jewelry, but I never wanted to run a business."

"Did you tell him?"

"Yes. Then you know what he told his friends? He said, 'I spent twenty years building this business, thinking my kids would take over and take care of me in my old age.' Now the business is going bankrupt, and he feels like he's failed us . . . or we've failed him."

"Your father has no right to expect you to fulfill his dream. It's not going to help him if you go down with the ship. This is your life, not his."

"You do know, whatever I do, I'll probably move to the Lower Forty-eight?"

"Yes . . ."

"So what happens to us then, you and me?" he asked.

"I don't know. What happens to us then?"

"You know I'm not interested in marriage."

"Why not?"

"Cara, I've never been able to sustain a relationship long-term. I can't promise to love someone forever. I don't even believe love exists."

"Doesn't exist? Come on! That kind of thinking has to be some kind of sickness."

"Maybe it is. All the more reason for me not to get married. Why do you want to hang around with an alcoholic, anyway?"

"Because I do believe love exists."

"I think *that* is a sickness."

One bitter night, a bonsai tree that belonged to Sean's dad appeared on their front stoop. The diminutive tree was dying, tiny inches of brown and drying twigs jutting this way and that. Anchorage was covered in frost, but when I found the bonsai it appeared untouched.

I carried it inside and asked Sean, "Do you think we could save it?"

"No. Once a bonsai tree starts to go there's little you can do."

I carried the tiny tree back outside and set it on the porch. I paused there a moment, took a deep breath of the chilled night air and let it out in small bursts like the chugging of a train, the way I used to when I was a girl, and watched the small, cottony puffs float away in the dark.

★ ★ ★

By spring, Sean and I barely saw each other anymore. I resigned myself to the idea that for many people life doesn't hold happy endings, only happy beginnings followed by reality.

Then came more reality. I wasn't there when it happened, but Sean called to tell me. One morning, his mother came downstairs from the house to the jewelry shop and stood mute in the doorway, wearing a worried frown, her mouth working as if she were trying to figure out what to say.

"What's wrong, Mom?" Sean asked.

"Grandma's not breathing," Tess said in a wispy voice.

Someone shouted, "Call 911!" and everyone ran upstairs to Grandma Mae's room.

Sean told me, "I shook Grandma and started yelling. There was all this commotion, and they wanted me to do CPR, and the woman on the phone was talking us through it, and she asked, 'Does she have false teeth?' She said someone needed to get the teeth out of her mouth. And I was reaching in Grandma's mouth to get her teeth . . . and it was just so, I hate to say it, but it was disgusting. None of us knew how long she'd been dead and I was about to do mouth-to-mouth, and all I could think was I didn't want to be there."

Just as he yanked her dentures out, the paramedics showed up. Tess, who had been standing riveted, shouted, "Stop! My mother didn't want any life-saving measures. She has a living will!" She disappeared down the hall and ran back with the living will in her hand. The chaos stopped and the murmuring began as everyone allowed death its place in the room.

That's when Sean decided it was time to leave home. A part of him had floated outside the scene and watched, and he could no longer deny what he'd seen: a house where financial demise, depression, and now death had run everyone down like a steamroller, flattening them like two-dimensional cartoons, floating down, down, down like paper. He knew his father was next, and he didn't want to follow. He asked me to edit his resume. Time was running out.

A few days after Grandma Mae's death, Sean's dad swung from depression to mania. He pulled out scissors, glue, and construction paper and began making a collage, a project that overran his entire living room. Too late did his wife realize he was also cutting up all their old family photos to create his dubious work of art. One day, the police called Tess to tell her that Stuart had gone to a thrift store, filled a shopping cart with odds and ends, and marched the cart outside without paying. It wasn't clear whether he'd turned into a kleptomaniac or his mind had drifted so far away he'd forgotten what he was doing. After that, he died his hair gold—not blond or yellow, but gold—and showed it off to everyone, cackling with delight at the color.

For Tess, the last straw was when he began inviting strangers to stay at the house, people who smelled of homelessness, booze, and wasted lives. He said that, as an A.A. member, he was just trying to help. Unable to coax him into sensible conversation or therapy, fearful of his odd house-guests who came and went at all hours, Tess left the house and moved in with her daughter.

Sean began spending more time at my place, hiding. But he couldn't avoid going home at least five days a week, because that was where he worked, at least until he found another job.

While he sent out resumes, I continued to save money for my global trek. Then my dad's wife fell into a coma. I didn't know that this family emergency—with its last-minute flights, unpaid leave, car rental, and expenses—would eat half the cost of a shoestring trip around the world. I thought I'd have to delay my dream. Then my grandmother mailed me the missing half as a gift.

"Mom, you need this money for retirement. I can't accept it."

"Yes you can. I have a good pension. I want to do this for you, while I'm still alive. I never had a dream. So your dream will be my dream, and you'll come back and tell me about it."

With that, the fulfillment of my goal required only the decision to go. I considered the possibility that this fantasy might save not just me, but Sean and me. I asked him to come with me. But he was afraid to spend his savings when his future was so uncertain.

"You can always get a job when you come back. Come on! Instead of sitting around here watching the business tank, you can have an adventure you'll remember the rest of your life!"

"I'm sorry, Cara, I know you want someone to come with you."

"Not 'someone.' *You.*"

"But it can't be me. It's just not realistic."

In July, he found a job in the Four Corners region of New Mexico. I began to hope that, if he wouldn't come with me, he'd at least ask me to go with him. "A lady waits to be asked," Mom once told me. I've never been good at waiting, but this time it seemed the right thing to do. Unless I let him ask me, how would I know if he truly wanted me? The question never came.

One day while he packed, I stood in the midst of a dozen boxes, surveying the disorder, motionless and pensive, until he stopped wrapping glasses in newspaper and stared at me, chewing his lower lip.

"So," I said, "you really aren't going to ask me to come with you?"

"I didn't think you'd want to. Besides, I couldn't do that to you. Farmington's a small town—there's no TV station, so what would you do? I won't be making enough to support us . . . I'm sorry, I can tell by the way you're looking at me that I'm screwing this up. Did you want to come?"

"What does it matter what I wanted? After that speech, I don't want it now. I don't want to be with someone who can't even be bothered to ask me to be with him."

"So it's over?"

"I don't know. You tell me."

"I don't want it to be over."

"So it's not over. But it will be, when you fly south."

"Right," he said. Then he shrugged and looked away, biting on his thumbnail. I hated when he did that. It made an ugly clicking sound. Turning back to look at me, he caught me staring at his thumb, and lowered it slowly. It was only the end of a relationship, but in the Last Frontier, if you squint long enough in the wrong direction, you can see the end of everything. And neither of us wanted to look anymore.

I'VE BEEN DINGLED
THIRTY-SIX YEARS OLD—DINGLE, IRELAND

I thought I left it behind in Alaska, but today in Ireland I once again visited the end of the earth. Sunshine transformed the Dingle Peninsula into the bright bliss of heaven as I biked around the Slea Head Loop. It took me to the westernmost point of Europe: the water-carved cliffs where the culminating energy of the Atlantic first crashes into land.

I locked my rental bike to a pasture gate and walked up a grassy slope, passing several sheep along the way. I soon found myself sinking and rising, wading through uneven grass up to my knees. As I approached the summit, the slope grew so steep I could crawl upward on hands and feet while remaining upright. At the top I looked north, where a crescent of jagged coastline curved into the distance toward Slea Head and the Blasket Islands. The ocean was a mad beauty, a blaze of furious white froth pounding the cliffs.

I arrived at a wreck of a wooden shack with gaping holes punched into its surviving walls and floors. Two couples were there, English by their accents. I maintained a discreet distance, and felt glad when they left. I not only wanted solitude, I craved a cold blast of loneliness.

I followed a narrow path along the cliff ledge, little wider than a footstep. The height was dizzying. I couldn't help but consider what it might be like to trip and fall off. There'd be a long time to think on the way down. I stopped to peer down a crevice that opened onto a view of the traveling sea and manic waves hundreds of feet below. The distant thunder of the ocean was soothing, though it vibrated the ground where I stood. I don't know why such terrifying power gives me peace. I suppose it's freeing to be reminded how little control we have over anything.

As I gazed, dreamy eyed, into the memory of all the waters I have met, I once again asked God to show me the purpose of my life and help me fulfill it. And, as I listened to the ocean's ferocious lullaby, I began to hear an answer. Since long before my odyssey began, to this moment staring at the place the ancients once thought of as the edge of the earth and the beginning of the unknown, only one desire has remained constant: my desire to be heard.

It is a compulsion so strong that it has driven the people I love to distraction: "I think part of the reason Grampa left was because of you. Because he couldn't stand all your arguing." . . . "When you keep going on and on like that, it makes me think about guns . . . and knives." . . . "I have to listen to you talk and talk, until you say everything you want to say. And if I don't, it's *'let me finish!'*" Throughout my life, the thing I've wanted most was to tell someone all I've seen and heard and felt. This has always been my curse. But now I understand: it is also my purpose.

Like the tide, to fulfill my purpose I need only flow in the direction that draws me onward. Like a wave, I'll glide along the paths of least resistance, jump over obstacles, and wear down walls. Like the surf, I'll whisper in the distance, and if someone draws close enough to listen, I'll roar. The ocean has a story to tell. And so do I.

★　★　★

I spent all day at the Café Lit, drinking tea and eating apple crumble with clotted cream, reading and writing and chatting with the regulars, but mostly waiting for Saoirse. It was closing time when he walked in, and I approached him to pay my bill and ask one more time for a job.

When I told him what I'd eaten, as usual he questioned me: "Did y' sit or stand? Did y' have sugar? Milk?"

Then I asked, "Have you given any more thought to whether you could use my help around here?"

He once again stood with his finger on his chin, thinking. He walked over to his son, and they whispered together. Then he walked back over to me, looked me up and down one more time, and said with his usual gruff warmth, "Come back tomorrow at nine."

Stunned at this unexpected success, I asked, "Come back to talk?"

"No, to work!" he said with a crooked smile.

"Oh . . . okay," I replied, hesitant but grinning from ear-to-ear.

"Can you?" he asked.

"Ye-e-e-s . . . Yes, of course. I'll see you tomorrow." I tripped over myself as I left.

"I have a job!" I spoke out loud as I walked down the street. "Oh my God! I have a job! I'm going to live in Ireland!" Then, as it sank in, "Fuck . . . I have a job . . . I'm going to live in Ireland?"

The Ballintaggart van was sitting at the bus stop, full of people, and I ran for it, grinning with elation and terror. I bounced onto a seat next to Gareth, turned to him and said, "I got a job!" A few people congratulated me, and someone slapped me on the shoulder.

"That's great!" Gareth said, but his eyes searched my face with concern. Although I was grinning, he must have noticed my eyes bulging with shock, because as we drove away he murmured, "Are you okay?"

"Yeah . . . I just can't believe it. Now I have to find a place to live." I'm sure I said more, but I can't remember what. My lips were talking about the job and living in Dingle, but I was thinking about my sister, Iliana, who just turned three a few days ago. I'd called to wish her a happy birthday. She'd told me that she'd had a piñata at her party. She'd learned so many new words. She'd asked if I could come play with her; she had no concept of a world so enormous that it might not be possible for me to come over tomorrow. I was thinking about all the drinkers I've met in Dingle. I went through nine winters surrounded by depressed, seasonal affective disordered, cabin-fevered alcoholics in Alaska. Do I want to do that again? I was thinking about Sean. But I no longer knew what I thought about Sean.

The peace I've felt in Dingle has vanished.

★ ★ ★

A person may give away all worldly possessions, don sandals and robe, and wander the planet, becoming in the process either a sage or a fool. I suspect it may be hard to tell the difference. When I go home, wherever that is, I suppose some people will expect wisdom from me, but it's likely most people will find me more foolish now than I was before I set out.

I wouldn't try to change their minds.

This morning I woke up early to start my new job. I was nervous about making pastries.

I still missed my sister, but I reminded myself that my father got married a few weeks ago to a woman with two daughters of her own. They're Iliana's family now; I'm simply the big sister who doesn't live at home. So there's no need to hurry back. I still missed Sean, but I reminded myself that he never exactly proposed. Again, no need to hurry back.

Before I set out for the Café Lit, I went to the hostel's payphone and called Sean.

"Hi-i-i-i!" he said in the sweet tone men only use with children or women they love.

"Guess what?" I said. My pulse leapt in my neck.

"What?"

"I got a job. I start this morning."

"Wow . . . " he said. "I thought something like that might happen. Congratulations."

"Thanks. It's not a good-paying job, but it's at this cute little café at the back of a bookshop where they sell Irish books. The owner speaks Gaelic. I mean, it's a great place . . . "

"It sounds great."

"But I don't know how I feel about it. I think it'll only pay about four Irish pounds an hour. And I wouldn't be able to see you for a long time . . . " He didn't step in to help me, so I spit out my next question, "AndIwanttoknowwhatyouthinkaboutit."

"*Ca-ra* . . . " he sighed, "I'm not going to do that."

"I'm not asking you to make my decision for me. But if you meant anything you've said, you definitely have an interest in it. And I have a legitimate interest in knowing your feelings, since this decision will affect our relationship. I was thinking about it all last night and I just couldn't come to peace with my decision. Then I realized that's because I want to go home. The problem is, I don't know what I'm going home to, or *where* to go home to." He said nothing, so I continued, "Two months ago you sent me an email that said 'Marry me, soon,' and I sent you three replies. But you never responded. I started to think maybe you didn't mean it."

"No. I meant it. But see, you've been doing all this traveling, and I keep thinking you're going to come to tiny little Farmington, New Mexico after seeing all these exciting places, and it's going to seem boring. I don't think you'll be happy here. I'm not even that happy here."

"Sean, if we don't like Farmington we can always move. All I know is, wherever I go, I'd be much happier living with you than traveling alone for the rest of my life."

"That's the other problem. I want to propose properly and do the romantic thing," the words caught in his throat, "but I can't do it while you're half-way around the world."

"So you're just waiting for me to come home before you propose?"

"Yes, of course," he said, with the characteristic sincerity I've learned to rely on.

"Okay. I'll come home."

We quickly declared our love, then I had to run to make it to the café on time. Even if I wasn't going to take the job, I owed it to Saoirse to tell him. As I hurried past the front desk, Wendy flashed a broad smile, revealing a crooked front tooth. "Going to your new job, then?"

"No, I'm only going there to tell Saoirse I can't work for him. I'm going home to get married!"

I just had time to register her gaping surprise, as she said, "That's the best news! Congratulations!"

"Thanks!" I shouted over my shoulder as I rushed out the door into the sunshine.

I ran almost the entire way to town, stuck on the idea that I had to show up on time. As I ran, I thought, "Now I can go home, because I know where home is: it's wherever Sean is, and he's not in Dingle."

When I arrived at the Café Lit, sweaty and out of breath, the door was locked. I knocked for several minutes before someone answered. It was Marcella, a young Spanish woman who just started working at the café last week. Saoirse wasn't in yet, but I told Marcella I couldn't take the job after all. She frowned but remained polite, saying, "This is too bad. Another woman was going to work today, but Saoirse gave her the day off because he was expecting you." I was surprised they planned to rely on me so heavily on my first day. Under the circumstances, I felt too ashamed to leave. So I told Marcella I'd stay for the day, for as long as she needed help.

With a sigh, she let me in. She showed me how to start the coffee, then took me upstairs to the kitchen to help her prepare the day's fare. Marcella was apparently born in a kitchen, and her sidelong glances made it clear I was hopeless.

She instructed me to cut vegetables for the sandwiches and slice apples for the pastry. This sounded simple enough, but when I put onions and carrots into the automatic slicer I used the wrong attachment, cutting thick slices instead of julienne strips. Marcella laughed and said we'd use them anyway. Then I squished a tomato because I didn't know how to use the tomato slicer. Now, it really wasn't my fault that it took me five minutes to peel a single apple; when a condescending Marcella attempted to show me how to use the peeler, she admitted it was dull.

The main problem was that I was still shaking in reaction to my second near-proposal in two months.

I was still destroying the apples when Saoirse and his son walked in. Saoirse looked gruff and cheery as usual. "Good morning!" he said.

"Good morning," I said, with a guilty smile—I liked him very much and I knew turning down a job I'd begged for wasn't likely to earn his respect—"I need to talk to you."

In the half-laughing, half-exasperated tone of someone who's been through this conversation at least a dozen times, he said, "No! I don't want to hear it! I don't want to hear it!"

Relieved that he was going to have a sense of humor about this, I rushed on, "I'm sorry. I called home this morning . . . "

"Oh no! Don't be doin' that. You should never call home." A twinkle lit his stern eyes.

"And I got another offer . . . " I continued.

"Ohhh no," he interrupted again, obviously enjoying the suspense.

"I'm getting married!" I said, beaming.

"Aw, that's the worst excuse I've ever heard," he said with good-humored disgust.

"No, it's true." I turned to Marcella, hoping for forgiveness. "Now, wouldn't you say that's a better offer?"

She only smiled, looking simultaneously pleased and disapproving.

"Well now, it might be a better offer and it might not be," Saoirse said. "It depends on who's making the offer."

"I promise I'll come back to Dingle someday with my fiancé so you can meet him."

"If you come back with him, he better be your husband, not your fiancé, or we'll know it wasn't a very good offer."

"I'm really sorry about inconveniencing you."

"Will you marry *me*, then?"

"Sorry, you'll have to get up earlier. I've already accepted the first proposal of the day."

Although I told Saoirse I'd stay for the day, Marcella and Saoirse's son politely suggested I might as well leave. I had a feeling they were relieved to be free of my dubious assistance—although I will say, at least I didn't ruin the scone mix. I thanked them for their understanding. Saoirse's son shrugged.

"Thank *you*. Most people who change their minds don't offer to help. Don't worry about it. It happens. And congratulations on getting married."

Those last words scared me. The idea hardly seemed real. But tonight my spirit is filled with the stillness that comes with a right decision.

Even if New Mexico isn't the right choice, this evening at Ballintaggart I saw the final sign that it's at least time to finish my journey. That sign was Jerry from the States. Jerry's been working in the kitchen of a local restaurant during the tourist season, but this evening he told me the restaurant is letting him go and he's having trouble finding a new job. Jerry is forty-five, but he looks fifty-five. Although his face, clothes, and hair have the rumpled look of all backpackers, on him the look doesn't communicate adventure, only a consummate weariness. He looks homeless. Maybe that's because he is. If I had any doubt about my decision, Jerry cured it. I pictured myself at forty-five, working in kitchens and hanging out with people half my age. It was an equally weary sight.

I'll miss Dingle's friendly people, spirited music, and numinous beauty. But I won't miss spending a long, cold winter working a low-wage job. I won't miss hitting the pubs each night amid people killing the blues with pints of ale. I won't miss sleeping in a lonely bed in a cheap room. I can always find friendly people, beautiful scenery, and lively music whenever I want, wherever I go, because I've swung the door to my life wide open, and there's no shutting it now.

People have always passed in and out of my life without my knowing why. This year they've left so many marks on me, my soul must look like *Lydia the Tattooed Lady*. Tomorrow I'll leave Ballintaggart behind, but the people I've met will come with me. An inky outline of their laughing, singing, open faces will remain indelible on the skin of my psyche.

Tonight in the music room, Gareth asked, "So, did you talk to your feller?"

"Yes."

"And did the conversation go all right?"

"It went better than all right. I'm going home."

"Good for you," he said with a firm nod. "Then it was probably all a good thing. It probably brought things to a head."

As news of my engagement spread through the hostel, I received congratulations all around, and requests for my story. The Irish Sisters sighed and pronounced it perfectly romantic: "It's just the best news!" Jerry the Cook listened with the skepticism of someone for whom wandering the world has changed from adventure to fruitless search to resigned transience. He blew a cynical raspberry, "Sorry, I don't believe in romance."

Gareth laughed, shaking his head.

"What?" I asked.

"It's just funny," he said. "One moment you're on the phone accepting this marriage proposal, and the next you're in the kitchen at this café chopping vegetables."

"And not chopping them very well, either," I said. "My grandma always told me if I didn't learn to cook no one would ever marry me."

"What a crrruel thing to say!" Vicki said, though I'd been aiming for a laugh.

"Anyway, you were right, Vicki: I was Dingled. And it took a prince to break the spell."

Soon the music started and there was no more need to talk. As music washed over me, I thought about my journey. From Anchorage to L.A., from China to Ireland, I've come farther in the past year than in my entire life before. I've traveled more than 25,000 miles, according to maps. Off the map, no lines of longitude or latitude can measure how far I've come. I still have a long way to go, to the Four Corners, where New Mexico, Colorado, Arizona, and Utah meet. I don't feel as if I'm going home. Rather, I'm going to yet another place where I'll be a stranger in a strange land. For me, it has always been this way. That's one of the reasons I considered staying away from the United States: in foreign countries it at least makes sense to feel strange and out of place.

But, although I doubt I'll ever feel completely comfortable anywhere, I no longer mind feeling uncomfortable. Why do we value one emotion over another? On this journey, in my deepest moments of loneliness and sorrow I've found profound beauty, as satisfying and healing as my greatest moments of love and joy. I've spent too much time as a worshipper in the American Cult of Happiness. That's only led me to an inauthentic life.

Although he may have broken the Dingle spell, the truth is Sean has yet to propose. Not to worry. Sean is not the only one I love. As my heart beats in rhythm with the drums of Ballintaggart, and my journey floats through me like smoke, I remember falling in love with someone else I met along the road. Myself.

AFTERWORD

I had planned a six-month solo trek around the globe, but it stretched to a year: eight months overseas and four in the States. My trip encompassed Alaska, Washington, Oregon, California, Mexico, China, Thailand, Nepal, India, Greece, Italy, Spain, France, Ireland, England, and New York. Even after that, I didn't stop traveling. It took me another year and four moves to settle into a place and a career that suited me. And it took Sean and me longer than that to get engaged.

Sean and I each had a little farther to travel on our separate journeys before we could grow together. His battle to become sober continued for a couple of years, and my battle to stop reshaping myself to suit others continues to this day. One gift from my global trek was that I ceased worrying about the search for love. I've discovered that in a planet of seven billion people, love is not scarce. For me, love is no longer something to search for, but a place to come from.

My trek became a training course in balancing self-efficacy versus mutual reliance, persistence versus flexibility. The longer I spent outside my comfort zone, the more I realized security is an illusion. That freed me to become an author, something I had wanted to do since reading *Little Women* in third grade, but which I once believed was reserved for extraordinary people. I had thought it would take a big ego to strive to be extraordinary. Instead, it requires humility, a willingness to say, "I'm not sure how, but I have something to share and I'm going to share it."

I filled fourteen journals during my trek, and reshaping them into a memoir taught me that it's possible to become the hero of my own story. I have committed to live the rest of my life that way. It's not easy. I used to find inspiration in the Confucius quote, "Choose a job you love, and you will never have to work a day in your life." I no longer see it that way. Great love requires sacrifice.

* * *

My trek ended with the big-city pleasures of London and New York, and then off I flew to New Mexico. Although I felt excited to see Sean's well-loved face when I arrived at the Albuquerque airport, I felt dismayed at my thoughts: "He looks older. Do *I* look that old?" There was a new gray hair or two at his temples, probably from worrying too much. There was a new line or two around my eyes from months in the sun. The planet kept spinning, and although I'd flown all the way around it in the opposite direction of that rotation, I couldn't stop it.

I didn't realize how tense I'd been for nearly eight months until I let it all go and relaxed against him. I almost fell asleep right there in baggage claim, leaning against his shoulder.

Sean took over my duffle into which I had stuffed my backpack. The duffle had picked up a duct-taped scar along the way after I'd dragged it through dozens of airports, train stations, and bus stations. It was the first time someone had carried that load for me, and I felt curiously light. As he dragged the duffle with one hand, he held mine with the other. His hand wasn't much bigger than mine. I'd never noticed that before. *We're so fragile*, I thought.

It was a three-hour drive to Farmington, a small oil town in the northwest corner of New Mexico. We traversed open desert, where intermittent mesas rose like giant anvils from flat terrain. There was so much sky it made me feel small. I tried to call on the inner quiet I'd found on my journey, but instead chattered about my adventures until I was hoarse. As always, Sean was a good listener.

When I fell silent, he said, "I'm still worried you're going to be bored with Farmington."

"I don't think I'm capable of being bored," I said. "Anyway, I'm just really glad to see you."

We drove down Farmington's Main Street, a microcosm of Small Town America: a line-up of dingy mom-and-pops, Wal-Mart, Kmart, a mall, a mesa, Taco Bell, Bank of America. Bored: the word carried a sense of relief. This dot on the map in the middle of a desert looked like a place where I would not feel compelled to get out and see stuff, a place where I could rest.

At Sean's studio apartment, I dropped my backpack in the entry and turned slowly to take in these new digs. Despite the ancient green-shag

carpet and nearly non-existent furniture, he'd managed to make his surroundings pleasant for a guy on a small income. Sean liked all things
Japanese, and the scant decorations reflected that.

I had mere seconds to take in my new home before we made love with
all the intensity of lovers long separated. Almost as good as the sex was
contemplating a long, deep sleep in a bed where I knew I'd be staying for
many nights to come, with no itinerary for the next day, or the next. The
future could wait. Let tomorrow be the first day of the rest of someone
else's life. I folded my shape into Sean's and slept the enviable sleep of a
child after a long day at play.

* * *

A month after I arrived, I broke out in hives. The unbearable itching made
me restless at night, scratching until I bled. I had never had hives before. A
friend suggested it was stress.

I was still waiting for a marriage proposal. But that wasn't what
worried me.

My feet still hurt so much from months of endless walking that I could
barely stand up in the mornings. For the first hour of each day, I hobbled
on both feet, as off-balance as if I had a nervous system disorder. But my
feet weren't stressing me out either.

We'd moved into another apartment, yet I still didn't think of it as ours,
but his. As an unmarried, unemployed woman, riding in the passenger seat
of *his* car, sleeping in *his* apartment, job-hunting and playing Mah Jongg
solitaire on *his* computer, I felt that nothing was mine, or ours. Just his.
But that wasn't what bothered me most.

Just before we moved, I'd been hunting for a can opener. Unfamiliar
with Sean's kitchen set-up, I randomly opened drawers. One drawer stuck
slightly, then gave suddenly, so that I heard the muffled thumpity-bump
of the contents rolling crazily around before I saw them: the drawer was
full of dozens of little corks, wine bottle corks. They rolled to a stop as I
stared dumbly. The world tilted. Panic rose in my throat. My eyes burned.

When I was overseas I got lost every day, but that was nothing compared
to this moment. I was not just lost, but a missing person. I slammed the
drawer shut, frightened I might fall in, never to be found again. Thoughts
rolled around my brain with the same crazy thumpity-bump as those corks.

I considered grabbing my pack and leaving. I had no car, but surely I could find a way to the airport. I had enough money for a ticket to L.A. I could fly back to Alaska. Or just go to a hotel for the night. *Anything!* my head screamed. *Just don't . . . stay . . . here!*

Then reason whispered, *Stop. Breathe. Think.* I borrowed Sean's bike, musing, *Even this isn't mine,* and rode to the nearby Animas River. The forest was turning to the yellows and browns of fall, but to me it was the color of little corks crunching beneath the bike tires like dead leaves, floating down the river like toy boats, left behind by the geese like droppings as they flew south for the winter.

Then the corks stopped rolling, and all seemed still but the river. I stopped the bike, stepped onto a small bridge over the gentle stream and looked down. The water rinsed away my panic as it whispered, *You're free.* Free. Even if every drawer I opened for the rest of my life was full of other people's corks. They weren't mine, after all. I could stay or go. The choice was mine. With that, I decided not to make a choice until I gave Sean a chance to explain.

When he came home I kissed his cheek, invited him to sit next to me on the bed, and told him about the corks.

Sean gave me a direct look. "Oh, those are from a long time ago. When I quit drinking, at first I broke down and drank some wine occasionally. But I haven't done that in a long time."

He'd never lied to me before, so I believed him. "Okay. I'm glad I asked."

But he was lying. Of course he was lying. He was an alcoholic. He started coming home drunk and provoking arguments. I felt betrayed, not by the drinking or the arguing, but by the lying from a man with whom I'd shared my deepest secrets, who had shared his with me.

★ ★ ★

I flew to see my family in L.A., where I borrowed my grandfather's truck. I spent the next two months driving Grampa's Toyota pickup around the Desert Southwest: New Mexico, Arizona, Nevada, and Utah. I couch-surfed with friends, trying to avoid overstaying my welcome in any one place. Then, just before the New Year, I received an offer to become a reporter at a small newspaper in Taos, New Mexico. The pay was less than I'd made during my first year out of college. I took it.

Sean and I spent New Year's Eve together in Chaco Canyon, camping among ancient Native American ruins. A few days later, I loaded the pickup with the two-dozen small boxes that held the only tangible remains of my previous life: mostly books, photos, and clothes. Then I climbed into the cab and rolled down the window to say goodbye.

Sean's eyes were damp, but he managed a teasing smile. "Drive fast and weave in and out of traffic."

"I love you, too," I said, then drove away.

I had a four-hour drive across lonely desert to think.

So I didn't get what I wanted that new year, but I wasn't some wandering mendicant waiting for life to give me a handout. I loved and I was loved—I found balance in that. I still had me—there was a beginning in that. I saw the rolling Sangre de Cristo mountains just ahead, shy peaks reaching from naked high plains into cold winter sky—there was beauty in that.

There, below the mountains, in the midst of the silver-green sagebrush, lay the crooked shadow of a deep crack in the earth: the Rio Grande Gorge. Ahead was the bridge that would take me to my new life. I pulled into the turnout and stepped out of the truck. The air was brisk but bracing after the stuffy heated cab. I walked to the middle of the bridge and looked down the battered curve of the gorge. Its rocky walls blushed at the chill touch of afternoon sun. Some 650 feet below, the great river looked small and motionless as a painting, the froth of the rapids wild brushstrokes of inanimate white paint. Then, as the roaring reached my ears and whispered, the water came to life.

★   ★   ★

I didn't stay long in Taos. I loved that soulful little adobe town nestled between mountain and gorge. Fell under the enchantment of hundreds of years of history passed down to the inheritors of Spanish settlers, Pueblo Indians, pioneers, utopians, and modern artists. Felt charmed when neighbors lifted a single index finger off the steering wheel to signal hello as we passed each other on remote roads. But it was the wrong fit, for several reasons: I felt uncomfortable with a colleague's ethics, and after my journey had shown me my true self I was less willing to compromise on my values; what's more, my small salary wouldn't even allow me to buy a used car, much less travel; and, I worked so many hours I had no time for the memoir I had decided to write.

So, after three months, I took a promising job as a TV reporter in North Carolina. That job sent me all over the state, from shadowy Blue Ridge Mountains to shimmering Outer Banks. Again, it was the wrong fit: I arrived in the midst of an ethics dispute between the news department and management; I was a loud, opinionated Westerner flailing amid soft-spoken, polite Southerners; and, although I love trees, I felt hemmed in by forest, surrounded, claustrophobic.

Seven months later, I accepted a job on the Great Plains, next to the Rocky Mountains, surrounded by the friendly but outspoken people of Colorado. Everything here felt open and untamed: the land, the people, me. From Colorado, I traveled the States as a field producer and writer for a TV show about artists who made functional art for homes. I went on to work for other shows on HGTV, Food Network, and Discovery Health. The traveling and writing were fulfilling, but after a few years, I wanted more free time to finish my memoir.

I went on to become a freelance author, editor, and writing coach, which gave me more freedom to set my own hours and call my own shots. Throughout my global trek, I had asked God to show me my purpose. Fourteen journals and more than twice that many waterways had whispered to me that I was a storyteller. Everything I've done since has been in service to that. How could I ask God a question and ignore the answer?

One reason my career has taken the shape it has is because travel is still important to me. During my world trek, I met Europeans on four- to six-week holidays. They convinced me that the standard two-week American vacation is almost uncivilized. Since then, my career moves have provided opportunities to travel for both work and pleasure. Because time is important to me, my income is humble, but since I have no children, my expenses are small. I drive an old car, buy few clothes, and live in a simple home, saving most spare cash for travel. Within two years after my solo trek, I visited Tanzania, Zanzibar, Malawi, and most of the 50 United States.

* * *

So how did Sean and I end up getting married? When I returned to Denver, it so happened he had already taken a job in Colorado Springs, about an hour away. We had kept in touch during our time apart, and he had done some counseling, some A.A., and some soul searching. He really *had* been striving to quit drinking since he'd left Alaska, and he finally did. With that, there was only one obstacle between us and a life together: his long-promised proposal.

In 2001 and 2002, he drove up to see me every weekend, and we often talked marriage. Then he found a job in Denver. Then he gave notice on his apartment. But he still hadn't proposed. On my birthday, I was out of town, but I had a feeling that when I returned he might surprise me with a ring. Instead, he showed up in a car packed full of his belongings.

That's where I drew the line. "You can't move any of your stuff into my apartment." He reacted with disbelief, but I assured him I was serious. I had warned him many times that I wouldn't live with him again until we were engaged.

Sean didn't protest much, just got in his car and drove his stuff all the way back to Colorado Springs. I almost felt sorry for him, but I knew if I didn't hold firm we might be stuck on that precipice forever. A few hours later he returned and took me out to celebrate my birthday at our favorite restaurant. There, he gave me a journal. Inside, he'd carved the shape of a solitaire diamond engagement ring into the pages. An actual ring nested in the hollow.

On the flyleaf, he'd written, "Will you marry me?"

Below that, I wrote, "Yes!"

He told me he'd had the ring for some time. He had just been wrestling with how to pop the question.

A year later we got married in front of three witnesses: a couple of friends and *Volcán Arenal,* an active volcano in Costa Rica. On our wedding night, Arenal erupted with the chugging sound of a train pulling into a station. Flaming red rocks carved fiery paths down the mountainside. The thrilling show was balanced by our relaxed contentment as we leaned into each other on our cabin porch, breathing in the exhalations of the tropical rainforest. We survived that explosive yet peaceful night, and more than eleven years of nights since, most of them in Colorado, but some in faraway places.

I still travel alone sometimes, but the best trips are now with my husband: Scotland, Peru, Guatemala, the Navajo Nation. Sometimes we return to Alaska where we first met each other, and where I began the long journey to meeting myself.

ACKNOWLEDGMENTS

It took a phenomenal amount of support to bring this book to life. Before I thank everyone, please allow me to apologize if I overlook anyone who helped me along the way. No doubt many more people deserve my thanks than I can possibly address in a few pages.

Many thanks to Caleb Seeling and Sonya Unrein for their dedication to authors in the Rocky Mountain region. I deeply appreciate them for giving my story an opportunity to find more readers and vice versa. Thank you to editor Debbie Vance for not only making sure this new edition looks pristine, but also for approaching it with all the delight of a joyful reader.

Thanks to Matthew Davis, for being the first person to believe in my story, and for his affection for "The Lost American." *For there is nothing lost, that may be found, if sought.* I'm grateful you found me, Matt.

Thank you to Andrea Dupree, Michael Henry, and everyone at Lighthouse Writers Workshop, without whom I would not have had so many opportunities to refine and present my work, or to make my humble leap into the world of published authors. The mentoring, support, and camaraderie I've found at Lighthouse have proved invaluable; it is a shining beacon for Colorado writers.

Thanks, too, to the Denver Woman's Press Club. It was lonely typing at home after so many years in noisy offices, and DWPC members not only offered support and encouragement, but delightful friendship and companionship that often kept me from going stir-crazy.

Loving thanks to my husband, Dale Jolley, for going well beyond our marriage vows in his support of my work and of me. He has heard almost every part of this book read aloud. Often he enjoyed it, sometimes he put up with it, and for both I'm grateful. Reading about your wife's love life certainly goes beyond the vow, "for better or worse." Perhaps it belongs under the category, "in sickness and health," for at some points the penning of my most embarrassing truths seemed like a sickness, or fit of madness, that turned our house into an asylum, with all its blessings and curses. Dale, no one could be a truer friend.

Many thanks to the friends and colleagues who read and offered feedback on my manuscript, or parts of it, in its various stages, from unwieldy tome to final version, to another final version, and another: Mark Graham, Nobuko Graham, Candace Kearns Read, Kimberly Drake, Heather Hovis, Sarah Stires, Leila Mar, Karen Foster, Lyn Jenkins, Gay Pinder, Tammy Kilgore, Cynthia Zieminski, Lori Howell, Barbara Roos, and Diane Regan, to name most of them. My loving gratitude to my departed grandmother, Caroline Lee, who clarified important background material and who always reminded me that she was proud of my work.

A special thanks to Tricia Hackel for giving me my first journal in Alaska. I probably would have kept putting off journaling about my Alaskan experiences if it hadn't been for her. Tricia's thoughtful and intuitive gesture became the cornerstone for the creation of this memoir, though I didn't know it at the time.

Thank you to all the fascinating, generous, intelligent, funny, colorful people I met on my travels: without you, there would be no story. I'm also deeply grateful to the friends and lovers whose lives have some part on these pages. Out of respect, I've done my best to disguise the identities of those who might be embarrassed by any of this memoir's content, and to create amalgams of different people where it helped maintain the pace for readers.

A memoir is fraught with the potential for unintended offense, but the gift of writing about one's life is the gift of finding grace even in the conflicts of our pasts. Please forgive me if you were present for any of the events I've described and remember it differently; I realize no picture looks the same to all people. It has never been my intent to make anyone look bad or foolish, but rather, to share my sense that none of us is alone in occasionally behaving badly or foolishly. Those who misbehaved on these pages have redeemed themselves with many acts of kindness, generosity, even heroism. I value every moment we've shared—the pain and tears as much as the laughter and joy. I believe we've learned much together, and since.

A book doesn't fulfill its purpose until it finds a reader. So thank you to all my readers for helping this book fulfill its purpose. I sincerely hope you've received something in return.